THE TOPOGRAPHY OF WELLNESS

THE TOPOGRAPHY OF WELLNESS

How Health and Disease Shaped
the American Landscape

SARA JENSEN CARR

University of Virginia Press
CHARLOTTESVILLE AND LONDON

University of Virginia Press
© 2021 by the Rector and Visitors of the University of Virginia
All rights reserved
Printed in the United States of America on acid-free paper

First published 2021

9 8 7 6 5 4 3 2 1

Library of Congress Cataloging-in-Publication Data
Names: Carr, Sara Jensen, author.
Title: The topography of wellness : how health and disease shaped the American
    landscape / Sara Jensen Carr.
Description: Charlottesville : University of Virginia Press, 2021. | Includes
    bibliographical references and index.
Identifiers: LCCN 2021010961 (print) | LCCN 2021010962 (ebook) |
    ISBN 9780813946290 (cloth) | ISBN 9780813946306 (paperback) |
    ISBN 9780813946313 (ebook)
Subjects: LCSH: Urban health—United States—History. | Environmental
    health—United States—History. | City planning—Health aspects—United
    States—History. | Epidemiology—United States—History.
Classification: LCC RA566.3 .C37 2021 (print) | LCC RA566.3 (ebook) |
    DDC 362.1/0420973—dc23
LC record available at https://lccn.loc.gov/2021010961
LC ebook record available at https://lccn.loc.gov/2021010962

Publication of this volume was assisted by a grant from Furthermore: a program of the
J. M. Kaplan Fund.

Cover illustrations: Paolo Mascagni, *Anatomia universa XLIV tabulis aeneis juxta
archetypum hominis adulti . . . repraesentata* (Pisa: N. Capurro "typis Firmini Didot,"
1823; *left panel*); antique illustration of human body anatomy: neck and head veins
(stock illustration/ibusca/iStock; *top/bottom panels*); Vitruvian Man (stock photo/
Vaara/iStock; *background*); William Pistor, Eng., "Map of New York City, drawn to
accompany the 4th annual report of the Health Department," 1874 (Lionel Pincus
and Princess Firyal Map Division, The New York Public Library, The New York Public
Library Digital Collections; *center foreground*).

To Maclean, Wyatt, Maya, and Lily,
who make my world brighter, greener, and happier

CONTENTS

ACKNOWLEDGMENTS

The seeds of my interest in how the built environment shapes health were originally sown when I was working at an architecture firm in New Orleans primarily doing healthcare facilities. Immediately after Hurricane Katrina, when the work turned to doing FEMA surveys of damaged buildings and recovery, I spent a lot of time walking around the then half-empty city and thinking about how the landscape itself was serving as a space of harm, healing, and social cohesion for the few that had returned at that time. When witnessing the difficult conversations and efforts regarding how New Orleans should rebuild, I had to confront the divide in perceptions between the architects/planners and the general public, as well as my own myopia. I was driven to see if the guidelines that dictate the design of almost every aspect of health care could somehow be translated to the landscape, which is what led me to pursue study in landscape architecture and environmental planning. The origin of this specific book was as a chapter in my dissertation at the University of California Berkeley, where I was trying to position what I saw as a growing trend in research and practice of "healthy" urban planning and design in other historical movements. The material proved much, much more expansive than a chapter, and this larger, longer study was born.

In 2017, I received a generous grant from the Mellon Foundation's Initiatives in Urban Landscape Studies, which funded a dream residence at Dumbarton Oaks in Washington, DC, where I was allowed the intellectual time and space to really develop the manuscript. A huge thank-you to my colleagues there, especially Jeanne Haffner, John Davis, Peter Ekman, and then-director John Beardsley, who gave incredibly incisive feedback on the structure and arguments.

Another thank-you to my editors at University of Virginia Press, especially Boyd Zenner, who was extremely patient with me extending deadlines through various life events, and Mark Mones, who took over this project after Boyd's retirement. Many thanks to Jane Curran for her heroic copyediting work on the manuscript.

I am also grateful for support from the Graham Foundation and Furthermore: a program of the J. M. Kaplan Fund, which came at crucial points in this book's journey, to fund image rights as well as printing and publication costs.

Most of all, I draw strength from my personal and professional circle. I have been so lucky to have valuable mentors throughout my academic journey, first and foremost Louise Mozingo, but also Linda Jewell, Judith Stilgenbauer, and Nicholas de Monchaux. Thank you to my former dean, Daniel Friedman at the University of Hawai'i at Mānoa, and department chair Daniel Adams at Northeastern University, for giving me the time and support to pursue this research. My New Orleans–based cheering squad always keeps me laughing and loved: Toni DiMaggio, Nick Jenisch, Mara LePere-Schloop, and Betsy Johnson are all talented and, most of all, humane designers who make positive impact on the world. Allison Lassiter, an amazing scholar and adventurer, has been a valuable and empathetic sounding board since our days in the PhD program at University of California Berkeley. My parents, Karl and Celia Jensen, instilled me with a deep sense of respect for the land and for other people and cultures. They and my in-laws, Bill and Shelley Carr, never questioned my various career shifts over the past years; hopefully their adorable grandchildren were an acceptable tradeoff. Due to the extremely niche topic, I'm sure none of them will read it, but our various wonderful nannies and babysitters have been perhaps most essential to this book's completion and deserve recognition. Connie, Alissa, Annie, Lindsay, Sabrina, Masha, and Eva kept my mind at ease as I knew our kids were well taken care of and loved.

Those three children, Wyatt, Maya, and Lily, have made getting the research and writing done more challenging but made the end product so much better by shifting my worldview and making me a more empathetic, if infinitely more tired, woman. Above all, none of this would have been possible without the unflagging support of my husband, Maclean, who has always pushed me to do better, given me space when I needed to step back for a bit, and been a partner in life in every sense of the word.

THE TOPOGRAPHY OF WELLNESS

Wellness and the American Urban Landscape

In 2016, Karen DeSalvo, interim secretary of the US Department of Health and Human Services, noted that public health had entered a new era, where "one's zip code is a better indicator of health than genetic code."[1] This is an epochal declaration from a government official, but not surprising considering that we are inundated with a plethora of competing lists of the "healthiest" places to live, geographically coded "Wellbeing Indexes," some scientific, some merely observational in nature. The Blue Zones Project, a private wellness consultancy, advocates for a preventative health model that comes from studying aspects of place in five communities around the world with the highest rate of centenarians, from Okinawa to Loma Linda, CA.[2] Empirical research on how the presence of trees, design of towns, and form of our workplaces and homes make us sicker or healthier has exploded in the past twenty years. However, all this data also reveals a troubling pattern in the United States. In terms of race, economy, and health outcomes, our neighborhoods are showing markedly more segregation and disparity. In an era where the primary causes of mortality are from chronic, environmentally influenced illnesses such as cancer, diabetes, and pulmonary and respiratory disease, the relationship between the landscapes we inhabit, our society, and our bodies is of renewed interest to the fields of public health, design, and planning.

The traditional view of health has traditionally been a binary—are you sick, or are you healthy? If you are sick, we often think the origin of that illness is etiologic, a linear chain of events that leads us back to the germ or gene causing the malfunction. In our new era, the complicated and often multifaceted origins of chronic disease have required an expanded, ecological view of health. The World Health Organization's Constitution of 1948 defined health as "a state of complete physical, mental, and social wellbeing, and not merely the absence of disease or infirmity." It states that health "is a fundamental human right and that the attainment of the highest possible level of health is a most important world-wide social goal whose realization requires the action of many other social and economic sectors in addition to the health

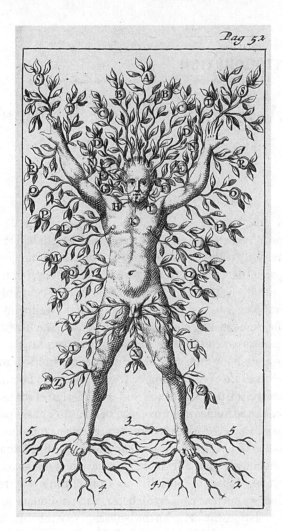

Fig. 1. John Case's *Compendium Anatomicum* (1695), which sought understanding of the human body through nature. (Wellcome Collection)

sector."[3] This accordingly opened up a new realm of research that looked not only at pathogenic factors of health outcomes, but economic, social, and environmental factors.

When it comes to issues of health, environment, and urban history, the lessons of the past are often forgotten by many Americans. Public health has had to confront several periodic eras of popular disinterest and federal disinvestment, often after epidemic crises are vanquished and therefore invisible to the general public. Public health is a long-term investment requiring years of preventive groundwork; to forget the epidemics of the past often leaves us unprepared and underfunded when the next, inevitable crisis hits. Moreover, concerns from the public health community tend to be discounted when they run up against interests of economic growth. Attempts to widen the scope of public health services have often been negatively characterized as "socialism," a consistent theme that dates back to the Sheppard-Towner Act of 1921, which sought to lower infant mortality rates and expand prenatal care to poor women; such criticism continues with today's political attacks on a nationalized healthcare system.[4] From germs to obesity, Americans tend to view most epidemics as a result of individual choices, and not a circumstance of social and economic structures. Apart from a few key victories over time, American health has rarely been viewed as an obligation of a society, or even a base human right.

The past few decades have seen an explosion of books and guides of how to build healthier and equitable neighborhoods. In turn, this renewed interest in the relationship between built environment and health is starting to be adopted into policy in many American major cities. Over 150 years ago, New York City conducted a sanitary survey to track the origins of cholera, typhoid, and yellow fever. In 2014, the city published a set of Active Design Guidelines, written to encourage physical activity in its buildings and public spaces. Whereas the first publication was a ward-by-ward accounting of built environment conditions to search for the source of epidemic disease, the latter embraces the new reality of chronic disease—that there are multiple levels of influence and impact surrounding us and the choices we make every day. Other books examine how to introduce walkability and density into the suburbs, and still more are working simply to establish the link and evangelize for an audience otherwise unaware of these connections. This book is not an effort to add to the guidelines of how to build healthy places, but rather to set the context for them. How have we attempted to build for health in the past, and what were the advances and unseen consequences of those movements?

It also serves to examine movements of design and planning for blind spots, particularly when those ideas purport to somehow improve the urban condition. The New Urbanist movement was founded on the idea that we needed to return to the "old way of planning." But to solely look to Garden Cities as a formal exercise, without its associated social and historical context, as well as how its ideals had been mutated in the past (and again, these mutations were often driven by competing interests in economic growth), we risk repeating otherwise unexamined fallout.[5] It is also worth noting that there have been many thorough accounts of both public health history and environmental/urban history, but they have yet to be combined in a narrative that shows their overlaps, divergences, and parallels. The fields of urban planning and public health became professionalized in the United States around the same time and were closely allied in order to combat the epidemic disease that wracked early American cities. From a policy standpoint, this helps us to understand the foundation of modern zoning laws, particularly those that separated industry from housing and dictated density. The history of American policies leaves literal lines on the earth, but there has not yet been a history of how these ideas manifested themselves in our on-the-ground experience. Even so, the progression of medical history often intersects with environmental histories. The rapid pace at which we have shaped our cities, towns, and landscape has inevitably manifested itself in our bodies, ranging from the tangible effects of air pollution and water quality to the more wide-ranging early twentieth-century general diagnosis of "nervousness" to today's in-depth studies on the long-term effects of stress. There are countless examples of ways we have tried to understand cities and ecology through our own bodies, from Hippocrates to Renaissance scientists to Aldo Leopold's land pathologies. Even so, reconciling the vocabulary of health, landscape, and ecology often reveals schisms among these fields. "Place" in public health is a relatively straightforward concept, simply referring to a geographic unit, whether it be a zip code or town. As historian Dolores Hayden points out, though, "place" is a more complicated concept to parse when we view it through the lens of cultural meaning;[6] "sense of place," so often used in design and urban studies, is perhaps even less understood. This is only one piece of vocabulary where the fields diverge; there are also fundamental differences in forms of inquiry, what is considered evidential, and day-to-day practices. Hayden posits that the study of this spatial realm necessarily embraces cultural and political geography, and she puts forth a call to view "urban landscapes as public history."[7] Public life, public health, and the public realm have a reciprocal relationship, and it is logical to tie them together in a narrative. In her canonical landscape history book, Elizabeth Barlow Rogers connected the body to landscape by noting how habitual movement is central to the study of archeology and how the spaces of pre-Columbian history were often designed around rituals.[8] John Brinckerhoff Jackson, in his essay "The Word Itself," points out that landscapes are synthetic spaces, reflecting the needs of a community and "a space deliberately created to speed up or slow down the process of nature."[9] This is key when it comes to reading landscapes as a way to understand changing concepts around health. We repeatedly see nature conceptualized as a tonic to urban ills, but only insomuch as it can be controlled and packaged to reflect an era's mores and preoccupations. When it comes to disease, though, landscapes are not merely a reflection of the times, but an actual vector of epidemics, which spread not only through contagion, but also due to social and physical conditions, a tenet that is even more true in the United States as chronic diseases have overtaken the infectious as primary cause of mortality. Moreover, disease and landscapes are both essentially spatio-temporal phenomenon—always changing, but linked by geography.

The relationship between public landscapes and specific health-relevant behaviors of course leads to larger questions of environmental determinism, which is explored in this text, but for now we accept the basic tenet of landscape theory that space is both born out of societal customs and simultaneously shapes behavior. The exploration of this territory can then yield useful insights into our state of wellness. Similarly, the history of architecture, landscape architecture, and urban planning is rife with Utopian schemes, some truly intended to be executed and some merely aspirational. What their tenets of health are and how they were translated and at times mutated in built form is important to discuss. We must also recognize Henri Lefebvre's definition of space (or place) as a function of economic and social reproduction, a city's public space being the stage for the reproduction of social relations.[10] American public space is more often than not a product of a capitalist society, and we see recurring patterns of "health" as enterprise. We see how the attempts to make spaces healthier often had to acquiesce to industry and real estate concerns, how health was marketed, or how health was leveraged to keep workers productive and to repress protest.

This book posits that the distinct urban landscape movements detailed here were reactions to specific urban epidemics. Obviously, we often deal with several health crises at once, but the interest here is why and when did these specific epidemics become focal or central to popular thought? Why did certain strategies to combat them come to the forefront? What did these landscapes reveal about scientific thought, namely pathology, and our social systems? By asking these questions of each era, how can we successfully bring wellness back to our built environment? All epidemics eventually develop a narrative that may or may not be rooted in epidemiological truth, whether it is by how it spreads, who it seems to affect the most, and ultimately, what kinds of places are perceived to incubate or prevent them. The text is split into two parts, corresponding to the shift from infectious disease to chronic disease. The first six chapters dissect, in chronological order, six different design movements that have each targeted a specific disease. The last two chapters discuss how our present-day physical and wellness landscape came to be and what is being done to reshape it. This approach attempts to link changing views of disease pathology to a shifting built environment. This book draws lines between each epidemic and its urban treatment, describing how those ideas were physically manifested in the American parks, public spaces, and housing prototypes of the late nineteenth to the twenty-first centuries. What is rarely discussed is how one movement exacerbated another epidemic; most prominently, how the original suburbs were modeled on an ideal of healthy lifestyles and today became a flashpoint for the debate on environments and illness, whereas cities followed the reverse timeline. Was this a function of changing disease, the actual environment, or a judgment of the people who live within them? Why do we attach certain physical elements to what we perceive as "healthy" or "unhealthy" neighborhoods, and why is there such a wide chasm in between them, both metaphorically, but increasingly literally, as well? Susan Sontag, in *Illness as Metaphor,* hypothesizes health as a locale; all of us inhabit "dual kingdoms" of wellness and illness, from birth, yet we think of the as two separate realms that we believe we or others inhabit as a result of our or their actions. Moreover, Sontag proposed that the less we know about a disease, the more we perceive it to be "morally, if not literally, contagious."[11] We still know little about the environmental influence of diseases that plague us most today, namely obesity and its related afflictions, cancer, and heart/respiratory disease, but we know it is there, and so if given the choice and resources, we distance ourselves.

It is also necessary to take a moment to discuss here the choice of the word "wellness" over "well-being" in the title. In contemporary discussions about health, especially as it encompasses social and environmental determinants, well-being is the term that is actually more widely used and even now is used to guide public policy, most likely because of its utilization in the WHO declaration. Nevertheless, a 2012 literature review in, somewhat ironically, the *International Journal of Wellbeing* notes a distinct lack of theory-based definitions of well-being. However, the construct is largely tied to an individual's self-reflection and happiness, the most classic definition being Norman Bradburn's 1969 scale of psychological well-being, which is itself linked to Aristotle's construct of eudaimonia. The authors note that recent research has provided a plethora of indices of how to measure well-being, most of them linking to self-satisfaction, purpose in life, environmental mastery, and autonomy—in other words, a feeling of control over one's life outcomes. However, these measurements are dimensions, rather than a definition. To address this, that same review conceptualized "well-being" as the center of a seesaw, with psychological, social, and physical "Resources" on one end and those same "Challenges" on the other.[12] This tracks with many other definitions of well-being as a form of personal balance, with the added nuance of well-being being a key factor for resilience in overcoming difficulties. Most of all, well-being is as much a mental state as it is physical. As such, it is a largely subjective measure and colored by personal experience. It is, therefore, much harder to discuss as it relates to populations, place, and landscape. While the built environment definitively affects mental health, that aspect is not explored in depth in this text; instead I choose to focus on physiological health and disease and how landscape has shaped those epidemics. There is, however, a growing and robust body of contemporary research and literature looking at the connection between landscape and mental well-being, which is touched upon in chapter 8.

"Wellness" has proven to be a more problematic construct but therefore offers more opportunity for interrogation. There is considerably less literature that attempts to define the word, even in relationship to well-being. Confusingly, in 2001, the US Department of Education, in conjunction with the President's Council on Physical Fitness and Sports, defined well-being as a component of wellness (when the above discussion seems to indicate the reverse), but crucially they note that "wellness results from healthy behavior."[13] Therein is the indication that wellness is viewed as a direct result of one's choices. Parallel to this concept, throughout history "wellness" has been tied to consumer goods, spiritual fulfillment, and other times "quackery." Nature, or returning to one's natural state, is also a consistent thread, but for a price. The late nineteenth-century craze for rural spas (discussed here in chapter 2), John Harvey Kellogg's sanitaria for biologic living, even up to John Travis's Wellness Resource Center in Mill Valley, California, founded in 1975, all centered wellness in their marketing.[14] Wellness, and not well-being, is the term most often seen in popular media, with an emphasis on the achievement of one's best self but pitched to populations of certain socioeconomic status.[15] Wellness's emphasis on personal responsibility also ties it more closely to moral imperative.

I choose to talk about landscape's relationship to wellness not just because it has evoked ideas about nature, but specifically because these same themes of commodification, morals, and achievement run throughout the places and epidemics discussed in this book. More pointedly, the urban landscape *should* be considered a tenet of well-being, a physical factor reflecting social needs that ensures quality of life and health equity. Instead, where we live is often seen as a consumer choice, a reflection of our values and behavior. The choice to focus on Americans' relationship with their own health and land is also deliberate, given our country's unique relationship with both. We view our health as the outcome of individual agency, from what we eat to what we do to where we live. If these are the choices that affect our health, then illness must be the result of bad choices. This is reflected at almost all levels of our culture, from how we approach healthcare policy and spending to popular thought. Meanwhile, the mythic American landscape is also an idea borne out of supposedly free agency, from homesteading to the right to private property untouched by government control, even if it was policy that has distinctly shaped it.

There are difficulties in constructing an intellectual history of a topic, particularly when it involves two fields that have largely been divergent for over a century. But I attempt to do so by concentrating on the ways ideas and theories were translated, made popular, and, in this case, often misinterpreted between fields. There are of course lags in dates, parallel but separate efforts to address problems, and competing theories, especially when discussing origins of and strategies to combat disease. In the spirit of Lewis Mumford's "generalism," I see this narrative as putting together fragments to find overall patterns, albeit at the risk of losing some detail.[16] This is about ideas, built work, and the oversights that occur between intentions and actions. I also feel strongly that this book should not be read as polemic on how to build healthy cities. It was, in fact, written as a reaction to a flood of urban design and planning literature I encountered in my research that purported to do exactly that, but without further exploration regarding the needs of specific populations, economic and environmental tradeoffs, and, most of all, a critical eye toward the history of building or altering neighborhoods for health. This book is instead offered as road map to how we got here and a reassessment and contextualization of precepts that have largely gone unchallenged.

Ultimately, this book explores how the intersections of public health and the public realm have formed American cities and neighborhoods, not only through a chronological examination of specific epidemics and their respective urban interventions, but also how our perceptions of place are based in changing understanding of urban systems, society, and the human body. Each approach reveals time- and place-specific ideas about the epidemiology of the built environment. From the infectious diseases of cholera and tuberculosis to "social diseases" of blight and crime, to the more complicated origins of the chronic diseases of today, each epidemic and its associated combat strategies of quarantine, elimination, or acupuncture has left its mark on the physical environment. Of course, in 2020, shortly after the draft of this manuscript was submitted, our relationship to our neighborhoods, our homes, and especially public space was upended by the COVID-19 pandemic. As I make the final revisions to this book, the evidence is still emerging on its contagion, but speculation on how it would change the buildings and landscapes we inhabit was almost immediate. Only a few months in, it also became clear that its spatial effects were starkly drawn by race, income, and immigration status. These patterns are not accidental, but inevitable due to years of exclusion and segregation from basic provisions of fresh air, fresh water, and green space. The narratives about what kind of place spreads the virus have emerged, retreated, and emerged again with each surge, reviving long-held conceptions about density, urban centers, and the suburbs regardless of empirical data. In the conclusion I reflect on how the pandemic response has only reinforced the need for a critical eye on common associations made between the built environment and health. I hope that this recognizance of the successes and failures in forming the public realm for wellness can form the basis for a more healthful, and much more just, urban landscape.

PART I

Infectious Terrains

1860s–1940s

CHAPTER 1

Waste and Super-Infrastructure in the Urban Landscape

The Origins of American Urban Landscape

The first urban landscapes of American cities were informal and uncontrolled. The most rapid urbanization of American cities happened between 1820 and 1860, a couple decades behind the English Industrial Revolution. The series of events that would follow in the United States would follow the same pattern as in London—an explosion of factories and other industries, a huge influx of migration, rampant disease, and a widespread campaign to eradicate it. As such, Americans would often look to the English for strategies on how to control the urban environment, with varying degrees of success. But the United States differed in its demographics, that is, a much more diverse and larger pool of immigrants, its landscape, and its closer ties to an agricultural past.

The shift of the economy meant a corresponding change of workers from farms to cities, but "urban life" was still very much tied to the rural, often a haphazard hybrid of industrial and agricultural activity. Livestock often roamed the streets as stables, slaughterhouses, dairies, and tanneries co-existed with factories. Organic, decaying matter wase emptied into the streets while the black exhaust of machinery filled the sky (fig. 2). Many accounts of this period describe the slaughterhouses and the activities of bone boiling, fat melting, and manure yards as part of the city's integral fabric. A sanitary survey of New York conducted in 1876 showed cattle roaming the street in front of a schoolhouse, with sky above them a flat gray and dirt ground beneath, a bull threateningly coming near a young schoolboy (fig. 3). This ramshackle hybridity was common to most American cities; stockyards and feedlots comprised much of the landscape of early Chicago. In San Francisco, a group of butchers collectively purchased land in the southeast corner of the city where the mouth of Islais Creek met the San Francisco Bay so offal and other waste could be washed out with the tides. In Boston, farmers harvested salt hay from the marshes in the shadow of factories from the city center. Often

Fig. 2. An illustration from the journal *Good Health: A Journal of Hygiene* points to the typical urban American backyard in the Industrial Revolution as a location for improvement, depicting open sewage, outdoor privies, livestock, and muddy soil (1886). (U.S. National Library of Medicine)

these industries were also clustered at the city's edges, not only out of interest for the citizenry's health, but so they could be adjacent to oceans, rivers, and lakes where effluent and solid waste could be dumped and carried away, a "solution to pollution by dilution."[1] The rapid pace of American industrial development also meant industry was largely a self-governing enterprise, with little oversight into their labor and also their waste management. Water and oceans appeared to be an infinite expanse and a convenient disposal strategy, especially to those cities with access to tidal waterways so waste could be flushed out every six hours. The construction of housing for incoming workers and other fortune seekers was similarly a laissez-faire enterprise, as was their own sewage and waste removal. A critical mass was soon reached.

In *McClure's Magazine,* engineer George Waring Jr. would say of New York City:

Before 1895 the streets were almost universally in a filthy state. In wet weather they were covered with slime, and in dry weather the air was filled with dust. Artificial sprinkling in summer converted the dust into mud, and the drying winds changed the mud to powder. Rubbish of all kinds, garbage, and ashes lay neglected in the streets, and in the hot weather the city stank with the emanations of putrefying organic matter. It was not always possible to see the pavement, because of the dirt that covered it. One expert, a former contractor of street cleaning, told me that West Broadway could not be cleaned because it was so coated with grease from wagon axles; it was really coated with slimy mud. The sewer inlets were clogged with refuse; dirty paper was prevalent everywhere, and black rottenness was seen and smelt on every hand.[2]

It was not long before a reckoning came in the form of disease. Cholera epidemics ravaged the United States in 1832, 1849, 1866, and 1874, as well as other diseases such as typhoid, yellow fever, and diphtheria. Cholera was an uncommonly violent disease; it could kill within a day and induced extreme vomiting and diarrhea, making those who witnessed it fear for its contagion. Many saw the murky waters and palpable filth of the city as no longer simply a visceral assault on the senses but starting to be embodied in themselves.

At this time cities were also still trying to figure out how to govern, but the first step taken by many municipalities were detailed studies into mortality, which quickly began to reveal a connection between locale, disease outbreaks, and economic class. They could look to European medical models of how to study and combat illness. London had also been confronted with its own series of cholera epidemics. During an outbreak in 1854, English physician John Snow mapped each occurrence of illness lot by lot. By doing so, he found five hundred people killed within 250 yards of a polluted well and was able to determine this water source as the epidemic's origin. This shoe leather method of deduction cemented Snow's reputation as "the father of epidemiology," and the idea that he found cause, origin, and defeat of

Fig. 3. The depiction from a New York sanitary survey shows livestock loose from a slaughterhouse in common contact with schoolchildren, indicating the hybrid agricultural/urban environment at the time (*1876 Sanitary Survey of New York City*).

a cholera outbreak through the sheer power of geography and dramatically breaking off the well's handle persists across the fields of urban planning and health. Snow's work was absolutely epochal, but these narratives give a significant amount of power to him and the map in and of itself, often as an argument for the deterministic possibilities of spatial representation. Archival evidence has shown that the story is more complex. He had many collaborators in his investigation and was already working off knowledge that the disease was ingested through water and not airborne.[3]

Fault lines of sickness were clearly drawn by economic class, though, and the study of the spatial distribution of disease and its relationship to class inequity dates back to the beginnings of urban industrialization. In 1662, English demographer John Graunt's *Natural and Political Observations made upon the Bills of Mortality* was the first to do a longitudinal study by looking at occurrences of death over time. Graunt categorized mortality data by age, sex, and location and looked at differences in mortality across the city of London. Comparing within sociodemographic groups allowed him to come up with a preliminary theory about groups vulnerable to certain diseases. Noting changes in causes of death also allowed him to forewarn the city government about future outbreaks, although this information mostly enabled the upper class, which had the mobility to escape to the country, to flee the city in time.[4]

Similarly, an 1863 mortality survey in New York City counts one death for every 35 inhabitants in 1863 for the entire city, but numbers differed significantly from ward to ward. In wealthier Murray Hill, the mortality rate was 1 in 60, but in the poorer immigrant neighborhood of the Sixth Ward the death rate was 1 in 24.[5] This large disparity alarmed officials enough to take on more detailed investigations of the city. This practice of the "sanitary survey" had become common during the Civil War, where surveyors would be sent out ahead of soldiers to map the land to be set up for camps. General guidelines would advise the military to avoid marsh lands (for their miasmic gases), not to lay out tents too densely, and to avoid humid winds.[6] Similar to Snow's mapping, many cities took on in-depth, block-by-block investigations into the urban environment. These went far beyond a simple neighborhood depiction and instead involved massive volumes of maps and narratives of every corner of the city. A five-hundred-plus-page report on the "Sanitary Condition of the City," published in 1865 by Council of Hygiene and Public Health of the Citizens' Association of New York, breaks down the city into twenty-nine districts, providing vivid descriptions of each landscape. The format of the subjects covered by each report, namely describing conditions of housing, businesses, and streets and enumerating incidence of disease, aided in the search for any correlations between the miscellaneous detritus of the city and illness. Called out as particular dangers were filthy streets,

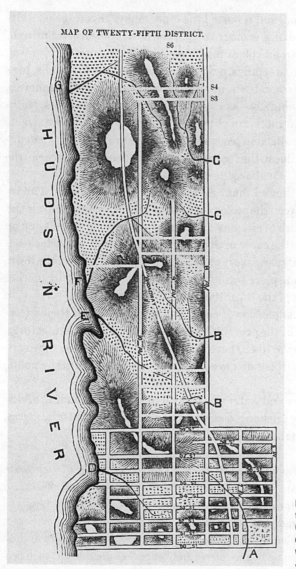

MAP OF TWENTY-FIFTH DISTRICT.

Fig. 4. The medical topography of the Twenty-Fifth District in New York City shows surveyors were closely examining the conditions of soil and waters near developed streets (*1876 Sanitary Survey of New York City*).

neglected garbage, overflowing sewers and drains, and neglected privies of homes. This practice of "medical topography," then a named field under the American Medical Association, was founded in 1855 (fig. 4).

Much attention has been paid to the conceptions of air, water, and waste during this time, but also discussed in detail are the literal ground conditions of each neighborhood. All the inspectors assessed the soil (or "nature of the ground") for its chemical composition, water retention, and the condition of streets and pavements and reported the topography. This revealed a city that is a patchwork of paving, geology, marsh, and dust, even an accounting of the Frankenstein-like ground plane made up of "bricks, mortar, slate, gravel, ashes, coal-dust, street-sweepings, oyster, clam, lobster, and egg shells, pig's hair, shavings, straw, glass, carpets, brooms, refuse materials from tanneries, crockery, bones, dead animals—as cats, rats, and dogs; shoes, boots, feathers, oyster cans, old tin roofs, tin clippings, etc. etc."[7] Cobblestone streets were deemed inferior to Belgian pavement, as they required too much maintenance, but primarily due to the fact that they held filth and dirt between the stones and rendered the air above the street impure as well.

These surveys also showed that New York's inspectors recognized an inherent connection between the ecology of the city's water, ground, and air and how it affected the health of citizens. One surveyor wrote his speculation on the literal landscape as the cause of the outbreaks, stating: "The surface-soil or street-dirt necessarily varies very greatly in the different parts of the town, being determined in one place by the non-occurrence of sewers; in another by the domestic habits of the inhabitants as to cleanliness or the reverse; in a third by the continual passage of cattle and the dropping of their excrements; in still another by the prevailing occurrence of certain manufactures, as of gas, leather, and the like. There can be no doubt that these very various modifications of surface-dirt are intimately connected with the public health."[8]

The condition of air and water was central to the understanding of disease, a theory virtually unchanged since Hippocrates's *Airs, Waters, Places,* written in 400 BCE. In the book he wrote:

And I wish to give an account of the other kinds of waters, namely, of such as are wholesome and such as are unwholesome, and what bad and what good effects may be derived from water; for water contributes much towards health . . . those who drink them have large and obstructed spleens, their bellies are hard, emaciated, and hot; and their shoulders, collar-bones, and faces are emaciated; for their flesh is melted down and taken up by the spleen, and hence they are slender; such persons then are voracious and thirsty; their bellies are very dry both above and below, so that they require the strongest medicines."[9]

The consumption of "bad waters" was obviously one health problem, but another was the air that emanated from waste left as the tides moved out, or as waste in streets and yards baked in the sun. "Miasma" was a loosely defined term that referred to a belief that illness could be transmitted through the air, the rancid smell being an indicator of its virulence. To this point, the direction of winds was also of utmost importance, especially as it related to the

Fig. 5. In a magazine illustration titled "The Silent Highwayman," Death is shown as rowing a boat on the River Thames, coming for the citizens of London via the water and air, which is thick with filth and disease (*Punch* Magazine, 1858).

swampy lands of many American coastal cities. The idea that the very air you breathed could mean your demise powerfully gripped those living in the city. In both the United States and England, cartoons often depict miasma as an ephemeral but all-consuming, giant specter of death looming over the cityscape. A cartoon from *Punch* magazine from 1858 depicts the Thames River thick with dead rodents, an urban skyline obscured by smog, upon which Death rows a boat (fig. 5). The association between bad water, bad air, and the threat of mortality was visible and clear to all citizens.

Dangerous Density

Air, water, and soil were the first battlegrounds of disease, but the other arena of combat, albeit a much more politically, morally, and economically complicated one, was housing. Specifically, most viewed the dense, hazardous housing conditions of the working class and immigrants as the locus of illness. Sanitary inspectors across all cities zeroed in on housing conditions, especially those of the working class. Tenements are routinely described as "perpetual fever-nests" by New York's sanitary inspectors in their survey. A journalist's account from 1865 described "the high brick blocks and closely-packed houses where the mobs originated seemed to be literally hives of sickness and vice," reinforcing the comparison of the poor to insects or swarms.[10] There was often a tangible change in air quality—some narratives observed less than two hundred cubic feet of "airspace" per person. The radical disparity in mortality between tenement housing blocks and middle-class and upper-class neighborhoods indicated that there was something about the character of the neighborhood that exacerbated disease, and most focused on the extreme density of these neighborhoods. Earlier medical research made a similar connection between disease and housing density during the yellow fever epidemic of the late 1700s, one reason why military sanitary surveys dictated specific distances between tents in camps.[11]

Better Tenements for the Poor, a committee report published for the city of Boston in 1846, noted the radical disparity between poor and wealthy neighborhoods. The book exhorted its presumably upper-class audience to understand that the plight of the poor, describing "the present crowded state of the poorest class of citizens, and the consequent physical and moral degradation: although it is generally known that Boston is a very crowded city, there are probably but few persons who are aware, to what extent this is the fact, and how severely the pressure is already felt by the most helpless class of community."[12] Social scientists, who were just beginning to explore the connections between environment and behavior, pointed to physical density as a risk factor for "moral contagion."[13] While later the sanitarians would make a case for new urban infrastructure by appealing to the desire of many Americans to be as cultured as Europeans, when it came to issues of class and worker welfare, the book leaned on the emerging sense of progressivism in the United States and the potential of American opportunity and expansion in opposition to Europe, noting that "if we apply these truths to the subject before us, we cannot but be struck with the fact, that in our large cities, a downward movement of the poorest classes has commenced, which, if it be not checked, must sooner or later lead us to a condition like that of the old world, where the separation of the rich and the poor is so complete, that the former are almost afraid to visit the quarters most thickly peopled by the latter."[14] Boston's population density was described unflatteringly as close to London's "54,626 persons in 370 acres," and in the Broad Street neighborhood, "a density of population surpassed, probably, in few places in the civilized world! One individual for every seven square yards!"[15]

The concern in ensuring better housing for the poor may not have been entirely altruistic. If the manuals and surveys printed during this time are viewed as a kind of propaganda for cleaning the city, many make their case by explicitly stating that these illnesses could encroach upon the wealthier districts of the city. *Better Tenements for the Poor* notes that the "influx of unacclimated foreign immigrants . . . render the air very impure, and expose the infants, who are compelled to breath it to disease and death. The influences of such circumstances are not confined to the places where they exist, but they are extended to the population in the neighborhood; and epidemics are

Fig. 6. Immigration is linked to the rise in urban disease in a cartoon entitled "The Kind of Assisted Emigrant We Can Not Afford to Admit," showing a skeleton in exotic clothing and a belt reading "cholera." The Board of Health and a line of cannons labeled as "disenfectant" are helpless in a small dinghy against the incoming ship (*Puck* Magazine, 1883).

generated which are no doubt injurious to the general health of the city."[16] The mortality of innocent children and babies was also frequently relied upon in order to stir people's emotions. The same report notes that in tenement neighborhoods, only 53.38 out of 100 children survived to five years of age, following with the assertion, "Can there be a doubt that a large portion of this terrible mortality arises from bad air, poisoning at once the lungs and the food of the infant?" It would also be remiss not to note that the productivity of the new urban economy was dependent on the sheer manpower of the workers clustered in tenements. Concern for their health and welfare may have been out of a concern to keep the economy moving upward.[17] *Better Tenements for the Poor* notes that the housing units to be improved were "investments made as investments, not merely as charitable subscriptions."[18] Of course, the less charitable view was that the immigrants themselves posed a threat to the general population; an editorial cartoon from *Puck* magazine in 1883 depicts cholera as a skeleton sitting on the mast of an incoming ship, with the Board of Health in a tiny dinghy and bottles of disinfectant at the dock. The caption reads, "The Kind of Assisted Emigrant We Can Not Afford to Admit" (fig. 6).

All the medical evidence to the contrary would not prevent the general public from associating health outcomes to individual responsibility. To many, the fact that disease outbreaks were so common meant an association between individual actions and health outcomes. Others were suspicious of the common immigrant condition of having so many family members to one unit, a fact that may not have been as culturally based as it was a necessity of housing availability and the reality of limited options. In his sociological study *The Philadelphia Negro* (1899), W. E. B. Du Bois laid bare this hypocrisy, writing, "At the same time color prejudice makes it difficult for groups to find suitable places to move to—one Negro family would be tolerated where six would be objected to; thus we have a very decisive hinderance to emigration to the suburbs. It is not surprising that this situation leads to considerable crowding in homes."[19] This was not solely confined to housing. Many immigrants also set up informal camps at the edges of the city, near the factories where they worked but also on the yet-unclaimed marshlands and banks of waters. Although tenement housing and waterside lowlands were known as hotbeds of disease, many saw those who lived there as a result of their willingness or choice to remain there rather than forced by circumstance. When England overhauled its "Poor Laws" in the 1838, a report by physicians Arnott and Kay divided causes of sickness as "independent" or "originating" in habits; the former attributed causes to drainage, cemeteries, and ventilation, that is, general conditions of the city, but the latter meant personal cleanliness, temperance, vaccination resistance, but most notably the state of their lodging. The economic conditions governing housing choice did not figure into the framing of disease.

Others posited that the "city" itself was an epidemic. *Better Tenements for the Poor* specifically saw the poor as victims of their environment, stating, "As to the influence of this crowding, on the moral health, there can be, we apprehend, even less doubt . . . not our intention to go into details, which would be equally shocking, and unnecessary . . . just as their physical nature becomes blunted, and hardened to the impurities about them, so their moral nature gradually accustoms itself to the sight of evil, and ceases, at last, to be offended, at what was originally shocking to it."[20] While health was tied to morality, those who lived in tenements or camps could not help but succumb to bad habits when surrounded by amorphous urban evils. Crusaders took it upon themselves to ensure health welfare for the poor out of a concern that was tied into our overall health as a society. The 1865 public health report from the Council of Hygiene and Public Health, quoting English physician Edmund A. Parkes noted: "Health is a boon, however, that must be sought and protected, especially in civic life, or it is soon alienated. So definite are the conditions upon which it depends, says one of the ablest teachers of hygiene, that 'it is undoubtedly true that we can, even now, literally choose between health or disease; not perhaps always individually, for the chains of our civilization and social customs may gall us, or even our fellow men may deny us health, or the knowledge which leads to health. But as a race, man holds his own destiny, and can choose between good and evil.'"[21]

INFECTIOUS TERRAINS

Miasma and Contagion: Implications for the Environment

Sanitary surveys and mapping confirmed that disease appeared most virulent in stagnant waters, marshy grounds, and tenements, but the vectors through which it spread were still largely unknown. The health crises that struck cities in the mid- to late nineteenth century were seemingly borne of myriad conditions—pollution, density, the nature of the urban ground itself. The variety of "filth diseases" and inconsistencies in patterns of how it spread required new inquiries and frameworks. In the 1600s, physician Thomas Sydenham, known as the "English Hippocrates," further articulated that foundational thinking by positing that disease manifested both as a condition of the environment and the disposition of the patient. Different illnesses originated from different sources; for example, plague, smallpox, and dysentery came from miasmic soil gases, while pleurisy and rheumatism came from atmospheric conditions, but the constitution of the individual predisposed them to the disease becoming fully realized.[22] Sydenham also furthered the theory of Hippocratic humoral models, a quadratic diagram of conditions that linked the workings of the body to the environment—blood, warm and wet, analogous to air; yellow bile, burning like fire; black bile, dry and cold like the earth, and phlegm, cold and wet like water. When these fluids and elements of the environment balanced, the outcome was health. Any imbalance, caused in the environment or by individual habits, resulted in illness.[23]

The theory of contagion, or that disease was spread through contact and particles, also served as a parallel course of reasoning. Many historical accounts of this period pit contagionists against the miasmists, often depicting contagionists as more scientifically advanced or even describing miasmists as "anti-contagionist." Girolamo Fracastoro's *On Contagion, Contagious Diseases, and Their Treatment* was published in 1546, so the theory had been around for some three hundred years by the time the cholera epidemic struck the United States. It is true that the major advances by Pasteur and Koch in the 1880s, aided by microscopy, were still in the beginning stages of exploration, but the miasmists weren't in any way blind to science. After all, many doctors who examined cholera patients didn't get the disease, so by observation the contagion theory alone didn't hold.[24] We now know that diseases have always been caused by microbes, and the newly dense conditions of cities, along with the close proximity to animals, exacerbated the conditions for disease. Even though John Snow definitively proved that cholera was contagious, or originated with a bacterium, miasmic theory was so strong that it was often grafted onto Snow's conclusions. Max von Pettenkoffer, a German scientist and hygenicist, subscribed to Snow's theory but still

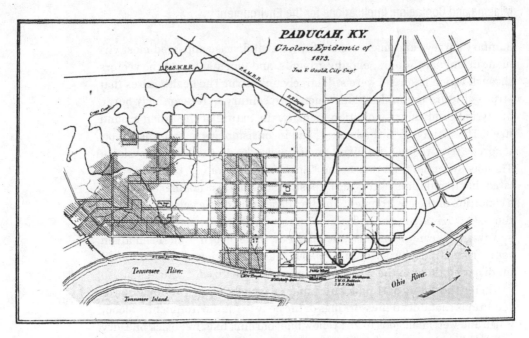

Fig. 7. The cholera map of Paducah, Kentucky, shows that there was still inconsistency on how the disease originated or spread, vaguely shading large block areas by the river. Despite John Snow's more exacting cholera mapping methods pioneered in 1854, Americans lagged behind in the epidemiological understanding of the disease (*Report to Congress on the Cholera Epidemic of 1873*).

hypothesized that sickness came when the germ itself was allowed to mutate through unfavorable soil and air conditions, so environmental conditions remained key.[25] Speaking to the above schism between medical researchers, Pettenkoffer famously and purposely drank a broth with cholera bacterium added in order to prove that the disease was not fatal without the predisposing conditions of the environment. Indeed, while he became ill with diarrhea, the stunt did not prove fatal.[26] Even the mapping of cholera shows uncertainty as to how exactly it spread. Although its origins in the United States were definitively traced to ships in ports, the same report on the state of the cholera epidemic in 1873 shows surveyors taking an exacting, Snow-like survey in Columbus, Ohio, and Lancaster, Kentucky, but another map of Paducah, Kentucky (fig. 7), depicts it as an indeterminate, amorphous shade over several city blocks. Yet another national map depicts it as simply a black line running along the Eastern Seaboard.

The idea that sickness originated from the relationship between the individual and environment, although not clearly delineated, had such a strong grounding in years of medical thought that attempting to change the physical quality of urban air and water was a plausible course of action. The general public didn't need a higher-level theory to explain why they were sick; it was tangible in the very atmosphere. Acceptance of contagion, or germ theory, in the United States lagged a couple decades behind Europe as well, for several reasons—a still emerging medical research culture, lack of university lab infrastructure, and stagnation in medical advances during the Civil War.[27] Different frameworks also had different spatial implications. Cholera was thought to cause inhalation damage from three hundred to four hundred yards away. Contagion could only occur at a much closer proximity or upon immediate contact. And while cholera and yellow fever dominate the epidemic narratives of this time period, by the 1880s death rates from pulmonary disease, tuberculosis, and pneumonia were markedly higher, as were typhoid and influenza. While cholera and yellow fever were thought to be related to conditions of the air, water, and soil, it appeared clear to the sanitary inspectors that cramped quarters exacerbated contagions. The New York City Sanitary Survey notes "typhus . . . owes origin to overcrowding, uncleanliness, and want of ventilation."[28]

The urgency of the epidemic required radical action, and coordinated sanitation campaigns proved to be effective by addressing both the predisposing conditions of miasma and the fast-moving vectors of contagion. The strategy of sanitation was also broadly understandable to people outside medicine and public health. Proponents could also tie cleanliness and bathing to a strong moral imperative. Bathing was not yet an entrenched cultural practice, but popular journals such as *Lady's Annual Register* and *Godey's Lady's Book* from the mid- to late nineteenth century depicted bathing as an aspirational activity. The importance of sanitation also encouraged the involvement of other activists and professions, especially middle- and upper-class women, engineers/architects, and temperance activists. Popular journals such as *Godey's Lady's Book* and *Ladies Home Journal* extolled the virtues of bathing and sanitation. The book *Women, Plumbers, and Doctors* (1865) by Harriette Merrick Hodge Plunkett, was a guide "showing that if women and plumbers do their whole sanitary duty, there will be comparatively little occasion for the services of the doctors." The book was essentially an introduction to plumbing aimed at women, putting the responsibility in their hands as main plumbing functions occur in kitchens, bathrooms, and butler's quarters—the "women's sphere." A report from the Twentieth Sanitary District of New York City asserted that to comprehensively combat the sanitary issue, the city needed a board of medical men with "associated engineers and architects of acknowledged ability, whose advice should at all times be sought upon questions coming within the sphere of their professional duties."[29] Leveraging the temperance movement, which was also led by women, sanitarians were able to convince activists that a consistent supply of fresh, drinkable water would lure away the general population from drinking alcohol instead. Most of all, they were able to harness the morality of sanitation to the morality of abstinence, uniting the two groups under a common cause.[30]

Medical texts would often point to miasma theory being "faulty," but this didn't mean that the actions to combat it weren't successful.[31] Even if yellow fever was caused by mosquitos and not bad airs and waters, the removal of the latter still effectively stopped its vectors. Many retrospective accounts of this time conclude miasma and contagion were competing ideologies that miasma "won," in the absence of a general knowledge of germ theory. However, this first example of the intersection of medical thought, popular concerns, and physical built environment interventions shows that these timelines are not linear or causal, but rather are overlapping and accruing. By end of nineteenth century, most scientists had identified specific germs for anthrax, plague, cholera, and so forth.[32] French and German scientists already made advances in bacteriology showing it was germs in the "filth," not filth in of itself, that caused illness. Germ theory did not erase the miasmists so much as that it clarified the argument. A multipronged strategy of sanitation and alleviating the density of industry and housing and cities addressed both ideas and were enough to radically remake the haphazard landscape of American cities. While miasmic theory guided the large-scale infrastructural transformation, contagion theory guided increased installation of sinks and privies in housing and an increased focus on individual responsibility for cleanliness.[33]

Many have characterized this search for disease causality as a war between miasmists and contagionists, or even contagionists and anti-contagionists. More accurately, it was a debate that has persisted to our present-day condition. Are public health crises best fought through an etiologic, linear course of action, attempting to find a single cause of disease, or an ecological, holistic one that encompasses broader systems of social status and economics? A contagionist stance was the former, looking at individual-to-individual infection and microbes; an anti-contagionist stance supported a social agenda. Even in the face of mounting evidence that the diseases of the Industrial Revolution originated with germs and not the generalized condition of the environment, some social reformers publicly rejected the theory as they were concerned it would take away the momentum behind larger social urban reform.[34]

Transforming the Urban Landscape and the Urban Body

Edwin Chadwick, a social reformer who oversaw the overhaul of England's landmark Poor Laws of 1834, was intensely interested in sanitation. After noticing disparities in health between the wealthy and poor, particularly after

1838 typhoid outbreak, he included sanitary measures as part and parcel of general welfare for the working class. Chadwick was an ardent believer that living conditions predisposed one to good or ill health and was driven by the desire for a permanent sanitary infrastructure. In the 1840s with surveyors and engineers, he conceived of a system that would not only carry away waste by gravity but provide a continuous feed of fresh water to flush it away from dwellings, as well as keep miasmic air from escaping. He also hypothesized that if streets were graded properly, then rainwater would also work to flush out waste. Basic sewerage components were being used at this time, but it was distributed and disaggregated in the form of private cesspools and outhouses, cleaned at their owners' behest, and waste removal was done by independent contract. Walter Channing's *A Plea for Pure Water* (1848) noted the constant failure and overflow of these private waste systems. Chadwick's revelation spread to the United States quickly, given the urgency of disease outbreaks and a willingness of newly formed municipal agencies to invest.

The dream of a sanitary city, built on cutting-edge technology and providing equitable health conditions for all, was the panacea for reformers of the late nineteenth century. British physician Benjamin Ward Richardson published *Hygeia: A City of Health* in 1876, which outlaid specific physical descriptions of a utopian city built on principles of health and hygiene, projecting "a city that shall show the lowest mortality." Richardson wrote his address as an admiring letter to Edwin Chadwick, and although Richardson recognized his manifesto as a utopian fantasy, he stated that it has the advantage of being a "new foundation, but it is so built that existing cities might be largely modelled upon it." The description of Hygeia reflects the main preoccupations with housing and miasmic gases for this era: houses are to be no more than four stories, density is limited to twenty-five persons an acre, streets are to be wide, ventilated, and "filled with sunlight," given the low height of houses. As in the sanitary surveys of New York, there are exacting details about soil makeup—clay at higher elevations, gravel at lower elevations for drainage. Streets are paved with "wood pavement set in asphalt," as "it is noiseless, cleanly, and durable." Transportation is confined to the underground, but other than that, nothing else can exist below the surface. Despite his lack of architectural or urban planning training, Richardson described every bit of the city down to house layouts and ventilation, hospitals, and public laundry operations. Discussion of people or daily living are curiously absent from his description—in fact, Richardson hoped for silent streets "though sufficiently filled with busy people"—other than noting that since the street can be flushed away with water every day, "gutter children are an impossibility in a place where there are no gutters for their innocent delectation. Instead of the gutter, the poorest child has the garden; for the foul sight and smell of unwholesome garbage, he has flowers and green sward."[35]

While not quite reaching the utopian heights of Richardson's vision, the sanitarians sought to reshape the physical landscape around these ideas.

The through line between Richardson and the on-the-ground transformation spurred by the sanitary movement is the inference of the top-down control of planning, design, and urban maintenance. The best strategy of controlling the spread of disease was controlling the urban environment and by proxy the behavior of people within it. The sanitary movement gave birth to the creation of many new categories of municipal departments such as public boards of health, urban planning, and sanitation, which banded together to combat illness.[36] This era also saw the first professional civil engineering programs in the United States, with the first degree granted by Rensselaer Polytechnic Institute in 1835. Technological and administrative prowess converged to set the stage for the major infrastructural endeavors of the late nineteenth century. All fields also enlisted infrastructural evangelists to build support for these projects. Engineer George Waring Jr. was often called upon to represent the newly formed National Board of Health in municipalities across the United States. Waring was credited with being the builder of the first separated sewer system in 1878, installed in Memphis, Tennessee, and the first to divide sewage and runoff into two pipes. He often consulted and designed sewerage systems across the country and published articles in popular media such as the *Atlantic Monthly* convincing citizens that investment in new sewer systems meant nothing less than their own humanity: "The evils arising from sanitary neglect are as old as civilization, perhaps as old as human life, and they exist about every isolated cabin of the newly settled country. As population multiplies, as cabins accumulate into hamlets, as hamlets grow into villages, villages into towns, and towns into cities, the effects of the evil become more intense, and in their appeal to our attention they are reinforced by the fact that in isolated life fatal or debilitating illness may equally arise, in compact communities each case arising is a menace to others, so that a single centre of contagion may spread devastation on every side."[37] In an editorial for *McClure's* in April 1897 he wrote, "It is not only through the children that the influence of clean streets has been felt by the people of the least intelligent classes. It has justly been said that 'cleanliness is catching,' and clean streets are leading to clean hallways and staircases and cleaner living rooms."[38] In 1894 Waring was appointed commissioner of the Department of Street Cleaning for New York and dispatched street sweepers and trash collectors in white uniforms not unlike healthcare workers, earning them the name of the "White Wings."[39]

Much like Paris's sewer system overhaul presented an opportunity to build Georges-Eugène Hausmann's grand boulevards, the new systems installed in the United States required straighter, longer streets for conveyance. The influence of European planning was not simply a technical exercise, though.

Richard Sennett's book *Flesh and Stone* notes how many eighteenth-century European cities prioritized circulation and movement via their street networks in the wake of physician William Harvey's discoveries about how the heart powered blood circulation. Dirt and grime were thought to clog healthy airs throughout the city, palaces and places of commerce acted as "hearts" that powered movement, and one-way streets were employed to maintain fast movement and mimic the directionality of veins and arteries. That influence is perhaps best seen in L'Enfant's 1792 plan for Washington, DC, especially in its many nodes and networked circulation. Although the metaphor would be much more extensively used in the latter part of the nineteenth century, L'Enfant also planned open space "lungs" at crucial intersections in order to inject the city with fresh air.[40]

At first, the new underground sewers took waste out of the street, but noxious gases still escaped into the air. The air expelled as matter decayed and dried was perceived to be just as harmful as the water itself so both sanitary engineers and many physicians advocated for steeply grading and paving surfaces to move water out and trap it underground.[41] The technology to move wastewater underground and garbage offsite unfortunately preceded the technology to treat waste. Urban waterways and bodies were already being used as a dumping ground for factories and now held the waste being conveyed away from the urban core. Over time, these naturally open waterways were contained in underground culverts and paved over. Sewers were often installed in water bodies, which were covered up and filled in. Even marshlands that otherwise were untouched by waste but still held brackish water and expelled stagnant air were filled in, which served the dual purpose of sanitizing them and accommodating urban expansion.[42] Not for nothing was one of George Waring's most well-known publications called *Draining for Profit and Draining for Health.* And as cities expanded, the infrastructure expanded with them, with outfalls further and further away from where people lived, effectively disconnecting them from the detritus of daily urban life. Philadelphia was the first city to build a public waterworks system in the 1790s, but technological advances and the sanitary movement notably hastened the construction of infrastructure in the late nineteenth century. New York and Boston built over a hundred miles each of sewers each between 1850 and 1870.[43] The proved success of these initial sewer systems would also give way to more construction as cities expanded farther still. In Newark, New Jersey, over two hundred miles of sewer were built between 1894 and 1910.[44] In Chicago, which was flat and muddy, many of the streets had to be raised.[45] Amazingly, much of the basic water infrastructure built during this time remains relatively untouched today in cities such as Pittsburgh, San Francisco, and New York.

Better Tenements for the Poor also had suggestions for overhauling worker housing and were explicit about form. The committee suggested limiting buildings in crowded parts of the city to be four stories high and to be built of iron-framed brick with slated roofs, copper gutters, and interior floors of hard pine, with the cistern on top, directly recalling Richardson's proposals for Hygeia. These specific materials were not necessarily proven to be more hygienic than others, but certainly the use of new, smooth materials that could be easily washed, with open sources of waters out of sight, gave the appearance of hygiene. In all, the change to the American urban landscape was so radical and comprehensive that even 150 years later, the improvements made during this time form the bones of the cities as we experience them today.

The building of municipal sewer systems became not only a mark of a healthy populace but also the first step in building a city that was civilized and had potential for economic, cultural, and social growth. An unidentified Baltimore engineer, albeit one who was competing for a sewer-building contract, credited Europe's extensive sewer system for low mortality rates and simultaneously its reputation as the center for the best "art, literature, science, and architecture."[46] The way our cities were transformed for sanitation is only the first case we will see of the United States looking to Europe for aspirational technology and design, or referring to London, Paris, Rome, and others as having solved the complex problems of urban disease and health. Of course, all cities had to grapple with the actual and human cost of infrastructural overhaul as well as how to address the clear links between poverty and disease. In the United States, although at this time most city services were privatized, water systems became public by necessity as no private firm could be convinced to serve an entire population, both rich and poor, purely out of concern for well-being.[47] In initial sewer installations, the city provided the line, but individual property owners had to pay to tap in. Many cities did not want to upset affluent slumlords by forcing them to hook up tenements, and as a result, poorer areas were still sometimes left behind.

The technological breakthroughs and seemingly objective sheen of "science" in both identifying the causes of disease and improving the environment also pushed aside more complicated questions of social responsibility, or poverty as a nonlinear, predisposing condition that made the poor more vulnerable to such diseases. Waring warned that true advancement could only be made if the entire city was considered, writing,

Public sanitary improvement is not the affair of the philanthropist alone, nor is the interest of the individual satisfied when he has made his own immediate surroundings perfect. Everything that can affect the health of the poorest and most distant of our neighbors may affect us; and, practically, the spread of disease in closely-built towns is more often than not, by the agency of public sewers, from the poorest classes upward, so that many a patient falling ill of contagious or infectious disease in the back slums of the city becomes the centre of a wide infection. The health of each is important to all, and all must join in securing it,—the public control, in the public interest, must extend to the sanitary condition of every household,—not among the poor alone, but at least equally among the rich. Indeed, from the greater complication of their plumbing work, the houses of the rich really require more careful supervision than do the simpler ones of the poorer class.[48]

Ultimately, while the environmental argument for health led to public intervention in the health crisis, the idea that disease disproportionately affected the poor because of insufficient hygiene habits or moral shortcomings persisted in popular opinion.[49] Many argued for social overhauls alongside the physical. An editorial titled "Ameliorating Poverty" from *Godey's Lady's Book* in November 1896 stated: "Private moneys have flowed like streams of water to the poor, with the inevitable result of increasing pauperism. Purely palliative measures had been tried at frequent intervals and proved ineffective. Now it has been asked, with a degree of pertinency, why there are palliative measures at all—why, instead, there is not a move made in the direction of complete social and industrial reform." Adding to Kathryn Staley's editorial, E. K. L. Gould, a member of New York's Improved Housing Council (IHC), again using density as a marker for ill health, added:

The solution of this problem will never be effected by tearing down a few overcrowded and unsanitary buildings, nor by mere police and sanitary regulation. The experience in the Paris slums, when great boulevards were run through the congested districts, showed very clearly that, left to themselves, the members of the slum-classes settle largely again in neighboring side streets, with the result that these are overcrowded and the rents increased. . . . In New York the conditions are these, in brief: Forty years ago the first legislative commission found them bad enough, and just a quarter of a century later, in 1881, it seems reasonable to believe, they had not improved, for a tenement-house committee was appointed and gave its warning.[50]

Conclusion

The template for how we frame, theorize, and debate the relationship between health and the environment was set in the American Industrial Revolution. Health was the medium through which cities were shaped and municipal governments imposed order. Sanitary surveys and medical topography

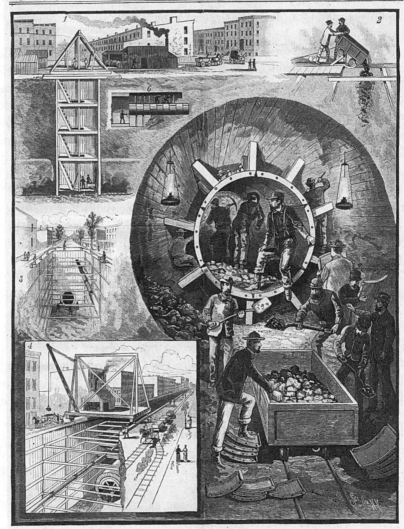

A GREAT SEWER BUILT BY AN IMPROVED METHOD OF TUNNELING, IN BROOKLYN, N. Y.—[See page 378.]

Fig. 8. Sanitary infra-structure gets the spotlight on the cover of *Scientific American,* indicating that cities taking steps to remake their urban landscapes to accommodate these pipes would be on the cutting edge of technology and enlightenment (*Scientific American,* 1885).

traced how existing landscapes of marsh and rock were transformed into city blocks, and defined the urban forms of industry and housing. The subsequent installation of sanitary infrastructure addressed the urgent issues of waste and water in the city but also widened and transformed the appearance of streets, smoothing over surfaces and reorienting grids to carry effluent out to waters (fig. 8). The sanitary campaign was indisputably a success. By the early twentieth century, infectious urban diseases had essentially been eliminated from American cities. The coordinated efforts to sanitize the city also played a major role in permanently institutionalizing municipal authorities for health, welfare, engineering, and physical planning, in turn expanding professional fields.

The early days of American cities showed the transitional seams between a rural and industrial economy. The new paradigms of health also crystallized the promise of urban life, where one was no longer in constant danger from physical hazards and disease, but where a quality of life could be ensured by the cutting-edge technology of sewerage. And as the natural coastlines were expanded with fill, and water bodies sent underground or enveloped by cisterns, cities also became further separated from their natural history. Instead they would be shaped to reflect an aesthetic of wellness that was first hardscaped and sanitary and later to accommodate large pastoral "breathing space" in the form of parks and beautification campaigns. The ability to embrace large-scale, humanistic thinking about health in order to draw connections, described by historian Sari Altschuler as "the medical imagination," characterized much of practice throughout the nineteenth century, an epistemology that can be seen in John Snow's landmark map. The "medical imagination" also helped practitioners at this time form convincing narratives about health, hygiene, and the urban environment that enabled its large-scale transformation.[51] However, it was also during this period American cities would move toward technocratic and scientific solutions over addressing systemic causes of inequity and disease. The tension between these approaches, especially as the United States began to form a decidedly more individualistic ethos around responsibility, health, and morality, would define the contours of the urban landscape as we know it today.

CHAPTER 2

Work and Play

Nature, Morality, Health

By the late nineteenth century, the epidemic disease wracking urban areas had been mostly eradicated thanks to the coordinated effort of public health campaigns, etiologic investigation, and massive infrastructural investment. Industrialization was not only about the production of goods but also about the increasing control of the elements that build the city. At the same time there appeared to be a sense of national anxiety of urbanization and growing ever distant from the American heritage of the frontier. There was a concurrent and growing interest in rediscovering a type of nature that was only accessible by leaving the city and civilization entirely. The longing for "nature" seemed to be a logical reaction against industrialization, but ironically, the leisure time allowed to people leaving the city was very much aided by technological progress. This chapter explores how integrating leisure and escape back into daily life was recommended for health but was also tied to moral imperative. The swift rise and decline of elite country resorts and towns offering elemental cures of air and water and the similarly short-lived playground initiatives in the United States were separate but parallel narratives built on the same ideas of building good character through leisure and opportunities to engage with nature, "nature" referring to both the physical environment and a state of mind. The utilitarian urban playgrounds, built in bare empty lots and surrounded by buildings, were a far cry from the remote mountains offering hay fever cures, but the strong movements behind both had similar goals of reclaiming the leisure time that industrialization had ostensibly taken from them and, above all, tapping into mankind's "natural" affinity for physical play and wilderness. What became clear in both cases was that the "correct" type of nature, either its physical properties or the kind of activity in which children engaged, was narrowly defined by a small subset of intellectuals.

Many historians have hypothesized different reasons for this sudden craze for rediscovering nature. The fondness for the pastoral in the form of art or parks appears to be universal, but immigrants and domestic new arrivals to the city still remembered their own rural background and began to feel regret for the unceasingly fast pace of their new lifestyles. The radical changes in the landscape, which happened within a couple decades, were distressing to even those who weren't directly displaced by infrastructural installation and slum clearing. Occasionally nature would try to violently reclaim the urban landscape as well, with cities prone to backup floods and pipe breakages. In Chicago, it was reported that fish both dead and alive occasionally came out of the faucets.[1] Some intellectuals, such as Henry David Thoreau, would publicly declare their uneasiness with the large-scale bending of natural resources to serve the urban population.[2] At the same time, the frontier of the American West had more or less been bridged by the building of railroads and settlement, making the wild accessible again.

The United States has always been defined by its perception of its wilderness, its vastness, and its agricultural history. But wilderness only exists as a contrast to civilization. Wilderness was associated with the sublime and sacred, a higher power that cowed man into good morals. This ideal was elevated by transcendentalists such as Thoreau, Emerson, and Hawthorne.[3] John Muir and Thoreau would credit nature as curing their consumption, the disease most associated with the urban condition. The urban man could only cure what he had become by immersing himself in the environment that he had forgotten, but these exhortations had distinct class associations. To conceive of nature or wilderness as an untouched resource neglected the history of the Native Americans who were removed from the land. Similarly, farmers involved in the day-to-day of agricultural work were not prone to idealize untouched land, as they intimately knew the work it took to transform it into something productive. Instead, the conception of healthy wilderness or nature was an image largely sold by intellectuals and other elite.[4] Nor was that position immune to the strain of American individualism and personal virtue. Thoreau's account of his time in nature, narrated in *Walden* (1854) is presented as a moral choice any man can make to preserve their own health and values. In his lecture "The Young American," Emerson expounded: "The land is the appointed remedy for whatever is false and fantastic in our culture. The continent we inhabit is to be physic and food for our mind, as well as our body. The land, with its tranquilizing, sanative influences, is to repair the errors of a scholastic and traditional education and bring us into just relations with men and things."[5] John Brinckerhoff Jackson elucidated that Thoreau's position was that man was "part and parcel of nature," a view that demanded a retreat from society and mutual responsibility.[6] This differs from his best-known anti-urbanist predecessor Thomas Jefferson, in views shared by later utopian plans such as Ebenezer Howard's Garden City and even Le Corbusier's Radiant City, which also advocated for the preservation of rural landscape, but in the interest of agrarian production and societal contribution.[7] These extreme ideas about wilderness and the inherent morality of primitive nature would reverberate through popular culture too, as seen in Theodore Roosevelt's demonstrative trips out West for hunting and respite. In 1913, a story that gripped the nation was that of Joseph Knowles, an illustrator who literally stripped off every modern convenience, including clothes, and went to live in the Maine woods for two months. When he returned he extolled the values of rejecting the mechanization of modern life and returning to nature. A Harvard physician was enlisted to report on his excellent health. Knowles would go on to command crowds of twenty thousand and write a best-selling memoir, *Alone in the Wilderness*. Although Knowles's performance is now widely thought to be a publicity stunt, he tapped into the anxiety of an increasingly urbanized population and a desire for a simpler life of solitude.[8] Nature as a place, and rediscovering the "nature" of humans, was sought as a salve for mental, physical, and moral illness.

Air, Water, and Sun Cures

Vis medicatrix naturae is the Latin translation of the Hippocratic idea "Nature is the physician of diseases." This thought persisted well into the nineteenth and twentieth centuries. Although the credo was more about the ability of both the ideal body and nature to regulate themselves, the idea of the elements as a consumable cure for illness became literal in the era's craze for nature resorts. In an 1886 book on "Hydrotherapeutics," Wilhelm Winternitz stated, "Nature alone can cure; this is the highest law of practical medicine, and the one we must adhere even when we have discovered a principle of cure second to it."[9] In an 1875 issue of the *Boston Medical and Surgical Journal*, Morril Wyman, MD, describes the conditions of "autumnal catarrh, or 'hay fever'" and presents the successful case of someone inhaling oxygen gas directly from a geyser spring for relief from his hay fever. Dissatisfied with the conditions of the city, elite urban dwellers sought to imbibe clean air, fresh water, and sunlight for a curious new crop of afflictions that seemed to only affect the upper class. Modern civilization seemed to breed an array of afflictions of "nervousness" ranging from exhaustion to increased sensitivity to climatic change, foods, medicines, and other irritants that appeared to be more acute during hot summer months. People with upper-class "indoor occupations" such as lawyers, dentists, merchants, and manufacturers, appeared to have the most frequent occurrence of disease.[10]

The relatively short-lived craze over hydropathy, or the "water cure," is an analog to the practical concerns of clean urban water supply in cities. Hydropathy focused on the use of mineral-rich waters, only found in rural areas. Like the sanitation movement, water cure theory originated in England, although curative bathing practices date back to Roman times. Actual water cure practice was a multistepped affair emphasizing fresh air, exercise, rest, and massage in addition to using water to wet linens and wrap them around the body for several hours at a time, as well as purging stomachs and bowels.[11] In other words, the "cure" could not be attributed only to water, but rather holistic practices of wellness. This was thought to cure skin afflictions and sores, digestive issues, joint pains, and the above-mentioned "nervous diseases." Although by the 1840s there were methods of water cure that could be done in one's home, the element of escape from the city and its ills was its most appealing aspect. Said physician James M'Cabe in 1823, "It not only refers to the diet . . . but also embraces air, exercise, society, or seclusion from society; and thus connects the physical necessities of the body with the moral influence of the mind." Once again, wellness was tied intrinsically to morality.[12] An 1862 edition of *Ballou's Dollar Monthly Magazine* exalted the "health sustaining effects of motorpathy, mountain air, and hot and cold baths" for "opium-eaters, arsenic-takers, etc." as well as "the low-spirited, dyspeptic, nervous, or organically weak."[13] Although many medical doctors were hostile toward spa medicine and hydropathy, particularly after it was proved that minerals could not be absorbed through skin, the practice even merited its own journal, simply called the *Water-Cure Journal and Herald of Reform*, which appeared from 1845 to 1861, and at one point had a circulation of fifty thousand.[14] Historian Marshall Scott Legan has also partially attributed the surprisingly widespread acceptance of hydropathy and other homeopathic cures to the populist mindset that characterized the United States after Andrew Jackson's election and its accompanying distrust of science and regulation.[15]

Another affliction that seemed to disproportionately affect urban professionals was catarrh. Loosely defined as a collection of "nervous diseases," mostly those affecting the respiratory tract, this disease was closely tied to place, time, and season. Physician Morell Mackenzie's book, *Hay Fever and Paroxysmal Sneezing* (1887), stated that those predisposed to the disease had "possession of a peculiar idiosyncrasy, but on what that idiosyncrasy depends is quite unknown . . . local abnormality affecting the structure of the mucous membrane, the capillaries, or the periphery of the nerves, but of too delicate a nature to admit of detection by available methods of research, cannot be determined." Mackenzie also noted the "idiosyncrasies" only seemed to affect English and Americans. Although germ theory was widening in accep-

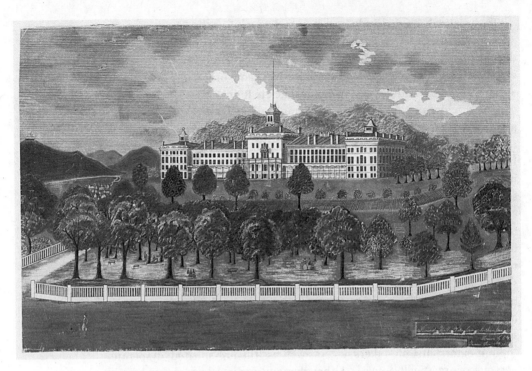

Fig. 9. *Round Hill Water Cure Northampton M[assachusetts]* by E. W. Farmer, 1856, depicts a medical institution based on hydropathic principles and opened by Dr. E. E. Denniston in 1847. The resort is positioned at the top of the hill to access better airs and is surrounded by carefully ordered trees. (Library of Congress, Prints and Photographs Division, Washington, D.C.)

tance, hay fever didn't show signs of contagion, meaning many physicians had to look at environmental causes.[16] While the etiology of the disease had not yet been pinpointed, anecdotally the symptoms seemed more attenuated in urban areas and during hot weather. An advertisement for the Round Hill Water Cure Establishment (fig. 9) in the *Boston Recorder* suggested that its presumably urban readers "escape the heated air and streets of our city, and seek for renewal health and vigor in the country."[17] In the book *The Adirondacks as a Health Resort* (1886), one Dr. Hooper is quoted as saying: "Change of air or climate is generally esteemed a most important means of preserving, improving, and restoring health. There are two classes of persons to whom it is usual to recommend the change. The one consists of invalids who suffer from no defined disease, but whose general health has been impaired by exposure to one or other of the many unwholesome influences which attend a residence in large towns; the other comprises persons suffering from some well-defined malady, such as chronic dyspepsia, chronic rheumatism, scrofula, pulmonary consumption, chronic bronchitis, and asthma."[18]

The westward expanse of the American landscape was dotted with many towns with natural hot and mineral springs that could provide this escape

The Most Picturesque Pleasure and Health Resort in California

MARK WEST HOT SPRINGS
With its Large and Beautiful Grape Arbor has no Equal in California.

Fig. 10. The advertisement for Mark West Hot Springs in California is typical of the era, showing a rural ideal, downplaying the urban development, and prominently featuring the mountain topography (1898). (Courtesy, the Sonoma County Library)

from the city (fig. 10). Far-flung locales such as Saratoga Springs, Palm Springs, and Calistoga, all in California, and Hot Springs, Arkansas, marketed the curative nature of their waters and swathed them in resort architecture largely in the Spanish Colonial Revival style, evoking dry, clean air. The growth of resort towns during this period was no doubt buffered by railroad expansion. The growing ease with which people with the attendant resources and time could escape the city only helped to solidify the binary of healthy country and sickly cities. These moves outward were also supported by the growth of a subset of research called "medical geography." In a way, medical geography was a natural outgrowth from the narrative sanitary surveys of the industrial era. Instead of describing wards of the city, books narrated the climatic and landscape conditions of towns in such a way that people looking to escape the city could gain a clear picture and glean anecdotal experience from others who had fled the city to cure their afflictions. The rise of pulmonary tuberculosis also spurred an interest in the relationship between climatology and disease; the American Climatological Association was formed in 1883, with a commitment to studying the origins of respiratory disease and pushing for climatology to be taught in medical schools. The connections between place and health were naturally and closely intertwined in most popular thought. Letters to the East Coast from family members who had moved to the West often referred to places as "sickly," "healthy," or "salubrious." Many still viewed health as an outcome of balance between body and nature, with the skin understood as an organ, but a porous one connected to all internal organs. As such, it would absorb environmental disturbances, so radical changes in the weather could spur sickness.[19] "Climate" was understood as an entity influenced by interconnections between trees, soil, and water. In a medical topography, all these elements had to be thoroughly described.

The findings of medical geography were disseminated in publications, often alongside maps and personal accounts of how these far-flung landscapes had cured their symptoms. Morrill Wyman mapped the literal topography of the disease in his book *Autumnal Catarrh* (1872), noting where his symptoms were the worst as he took a cross-country train trip. The spatial investigations originated by the sanitary surveys became regional. Spread over a wider area, they lack the epidemiological preciseness of John Snow's maps but provide a qualitative narrative of place, landscape, and nature. In a map of the White Mountains (fig. 11), an area of New Hampshire popularized for its hay fever resorts as well as the writings of Emerson and Hawthorne, Wyman delineates

Fig. 11. *White Mountains from Conway, NH* by David Johnson, 1851–52, depicts a hay fever resort set in a romanticized rural landscape. (Oil on canvas, 40.64 × 58.42 cm 16 × 23 in.], Gift of Maxim Karolik for the M. and M. Karolik Collection of American Paintings, 1815–1865, 62.276; Photograph © 2021 Museum of Fine Arts Boston)

INFECTIOUS TERRAINS

areas of catarrh as one amorphous colored area overlaid on the southern area of a topographic map. It is unclear what environmental features could be related to the epidemic, just as the factors contributing to the illness remained unclear for years. What did last from this cartography of hay fever and water cures was a theoretical relationship between city and country, where the former was seen as an incubator of disease, the latter the cure. The medical topographies were not so much a causal investigation but descriptive texts that were meant to help people suffering from these maladies explore and understand the potential of new locales from the safety of their home. There also appears to be evidence that cities would commission such topographies in a bid to attract new settlers. In *The Health and Wealth of the City of Wheeling* (1871), a Dr. James Reeves described this West Virginia town in terms of its economic potential, environmental health, but also urban morality. In his address to the town's mayor, Reeves stated, "If, in my topographical survey, I have exposed sanitary defects and disadvantages which attach to the city—have spoken plainly of evil practices which, unfortunately, form part of the heritage of all cities and large towns—I have also made known a greater number of truths concerning the virtuous character of the people of Wheeling, as well as their business prosperity and happiness." Reeves outlined the elevation, natural resources, plant list, geological stratification and soil. The state of the city's drainage and sewerage, extending to private privies, was of course discussed. Reeves discussed the numerous refineries, manufacturing plants, and slaughterhouses in the city but also assured potential residents how they were cleaned or kept away from the residents. These were presented in conjunction with a directory of physicians, a history of epidemics (cholera, scarlet fever, diphtheria, etc.), and the presence of immoral activities, called out specifically as prostitution, "self-abuse," and abortion. Berkeley Springs, another West Virginia town, was depicted in a painting as situated just beyond a protective barrier of trees, with a mountain backdrop, the buildings of the town itself relegated to the very bottom of the frame to devote more space to its blue, clear skies (fig. 12). A collection of accounts of the town from the 1840s notes the friendliness and moral character of its citizens in contrast to other increasingly more crowded resort towns, concluding "the more populous they are, the less sociable."[20]

For the elite, medical topography also served as a brochure for a wellness vacation. In these volumes, the intersections between nineteenth-century concepts of nature, morality, and health are clear. The subtitle of Joseph W. Stickler's *The Adirondacks as a Health Resort* (1886) states that it is "Showing the benefit to be derived by a sojourn in the wilderness, in cases of pulmonary phthisis, acute and chronic bronchitis, asthma, 'hay-fever' and various nervous affections." Instead of a view of the region through one expert's eye,

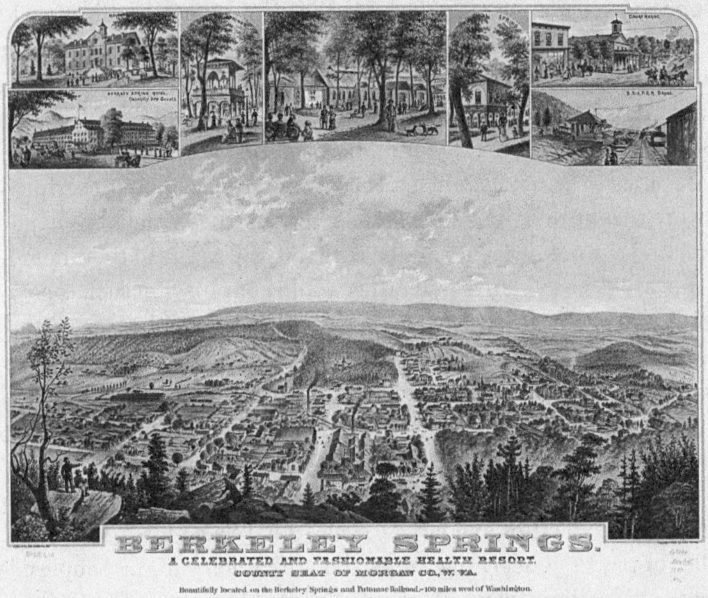

Fig. 12. In a poster titled "Berkeley Springs, West Virginia, a celebrated and fashionable health resort" by John Moray and A. Hoen, 1889, its mountain topography, large expanses of clear sky, and trees are prominent with vignettes of small-town life above. (Library of Congress, Geography and Map Division, Washington, D.C.)

the book is a collection of testimonies from people who went to the mountain range for treatment of various "pulmonary affections," along with the observation that year-round residents do not have hay fever, diseases of the throat, respiratory diseases, and diseases of the nerves. Like any dutiful geographer, Stickler placed the resort in space, latitude and longitude, and between major water bodies and mountains, and provided elevations and seasonal climate changes. The water's purity was judged by its transparency. A few key passages reveal that a healthy landscape was narrowly defined in the eyes of its advocates. Stickler noted the silence and temperate environment, and in a section titled "Seclusion from Temptation to Harmful Indulgence" he extolled the quiet campfire dinners in place of dinner parties (i.e., an urban activity). Camping, rather than staying in a resort, was encouraged, and overall Stickler's proposed cures hewed much more closely to the asceticism of Emerson's and Thoreau's sojourn. Actually viewing agricultural activity is simultaneously too industrial, too uncivilized, and too destructive a venture to promote health, however. In a featured essay about the Adirondacks topography, the Reverend Joseph T. Duryea described the region: "The vegetation is mostly arboreal, and the grasses and other plants do not secrete the materials for such fermentation and putrefaction as may be detected in heaps of potato and tomato vines, and other such products of thickly settled and badly managed farming regions." Just as the sewerage programs of the

Industrial Revolution deposited waste into rivers far out of sight, the messy work of healthy human habitats had to be hidden to be accepted.

Even if there was a prevalent mistrust of science, endorsements of doctors were key to the popularity of hydropathy and therapeutic rural resorts. In 1899, Dr. James M. Crook published an extensive guide entitled *The Mineral Waters of the United States and Their Therapeutic Uses,* which claimed to be the first to locate all 2,822 mineral springs and wells in the United States, listed state by state with each located by latitude and longitude and in many cases its mineral content broken down in grains per gallon. A good portion of these springs are noted to have hotels built nearby, and in the case of many western states, it bears special mention when there are not, perhaps inadvertently signaling economic opportunity. The Round Hill Water Cure Establishment was in fact run by one H. Halsted, MD, both the "proprietor and physician," with his particular success in "women's diseases" noted in an 1860 advertisement in the *New York Illustrated News.* The way these resorts were advertised blurred the line between vacation and medical treatment. The Round Hill resort notes that at the dining hall "two tables are set; one furnished with all the luxuries of a first class hotel—the other with a plain diet recommended to invalids." Furthermore, the resort notes its extensive program of amusements, among them music, dramatic readings, and horseback riding, but with the purpose of "whatever tends to render the mind cheerful and happy, and to draw it away from dwelling on bodily aliments."[21] A lithograph of the resort showed it sitting upon a hill ("200 feet" from the presumably miasmic airs of the Connecticut River, an advertisement is careful to note), surrounded by orderly planted trees. Crook's massive volume on mineral springs, Halsted's promotional material for his resort, and countless other medical geographies took great pains to describe trees, mountains, and other bodies of water, but they are not heralded for their environmental or health performance so much as providing views for delight, amusement, or contemplation. The aesthetics of these resorts were meant to soothe nervous urban dwellers as their waters cured their physiological dysfunction.

Ironically, the rural landscape many sought was increasingly urbanized by the economy of health. Wyman writes that the "dust and smoke of a railway train" is noted as the most prominent and general cause of sneezing paroxysm along with strong light. Ragweed, a known allergen, sprung up in places where soil was disturbed.[22] Moreover, disease literally shaped the landscape as these small towns were transformed into hotels, larger towns, and other land use. Western cities such as Phoenix and Denver grew significantly by specifically recruiting asthmatics. Dr. Charles Denison's *Rocky Mountain Health Resorts* (1880) advertised Colorado as the "Switzerland of the Americas," evoking images of both clean mountain air and the superior moral values of Europeans. This was a common tactic in these tomes, which were part medical geographies and part travel brochure. Crook also frequently invoked more established European spas as models for American ones. It was estimated that up to a quarter of people who settled in Colorado, Arizona, and California during this time did so due to for their health or a family member's health. Ironically, agriculture and increasing irrigation supported plant growth in the future, and many developed allergies.[23] By 1890, Denver had grown by almost a third, with almost thirty thousand people moving there to treat consumption. This rate of growth would persist for the next three decades.

There is no doubt that health resorts were only available to the elite. After all, treatment required a ticket out of the city and weeks or even months of treatment, time and money not afforded by most of the urban laboring class. The origins of hay fever and other nervous afflictions were difficult to pinpoint, and in fact so were its exact afflictions, but when the only "cure" was to escape the city, many were only too eager to seize upon it, not only as a way to address their illnesses, but as a status symbol. An editorial by a Mrs. Hopkinson in the March 1867 *Godey's Lady's Book* discusses "the water-cure in Prussia" and adds: "A Frenchman has established a *Sun Cure*. It is very simple, and is said to be very effectual as a remedy in obstinate cases of disease. The patient is seated in an apartment at the top of the house, which apartment is completely glazed. Nothing is allowed to supervene between Apollo and the surface of the patient. It is to be supposed that the reception rooms of the god are single—at all events we do not hear of the patient's receiving his visits in a social way. But the effect of the direct rays of the sun is said to be very peculiar and sanitary. . . . Our countrymen enjoy change of place and change of air. We like to plunge at Newport, to climb at Franconia, to pour libations at Saratoga to Hygeia. We like to give money for things, and have our money's worth. Why should we bathe in this miserable brook Jordan which runs before our very doors? Are not Abana and Pharpar better."

All About Santa Barbara, CA: The Sanitarium of the Pacific Coast (1878), a promotional pamphlet for a tuberculosis clinic, warns:

Persons predisposed to consumption ought not to be allowed to live in cities. The absence of sunlight is a frightful cause of the prevalence of the disease. The streets are so narrow and the houses so high, that sunlight seldom reaches the sitting rooms. The schoolhouses are so situated that children can scarcely ever see the sun. The sun is the source of all light, life and beauty, and Is as necessary to give color and health and life to animals and plants. It corrects musty smells, so prolific of disease. There is no surer way of promoting consumption than by the exclusion of sunlight. Sedentary life and inactivity, impure air and the absence of sunlight in cities produce a fearful mortality.

Even with urban improvement projects in both Europe in the United States, the increased utilization of population data and medical topographies still revealed higher mortality rates in the city than in rural areas, strengthening those associations between density and disease.[24]

The health resort was a relatively short-lived phenomenon in the United States. Many of the towns fell into ruin with discovery of penicillin and more internal methods of treating illness. Strangely, the affliction of hay fever began to fade from popular thought; some advancing the theory that it was caused by abnormalities in nose structure reflected medicine's turn in general toward individual and internal. It is not surprising that as germ theory and a new era of scientific rationalism began to define the medical community, the medical topographies, written by doctors acting as surveyors and landscape narrators began to fall out of favor. Moreover, the field was always somewhat defined by its adherents' defensiveness. One C. Barham wrote a letter in 1850 to *Provincial Medical and Surgical Journal* regarding the state of the field of medical topography. Seeing the practice as an important corollary to sanitary science, he argued for more rigid methodology. Instead of point-in-time descriptions, he advocated for more longitudinal observations, at least over two years, and wrote: "Let the work specially undertaken by our Association be a simultaneous record of the health of the population in certain selected localities, during a fixed period . . . the daily registration of the phenomena of disturbed vital organisms—those of animals and plants as well as of men—should make the nearest practicable approach to regularity and precision considered indispensable in meteorological observations." Buffalo physician F. R. Campbell also critiqued germ theorists' dismissal of environmental causes, stating: "All are busy searching for specific germs; by their constant microscopical labors they have become intellectually myopic, and cannot see that there may be causes of disease which it is impossible to place beneath a cover glass."[25] Nevertheless, medical geographers were now forced to specify pathology of their environmental diseases in an era that demanded microscopic studies and explanations, and the significant body of literature dwindled.

Children's Health and the Playground Movement

Epidemic urban disease was mostly under control by the early 1900s, but the idea that cities cultivated poor morals persisted. Just as sanitarians during the Industrial Revolution made their case for intervention by focusing on the mortality of infants and children, a new "child saving" movement emphasized how the morals of urban youth were most vulnerable to the corrupting, all-encompassing influence of the city. Luther Gulick, who would go on to become the president of the Playground Association of America, reached out to *Good Housekeeping's* audience of mothers in a 1909 editorial titled "Why Have Playgrounds?," by noting the actual and moral danger of the streets, citing that one-third of all accidents to city children happen in the streets, and by stating ultimately, "Playgrounds stand for law and order; the street corner gang stands for anarchy and disorder." Above all, playgrounds were a tonic for the ills of the city; a pamphlet advocating for playgrounds in Philadelphia built on the successes of the actual and social sanitary movement by stating, "Adequate play space is a sanitary measure as much as pure water and clean streets. Since disease and subnormal vitality are the primary causes of a large percentage of poverty, well directed play is a preventive of poverty, and an important factor in the solution of the problems of the city."[26]

Additionally, the increasing use of child labor in factories made many reexamine what a child's formative years should entail. It is key to note that these activists were not against child labor itself. Henry S. Curtis, former secretary of the Playground Association of America, didn't necessarily view the fact that children were working as a negative development; in fact, he felt that the decline in farm work for American children was a detriment. However, he thought the type of work industrialization offered was to blame. Rather, he said, "These [child labor] laws have been made necessary by modern conditions, but it is not so much that work in moderate amounts is harmful to children, but that the work which is available for them is work of a monotonous, uninteresting kind which is destructive both to soul and body for man and child alike."[27] Similarly, G. Stanley Hall decried not the fact that children had been enlisted in the Industrial Revolution, or their working conditions, but the plague of industrialization as a concept, noting the emphasis on the quantification of industrial efficiency "was a culmination in the field of industry of acute Americanitis, set forth in the gospel of greatest results by least effort."[28] In an article for *Public Health Journal* in 1913, titled "The Value of Playgrounds to Community," anti-poverty activist Jacob A. Riis said, "There is an unsuspected connection between lack of play in young years, child labor, and trampery. . . . The boy without a playground is the father of a man without a job. Force him into a shop in his young years, when he should be out at play, and he will be the father of the man who doesn't want a job!" He added, "strenuous as is the life of our people, the great danger in the American city is not in overwork, nor in intense work, but in the relaxation of our people . . . not until we care for the relaxation of the nation may we boast of a permanent and virile civilization"[29] (fig. 13).

The movement to introduce physical activity back into children's lives was led by activists primarily in social work, child psychology, education, and anti-poverty movements. Many were also specifically tied to the Chicago

Fig. 13. Boys pushing wheelbarrows and a simple dirt lot in an early playground in an area of New York City called Poverty Gap, photograph by Jacob Riis, 1890. (Jacob A. Riis / Museum of the City of New York, 2001.41.4)

Settlement House movement such as Riis, Jane Addams, Lillian Wald, and Graham Taylor, which further tied the activism to the plight of those living in tenements. Like other Progressive Era design movements, the playground movement epitomized the odd intersection of scientific hypothesis and moral instruction, here applied to the study of children. The intellectual drivers of the movement, among them John Dewey, G. Stanley Hall, Henry Curtis, and George Johnson, all had backgrounds in education and psychology. Luther Gulick, another leader, was contemplating a career in ministry but saw the future of organized play as a similar salvation to the nation's children, putting physical exercise and moral discipline hand in hand.[30] Many of the aforementioned activists ended up in the Playground Association of America (PAA, established 1906) and were considerably boosted by funding from the Russell Sage Foundation, the philanthropic organization founded in 1907. They were volunteers but hoped to turn the building and administration of playgrounds into a state responsibility and permanent fixture of public policy. Reflecting the embrace of these ideals at a national level, the first honorary president of the PAA was President Theodore Roosevelt. Local groups were similarly staffed by upper-middle-class professionals and elite, all volunteering time, but for the most part dedicated to the mission of working with local groups. The Chicago Playground Association included businessmen, welfare workers, a juvenile court judge, and landscape architect Jens Jensen but undertook the work of investigating city conditions and forming neighborhood committees. Even Frederick Law Olmsted was involved with the Chicago playground system at some points, laying out fourteen small playgrounds with the South Side Park Commission.[31]

These leaders advocated for a very specific kind of play, both highly prescribed in program and distribution. The organizations did succeed in passing successful policies that ensured access. A model law many would come to adapt was a 1887 "small parks" statute in the state of New York "to provide for the location, construction, and improvement of additional public parks in New York City," giving the Board of Street Opening and Improvement power to close streets, assess damages to owners of land taken for parks, and place taxes on land with little restriction on powers (fig. 14).[32] The board was a result of a recommendation by the Tenement House Commission, no doubt a strategy to reduce the density of these neighborhoods. Almost twenty years later, in 1908 the Massachusetts Legislature declared that every city with a population of more than ten thousand should provide and maintain at least one public playground, and one more for every twenty thousand, and the law was used as a model in advocacy material in Philadelphia and other cities.[33] The directive was closely tied to the improvement of health; the Massachusetts directive gave as guidance to the Department of Public Parks to "construct the said parks in such manner, and to erect and furnish therein for

Fig. 14. Orderly play at a vacation playground at 66th Street and 1st Avenue, Manhattan, photograph by Jacob Riis, 1902. While children were encouraged to rediscover their "nature," play was often segregated by sex, heavily programmed, and closely supervised. (Jacob A. Riis / Museum of the City of New York, 90.13.1.121)

public purposes, for the health, comfort, and instruction of the people."[34] In Philadelphia, the Health Department was closely involved with the project, recommending that parks should be located near public schools so they would maximize usage as playgrounds.

Not only was the placement of playgrounds highly regulated, but so was the type of play advocated for—leaders sought to combat the perceived anarchy of street games with organized activity. Many of the foundational ideas can be found in Henry Curtis's *The Play Movement and its Significance,* published in 1917. Curtis was a secretary for the Playground Association of America and later supervisor of the District of Columbia. Although Curtis argues that is in children's nature to play, that play must be highly organized, such as in team sports or prescribed activities. He fails to elaborate on his claim that even cats "organize" games for their kittens, but nevertheless he stands by a thesis shared by the other intellectuals involved with the movement that children needed to simultaneously reclaim their "natural" tendency toward play but also be shaped into upstanding young adults of the next generation. Two editorials in the PAA's publication *The Playground,* "Play as an Antidote to Civilization" by Joseph Lee and "Play as a Moral Equivalent of War" by George Johnson, demonstrated where these two ideals may come into conflict. Hall believed in tapping into "primitive" psyche, which was linked to better morality, implying that the city and modern modes of work were the corrupting influence on otherwise innocent children. Despite the bemoaning of industrialization and efficiency, "play" as defined by the PAA is quantified and even "efficient" per Curtis's exhortation; in a section called "Play Efficiency" he calls for playgrounds to be laid out in sections for children of same age and sex. Despite the discussion about children discovering instinct, a key component to the play agenda was to fill up time to prevent idleness, and there was an emphasis on qualified supervision from an education or other professional (in some promotional materials, only referred to as a "he").[35] Curtis prescribes a minimum of "five hours of play and physical training each week, over and above the fifteen-minute recesses during the morning and afternoon, and the noon intermission, shall become a part of the program for each grade of the elementary and high school."[36]

The battle against idleness was tied up in the moral foundations of the movement. Honorary PAA Theodore Roosevelt claimed, "Playgrounds are necessary means for the development of wholesome citizenship in modern cities." Team sports played on these playgrounds were practice for good social behavior. Riis would add that if cities were to follow the philosophy of the PAA, "be sure that it will repay you a thousand times in the days coming, in good citizenship."[37] Above all, activists liked to point out how playgrounds were a deterrent to crime. Said Curtis, "Stunted bodies often result in unde-veloped minds, and these in warped morals. . . . The Public Playground is the greatest deterrent of delinquency and lawlessness among children. It stands for body and character building and produces better children, homes, morals and citizens. On the score of public economy alone the playground is a neces-sity."[38] An oft-cited statistic in literature noted that in one district of Chicago, juvenile cases decreased 44 percent with introduction of a playground.[39] Like the sanitary movement, the participation of women was also crucial in com-municating the concerns of childhood dangers to the public. Not only were women seen as inherently more "moral," but their established roles in the related fields of education and social work, as opposed to other professions, meant they were relied on as experts and supervisors.[40]

Writing about play and playgrounds emphasized the danger of the streets, where children would otherwise play if bereft of structured playgrounds. In this era, although "streets" had been cleared of waste and cholera, they still represented the battleground of the city. Curtis noted, "On the physical side the street means degeneracy. It stands for an overstimulation of nerves, for heat that is almost past endurance at times, for air that is charged with nox-ious dust and germs, among which the germs of consumption find a promi-nent place. The analysis made in 1907 showed more than 100,000 germs to the cubic centimeter of air taken from near the curb on some of the down-town streets of New York."[41] He objected to cobblestone and block pavement as the joints between them still held dirt and germs and also presented risk of injuries such as sprained ankles. While he preferred the growing use of automobiles, noting that drivers are required to have licenses and therefore are more qualified to navigate streets than common wagon drivers, he did note their danger to pedestrians if speed was not regulated. Curtis also noted the chain of events in street play that led to delinquency, echoed by many of his fellow playground advocates. Children who play in the streets were thought more likely to cause accidental damage to adjacent buildings, lead-ing to arrest. Curtis said street games like baseball make policemen become a "natural enemy" and lead to a childhood of antagonism toward law enforce-ment. He also noted those engaging in street play tend toward "loafing" be-cause the games are broken up frequently by traffic. In essence, "it is not the play but the idleness of the street that is morally dangerous."[42]

Organized play was thought to be a tonic not just to behavioral issues but also to actual infectious diseases and altered physiology wrought by modern culture. Promotional materials to establish a playground board in Philadel-phia read, "The International Conference on Tuberculosis adopted a resolu-tion that "playgrounds constitute one of the most effective methods for the prevention of tuberculosis, and that playgrounds should be put to the fore in the worldwide propaganda for the diminution of its unnecessary destruction of human life."[43] John Collins Warren, professor of anatomy and surgery at Harvard University, described how too much leisure time distorted the bones and spines of children as they grew, in his treatise *Physical Education and the Preservation of Health* (1846): "Nature has destined that the physical and intellectual education of man should be conducted in very different modes. The culture of the mind requires the early, constant and well-directed efforts of an artificial system. That of physical faculties is fully effected by the powers of nature. . . . Unhappily, our state of civilization, while it has copiously supplied the means of intellectual improvement, has, nearly in the same ratio, raised obstacles to the development of physical powers."[44] He echoes the medical community's support for established playground boards, noting that in most municipalities popular votes had almost always passed for taxes and the establishment of commissions.

Most pin the origins of public play structure design to the "sand garden," or what we would call sandboxes, a German idea that was adopted by many settlement houses. The first sand garden was erected in Boston's North End, a project of female philanthropists to benefit newly arrived immigrant children.[45] These soon expanded into "model playgrounds," the first one at Jane Addams's Hull House in Chicago, where an adjacent tenement building was torn down specifically to accommodate the play area. The goal of the model playgrounds was to carefully observe which equipment was most used and how children played, in effect small laboratories to advance the theories of play.[46] The model playground program led many to attribute the play park, with its emphasis on different types of play and equipment for sex and age, as a distinctly American invention.[47] These first playgrounds were fairly utilitarian in character. The ground was often just dirt, the same structures— seesaws, maypoles, swings—built simply out of metal pipe and chain. There was some disagreement among advocates about what an ideal playground would evoke. Charles M. Robinson and landscape architect Frederick Law Olmsted thought they should be more pastoral in quality, like the latter's grand urban parks. While those parks and playgrounds had the same goal of an escape from city life, the larger parks were aimed at adults to immerse them in nature with some active play areas, whereas the goal for the playgrounds was to be easily accessible and supervised spots for regimented activity. As the playground activists focused on vacant lots as a strategy for building and distribution, they were also necessarily hemmed in by surrounding development. The criticism of these utilitarian lots was rebutted by Curtis, who dismissed the old adage "it is better for the grass to grow green over the children's graves than yellow under their feet," or worries about free play ruining the grass, by saying, "Park lawns have no other considerable use, except for

Fig. 15. "Boys Enjoying the Amusements of a Public Playground," photograph by Lewis Hine, 1915. As urban playground building movements became more widespread, the landscape remained simple (often remnant lots), but the equipment encouraged more active play—at least for boys—such as the pommel horse seen at the right. (Courtesy of the George Eastman Museum)

play. There is no great landscape effect from a broad and empty meadow. The introduction of a few sheep or cows always adds greatly to the scenic charm, but there is nothing else that has quite the landscape value on an open lawn that children have."[48]

As the playground associations expanded and became flusher with money, the requirements for play parks would become even more programmatic, with the infrastructure to match. Curtis's ideal playgrounds included "a space set aside solely for the use of boys and girls under twelve years of age, under the charge of a woman teacher . . . [and would] contain sand piles, swings, baby hammocks, and other suitable apparatus" (fig. 15). Should there be space, it should also include separate boys' and girls' gymnasiums, fields for playground ball or baseball, running track, wading pool, and finally a recreation center "fenced in and bordered with trees, shrubs, and flowers. Not only is such a recreation centre not a nuisance . . . but it is a creditable adornment to, and improvement of any neighborhood."[49]

It is also worth mentioning that after Curtis noted the danger of street play, he also devoted a lengthy chapter to using street space and other interstitial spaces for play. Recognizing the lack of open space in denser urban areas, he concedes: "There are five possible solutions: The setting aside of certain streets for play; the clearing out and improving the interior courts; the utilizing of all vacant spaces; the larger use of the roofs; the building of more recreation piers or skyscraper playgrounds; or in all of these means together."[50] By 1911, the PAA had renamed itself the Playground and Recreation Association of America (PRAA), and its report from 1913 noted that although streets were undesirable, it was impossible to completely remove children from them. It proposed expanding its programs to "organized street play" in twenty-six cities in 1915, but under controlled conditions such as scheduled closures and speed regulations. Taking note of the street environment, Curtis also calls for planting trees, saying:

The shade will cool the air on the streets and prevent the burning reflection from the asphalt. The leaves of the trees will take up a part of the carbonic acid gas and thus improve the quality of the air. With this natural shade, the streets will be vastly improved for children's purposes. A few years ago the New York Medical Association passed the following resolution: "Resolved that one of the most effective ways of mitigating the intense heat of the summer months and diminishing the death rate among the children is the cultivation of an adequate number of trees on the streets."[51]

He ends by proposing two unconventional locations for playgrounds and parks—predating New York's High Line by more than ninety years, he suggests building on elevated structures, such as railways, and also the aforementioned "skyscraper playground," which would move the play structure from the street and ground entirely (fig. 16). Curtis's vision was for a twenty-story building, with businesses and retail on the bottom five to six stories and with the above floors used for swimming pools, other recreational gymnasiums, and playgrounds on roofs.

As with any social movement, the playground advocates had to appeal to philanthropists and private business to make their argument. A special park commission for the city of Chicago issued "A Plea for Playgrounds" in 1905 with a special chapter on "Municipal Playgrounds as Child Savers and Money Savers." On a pragmatic note, Curtis urged potential backers to invest now before land values go up—better to develop "when the ground costs a thousand dollars than to wait till it costs a million." The popularity of playgrounds in the early 1900s actually meant their very construction increased value.[52] In the end, the playground movement could be recognized as a success. The Yearbook of the PRAA in 1918 notes that in a survey of 1,121 cities, 3,944 documented public playgrounds were built. Between 1880 and 1920, governments spent $100 million on organized playgrounds.[53] Like almost any American social movement aimed at the poor, playground activists also had to fight accusations of socialism but were able to buffer those arguments with the wide array of businessmen and merchants on their boards. Almost everyone could find a common ground in children's salvation. The playground movement actually predates the Fair Labor Standards Act, outlawing non-agricultural child labor in 1938 and was no doubt the beginning of a larger "child-saving" movement. Ultimately, funding decreased over time not due to lack of concern or because the issue of children's health had been "solved," but rather

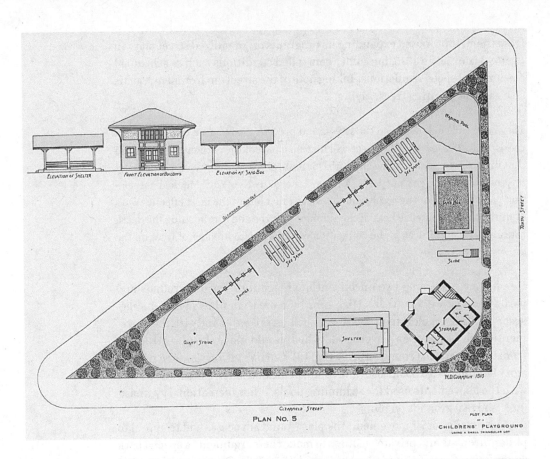

PLAN No. 5

PLOT PLAN
OF A
CHILDRENS' PLAYGROUND
USING A SMALL TRIANGULAR LOT

Fig. 16. The 1910 publication *Playgrounds for Philadelphia* showed more elaborate buildings and landscaping, as well as ideas of how to build in unconventional spaces. This is a plan for a "Children's Playground using a small triangular lot" and the resulting constructed landscape.

because federal and municipal dollars started to be diverted to the war effort. In fact, many of the play parks built during the early 1900s became grounds for military exercises and camps.

Like the sanitary movement, the playground movement focused on the poorest citizens perhaps out of concern that the corrupting influence of the city would spread like epidemic disease. Although moral behavior had no epidemiology, activists thought the solution was to instill immunity in childhood. Said Addams in her own treatise, *Youth of the City:* "Let us know the modern city in its weakness and wickedness, and then seek to rectify and purify it until it shall be free at least from the grosser temptations which now beset the young people who are living in its tenement houses and working in its factories."[54] Even so, the movement was not the same sort of top-down instillation of moral values that drove the sanitary movement and large urban parks during the previous Progressive Era. They aimed for accessibility, not just in distribution, but in seeking to provide space and equipment not only for the active and able bodied, but also the "weakly, the anemic, and the tuberculosis children who need the outdoor air and exercise the most."[55] Playgrounds were a form of social control but also responded to immigrant demands.[56] In "A Plea for Playgrounds," the discussion of Chicago neighborhoods yields the insight that "the 19th ward, west of the river, between Van Buren and 12th streets, is the home of a cosmopolitan population. Thousands of Greeks, Italians, Syrians, Bohemians and Jews are crowded into some of the most dilapidated and unsanitary dwellings to be found anywhere. These people came from sunny and picturesque lands, where pure air, sunshine and open spaces were their birthright."[57] The playgrounds would also play host to ethnic festivals, celebrating diverse identities rather than trying to erase them.[58] Playgrounds were largely built from volunteer labor, which indicates there was some interest from neighborhood groups, and the PAA used extensive recreation surveys and other ethnographic methods.[59] Unlike the paternalism and control of the top-down planning that characterized the city planning and parks building of the Progressive Era, playgrounds of this time were largely built by women and volunteer labor, ingraining community needs into the designs. Social welfare was not always a form of control, when performed from the ground up, and offered real ways for empowerment and uplift.[60]

Conclusion

The parallel trends toward nature resorts and playgrounds in the late 1800s and early 1900s may appear, on the surface, to be wholly different movements, but the ideology driving them was startingly similar. The first appealed to elite urban adults who sought to escape the city. The latter was a movement giving urban children, especially poor and immigrant youth, access to play in their own neighborhoods. The two movements were linked by a distinct antipathy for the corrupting influence of the city, particularly the rash of "nervous" diseases only seen in urban dwellers. They also propositioned a nature/city binary of both a literal and psychological nature. Materials advertising nature resorts were explicit about the physical maladies that would befall citizens of the industrial city, whereas the leaders of playground movement made their argument by emphasizing the moral pitfalls for children who could not escape city streets. Both encourage a return to "primitivism," or humankind's true nature, as a response to the urban economy. Although they espoused this theory and evoked a nostalgia for the country's rural landscapes of the past, in practice they advocated for a type of highly structured or civilized nature as "healthy" or "salubrious" landscapes for health. Playground advocates wanted children to tap into their "natural" instincts for play, but only in the context of highly prescribed activity or team sports. Nature resorts were designed around allowing patrons to literally ingest and embody the rural landscape's air and water to cleanse their bodies of urban diseases, but only against the backdrop of manicured fields, elegant baths, and painterly settings of mountains and lakes, without the messy reality of agricultural processes or wilderness.

Most of all, both movements served as a backlash to the round-the-clock efficiencies and production demanded by the Industrial Revolution. Both sought to introduce leisure back into lifestyles, not simply as a matter of overall well-being, but for actual physical health. By warning how new occupations and an increased focus on education were literally changing our physiology, leaders in the medical community asked Americans to pause and reconsider the effects of urban culture. But it cannot be overlooked that the embrace of fresh air and water cures was a luxury only available to the elite. To change one's location, especially only on a seasonal basis, required flexibility in work (something not afforded to factory workers) and money for train tickets, lodging, and food. There were strong moral underpinnings in the exhortations to reconnect to nature as well, supported by the writings of Emerson, Thoreau, and others. By not addressing the class issue in discussing who had the opportunity to go to these resorts and who didn't, the associations between poverty, morality, and ill health remained implicit. The playground movement, on the other hand, was in many cities a ground-up, volunteer operation and was specifically aimed at uplifting the children of the working class, but overall it aimed to do so by introducing them to activities acceptable to the upper class. Moreover, there were still significant disparities of where these efforts to remediate the urban landscape were made by race. Between 1890 and 1910 Baltimore made significant attempts to address a tuberculosis crisis by installing a citywide sanitary sewer system, improving housing, and building playgrounds and bathhouses. As the latter facilities were only accessible to whites, the death rate from smallpox and tuberculosis for the black population was over twice that of whites.[61]

Soon, though, the science of wellness started to coalesce around germ theory and internal pathologies of disease. Air and water cures, always viewed as somewhat faddish and of unstable foundation in pathology, faded from prominence, and so, too, did the prosperity of resort towns wane. Theories about children and play turned increasingly toward psychology over the effects of physical activities. The introduction of child labor laws in 1938 was a successful conclusion to the activism that marked the decade. However, the Great Depression and World War II would stymie federal funding and strain city resources for municipal programs, and many city playgrounds would start to give space and programming over to military bases and activities.[62]

CHAPTER 3

Purified Air in the Progressive Era

Science, Cemeteries, and Society

Most histories of public health and design point to the Progressive Era as the apex of connecting the two fields. It cannot be denied that the sanitary movement was a great success in stopping infectious disease and in discovering links between environment and health outcomes. The ground had been paved smooth and cleared of waste and stagnant water. Populations, industry, and economy continued to grow. The exertion of control over natural elements via engineering set the stage for unlimited urban expansion, and with early diseases such as cholera and yellow fever mostly eradicated, the shapers of cities could turn more attention to how the landscape affected health through more indirect pathways, in particular the way it influences behavior. A longing to recover nature in cities and speeches and writings by prominent intellectuals posited that parks needed to be an integral part of the American city to insure health, control density from spreading, and clean the air.

Furthermore, "scientific" planning could not only physically cleanse cities but also improve the human condition and uplift lower classes. "Science" is used frequently in writings and advocacy during this time to give weight to decisions that would play out in the public sphere. While today we would define a "science" as based in empiricism and deduction, in the Progressive Era it was often an umbrella term indicating a combination of efficiency and enlightenment. One of the most popular books of this period was Frederick Winslow Taylor's *The Principles of Scientific Management* (1911), which stressed "clearly defined rules, laws, and principles" for "maximum prosperity for the employer, coupled with the maximum prosperity for each employee."[1] Taylor's science indicates that any task can be maximized according to formulas, mathematical science, and proper delegation of tasks, from large-scale organization to even shoveling. Similarly, Walter Dwight Moody, managing director of the Chicago City Planning Commission, thought scientific management could be applied to the nascent field of city planning, not necessarily in terms of the scientific method; he felt "the science of planning is the development of cities in a systematic and orderly way."[2] Warning that the idea of city planning had become a "fad," the term linking efforts as disparate as a few street improvements to more comprehensive transport and civic center plans, he asserted, "Of all the American cities that have attempted city planning, hardly a dozen made any real progress because of their failure to realize the fundamental value of scientific promotional effort. Misapplied energy has also been a common fault. Two-thirds of all the failures in city planning in this country are due to these two causes."[3] Moody mentions health repeatedly in his book *What of the City?*, albeit almost purely in terms of capital. Moody supports the building of "parks, playgrounds, pleasure piers, and bathing beaches," but for their value in increasing the efficiency of the population (i.e., workers), of which "commerce" is a beneficiary. The Chicago Drainage Canal is lauded as an example of health preparedness, and Moody pointed out that its construction cost of $60 million was a savings over what he estimated could have been $75 million due to typhus deaths since its building. Safeguarding the health of citizens, he says, is "safeguarding the nation's greatest asset."[4]

The successes of the emergent planning and public health fields alongside their scientific credibility meant that the professionals still wielded considerable influence, if not more so, in shaping the growth of cities. At a planning conference Henry Morgenthau, banker and real estate figure, said it was the duty of the city planner to eliminate breeding places of "disease, moral depravity, discontent, and socialism."[5] The job of a planner was to impose order on an uncertain, messy, seemingly threatening world—not just to eliminate epidemics, but elevate the moral morass of the inner city. Planners and designers were closely entwined with the urban public health institutions, making them de facto experts on urban health crises. Even though the issue of waste and stagnant water had been engineered out of cities, leaders still struggled with the continuing problem of increasing density, tenements, and widening class divisions, which demanded more complex solutions than a sanitation campaign or hard infrastructure. The human condition was not nearly as visible as cleaned streets or quantifiable cholera cases, yet it cannot be denied that enlightenment, social justice, and the image of a civilized American city had a unifying aesthetic.

Sanitary infrastructure had imposed order upon the urban fabric, and most cities found their next priority was to inject green in the form of parks, tree planting, and landscaped streets. Strangely enough, the precedent for large urban parks, and how they could serve the health of a society, was realized in cemetery design in the mid- to late 1800s. Prior to then, many cities buried their dead at city churches. The lessons learned from the yellow fever and cholera epidemics gave many pause regarding placing disease-ridden cadavers back into the ground. In the soft, swampy soils of New Orleans, the dead were even buried in individual above-ground stone crypts, not only to prevent disease from spreading through the ground, but because so many became traumatized when during severe rains the high water table would push coffins back up above the surface or knock against the stone slabs that covered gravesites. Dr. Jacob Bigelow, a Boston physician, advocated for cemeteries to be placed outside city limits, and Mount Auburn, the first such "rural cemetery" was built in Cambridge, Massachusetts, in 1831.[6] Mt. Auburn was expansive and picturesque, with winding paths free of the urban grid plan to fit the existing topography. The Massachusetts Horticultural Society also established an experimental garden alongside the cemetery. These cemeteries would prove to be wildly popular, with stagecoaches often lined up outside them on the weekends waiting to enter for a leisurely drive.[7] Ironically, considering these cemeteries were originally moved outside cities because of their "bad air," they became a place where people would go for fresh air and walks, much to the discomfort of their designers and medical professionals.

Others saw the recreational use and pastoral environment of cemeteries as a correction to the negative influence of cities and the modern age. Wilson Flagg, in "Moral Influence of Graves," wrote:

We come here . . . to think more earnestly of the higher purposes of life, of its transient duration . . . we need not to be the disciples of a theological faith to feel the truth of these remarks, or to understand the benefit we derive from scenes that tend to conquer an excess of frivolity, or to moderate that entire devotion to mammon which, like intemperance and vice, has ruined many a noble heart. Many a mind is destitute of philosophy because it has not been trained in a school of wisdom; and many a soul is destitute of virtue, because the multiplied cares of fortune and ambition crowd out every thought of other things.[8]

Andrew Jackson Downing, who had held the Greenwood Cemetery in Brooklyn to great acclaim upon its opening, thought people were too joyous and not engaging in enough contemplation during their visits.[9] He also objected to the aesthetic mismatch between "hideous ironmongery" of the cemetery and people's recreation, but he was one of the first to point to cemeteries' popularity as an indication that people would use parks if built at the same scale and if offering the same pastoral feel. Both Flagg and Downing felt that parks should be a truly public (and corpse-free) amenity available to all, they both noted that cemeteries are essentially private enterprises in that they were funded by the purchase of lots. Poet William Cullen Bryant, who also served as the editor for the *New York Evening Post* from 1827 to 1878, agreed and often used his considerable platform to advocate for urban improvements. He shared his experiences from abroad and speculated on how the American city could achieve the greatness of European cities. In his book *Letters of a Traveller,* he discusses the parks of London thusly:

Nothing can be more striking to one who is accustomed to the little inclosures [*sic*] called public parks in our American cities, than the spacious, open grounds of London. . . . These parks have been called the lungs of London, and so important are they regarded to the public health and the happiness of the people. . . . The population of your city, increasing with such prodigious rapidity; your sultry summers, and the corrupt atmosphere generated in hot and crowded streets, make it a cause of regret that in laying out New York, no preparation was made, while it was yet practicable, for a range of parks and public gardens along the central part of the island or elsewhere, to remain perpetually for the refreshment and recreation of the citizens during the torrid heats of the warm season.[10]

Bryant also attributed to parks the low crime rate in London, relating the story of another American in the city who was taken aback by the fact that his landlady did not bother to lock her lower shutters. It is worth noting that Bryant chose to juxtapose the narrative of parks, police, and a story of laborers searching for food. The latter story served as a possible harbinger of the divide to come in cities, and he ended the letter with this statement: "I hear it often remarked here, that the difference of condition between the poorer and the richer classes becomes greater every day, and what the end will be the wisest pretend not to foresee."[11] Bryant was troubled by both the threat to open space in New York and the trend of the elites leaving the city entirely for summer and recreation, leaving distinctly striated classes occupying public space.[12]

Andrew Jackson Downing, who by this time had made his name producing architectural pattern books on rural living, would also publish extensive writings advocating for great American public parks. His earlier works reveal his predilection toward pastoral landscapes and a rigid aesthetic, but his advocacy for open space revealed that he considered the intersections of morality, civic pride, and health. Bryant and Downing published one of their conversations in Downing's *Rural Essays,* with Downing writing in the voice of an American traveler who had been abroad for five years and Bryan his interviewer. After some traditional boosterism praising the "wonderful, extraordinary, unparalleled growth of our country," comparing the it to "the moving and breathing of a robust young giant, compared with the crippled and feeble motions of an exhausted old man," Downing followed with the caveat that Europeans, particularly French and Germans, are far more "republican" in their social life.[13] They excel in "public enjoyments, open to all classes of people, provided at public cost, maintained at public expense, and enjoyed daily and hourly, by all classes of persons. . . . I am thinking of public parks and gardens—those salubrious and wholesome breathing places, provided in the midst of, or upon the suburbs of so many towns on the continent—full of really grand and beautiful trees, fresh grass, fountains, and in many cases, rare plants, shrubs, and flowers."[14] In yet another example of American intellectuals' tortured relationship with European precedents, the men strove to translate European trends while seeking to form a distinctly American ethos toward urban green space. Downing cited the superiority of Paris, Vienna, Munich, and Frankfurt in providing public amenities for their residents. Bryant and Downing extolled the physical character and perceived social benefits of these parks but also debated the European history of parks as shows of power from royalty as opposed to "our ideas of republican simplicity."

The size of the park was a key argument for all involved. A large park would bring the benefits of the country into the context of the city, to allow its citizens to escape the concrete and steel and be fully immersed in the green space. In Downing's "The New York Park," the original proposal by Kingsland of 160 acres was declared to be too small, and a minimum of 500 acres was proposed as an alternative. He dismissed the current state of the city, saying:

Deluded New York has, until lately, contented itself with the little door-yards of space—mere grass-plates of verdure, which form the squares of the city, in the mistaken idea that they are parks. The fourth city in the world (with a growth that will soon make it the second), the commercial metropolis of a continent spacious enough to border both oceans, has not hitherto been able to afford sufficient land to give its citizens (the majority of whom live there the whole year round) any breathing space for pure air, any recreation ground for healthful exercise, any pleasant roads for riding or driving, or any enjoyment of that lovely and refreshing natural beauty from which they have, in leaving the country, reluctantly expatriated themselves for so many years—perhaps forever.[15]

Downing also argued that the "breathing zone, and healthful place for exercise" of the park had to be large enough to accommodate future growth.[16] Appealing to the science of Progressive Era ideals, a large park was sold as something that would work mechanistically and biologically, cleaning the air, "a green oasis for the refreshment of the city's soul and body,"[17] but it needed sufficient room to operate. Such a large park could only come from a city's public investment and administration.

Although the image of parks as "lungs of the city" is popularly attributed to landscape architect Frederick Law Olmsted, the metaphor was frequently used by others in advocating for an integrated park system, that is, a network of green space that would oxygenate the entire city across all economic strata of neighborhoods. Some attribute the metaphor to William Pitt the Elder, the British prime minister from 1766 to 1768, and the phrase was repeated in several British popular media outlets throughout the early 1800s. Codes demanding public parks and walks in England were often proposed in the wake of the cholera epidemic, and Victoria Park was specifically built to serve a sick working-class population and, as in the United States, to serve as a buffer to prevent more upscale parts of London from contagion.[18] An 1839 editorial titled "The Lungs of London" from *Blackwood's Edinburgh* magazine, describes each of the great parks of London as a travelogue, referring to them as "respiratory organs." In an essay about Honolulu's expansion, James Jackson Jarves wrote in *The Polynesian* in July 1844: "as the town increases . . . a central spot should be reserved and trees planted for this purpose. It is highly necessary for the comfort and health of all classes that ventilators, or lungs, as these squares have been called should be left in all cities."[19]

John H. Rauch, a physician and president of the American Public Health Association (APHA) from 1876 to 1877, was intensely interested in how diseases were spread or mitigated through landscapes. One of his first publications was *Intramural Interments in Populous Cities and Their Influence upon Health and Epidemics* (1859), in which he warned against turning a large cemetery into what we now know as Lincoln Park, citing historical examples from the Ancient Greeks to sixteenth-century France on prohibitions on burying the dead within city limits. Rauch warned, "Emanations or effluvia from dead bodies, or the exhalations and exudations for living but diseased bodies, or the exhalations and exudations of living but diseased bodies, may excite in the fluids of the system fermentative action, resulting in functional derangement or organic lesion."[20] A few years later, Rauch published *Public Parks: Their Effects upon the Moral, Physical and Sanitary Conditions of the Inhabitants of Large Cities, with Special Reference to the City of Chicago* in 1869. He collected anecdotal evidence from Rome, slave housing in Alabama and Washington, DC, among others, that plants could guard against malaria and other fevers, particularly when placed between dwellings and bodies of water. This observation led him to believe that when positioned in a "belt," trees could form a physical barrier to disease. He notes even a field of sunflowers having a similar effect and extolled the "preventive influence of trees," discussing how leaves "collected" malaria but also how cutting them down for development released gases.[21] Rauch provided detailed month-by-month mortality tables for Chicago from 1862 and 1865 through 1868, first by disease and then against records of winds, temperature, and rains. Special attention was paid to throat and lung diseases, especially consumption (the "most common and fatal"), but Rauch noted the deadliest were the acute diseases of bronchitis and diphtheria. Rauch noted that miasmic thinking was still very much a part of medical thinking, even alongside contagionist perspectives, by discussing how winds could "blow the seeds of disease" over unhealthy neighborhoods so that even people in distant neighborhoods can become ill. He hypothesized how the worst winds were the humid currents from the southeast, and that humans needed 333 cubic feet of fresh air a day for proper respiration.

Rauch ended his book musing on the link between landscape and neurology, which was at the time yet largely unexplored territory. He concluded that the new urban condition was "an age of great mental activity" and "nowhere is the mind more stimulated than Chicago," and that in a physician's opinion, "judicious use of the organ increases its power and confirms its health but excessive exercise which requires an undue share of vital energy leads to an unhealthy conditions," which can only lead to ill effects.[22] Rauch placed a special emphasis on the city's constant pursuit of wealth as requiring an urban space for mental restoration and physical activity to restore balance to the modern man; the population of concern, of course, a specific kind of upper-class white man who would be most concerned with building capital. Rauch says as much when he states that nervous conditions affected men more significantly than women, particularly the higher mortality witnessed during "speculative excitement of 1856" and "financial revulsion" of the following two years. His concern for (again, upper-class) women is due to their rate of consumption, resulting from "more sedentary lifestyles."[23]

The concern for mental health was tied very much to improving the moral character of urban dwellers. If the upper class were in good health, they could set a good example for the working class. While physically the intent of these massive park and tree planting initiatives was to alleviate density and cleanse the air, the recreation and refuge they offered was thought to alleviate the downtrodden condition of the city. Downing ostensibly sought to burst bubbles of privilege when he said it was "both curious and amusing to see the stand taken on the one hand by the million, that the park is made for the 'upper ten,' who ride in fine carriages, and on the other hand, by the wealthy and refined, that a park in this country will be 'usurped by rowdies and low people.' Shame upon our republican compatriots who so little understand the elevating influences of the beautiful in nature and in art, when enjoyed in common by thousands and hundreds of thousands of all classes without distinction!"[24] That statement also revealed that the underlying aim of the public spaces was not to allow the working class or immigrants to participate in activities they wanted, but instead to elevate them to the more genteel leisure of the upper class. Said Downing, "Out of this common enjoyment of public grounds, by all classes, grows also a social freedom, and an easy and agreeable intercourse of all classes, that strikes an American with surprise and delight. . . . By these means, you would soften and humanize the rude, educate and enlighten the ignorant, and give continual enjoyment to the educated."[25] Fresh air, green space, efficiency, and enlightenment characterized the urban landscapes of the Progressive Era, both real and imagined. Moody also asserted that "attractive surroundings encourage good morals."[26] These beliefs set the stage for a triumvirate of men who are still most closely associated with the aesthetics of wellness in the urban landscape: landscape architect Frederick Law Olmsted, planner Daniel Burnham, and social reformer Ebenezer Howard.

Burnham, Olmsted, and the Aesthetics of Purified Air

The preeminent planners and landscape architects of the Progressive Era were bolstered by the scientific advances of the Industrial Revolution but would formulate theories and aesthetics of health that many still ascribe to today. Parks became "breathing rooms," and streets were widened and smoothed as a function of their new underground infrastructure, but this also allowed more air and light into the corners of the city. The aesthetics, motivations, and contradictions of Progressive Era urban landscapes are perhaps best epitomized by the period's preeminent landscape architect, Frederick Law Olmsted, and city planner, Daniel Burnham. These men and others grafted green onto the new veneers of steel, iron, and asphalt that unified the messy and piecemeal approach to urban waste. Olmsted has especially been widely associated with public health due to his well-known history on the US Sanitary Commission and extensive writings specifically regarding the public health benefits of parks. Olmsted had a unique platform for a landscape architect, not only from the Sanitary Commission writings but also as the managing editor of *Putnam's Monthly Magazine of American Literature, Science, and Art*.[27] Other sanitarians were also instrumental in shaping the canonical parks of this era. Sewerage expert George E. Waring Jr., who had a thriving consulting business, worked in the office of Olmsted and Vaux as the agricultural and drainage engineer for Central Park. Although their ideas were primarily formed by surveying military camps during the Civil War, they directly translated the distressing conditions of these encampments to the problems of the American city and waged their own campaign to alleviate density and bring fresh air back into the city. Burnham's connections are less explicit, and in fact a reading of *The Plan of Chicago* as published contains few references to those benefits, but the examination of his plans reveal popular thinking about physical planning, morals, and behavior that was popular in the Progressive Era and resonates today. Olmsted's parks and Burnham's city plans both explored the intersection of urban landscape, beauty, and human improvement.

The need for parks in the city was usually described in strictly utilitarian terms. Historian Jon A. Peterson noted, "The park proposal represented an anti-pollution device more than a public space concept. In short, comprehensiveness sought pertained to health factors, not to the city's commercial, circulatory, recreational, or domestic requirements."[28] Little is written about how these landscapes should function beyond providing a dose of nature back in the city, and less about how it should look beyond feeling "airy" and "dry." In the New York Sanitary Report, parks are referred to as "valuable breathing spots."[29] Later the report states, "Nature is lavish of air, and sunlight, and water—they all come from her hands pure and unmixed; and man must receive them and use them in the same bountiful measure in which they are bestowed, if he would maintain a standard of perfect health."[30] Peterson also notes that the move to address the city as a whole also signaled the first inklings of what he calls "townsite consciousness," or the health implications of a city's site and structure as a whole.[31]

Olmsted is rightly credited as seamlessly coalescing health, social justice, and ecology in his works. Known as the father of landscape architecture, he frequently moved back and forth between practice, public service, and publication. Olmsted was more visibly political in his early years and published a great deal of writing alongside his built work.[32] While Olmsted and Vaux's Greensward plan for Central Park was selected in 1858, his actual work on the Sanitary Commission began in 1861, after he departed the project largely due to irreconcilable differences with the park's board of commissioners.[33] He returned to full-time practice in 1865 but also served as chairman of the American Public Health Association's 1872 committee on "sanitary value and uses of shade trees, parks, and forests."[34] There is no doubt that Olmsted's work as a public servant influenced the social bent of his work. Olmsted deeply understood the importance of cross-disciplinary work in both physical and scientific fields and was even one of the founders of the American Social Science Association (ASSA).[35]

Olmsted's innate anthropological and scientific eye served him well across the many disciplines in which he served. His initial survey described the Central Park site as "squalid," swampy, and littered with squatters' shacks and large rocks. Olmsted's experience with the department convinced him that the generalized slum conditions seen in working-class neighborhoods were the root causes of disease but were also amplified through density, resulting in mass contagion.[36] This obsession with alleviating density through green space was one of the most consistent threads throughout his writing.

In reference to planning and reinforcing military camps, he characterizes walled medieval cities as places of disease. He calls for "the abandonment of the old-fashioned compact way of building towns, and the gradual adoption of a custom of laying them out with much larger spaces open to the sun-light and fresh air," which would yield greater immunity from "the plague and other forms of pestilence."[37] If people are too close together in walled quarters, "a certain gas, which, if not dissipated, renders the air of any locality at first debilitating, after a time sickening, and at last deadly."[38]

There is also no doubt that Olmsted's knowledge of natural systems also made him an ideal advocate for the environmental remediation power of parks. Environmental historian and landscape architect Anne Whiston Spirn noted how his mastery of ecological processes led him to construct works with a "natural" aesthetic, but in fact they enlisted massive amounts of labor and were meant to work mechanistically to improve air and clean water. While she also argues that he was less successful in matters of social or economic analysis,[39] it is true that his writing is most precise and engaging when describing the biological connections between nature and the body, while at the same time wrapped in the language of science and industrial efficiency popular at this time. In his paper "Public Parks and the Enlargement of Towns," presented to the ASSA in 1870, Olmsted wrote, "Air is disinfected by sunlight and foliage. Foliage also acts mechanically to purify the air by screening it. Opportunity and inducement to escape at frequent intervals from the confined and vitiated air of the commercial quarter, and to supply the lungs with air screened and purified by trees, and recently acted upon by sunlight, together with opportunity and inducement to escape from conditions requiring vigilance, wariness, and activity toward other men—if these could be supplied economically, our problem would be solved."[40] Olmsted worked with sanitarian and public health officer Elisha Harris on the first plans for Staten Island (1871); in a report on the project they suggest trees formed a barrier to malaria and absorbed excess moisture, and they talked about shade regulating the microclimate—a concern as rapid heating was thought to release gases from soil.[41]

The concept of public landscape as machine would become even more literal in his design for Boston's Back Bay Fens. Boston's population had grown by more than a hundred thousand between 1800 and 1855; as a result the Back Bay, then a shallow saltwater bay, had become what was described by the *Boston Globe* and several other accounts as a "public health menace," filled with sewage and other waste as well as effluent from Stony Brook and the Muddy River. The Back Bay was filled in as part of a massive land-making movement that not only covered up the water body but provided ample new land for building houses closer to the city center. City commissioners were faced with a complex engineering problem, and because the reputation of the Back Bay was so negative, they had to make sure the new neighborhood conveyed a sense of good health and social aspiration. Wide avenues and trees were planned, along with educational institutions and an edict that the neighborhood never become too "overcrowded." Initial plans for the Back Bay preserved 43 percent of the land for streets and parks, most notably Commonwealth Avenue, a wide boulevard with a generous swath of occupiable green space down the center.[42] Olmsted was commissioned in 1877 to further improve the neighborhood with a park, but he also ensured the landscape itself would help protect against further flooding and sewage backup, by installing a tidal gate and planning a pump station, designed by famed architect H. H. Richardson. Olmsted also used one of the water bodies as an open sewage interceptor on the city side in case of heavy rain and overflow and planted trees that could withstand flooding and brackish waters in these events. The rest of the park had separated paths for strolling and driving. Olmsted's design for the Fens was decidedly less picturesque and grand than Central Park's design of twenty years earlier, which raised some objections from nearby residents. An anonymous 1884 editorial in the *Boston Globe* said that allowing for the passive retention of overflow would only "have the effect of making the surface of the pond anything but pleasant to the eye, as there will be nothing picturesque in a green scum of filth, which will constantly accumulate, and in the years to come, in all probability, it will be the source of deadly miasma." In conclusion it stated, "Olmstead [*sic*] said once the view from the railroad trains, passing by at 40 miles an hour, would be one of 'sylvan beauty' but I cannot see what there is beautiful about it at present after all the money has been spent."[43]

Ecological function is not always compatible with more widespread perceptions of beauty and health, and the common thread through Olmsted's plans is that they are thoroughly biological in nature, blending function with grander ideas about the intertwined systems of nature and the body. Lakes and masses of trees can be read as organs, with gradients of openness and enclosure in its circulatory routes carrying the benefits of nature to each corner. The carefully modulated paths for pedestrians and carriage echo nervous systems of the body. A walk in Olmsted's parks was akin to exploring one's one circulatory system, placing the patron in closer touch with their internal systems and external nature simultaneously. Olmsted also embraced the "townsite consciousness," even if at first he saw his parks as stand-alone organisms, a respite from the city where people would passively reap the benefits of nature and participate in genteel activities. Later he would see the importance of connecting to other municipalities and would include transportation as a key component of his plans.

When it comes to thinking about the democratic and health-based underpinnings of Olmsted's work, it also must be seen in context with the writings of Andrew Jackson Downing, in particular *Rural Essays.* He worked closely with Olmsted and founded an office with Olmsted's longtime partner Calvert Vaux before Downing's untimely death in 1852 at the age of thirty-six. Like Downing, Olmsted also idealized the rural; there are letters showing he encouraged his brother to study farming instead of continuing in academia.[44] Olmsted's driving force was to bring pieces of rural (and morally superior) life to urban areas—in one writing he even expressed a desire to bring back sheep.[45] While walls of trees around his park do serve a purpose as an ecological barrier, they also wall off the city. He envisioned the park as a place

to which people may easily go after their day's work is done, and where they may stroll for an hour, seeing, hearing, and feeling nothing of the bustle and jar of the streets, where they shall, in effect, find the city put far away from them. We want the greatest possible contrast with the streets . . . the greatest possible contrast with the restraining and confining conditions of the town, those conditions which compel us to walk circumspectly, watchfully, jealously, which compel us to look closely upon others without sympathy. . . . We want depth of wood enough about it not only for comfort in hot weather, but to completely shut out the city form our landscapes.[46]

The common through line when discussing the social justice aspect of Olmsted's parks is that they are "democratic," but this glosses over his more complicated views on morals, class, and recreation as well as his many stipulations on right and wrong ways to use his parks. He did believe that his parks should be used by all. In his publication *The Spoils of the Park: With a Few Leaves from the Deep-Laden Note-Books of "a Wholly Unpractical Man"* (1882), which largely laments the "inefficiencies" of the management of Central Park, he also expresses disappointment that there were so many wealthy drivers and riders, "that part of the population who least need to have the opportunities of rural recreation brought to them."[47] He convinced the Central Park Commissioners that the park needed surveillance, under his own supervision, as people "will need to be trained in the proper use of it, to be restrained in the abuse of it."[48] In its early days, visitors to the park were not even allowed to walk on the grass or use rude language.[49] In "The Justifying Value of a Public Park" he decries the example of pool rooms, grandstands, and stables being installed in an European park, calling them "popular diversions of the class which we elsewhere look to Barnum to provide."[50] He had a disdain for boisterous activity, particularly of working-class men; an aside in his presentation to the ASSA talks about "young men in knots of perhaps a half dozen in lounging attitudes, rudely obstructing the sidewalks. . . . There is nothing among them or about them which is adapted to bring into play a spark of admiration, of delicacy, manliness, or tenderness."[51] Olmsted's parks were deliberately light on recreational programs because they were meant to be understood as works of art, passively uplifting society, and a testament to the power of landscape in and of itself, but could only be appreciated by an elite class. In a document written for his design for Mount Royal, Montreal, he said, "if it is to be strewn with lunch papers, beer bottles, sardine cans, and paper collars and if thousands of people are to seek their recreation upon it unrestrainedly, each according to his special taste, it is likely to lose whatever of natural charm you first saw in it."[52] Of course, in later renovations, Central Park would add recreational areas; a 1910 renovation of the Back Bay Fens by Arthur Shurcliff included ball fields and a more formal rose garden; and by the time Olmsted had designed Boston's Franklin Park, the last piece of the Emerald Necklace, he himself had acquiesced to the pressure for including more active programming but expressed a desire for no men's athletic teams, activists, or speechmakers and for physical activity to be confined to specific spaces.[53] Olmsted's views on parks as a public health amenity were couched in the paternalist tone of Progressive Era ideals. He was not above casting the argument for parks in the interest of increased worker capital, writing, "The lives of women and children too poor to be sent to the country can now be saved in thousands of instances, by making them go to the Park. . . . The much greater rapidity with which patients convalesce, and may be returned with safety to their ordinary occupations after severe illness, when they can be sent to the Park for a few hours a day, is beginning to be understood. The addition thus made to the productive labor of the city is not unimportant."[54] Although the land for Central Park and his other public landscapes was secured long before Olmsted's involvement, it cannot be ignored that the building of many of his parks came at the cost of razing swaths of land occupied by working-class neighborhoods and under the guise of preventing the perceived spread of disease from them. Olmsted was a well-known abolitionist; in the 1850s he traveled through the South to write a series of articles for the New York Times that vividly described the environmental and social conditions of "The Cotton Kingdom" as an argument against slavery. This nuanced discussion of race is largely invisible in his own writing about the conditions of his projects in the North, and even in several contemporary accounts of his career. Central Park was built on the grounds of Seneca Village, a thriving and prosperous African American neighborhood that fought the removal of their homes and their church in court. The popular press instead portrayed the neighborhood as a ramshackle slum; an 1856 edition of the New York Daily Times noted that the park will be built upon a settlement of "Ebon inhabitants" and "Celtic occupants," noting that the former at least presented a "pleasing contrast" to the latter "in common with hogs and goats" (figs. 17–20). The article dismissed their resistance by

Fig. 17. *Harper's Weekly* depicted the *Squatters in Central Park*, Irish immigrants and African American residents of Seneca Village, in this sketch by D. E. Wyand, 1869. Their supposed moral failings and poor health were leveraged as an argument to displace them for the park's development. (Library of Congress, Washington, D.C.)

Fig. 18. Central Park in its early stages of completion, still a largely barren, rocky landscape (1862). (Courtesy of the National Park Service, Frederick Law Olmsted National Historic Site)

Fig. 19. (*above*) A bird's-eye depiction of Central Park, emphasizing its "natural" topography and features (printed by F. Heppenheimer, 1863). (Courtesy of the National Park Service, Frederick Law Olmsted National Historic Site)

Fig. 20. (*right*) The completed Central Park, the tree line hiding the urban context and invoking a healthy pastoral ideal (undated). (Courtesy of the National Park Service, Frederick Law Olmsted National Historic Site)

noting that they are of "simple minds," and that their inevitable removal will be "effected with as much gentleness as possible." Noting the draining of the marshlands to build the park, the article concluded that if "other inmates of the shanties do not die of the yellow fever this Summer, it will only be because Death himself hesitates to enter such dirty hovels."[55] Nevertheless, the park's construction continued apace. Workers building a new entrance to the park in 1871 even found a coffin containing the body of a Seneca Village resident, wholly unaware they were building on top of a cemetery.[56] It was not until 2019 that the City of New York announced it would build a monument to the Lyons family, one of Seneca Village's prominent residents, in Central Park.[57]

Most historians easily associate Olmsted with health goals, given his experience and direct writing about the subject. Less mentioned is the role of planner Daniel Burnham, chiefly in his plan for Chicago, coauthored with Edward Bennett and published in 1909. The illustrations of Burnham's plan are oddly bereft of landscape, and in the writing he seems to dismiss the "remorseless enforcement of sanitary programs." Even so, he concludes: "We now regard the promotion of robust health of body and mind as necessary public duties, in order that the individual may be benefited, and that the community at large may possess a higher average degree of good citizenship . . . the returns will come in the shape of increase of health and joy of living for all the people; and incidentally the value of every real estate holding in the city will be enhanced."[58] One also only has to look at his earlier plan of the White City in the 1893 Columbian Exposition to see how he was taking the values of light and sanitation from the utilitarian form infrastructure to a design aesthetic. The plan for the city takes "townsite consciousness" to the urban scale, connecting it through circulatory systems of tree-planted boulevards and networked green space.

Burnham also wrote about parks as a specific tonic to increasing urbanization and stated, "Fifty years ago, before population had become dense in certain portions of the city, people could live without parks; but we of to-day cannot." His ideas about public health through design and planning can also be better understood when seen in the context of not just his contemporaries and his own work, but the auxiliary publications related to the plan. The actual book was an expensive (twenty-five dollars at the time of publication) and unwieldy, albeit handsome, volume put out by the Commercial Club of Chicago (CCC), making it largely prohibitive to the mass market.[59] The CCC then hired Walter Dwight Moody in 1909 to produce a public version, which would be known as *Wacker's Manual for the Plan of Chicago* and was to be read in conjunction with the first published plan. Its namesake and benefactor, Charles Wacker, hoped it would be used in schools as part of an eighth-grade civics curriculum to teach concepts of patriotism, virtue, and civic interest.

Although not a planner himself, Moody took it upon himself to promote the power of planning to the citizens of Chicago, to the extent that he also used social psychology techniques to build stakeholder interest. The eighth-grade level was in fact selected as the audience since psychology research had shown that children were most impressionable at this age.[60] It was largely up to Moody to talk about economic and health benefits of the plan to the general public in a more accessible version than the decidedly elitist tone and rollout of the original book. Moody casts a relentlessly cheery yet pragmatic picture of the plan's benefits, promising that "the Plan of Chicago solves our vital problems of congestion, traffic and public health."[61] Addressing the urban concerns of the time of density and fresh air, he promises that "good order, cleanliness and beauty will result in saving time, doing away with the smoke evil, banishing unnecessary noise and dirt, promoting good health, assuring happiness and prosperity to the millions upon millions of people yet to live in and visit Chicago."[62]

The power of city planning to beautify and uplift populations was also clear in Burnham's admiration of Georges-Eugène Hausmann's plan for Paris, directly referred to in the plan. Burnham talks about how Old Paris, with "its dirty, crowded, ill-smelling narrow, winding streets, the hotbeds of vice and crime," had been transformed through grand, tree-planted avenues.[63] Moody affirms this was the template for Chicago, writing that Hausmann's plan is the "most beautiful, healthful, convenient, and prosperous city in Christendom."[64] The praise for European models of health and control echoes how the sanitarians of the Industrial Revolution looked to the British for engineering solutions. Commonwealth Avenue in the Back Bay was also very much modeled on Hausmann's boulevards to convey standards of fresh air, green, and enlightenment. It should be mentioned that Hausmann's long boulevards were also a convenient way to eliminate blighted housing, quarantine what was left, facilitate surveillance, and deploy military quickly to all corners of the city. Burnham's were, more optimistically, meant to craft aesthetic experience and streamline transportation (fig. 21). Most of all, he wanted the boulevards to lead to places for public gathering to build community and civic spirit. Much like Hausmann's streets led people to parks and landmarks in Paris and to famous monuments in Washington, DC, Burnham's grand boulevards often terminated or intersected in grand outdoor spaces (fig. 22). In his ultimately unbuilt plan for San Francisco, Burnham justified his radiating boulevards from Market and Van Ness by stating they would bring the city into "miraculous formal equilibrium" (equilibrium being a goal of health and echoing the perceived balance of nature), and he designed a continuous park strip leading to Golden Gate Park.[65] Burnham and Moody had a much more charitable view of vigorous exercise, particularly in its relationship to

Fig. 21. Daniel Burnham's depiction of a grand boulevard in Chicago. Trees and landscape are subservient to the urban axis, which is reinforced by buildings (1909). (Plate 112, Historic Architecture and Landscape Image Collection, Ryerson and Burnham Archives, The Art Institute of Chicago, digital file #80380)

upstanding behavior. Moody would write, "Science tells us, further, that recreation is a necessity for the people. If proper and moral means of recreation are not provided in our plan, therefore, we may be certain that in the future Chicago, the people will become inferior in morals, mind and even in physical size and strength to the people of the present Chicago."[66] And later he stated: "It is this strain of city life which increases insanity and brings weaknesses of many kinds to shorten life and deprive the people of their vigor. The best way known by which a community may lesson these ills or do away with

Fig. 22. Daniel Burnham speaks extensively about the value of green space and trees and their relationship to health in the *Plan of Chicago*, but the illustrations are curiously bereft of landscape (1909). (Plate 132, Historic Architecture and Landscape Image Collection, Ryerson and Burnham Archives, The Art Institute of Chicago, digital file #80376)

them, is by increasing park areas and by creating conditions which invite the people to an athletic, out-of-door life."[67]

Burnham's advocacy for the importance of green space also belied the lack of presence in the plan. He advocated for parks to be equally distributed ("one acre for each hundred people") and networked; he was successful in getting the Special Park Commission in the Chicago City Council to pass a resolution that recognized parks' value in "preventing crime, promoting cleanliness, and diminishing disease."[68] Burnham and Moody knew the importance of bringing nature into the city, albeit still positioning it as oppositional to the urban condition itself. Speaking of the Forest Preserve Enactment in Illinois, Moody would say: "In demanding forest preserves the people of Chicago show that they understand the importance of conserving public health. They know what relief Nature affords in its fields and forests from the wear and tear of city life. There has been much agitation in recent years for the 'conservation of natural resources.' Our people realize that the most important national resource is the health of the people."[69]

For all the health values espoused in Burnham's plan, there is shockingly little regarding housing and social welfare, for which he has been highly criticized. The aesthetic of reformation was largely cosmetic or only concerned with health and welfare to the point to which it supported the design or increased capital. Housing, particularly tenements, are absent from the plan, although "tenements" were in an early outline.[70] There in fact lies a large question about what exactly populates the gleaming streets and how the parks are accessed. Apart from the absence of houses, Burnham also advocated for moving industry out of the urban core and sending rail underground, and he even moves single-family homes outside the city, showing each suburb as a self-contained community centered around a school, playground, and public library. Historian Margaret Garb indicates that this may be gendered. Traditionally, those practicing in public health and planning tended to be male, looking at issues of medicine, transit, and production, while many housing social reformers were female.[71] Burnham was of course most concerned with beauty and aesthetics, believing it enough to uplift morals and improve the environment. Moody tried to counteract this perception by selling *The Plan* as "The City Practical" and touting its efficiency aspects. Even so, critic Lewis Mumford called the Burnham approach in Chicago "municipal cosmetic," comparing it to the planning of totalitarian regimes and criticizing it for ignoring housing, schools, and sanitation. Similarly, historian Peter Hall argued that the City Beautiful movement portended future practices of exclusionary zoning and was "planning without social purpose—even with a regressive one," as planning became further untethered from basic societal goals such as housing the poor.[72] Ultimately, Burnham's City Beautiful gave way to the "City Functional," emphasizing zoning to benefit business over aesthetics and even health when there ultimately wasn't enough money to realize them on a grander scale.[73] Even so, the work of Olmsted and the visions of Burnham and Bennett, supported by Moody's advocacy as well as Rauch's scientific credibility, gave weight to the idea of parks, trees, and other urban green spaces as necessary to the health and morals of citizens, a conjecture that would be given much more weight in the next century when interest in health and built environment surged. Collectively, they also crystallized an aesthetic of healthy urban landscapes that ranged from highly ordered to just pastoral enough. The ideal projected by this aesthetic is one that erases industry and its pollution and instead injects fresh air into dense cities. This is inarguably a positive, but we cannot ignore the fact that this alleviation often came at the cost of razing or ignoring working-class neighborhoods. These aspects of achieving the Progressive Era vision are often overlooked for what seems, to our present-day perceptions, a prescient view of green space as essential to wellness and citizenship.

The Move Outward

Parks and streets could only do so much to alleviate the density of cities, and over time transportation, land shaping, and home-building technology made the move outward to suburbs a more viable option to more people. The early suburbs were built on an image of salubrity, the opportunity to live within the purified air of the city parks. Olmsted himself designed several early East Coast suburbs, and his and Burnham's ideals reverberated beyond the places in which they had a hand. More so, these early suburbs and their relationship to landscape and health were shaped by Ebenezer Howard, a British social reformer, who in 1898 wrote *Garden Cities of To-morrow* (1898). Howard's professional background was in stenography, but as a young man he had attempted farming on a homestead in Nebraska. When that enterprise failed, he returned to England and worked as a court reporter. His work put him in touch with many social reformers, and his book would draw connections between the moral fortitude ostensibly built through agricultural life and the social and health issues of urban life.

The Garden City model is purposely noncontextual as to be universal with only five highly figurative diagrams. Perhaps most well known is the "Three Magnets," which shows the advantages and disadvantages of "Town" and "Country" (respectively, "closing out nature, social opportunity, high wages, foul air, murky sky" and "lack of society, beauty of nature, lack of drainage," to name a few) and the Garden City, a "Town-Country" that triangulates them with the best of both with "low rents, high wages, pure air, pure water, good drainage, bright homes and gardens, no smoke, no slums." Its formula is highly prescriptive—six wards of 32,000 each, radially arranged around a city center of 58,000, connected by trainways and boulevards 120 feet wide and surrounded by a greenbelt 420 feet wide, meant to hold the Garden City to its perfect size and population. The plans promise a "smokeless, slumless town," promising escape from both polluted air and disease-ridden working-class housing.[74] The level of detail that Howard has in his plans and the zealot's belief in its impact make it unclear whether Howard thought of the Garden City as utopian. Its description of the landscape appears directly influenced by Richardson's *Hygeia,* specifying low population density, good housing, wide roads, underground railway, open space, and the attendant health concerns of the time, clean air and no standing water. Howard detailed the economics of the Garden City as much as he did the landscape; in his conception the town would be sustained through a system of payments to a general welfare fund after mortgages were paid off and funneling increasing land values back into community amenities, including pensions for the town's elderly. The level of preciseness regarding proportions, finances, and labor indicate that he conceived of it as a workable template. As someone deeply entrenched with social movements, Howard also understood that the landscape of the Garden City was as much about the systems that created and maintained towns as it was about the material landscape.

The social underpinnings of the Garden City would rarely be seen in their translations, as well as the model's intention to be an urban system of smaller towns and central city. The first built Garden City, in Letchworth, England, was the result of a competition held by The First Garden City Limited, a private company with the express purpose of testing Howard's ideals. Raymond Unwin, a British engineer, architect, and planner, was the link between Howard's words on the page and their realization, as the appointed architect of Letchworth. He became the preeminent expert on building Garden Cities but made his own tweaks to Howard's template that were concerned with healthfulness but also cost efficiency, mainly in the reduction of roads. His 1912 pamphlet, *Nothing Gained by Overcrowding!: How the Garden City Type of Development May Benefit Both Owner and Occupier,* was adopted by England's Ministry of Health as a guide for model housing. Unwin showed how a less dense housing plan is more cost effective as it gets rid of roads, which Unwin proposed be given over to green space. He acknowledged that utilities would be more expensive to extend out to the city later but asserted that roads are the primary drain on finances.[75] Unwin also discussed how the radial street layout proposed by Howard not only differentiates the Garden City from the urban grid but also saves road costs and keeps everything within a walkable distance.

Ultimately, Unwin neglected to translate much of Howard's economic ideas in favor of formal styles and guidelines written as a direct rebuke to urban living, chiefly the dense living conditions, as stated clearly in the pamphlet's title. A specified minimum distance of seventy feet between houses, or twelve houses per acre, not only served to let miasmic airs dissipate and guard against the contagion of person-to-person contact, but also guaranteed a degree of sunshine and fresh air. Unwin also had to grapple with increasing use of the automobile; fearing pedestrian safety, he sought to reduce auto land use by cutting down the amount of road area from 40 to 17 percent of available land area and subsequently raising garden and open space land from 17 to 55 percent.[76]

Unwin adopted the form of the Garden City without Howard's socioeconomic goals intact, and they were additionally refracted through the lens of American morality and real estate capitalism by Olmsted and planners Clarence Stein and Henry Wright, who designed Radburn, New Jersey, between 1928 and 1929. Stein and Wright were also influenced by the work of sociologist and planner Clarence Perry, who attached social ideals to the concept of the neighborhood unit and in his 1929 monograph further crystallized the concept of an ideal town based on school catchment area of a half-mile radius. Perry also emphasized the importance of a town square holding a flagpole and annual readings of the Declaration of Independence—implicitly, the idea was that immigrants would move out of the city and be civilized and assimilated by the form and planning of the neighborhood.[77] Like Unwin, Perry also had a great deal of distaste for the automobile; his advocacy for the neighborhood unit was in fact a way to combat the "menace" he saw in its rise in popularity. On the other hand, Stein and Wright, while keeping much of Howard's and Unwin's tenets, particularly regarding density and a country home aesthetic, chose to accommodate the automobile but would separate pedestrian pathways from vehicle roads, allowing developers to sell Radburn as "A Town for the Motor Age."[78] Stein and Wright would later experiment with bringing the form and planning of the Garden City to public housing complexes in the United States, discussed in more detail in the next chapter.

Ultimately Howard's ideals were cast aside in favor for the aesthetic of rural life rather than its labor and systems, for romantic cottage houses and personal realms of green space never utilized for productive farming per Howard's intent. Nor did the self-sustaining craftsmen he envisioned materialize. The centers of industry remained in the city, making it inconvenient for their laborers, arguably most in need of healthful environments, to live there. These towns instead became the template for the eventual American suburb. New suburbanites were loath to readopt sustenance farming. Restrictive greenbelts were antithetical to the unfettered expansion promised by new capital and transportation systems and were done away with. American suburbs instead acted as corollaries to the cities from which they radiated out, remaining dependent on the city as an economic center.[79]

This fulfilled Burnham's vision of the city becoming increasingly commercial and elite residents having the mobility to move out to the suburbs. Olmsted was also steadfast in declaring that the built-up nature of cities was always going to be inferior to the country when it came to the health of citizens, going so far as to declare that density would change the very physiology of those who dwelled within:

In the interior parts of large and closely built towns, a given quantity of air contains considerably less of the elements which we require to receive through the lungs than the air of the country or even of the outer and more open parts of a town, and that instead of them it carries into the lungs highly corrupt and irritating matters, the action of which tends strongly to vitiate all our sources of vigor—how strongly may perhaps be indicated in the shortest way by the statement that even metallic plates and statues corrode and wear away under the atmospheric influences which prevail in the midst of large towns, more rapidly than in the country. The irritation and waste of the physical powers which result from the same cause, doubtless indirectly affect, and very seriously affect, the mind and the moral strength; but there is a general impression that a class of men are bred in towns whose peculiarities are not perhaps adequately accounted for in this way.[80]

Olmsted said, in dense parts of town, we need to avoid collision and "constantly to watch, to foresee, and to guard against their movements." This endless calculation, "not so much for their benefit as our own," would harden men.[81]

When the Garden City was translated to American suburbs, it didn't combine city and country life in one town, as was Howard's intent, but acted as both a dependent corollary and a simultaneous rebuke to the cities. Cities were for work, the suburbs were for living, and new transportation infrastructure allowed more and more in the middle class to do so. This model was in place long before Howard's pamphlet made it to the United States. Burnham and Olmsted had long sought to soften the lines between the industrial city and the pastoral ideal of country, first by bringing nature into the urban fabric, but later through their speculations on the suburbs. Olmsted and Vaux's plans for Riverside, Illinois, were designed with the commuter in mind, radiating off a promenade connecting the town to Chicago designed for a pleasant journey home for the city worker (fig. 23).[82] Architect Andrew Jackson Davis and owner Llewellyn Haskell, in advertising the new suburb of Llewellyn Park, New Jersey, advertised "healthfulness of climate . . . with special reference to the wants of citizens doing business in the city of New York, and yet wishing accessible, retired, and healthful homes in the country."[83]

Early suburbs, predating widespread car ownership, also adopted winding roads in a way to be markedly different, and healthier, than the layout of the city. Downing railed against "the gridiron" for not providing enough light and air, or space around grand buildings to admire, and noted that it would not work with the rolling hills of natural topographies.[84] Olmsted sought to order the irregular topography with streets of the twenty-third and twenty-fourth wards of the Bronx with larger, irregular block sizes by citing health reasons: "The practice [of the grid] is one that defies the architect to produce habitable rooms of pleasing or dignified proportions, but this is the least of its evils, for in the middle parts of all these deep, narrow cubes, there must be a large amount of ill-ventilated space, which can only be imperfectly lighted through distant skylights, or by an unwholesome combustion of gas. This space being consequently the least valuable for other purposes, is generally assigned to water-closets, for which the position is in other respects the worst

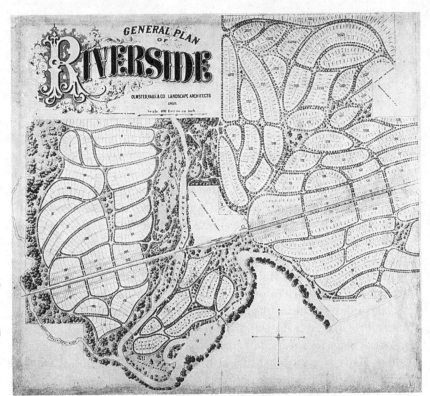

Fig. 23. Olmsted and Vaux's plan for Riverside, Illinois, made a definitive break from the gridiron plans of cities, with the urban form almost biologic in pattern with buffers of trees and landscapes in between (1869). (Courtesy of the National Park Service, Frederick Law Olmsted National Historic Site)

that could be adopted."[85] Henry Stebbins (formerly on the Board of Commissioners of Central Park and Department of Public Parks) criticized the plan for being too extravagant. Stebbins said plans were "irregularly warped and curved" as well as "tortuous" and "fanciful" while disregarding the "principle of obtaining direct and rectangular streets to as great an extent as the geography will permit."[86]

The canonical healthy American urban landscapes were dominated by only a few voices, but they persist today as the models of health to which many want to return. It is always worth remembering that the Progressive Era designers, planners, and thinkers who set the template for our modern-day suburbs sought not only to bring in fresh air and green space to towns but also to reclaim the morals they saw inherent to a rural life from which more and more people were growing distant. The ideal rural-urban hybrid would not only bring good health but instill a civic spirit. Ironically, the concept of individualized plots of green and the levers of policy and investment that enabled the elite and middle class to move out of the city instead fostered physical separateness, among the suburban dwellers themselves and between the "suburbs" and the "city" as physical places and in the popular imagination.

Conclusion

Many historical accounts of built environment and health tend to hold up the Progressive Era as the apex of collaboration and distillation of health conveyed through urban landscapes.[87] The period has been examined in detail or mentioned in contemporary empirical studies, often as a way to frame the contemporary resurgence in interest in green space and air and water quality, physical activity, and town planning. No doubt designers that are interested in the applications of these principles also look to the latitude and acreage that was granted to Olmsted and Burnham in their work, as well as the faith and capital behind creating entire towns from ground up. The designers were riding a larger national wave of desire for change and enlightenment, even if it often came wrapped in a decidedly conservative morality.[88] Judgment about what is "right" or "wrong" (or "healthy" or "unhealthy" behavior) goes hand in hand with any kind of positivist view of the environment. The dimension of this work is likely overlooked because landscape and urban planning were mediums where disapproved behavior was not actively policed from the top down; rather it replaced environments where social and physical ills festered with environments that provided no space for them. That ethos extended to the actual erasure of urban water bodies, undesirable land, and especially tenements and neighborhoods populated by immigrants or people of color, in the name of preserving health for an elite population. In an editorial for *The Albion* entitled "The Lungs of London," an unknown author wrote: "At home, the health, which is the life of the great mass of the population, is not considered worth a thought, except at times of impending danger, when thought is vain—when the pestilence rages in the midst of us, we run wildly about in search of relief—when having completed its ravages, it finally disappears from our towns and our cities, we are too happy to dismiss it also from our thoughts, and to forget all enquiries as to the means of prevention for the future, in congratulation on our preservation for the present."[89]

In the present day, Olmsted's legacy also becomes more complicated. He was an outspoken abolitionist, but many of his parks came at the cost of clearing out black and immigrant neighborhoods. He believed in the democracy of public spaces but openly promised municipal leaders and businessmen that they would raise property values. He advocated for places where all economic classes could mix, but for the purpose of the upper class to refine the working class. The indisputable lasting power of their work is a testament to Olmsted's and Burnham's talents as master technicians and their distinct design view, but the refusal to examine their motives further often obscures the paternalism inherent in their work and philosophies. Olmsted's extensive writings show his obsession with how his works would be maintained and surveilled. While they were indisputably visionaries, their ideas about morality and acceptable behavior also reflect a rigid control that aligned them with the larger aims of the Progressive Era.

The parks and town plans of this era also showed that Americans continued to look to Europeans for how to address health and for design precedent. Bryant and Downing specifically built a campaign around parks by talking about the superior morals and parks of the English; Olmsted's more formal parks as well as other popular parks of the time emulate English pastoral motifs.[90] The streets and boulevards of Paris, and their implicit control of the environment, are echoed in Burnham's *Plan of Chicago*. These landscapes were also filtered through the still recent rural and agricultural heritage of the United States, and certainly some of Olmsted's more "experimental" work, such as the Back Bay Fens, recalls the wilder and more varied character of the American urban landscape.

Finally, these landscapes persist because the concept of miasma and clean air and its relationship to green landscapes was, and still is, so palpable. Miasma theory was accepted by the urban practitioners mentioned here and by the general public well into the early 1900s, even though the medical and most of the public health communities had largely shifted to a germ theory perspective by this time.[91] A major shift in pathological thinking and political attitudes would effectively dissipate the environmental ethos of Progressive Era healthful landscapes. *The New Public Health,* written in 1916 by Hibbert Winslow Hill, called for a revolution in public health that was distinctly more etiological in nature, saying that the old ways of practicing were not rigorous enough to uncover sources or vectors of disease and had overlooked other origins of illness such as insects, hand and mouth contact, and food while "dirty clothes, bad smells, damp cellars, leaky plumbing, dust, foul air, rank vegetation, swamps, stagnant pools, certain soils, smoke, garbage, manure, dead animals, in fact everything physically, sensorially, esthetically, or psychically objectionable, were lumped together as 'unsanitary' without much distinction of 'source' or 'route,' and were regarded as a sort of general 'cause of disease' to be condemned wherever found, 'for fear of epidemics.'"[92] Hill had a point that the miasmic platform allowed for the broadest of generalizations to justify sweeping physical changes, but the outright dismissal of urban improvements would define medical thought for decades to come. To be exact, he also wrote, "the great public-health fallacy of the nineteenth century consisted in the devotion of nearly all the effort to man's surroundings; of almost none at all to the man himself."[93] All disease originated with the individual body and should be treated at that level. Hill called for governments to devote more energy to epidemiological research than social and environmental improvements.

Hill's screed came at the same time the moralism and underlying conservatism of the era would be brought to the forefront of American attitudes, as well as the rise of the American Medical Association (AMA). In 1922, the Sheppard-Towner Act, which funded prenatal and child health centers and staffed them with female doctors and nurses, came under fire from the AMA, which declared it a socialist scheme.[94] The organization's rising power and profile led Congress to eliminate the funding for these health centers in 1927. This would be a recurring theme in the coming century, as social programs were rejected or eliminated in favor of individualized medicine. This was not only due to a change in theory, but as the medical and public health fields started to cleave, physicians sought to protect their interests and take over established public health structures. Recounts Samuel Hopkins Adams in his 1908 commentary "Guardians of Public Health" in *McClure's:* "a medical politician who served on the public health committee of the legislature addressed this question to a body of physicians who had come there to appeal for certain sanitary reforms: 'What do you want of laws to prevent people from becoming sick? Ain't that the way you make your livin'?'"[95] This observation may have been glib, but it predicted a future where health would be focused on treating individual bodies instead of the design of settlements, towns, and cities, an idea that would eventually be repeated in architecture, urban planning, and landscapes of the mid- to late twentieth century.

CHAPTER 4

Germ Theory and Environmental Compartmentalization

The Etiological Individual

From the explosion of tenement housing in the Industrial Revolution to the real estate crises of today, dwelling has historically been the most contested space of wellness, the center about which our arguments about equity and morality in the city revolve. In the modern era, thinking about health turned from *ecological,* with consideration of multiple origins in the environment, to more explicitly *pathological,* seeking a linear etiology between single origin and outcome at the individual level. This shift in thinking to a biomedical model of the city was eagerly taken up by urbanists and architects seeking to address knotty urban issues such as traffic and housing. Even so, most historical accounts of health and built environment often point to the modern era, loosely defined here as the late 1920s to the early 1980s, as a period where health and design were irrevocably split, with the generalized reasoning that as germ theory became more widely accepted, the public health field no longer sought answers in environmental design, and designers and planners lost interest in designing for health and were instead taken with advances in building materials and systems.

As such, the modern era is often glossed over as a period of stagnation in connecting design and health, as the fields advanced on their own trajectories. In his essay "Epilogue: Airs, Waters, Places; A Status Report," medical historian Charles E. Rosenberg notes:

By the mid-twentieth century this accustomed epidemiology of place had become decreasingly central in Western medicine, not so much forgotten as moved from center stage. It had become a supporting player in a little-questioned narrative of progress toward an increasingly inward and ultimately biochemical and biophysical understanding of the body. But the body that we have come to know so much about in the controlled environment of the laboratory, through bacteriology, physiology, biochemistry, biophysics, and, more recently, genomics, is a body ordinarily abstracted from its particular surroundings. The situated body had become by the mid-twentieth century the concern of marginal specialists, the focus of workers in tropical medicine, of public health advocates, of practitioners of military medicine."[1]

Rosenberg's singling out of "public health advocates" is key. The field was still concerned with issues of place, specifically dwelling. In 1938 the APHA still had a committee on the hygiene of housing, which published the report *Basic Principles of Healthful Housing.* The guide was four sections, respectively emphasizing physiological needs (thermal comfort, sunlight, aural environment), psychological needs (privacy, community life), protection against contagion, and protection against accidents.

Even if the respective fields of medicine, public health, and design and planning began to split, it did not stop architects from borrowing the metaphors of cellular-level science harnessed to mathematical formulas for sun, fresh air, and green space to optimize dwelling. A good deal of American public housing complexes built between 1930 and 1960 bore the brunt of this inquiry and experimentation. This was due to a confluence of factors: a revived interest in scientific social housing in Europe, the nascent "houser" movement in the United States, and a government eager to address urban issues through technocratic solutions but less interested in maintenance or community integration. Applying these ideas to public housing complexes was perhaps also alluring as they constituted their own internal landscapes, an urban plan in miniature where sociologists and architects could claim to test the relationship between built environment and health, particularly on those supposedly most in need of intervention. The explicit message was that the highly vulnerable residents of these complexes could also have their lives improved by controlling their "unhealthy" behavior through design.

Medical Models of the City

As seen in the Progressive Era, planners and designers often seized on medical ideas and metaphors to drive their work, even if those ideas consistently lagged behind predominant thinking in the health community by a couple decades. Although the fields drifted farther apart in terms of actual collaborative effort, the pull to legitimize the design fields and "solve" the problem of the city through scientific models was stronger than ever, even if the metaphors themselves became more tenuous. The technocratism underlying the works of Olmsted and Burnham was softened by a pastoral and City Beautiful aesthetic, but in the 1920s and 1930s it came to the forefront to result in urban landscapes that were almost clinical in nature. The idea that cities were the origin of disease persisted, especially as the elite moved out to the suburbs. And although epidemic disease was not the crisis it had been in the previous century, many became concerned with the social ills that appeared to reside there. Urban sociologist Robert E. Park would make a direct analogy to the previous scourges of infectious illness, saying, "Vices undoubtedly have their natural history like certain forms of disease. They may therefore be regarded as independent entities, which find their habitat in human environment, are stimulated by certain conditions, inhibited by others, but invariably exhibit through all changes a character that is typical."[2]

The city continued to be an ever-growing and unknowable entity, and its future was further thrown into flux by the uneven outmigration to suburban areas. Furthermore, the growing use of automobiles belched pollution into the air, slowed the streets, and presented an increasing threat to pedestrians. Only forty years after the successes of sanitary infrastructure and urban beautification, planners bemoaned the breakdown of pipes and flooding of streets and felt an ever-present concern that population density would degrade the quality of urban living. Contagion was not so much the concern; rather, it was the mental toll that "crowding" would have on urban populations. Planner Clarence Stein, in an editorial decrying "Dinosaur Cities," says: "The day of the palliatives and the patent medicines is passing. In city growth as in the fight on disease. We must do all that is necessary to combat the forces of congestion at their source."[3] However, in other editorials alongside Stein's in a Lewis Mumford–edited 1925 edition of *The Survey,* it becomes clearer that the planning profession's concerns for health came alongside an anxiety about neighborhoods being built beyond their control and the strain it would place on municipal infrastructures that were struggling to keep up. In an essay entitled "The Road to Good Housing," Stein's frequent collaborator Henry Wright warns that continuously building out from the city is not the answer to escape tenement life, saying, "In pursuit of the ideal home people use the automobile to escape beyond the borders of the city and beyond its restrictive building codes and accept the inconveniences and often risk the dangers of bad sanitation and an inadequate water supply."[4]

The relationship between the human body and nature, and what it means for the health of both systems, has been a consistent area of inquiry, but how cities fit into the equation has shifted over time. Was the city an ecological model, with people acting like flocks of birds or herds within? Was the city a medical model, with streets as its arteries and green space as oxygen supply, or was the city in and of itself like a cell? The underlying notion to all these models was that somehow the city had to get back to a "balance" that seemed inherent in ecosystems and healthy bodies but had not yet been achieved on the urban level. Although tuberculosis was epidemic in the United States during this time, planners and designers appeared more concerned with the decay of civics. Wright makes a plea for community planning over sprawl as social ordering and sensible resource management, saying: "Planned housing of this kind is able to achieve the sort of honest individuality that comes from performing adequately one's own part in a larger whole: each house is, as it were, a good private citizen, with its individual entrance, its individual porch, its individual drying green, its complete sense of privacy, and at the same time it performs its civic obligations it supports a park, a playground, a tennis court, swings, slides, wading pools. Above all, no house attempts to shout down its neighbors by reason of special size or style."[5]

Ecologist Aldo Leopold also frequently used bodily and wellness metaphors to communicate the importance of environmentalism. In a posthumously published 1946 essay, he presciently discusses "the symptoms of disorganization, or land sickness," including increased flooding, lower crop and forest yields, and sudden outbreaks of pests and disappearances of other species.[6] Conversely, his contemporary, physician Walter B. Cannon, also used ecological metaphors to describe individual and population health, proposing that both naturally seek a state of homeostasis, but the health of the individual is only assured when the larger population is also healthy. Illness in the body, or unexplained catastrophe in a biome, signal a disruption in these ostensibly self-regulating systems.[7]

In his book *The City: Its Growth, Its Decay, Its Future* (1943), Eliel Saarinen implored planners to bring "organic order" to "urban communities," saying: "In doing so, we find ourselves in much the same position as a doctor, who, to be able to maintain organic functioning in the human body, must be familiar with organic processes in general. Analogously, we must learn to understand these general organic processes so that we may be able to maintain order in the city's physical organism."[8] Saarinen illustrated his volume with drawings of cells, blown up to look like a suburban plan, hypothesizing that as cells divide and grow, so should professionals look to that model in order for healthy city growth.

Design and planning often borrowed metaphors from medicine, but in this era they also began to take cues from the emerging fields of sociology and ecology, essentially a grab bag of scientific concepts that could be used to legitimize their work. Those fields were also closely intertwined at the School of Sociology at the University of Chicago, led by researchers Robert Park and Ernest Burgess. Park and Burgess also believed that there were underlying systems of individual and group behavior and the innate relationship of people to natural systems. They assigned texts by plant and animal scientists alongside those on social theory and studies, going so far as to name their subset of research as "human ecology." Burgess is also credited with designing the "zonal model" of cities, depicting the city's structure as a series of concentric rings (fig. 24). The model describes a taxonomy of labor, population, and housing in the city, with ethnic neighborhoods occupying the center, apartments of "workingmen" in the next ring out, and then respective "residential zones" and "commuters zone" occupied by single-family dwellings.[9] The use of a circle echoes Ebenezer Howard's model of spokes and self-contained communities. It also implies that like an ecosystem or individual, the ideal state of the city is stable, balanced, and static. While not meant to be literal to the physical form of the city, Burgess's model further solidified a suburban and urban binary and persists as an image throughout urban history up to today. Retrospectively, thinking of the city as definitively stratified was also a way to "scientize" the nascent field of urban sociology. Categorizing areas of the city and the people within as such made it easier to determine control groups and compare conditions and outcomes against each other.[10] The adherents to the Chicago School believed analogies to natural systems were predictive in another way—as the city appeared to slip into crisis, they believed they were studying American cities at their "apex" or "climax," indicating a system soon to fall in entropy or be replaced by another.[11]

Although their models of the city echoed each other, the perspective of the relationship between environment and behavior differed significantly

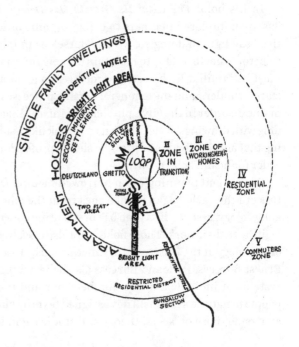

Fig. 24. The Burgess zonal model of urban ecology is deceptively simple but relays many of the underlying theories of the time. It shows the city as a closed-loop system (ecological) but as a cellular structure (biomedical) with "slums" confined to a declining center in danger of spreading outward (*The City: Suggestions for Investigation of Human Behavior in the Urban Environment*, University of Chicago Press, 1925).

INFECTIOUS TERRAINS

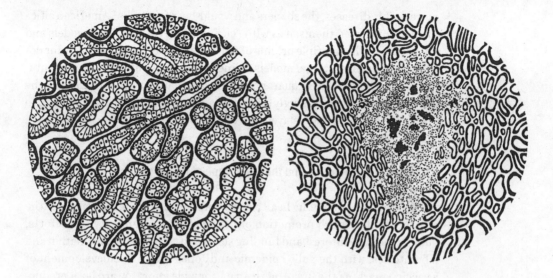

between designers and sociologists. Saarinen implored architects and planners to better understand the underlying systems of cities so order could be imposed on a chaotic city by physical planning (fig. 25). Park's observations show that he believed the physical environment of the city is born out of social interaction, saying: "The neighborhood exists without formal organization. The local improvement society is the structure erected on the basis of the spontaneous neighborhood organization and exists for the purpose of giving expression to the local sentiment."[12] He goes on to state: "In American cities the attempt has been made to renovate evil neighborhoods by the construction of playgrounds and the introduction of supervised sports of various kinds . . . these and other devices which are intended primarily to elevate the moral tone of the segregated populations of great cities should be studied in connection with the investigation of the neighborhood in general. They should be studied, in short, not merely for their own sake but for what they can reveal to us of human behavior and human nature generally."[13]

By the 1920s, virulent infectious disease had been eliminated from most cities. C.-E. A. Winslow, in a 1926 report entitled "Public Health at the Crossroads," written for the *American Journal of Public Health,* enumerated cases of urban disease by comparing New York City health records in 1875 and 1925. He found that diseases such as diphtheria, croup, and scarlet fever had decreased by more than 95 percent, and tuberculosis by 79 percent. On the other hand, incidences of cancer and heart disease increased by 176 percent and 187 percent, respectively.[14] These latter diseases were degenerative, breaking down the body over a longer period, and therefore perhaps were not on the radar of designers or even sociologists yet. In the absence of these

Fig. 25. Eliel Saarinen's models of city growth and planning used cellular and biological patterns literally to show what "order" and "decay" looked like in urban planning (*The City: Its Growth, Its Decay, Its Future,* 1943).

more visible diseases, the shapers and would-be reformers of American cities instead concerned themselves with "curing" behavior. Without models and knowledge of the multiple origins of chronic disease, their strategies for doing so followed traditional models of linear pathology, and when that eventually failed, they turned to quarantine and elimination. While models for the city itself became increasingly ecological and systems based, the approach to disease, even social ones, stayed narrow and direct.

Pathological Architecture and the Landscape of Public Housing

In the previous era, public health had meant ensuring the sanitation of the environment through promotion of personal hygiene and citywide efforts, but increasingly interest and funding started to turn toward vaccination and laboratories, with the polio epidemic and Jonas Salk's 1955 development of a vaccine marking the first American nationwide effort toward both producing and promoting vaccines.[15] Widespread acceptance of germ theory shifted the study of public health from external to internal causes, and more implicitly, from the state to the individual.

It would be more accurate to characterize this so-called split as a change of the scale of intervention, a turn toward addressing the individual instead of a population, single microbes rather than the external environment. In the wake of this shift, architects and planners struggled to determine what the demand for scientific epistemology meant for their field, beyond embracing new advances in building technology. The increased use of steel, elevators, and plumbing systems meant that architects were able to build bigger and with increased control of the internal environment. Rather than having to confront the messiness of the urban context, they could focus on the scale of the individual building, which now could be thought of in vertical, self-contained cities, where waste, air, and light could be transported, cleaned, and portioned with maximum efficiency. "Sanitation in Modern Architecture," a 1934 article on the building of skyscrapers, outlines specifically how new engineering technology influenced architectural form. Just as the sanitary era hid and conveyed waste under the streets, the book decrees that skyscrapers should relegate their wastewater pipes to a mechanical central core, a vertical manifestation of the urban strategies of the past. Concealing the inner workings of the building also allowed for continuous glass facades to allow sunlight into tall office towers. To deal with impure urban air (now caused by autos rather than waste), a tower was to be significantly set back from street, to allow wind to blow away the congestion of the traffic.[16]

Formally, fresh air and sunlight remained a key design principle, but the treatment of these elements became vaccination-like in its application. Le Corbusier's designs, and indeed much of modernist architecture, shows the influence of tuberculosis sanitoriums, which had come into widespread use in the late nineteenth and early twentieth centuries. If the pastoral landscapes of the Progressive Era were characterized by their purified or clean air, modernist architecture took it a step further; their buildings and even landscapes communicated seamless, gleaming sanitation.[17] The sanitarium was an advancement on health resorts for a germ theory era, narrowing their focus to consumption rather than the vague litany of urban afflictions the prior structures aimed to address, as well as a more rigorous treatment regimen.[18] This speaks to the severity and more exacting diagnosis of the disease, but even with the significant advancements in germ theory, the success of sanatoriums and their design proved that sun and fresh air actually were medicinal. Their design was closely linked to practice; the white walls and floors and use of smooth materials not only gave the appearance of sterility but also allowed for easy cleaning. Even so, their use of the environment was still largely holistic; the idea that they could be quantitatively "dosed" for healthy living appears to be purely an invention of architects. The influence of sanatoriums on social housing, specifically, might also speak to the fact that the disease was largely thought of as one that primarily afflicted the working class.

The International Congresses for Modern Architecture, or CIAM, the best-known organization of modern architects, founded in 1928, was driven by a common interest in how modern architecture could address the chief social problems of the era—namely transport, housing, and health. Representing seven European countries, the organization's design solutions had a distinct socialist and scientific bent, although it was not too long before some of its members, most notably Walter Gropius, departed for the United States, and the political side of the organization would wane. Its landmark document, The Athens Charter of 1933, was meant as a set of urban codes ensuring wellness and equity through design, the implication being that architects were so committed to the common good as to be above the taint of political power and corruption.[19] The doctrine dictated guidelines ranging from the scale of city planning to dwellings, with specificity as a proxy for "science." Among the provisions are that builders must show plans proving sunlight enters a house for "a minimum of two hours on the day of the winter solstice. . . . To introduce sun is the new and most imperative duty of the architect."[20] A later book, *Can Our Cities Survive?*, published in 1947, also shows a much stronger stance on providing active recreation in open space than seen in the more passive designs of Progressive Era parks. In an entire chapter written on the importance of recreation, the authors showed an expansive grid of recreational activity broken down by age group, a periodic table of sport.

Architect and CIAM member Le Corbusier was intensely focused on the singular body and the optimization of the individual and its implications for architecture and landscape. *Le Modulor* (1948) reimagined the Vitruvian Man for the Modern Age, showing how the dimensions of the human body could be used to proportion homes, furniture, and even transportation. Le Corbusier also proposed exact cubic meters of air, sunlight, and open space needed per resident, as the basis for entire speculative developments. He stipulates 14 square meters per occupant for each "cell" (apartment), 12 meters of plate glass window, 4 meters 50 centimeters split by a mezzanine level for height of the space, air at 64.4 degrees Fahrenheit, 8 liters of air to go through the rooms every minute for "exact respiration," 1000 people per hectare, and that each resident would need to walk no more than 100 meters to transportation (elevator or taxi).[21] In *Towards a New Architecture,* he notes that in a tower, "starting from the fourteenth storey you have absolute calm and the purest air" (begging the unanswered question of who is relegated to the first through thirteenth stories).[22]

Towards a New Architecture (1923) was written only a couple decades after Ebenezer Howard's *Garden Cities of To-morrow,* but it directly rebuked its math and proposed its function could be contained in a single housing complex. Le Corbusier notes: "400 square yards allocated to each inhabitant of a garden city, we find that the house and its outbuildings take up 50 to 100 square yards; and 300 square yards are given up to lawns, fruit and vegetable gardens, flowerbeds, etc. All this involves an absorbing, costly and laborious upkeep. The result is often a few bunches of carrots and a basket of pears. There is no space left for games or sports." He instead proposes 150 square yards per house for "industrialized and intensive" agriculture . . . giving a large yield . . . the artisan here becomes his own agricultural labourer and produces an important part of the food he consumes. Architecture? Town planning? The logical study of the cell and its functions in relation to the mass may furnish a solution rich in results."[23]

Le Corbusier's use of the word "cell" is also notable. The word is not meant to evoke a solitary dwelling, but rather the smallest unit of the human body, in his mind the perfect self-regulating machine. It also shows an effort to relate the science of architecture to advances in germ theory and modern medicine. The body metaphor is evoked several times in *The City of Tomorrow and Its Planning* as well, reviving the persistent metaphor of open spaces as lungs and the other components of the plan as organs and biological systems as well.[24] *Towards a New Architecture* culminated in the proposal for the Freehold Maisonettes, where flat roofs, deep patios, and white floors and walls reflect sunlight into the far reaches of their units. Perhaps most telling of the turn toward individualization, each unit also features a balcony garden "completely shut off from its neighbor."[25] The hanging garden is not so much a garden than it is an outdoor room, plants confined to planters and walls on the side.[26] Multifamily housing is no more than the individual dwelling, scientifically portioned out for the individual, multiplied and scaled as necessary. Interestingly this is in contrast to the APHA's guide to healthful housing, which specifically stated, "The housing needs of a population are not met by devising standard 3 and 4 and 6 room unit plans and repeating them endlessly without variation simply because they are efficient users of space and have an economical relation to plumbing stacks and stairs."[27] In the most notable shift in how disease and pathology were conceptualized in the modern era, Le Corbusier's proposals show no fear of unit density. Infectious disease was largely thought to be eradicated, and contagion was less a concern. This is also reflected in the APHA document, with protection against illness met with clean water supplies, pest control, safe food storage, and enough sleeping space for each resident, rather than specifying densities. The specter of density, or more precisely overcrowding, as a condition for disease was still somewhat present, but CIAM asserted the main danger came when "there are more persons than rooms," but a high density was possible without "overcrowding" if a district were "properly planned."[28] Housing became a puzzle of efficiency, divorced of political, social, or economic context. Le Corbusier even proposed that someone with the qualifications to understand "scientific principles," not elected officials, should oversee the operations of the housing development.[29]

"Scientific" housing meant the embrace of the machine age, and Le Corbusier was also motivated by the possibilities of mass production to make a giant complex, where all social life was internal to the building itself, a vertical city that would liberate people from the congestion of the street and reduce the danger of pedestrian and automobile accidents (fig. 26). With one of the fourteen principles of the Radiant City entitled "The Death of the Street," his intention was clear. The functions of socialization, exercise, and transport once relegated to the public realm would be safer if transferred to corridors and vertical shafts. What is left of the urban landscape is simply a flat green plane at the base of the building, healthy by virtue of simply hosting grass and trees, and a vague idea of recreation, without specific programming in order to be flexible in use. Le Corbusier recognized the purpose of the street as a site for social contact but attempted to recontextualize it within the building itself for the protection of the buildings' citizens. For all the advances made in medicine in the early twentieth century, the concept of environmental health was still mostly confined to bad airs and waters, now

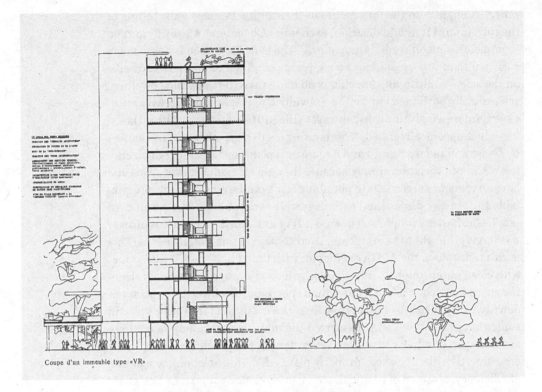

Coupe d'un immeuble type «VR»

Fig. 26. The model and section of Le Corbusier's Ville Radieuse (Radiant City) shows the scale of the residential buildings and their relationship to the street. The perforations in the building envelope were meant to light the corridors of the building, a safer alternative place for people to socialize than the street. The landscape is remote to the building's inhabitants (1933). (© F.L.C. / ADAGP, Paris / Artists Rights Society ARS], New York 2019)

driven by the increased use of the automobile. Although based on the scale of the individual, Le Corbusier was an avowed socialist; part of the driver of the anonymous architecture of his speculative urban developments was to create communities that were classless in order to achieve social and health equality. The end result, though, is ruthless in its neutrality. Not betraying any culture, taste, or aesthetic, the buildings were literally cleansed of the possible messiness, or richness, of place.[30] "Green" was not an unconsidered factor, but it was conceived as a quantifiable unit that only had to be delivered to residents in its most basic form, equal to light and air. Its mere presence was thought to be enough to provide restorative benefits, and did not need to be further designed. *Towards a New Architecture* depicted superblocks buffered by identical lines of trees and standardized rectangular green paces, each with an identical recreation court and arbitrary paths winding across. The greenery reinforced the linearity of the plan but also buffered automobile thoroughfares. Le Corbusier's copious use of trees reflected a particular view of urban forest as an indicator species for human health as outlined in

CIAM's *Can Our Cities Survive?*, which related population density to crowding and, therefore, less space for trees to grow. The book concludes, "the absence of trees is an index to substandard living conditions," pointing out that the highest income districts in an Amsterdam case study had the most trees per capita ("9 trees to every inhabitant"), a poor district the inverse ("one tree to every 27 inhabitants").[31]

Contrary to how most would frame Le Corbusier's consideration of the public realm, a 2013 Museum of Modern Art exhibit in New York City on his work subtitled the show as "Embracing the Landscape." Even so, Le Corbusier's drawings and buildings still only show the landscape as contained and remote, viewed through the horizontal windows of his towers, or merely serving as a neutral plane for structures.[32] By keeping the landscape at arm's length and farther from the intended residents of his buildings, he also rejects the wilder and unknown aspects of nature, pollen or other allergens that may come from trees, or the consideration of designed landscapes as a part of the larger and messier ecosystem. His landscapes read as "sterile," not purely in a pejorative sense but to describe the germ phobic and medicinal thinking of the era, reflected in building types from sanatoriums to housing.

Le Corbusier's only built work in the United States is the Carpenter Center at Harvard University. How then, did his ideas become the standard for midcentury American public housing? There is very little literature directly linking his specific work and writing to public housing prototypes in the United States, but many leaders in the American public housing movement were specifically taken with the style of CIAM's social housing, perhaps in part because it represented a clean break with existing urban slums and gave the appearance of technological advances.[33] The challenge of public housing epitomized several goals of modernity. Buildings could presumably address large-scale social goals through the power of technology and formulas, concrete and grass.

The 1937 Public Housing Act in the United States energized the design and planning professions, so it is unsurprising that several design publications from this time showcased public housing as beacons of progressive architecture, touting not only their use of materials and budgets, but discussing how their intention to uplift the lives of residents within. A 1940 *Architectural Forum* editorial asked, "Are the Standards of USHA [United States Housing Authority] Projects Too High?" and in response stated, "Frequent is the argument that costs could be lowered by eliminating all amenities from slum clearance and low rent housing projects. This school of thought would lop many a square foot off USHA's minimum room areas, would do away with landscaping and architectural ornamentation, would devote no interior space to recreation and community activities and would reserve much smaller areas for outdoor recreational facilities. . . . No public housing program of new construction that does not produce attractive, safe, healthful, modern living quarters is worth its salt."[34]

These publications also posited public housing as an opportunity for private investment, noting that the density of dwelling units could reap profits as well as do good. A 1938 *Architectural Forum* article on a development built by Metropolitan Life Insurance Company notes: "Symbolically flanked by tight-packed apartments, this 120 acre Bronx site will presently demonstrate that air, light, grass, trees and modest rental can pay an economic as well as a social return.... Low-rent housing [Metropolitan] views as its greatest opportunity to further the wellbeing and health of the nation. That it can combine social objectives with a secure, reasonable return for its fifty-million-dollar investment . . . gives special impetus to the program in a period when no other investment legally open to insurance companies presents these qualifications."[35] That language obscured how Metropolitan Life Insurance Company would protect its capital in much more insidious ways, though; the company's Stuyvesant Town in Manhattan infamously banned Black tenants until the 1950s.

Some of the more successful executions of 1930s-era healthful public housing are still intact today. Most often they linked CIAM's vision of sanitary modernism to Howard's Garden City ideals. Harbor Hills Housing in Lomita, California, was designed by Reginald D. Johnson with Henry Wright's frequent collaborator Clarence Stein as consulting architect, had 300 units occupying a green, hilly site, which allowed for the one- and two- story homes to take in light and have immediate access to green space, and the articulated horizontal bands and multipaned windows are reminiscent of Viennese architecture (fig. 27).[36] Lockefield Gardens in Indianapolis, Indiana, designed by William Russ and Merritt Harrison, also directly referenced European prototypes and were sited to form small pedestrian alleys between

Fig. 27. The buildings of the Harbor Hills Housing Project in Lomita, Los Angeles County, California, similarly showed European influence and were sited on a hilly topography to maximize sun and fresh air exposure. Clarence Stein, an influential figure in American neighborhood planning, was a consulting architect on the project (c. 1933). (Library of Congress, Historic American Buildings Survey, Prints and Photographs Division, Washington, D.C.)

Fig. 28. The Lockefield Gardens public housing in Indianapolis, Indiana, was directly influenced by European social housing in its scale, design, and detailing (buildings completed in 1933, photo taken in 1980). (The Indiana Album: Joan Hostetler Collection)

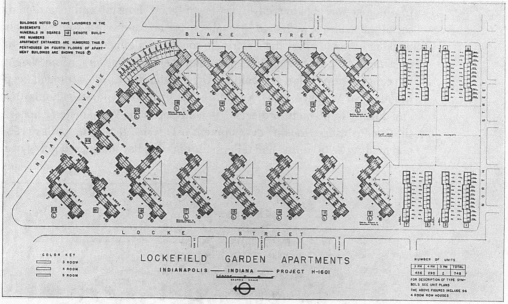

Fig. 29. The orientation of the Lockefield Gardens residences formed an internal courtyard and pedestrian way linking the entire development, but the rotated L-shape gave each building its own outdoor space as well as ensuring sunlight in each building. (Library of Congress, Historic American Buildings Survey, Prints and Photographs Division, Washington, D.C.)

the two-story townhouses at one end and a series of smaller courtyards and a large green space central to the taller buildings, with each L-shaped building slightly rotated for maximum sun exposure (figs. 28, 29).[37] Both these complexes are still in use today, the latter as a renovated complex now owned by the Indiana University–Purdue University Indianapolis campus as both student and private apartments. These strategies were also deployed to some success in far larger complexes. The Williamsburg Houses, or Ten Eyck Houses, in Brooklyn, New York, by William Lescaze and Raymond Shreve and completed in 1938, contain over 1,600 units but are broken up into H- and T-shaped four-story buildings rotated 15 degrees off the surrounding urban grid (fig. 30). The resulting effect is a networked series of courtyards that belong to each building but form a continuous flow of open space, softened by its material palette of earth-toned brick and articulated horizontal banding. The complex even features a school and playground at its center, recalling Garden City principles (fig. 31). Largely regarded as one of the most successful designs of early New York public housing, the care taken to detail the facades and create a hierarchy of landscapes and communal spaces softens the massive scale of the development.[38]

It is also worth noting that Henry Wright served as the chief architectural consultant to the Public Works Administration from 1933 to 1934, a position in which he was able to apply his ethos of "good" housing and its attendant social and health benefits. Additionally, in the micro-urban systems of public housing he could exert the control he sought in planned communities, increasingly rare in the race to expand outside of city borders. After Wright, the consultant position was held by Alfred Fellheimer, who, although keeping many of Wright's ideas, was more concerned with how to standardize and quickly implement projects.[39] In contrast to the Williamsburg houses, the Queensbridge Housing development in Queens, New York, built in 1939 and holding 3,000 units, had taller buildings and flat surfaces looming over

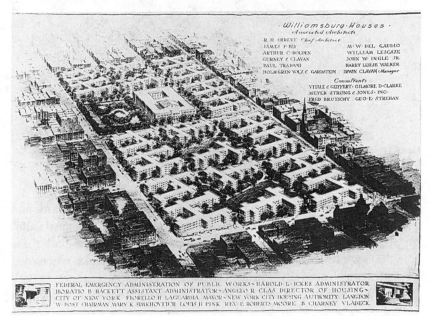

Fig. 30. The Williamsburg Houses echo the sterile, European modernist aesthetic seen in much public housing at this time but kept the scale of the buildings to a mid-rise of four to five stories and mediated the scale of the shared courtyards to the buildings with trees. (Courtesy NYC Municipal Archives)

INFECTIOUS TERRAINS

flat, central courtyards. Placing an early rendering of Queensbridge next to Le Corbusier's Plan Voison (figs. 32–34) shows how the same base ideals that guided more humane housing prototypes—separation of pedestrians and autos, crossbow plans for maximum sun exposure, increased density to maximize green space—could instead feel oppressive when efficiency and maximalization were prioritized.

Although largely devoid of actual people interacting in the spaces, Le Corbusier's drawings did evoke a city of the future—hygienic, peaceful, every piece with function and purpose. The realization of the ideas in brick and mortar failed to cohere, in a large part because of the inattention paid to the landscape and assumptions about the behavior of housing residents. In the sanitary movement, public health and planning came together to think about the city as a series of systems, comprehensively clearing slums, disposing of waste, and paving over streets and streams and simultaneously conducting widespread hygiene education campaigns.[40] In contrast, public housing design exemplified a trust in environmental determinism, precise interventions, and formulas, exhibiting a belief that if provided the correct amenities, residents would simply act accordingly and healthfully.

Almost all these housing complexes adopted the superblock concept, relegating traffic to the outside and containing only pedestrian paths within. In Le Corbusier's vision, this was to accommodate future public transportation technology, but in the context of larger cities, setting the housing within major arterials only created a barrier between residents and surrounding urban

Fig. 32. Le Corbusier experimented with forms that would access better air and light and allow for super sanitation systems in Plan Voison, although it remained a hypothetical scenario (1925). (© F.L.C. / ADAGP, Paris / Artists Rights Society [ARS], New York 2019)

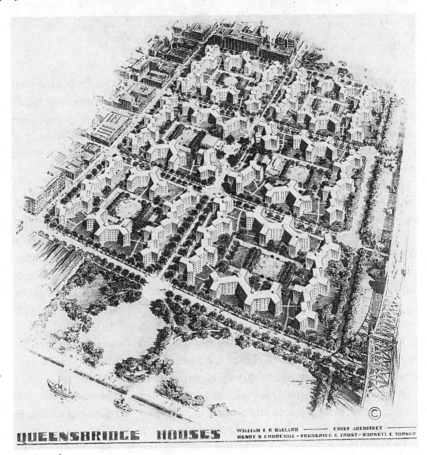

Fig. 33. Although Le Corbusier's Plan Voison was a hypothetical business district, there is a clear influence on the Queensbridge Housing in New York, one of the largest housing projects built in the 1930s (Louis H. Dreyer, 1939). (Courtesy NYC Municipal Archives)

Fig. 34. While the base principles of building orientation and form to access sun and fresh air remained consistent, the conception of public housing as an individualized unit shows that the resulting urban landscape of housing is lacking. The scale of the buildings in Queensbridge, their detailing, and trees and green space matter in terms of social cohesion and health (1939). (Wurts Bros. / Museum of the City of New York, X2010.7.1.16653)

fabric, as did the use of a markedly different architectural style and scale than the context of the neighborhood. Catherine Bauer was a leading "houser" and the movement's most clear-eyed advocate and critic when it came to the translations of European prototypes in the United States, most notably in her 1934 book *Modern Housing.* She noted in a 1957 issue of *Architectural Forum:*

There are also more subtle social reasons for the lack of enthusiastic acceptance. Public housing projects tend to be very large and highly standardized in their design. Visually they may be no more monotonous than a typical suburban tract, but their density makes them seem much more institutional, like veteran's hospitals or old-fashioned orphan asylums. The fact that they are usually designed as island— "community units" turning their backs to the surrounding neighborhood which looks entirely different—only adds to this institutional quality. Any charity stigma that attaches to subsidized housing is thus reinforced. Each project proclaims, visually, that it serves the "lowest income group."[41]

She further elaborates, "The basic ideas that stemmed from the British garden city planners, and were rationalized by the Bauhaus school of modern architects, contributed vital concepts to American housing. . . . But in grasping for modern principles of large-scale community design, we embraced too wholeheartedly functionalist and collectivist architectural theories that tended to ignore certain subtler esthetic values and basic social needs. . . . The mistake, again, was to jell both policy and practice in rigid formulas that prevented further experimentation to adapt and humanize these principles in suitable terms for the American scene."[42]

The 1949 Urban Redevelopment Act deemed much of the cleared land in city centers too valuable for housing and instead intended it to be improved with civic centers, schools, or retail. Consequently, new public housing was often built on land on the outskirts of the city.[43] The features of modern housing meant to promote health instead presented new dangers, largely due to subpar maintenance. The wide and labyrinthine corridors meant to replace the street and encourage leisurely interactions between residents were instead dark and confusing, allowing for intruders to hide and attack. Skip-stop elevators, ostensibly meant to encourage physical activity and sociability while increasing mechanical efficiency, often broke down and were undersized. Steam piping left exposed to reveal the technological systems of the building often burned children playing around the building.[44]

Nevertheless, for some time, many progressives were determined to find empirical evidence supporting this way of building. In a 1940 issue of the *American Sociological Review,* F. Stuart Chapin, in "An Experiment on the Social Effects of Good Housing," presented reams of data purporting to show improved aesthetics and improved psychological health among the residents of a housing project in the Sumner Fields Homes of Minneapolis. The scales of "morale," "general adjustment, "social participation," and "social status" were self-reported. A total of 239 residents were interviewed, and the sheer amount of numbers and loosely defined scales cloud any real conclusive analysis, but the "science" of the study gave housing proponents increased leverage, even after Chapin published a follow-up study one year later showing no real difference in morale or psychological adjustment among the rehoused. He did note that there were significant changes in "social status," but this is curiously defined as the cleanliness of individual dwellings. There is little inquiry into the complex as a larger system.[45] By 1968, The National Commission on Urban Problems had a largely negative assessment of American public housing. At several times they decried the high-rise buildings, "which make a better communal life very difficult and which identify the occupants as dwellers in 'poor town,'" and chastised developers for a "comparative neglect of the importance of design and of beauty, which are elements in the good life along with space, light, and shelter."[46] In other words, the mere delivery of amenities was not enough.

Conclusion

The thrust of the modern era could be characterized as a society seeking to better the individual via technology and generalized, mass-produced solutions. Henri Lefebvre had a dim view of this era, writing in "Reflections of the Politics of Space":

A more hidden postulate was the following: The objectivity and "purity" of the space of urban planning an object of science gave it a neutral character. Space passes as being innocenter, in other words, as not being political. This container only had existence through its contents, only had value through this content, thus formed as the objectivity and neutrality of mathematics, of technology, and without doubt a logic of space. The science of space therefore became the crown and the content itself of urban planning theory. But this is where the problems begin. Effectively, if this science is a science of formal space, of a spatial form, it implies a rigid logistics, and this science would consist of nothing but the constraints placed on the contents (the people)![47]

Later, he is much more blunt, stating: "The pressure of techniques, technicians, technocrats, epistemology, and the research of a purely technical or epistemological order resulted in an intellectual terrorism."[48]

Nowhere is it more difficult to sever design from politics than in public housing. In *The Death and Life of Great American Cities* (1961) Jane Jacobs notes that advanced statistical formulas made it easier to calculate material, budget, space, and energy but could not calculate the social costs of uprooting families, nor the public housing environment itself. In many countries, but especially in the United States, the poor have always been subject to experiments ostensibly meant to improve their health. The promise of public housing was precisely this, an experiment. Le Corbusier devoted a great deal of time to studying human proportion, but when it came to relating the environment to the individual body, his units were at best arbitrary; Bauer noted the movement's "certain weakness for expertise: sun-and-air specialists, standardization specialists, experts in modern spatial aesthetic," as difficult to coalesce into a complete solution.[49] It is notable, though, that there is no overlap or references between the modernist housing codes and the guidelines for healthful housing from the American Public Health Association, although they were published almost simultaneously and show the same enthusiasm for sun, thermal environment, and sanitation.

Landscape somehow defies this quantification, though. Just as social housing is more than the sum of individual living units, public health is not merely ensuring that each individual is free of disease. The landscape of any group of dwellings bears the responsibility of social cohesion, access to nature, and recreation. These interactions could not be calculated and require an articulation that goes beyond mere square footage. It must be understood as a holistic system rather than vaccination-like units of delivery.

In his article "High Ambitions: The Past and Future of American Low-Income Housing Policy" (1996), Alexander von Hoffman noted that the failure of American public housing was in how much stake it placed in environmental determinism and its high expectations. Less discussed is our larger national discomfort with addressing poverty and public health in tandem. European social housing was the model for these complexes, but when transplanted to a culture that largely distrusts the state (particularly when it comes to welfare) and a conviction that one's state of well-being—physical, social, financial—is the sum of one's own choices, they were perhaps always doomed to fail, especially alongside deliberate neglect and racism. The design itself was meant to influence behavior, but that was as far as provisions went. Poverty itself was thought of as the disease. The implication in much of American public housing, and as it continues today, is that it is temporary, a place to pass through until one has been "cured" of their dependence on the government. Although the supposed disease was mostly metaphorical, it was still manifested in the decidedly clinical designs of their internal landscapes. Historian Charles Davis II, in his book *Building Character: The Racial Politics of Modern Architectural Style* (2019), also demonstrates that the more widely espoused theories of public housing and its power to rehabilitate populations were concerned more with the assimilation of white immigrants, whereas the housing of Black communities was in the interest of keeping them separate. Williamsburg Houses, held up as a model of the best of Modernist public housing, purposely excluded Black residents, who made up only 34 of 1,622 residents, only enough to skirt federal segregation laws.[50]

Moreover, as disease became increasingly disconnected from the environment and its causes more amorphous, the concept of preserving health was increasingly used to explicitly exclude minorities and immigrants from neighborhoods. A 1922 housing covenant for Silver Spring, Maryland, read, "For the purposes of sanitation and health, no owner will sell or lease the said land to anyone of a race whose death rate is at a higher percentage than the white race."[51] Germ theory and the language of quarantine were extensively used in Baltimore's residential segregation ordinance of 1910, which kept Blacks from moving into blocks that had a white majority of residents, even when a series of coordinated actions by the city had excluded Blacks from healthcare access and neighborhood improvements.[52] Similarly, in San Francisco's Chinatown, disease was used as a justification for the Department of

Public Health to repeatedly raid and control the neighborhood's boundaries, and medical inspections and largely fabricated assessments on nearby Angel Island were also used to keep Chinese out of the city all together.[53]

The constant contradiction of American politics is the use of government control to enforce divides and the simultaneous fear of government control, especially when it comes to economics. In the 1910s, the American Association for Labor Association, with support from key figures in the still newly formed American Public Health Service (APHS), made the push for a national system of welfare. But by the 1920s and 1930s, the Republican-controlled government, alongside an increasingly empowered American Medical Association, decried the campaign as socialist scheme. The growing suspicion of the public health profession and political opposition to funding would effectively put an end to its Progressive Era heyday. Accordingly, during the Depression, rates of suicide, mental illness, and infant mortality rose sharply, with little infrastructure to address these crises.[54] And although the APHS enjoyed a brief infusion of funding and power during the New Deal, funding toward medical interventions rather than preventative population measures would leave the public health profession and its more expansive aims of economic and health equity in a constant battle.

PART II

The Chorography of Chronic Disease

1950s–Present Day

CHAPTER 5

Urban Decay and the Metaphorical Cancer of Blight

The Maligned City

Anti-urban perceptions persisted throughout most of the twentieth century, a paradigm that peaked in the period of 1960 through the 1980s in the urban crisis. Morton and Lucia White's *The Intellectual versus the City* (1962) attributed this particularly American attitude as dating back to Jefferson's distaste for the city and consistent nostalgia for the agrarian United States and constructs of its "wilderness." Although we often think of the architecture and urbanist elite as pro-city, the Whites point to Frank Lloyd Wright and his mentor Louis Sullivan as contrary to this perception, noting Wright's frequent referrals to Jefferson's depiction of cities as cancerous growths on the landscape and his fondness for quoting the Transcendentalists.[1] Of course, what Jefferson and Wright had in common was a desire to order the wilderness into gridded systems for agrarian production, to which they both attached a romantic view of man's place in society. These leanings were made most clear in Wright's evolving designs for his utopian proposal of the Broadacre City, which was first presented in 1932 with his book *The Disappearing City* and fleshed out more completely in his last book, *The Living City* (1958). The Broadacre City surrounded each family with its own acre of land for farming. The other predominant features of the landscape are elevated freeways, the occasional slim tower, footprint light on the landscape, and drone-like transportation vehicles overhead.[2] The expanded use of the personal vehicle and enhanced transportation infrastructure offered even more opportunity for those with means to move even farther outside the city or even early twentieth-century suburbs; among the urban and design elite the concern of the midcentury was "decentralization" and the associated deterioration of the city. The continued outward move was the concern of Lewis Mumford's essay "The Fourth Migration," put in the context of the first three American migrations—westward expansion, the Industrial Revolution and urban influx, and now initial suburban settlement. Or in Mumford's words,

"The first migration sought land; the second industrial production; the third financial direction and culture."[3] The basis of the Fourth Migration was technological revolution, especially the automobile, which made the "existing layout of the city and the existing distribution of population out of square with our new opportunities."[4] In his book *The Last Landscape* (1968), William H. Whyte upended the famous Unwin essay in his chapter "The Case for Crowding," which was primarily concerned with the inefficiencies of continued sprawl, and laments, "a lot of nonsense is heard these days about the psychological effects of living too close together in cities, or of living in cities at all for that matter. . . . What about undercrowding? The researchers would be a lot more objective if they paid as much attention to the possible effects on people of relative isolation and lack of propinquity. Maybe some of those rats they study get lonely, too"[5] (figs. 35, 36).

The health of the city itself was threatened by the apparent trend of decentralization. Victor Gruen's *The Heart of Our Cities: The Urban Crisis; Diagnosis and Cure* (1964) was entirely built on bodily metaphor, comparing a taxonomy of development types to different organs:

Though the word "anatomy" is primarily a medical term, it may be usefully applied in dissecting the "body urban" because, like everything nature has supplied us with, or what man in imitation of nature has produced, the body urban has certain characteristics of organic construction in common with the human organism. . . . As cityscape we regarded the clearly defined area in which man-made structures were

Fig. 35. *Fifth Ave at 110th St East Harlem,* photograph by Camilo Jose Vergara, 1970, shows urban residents living among physical blight in New York City. (Courtesy of Camilo Jose Vergara)

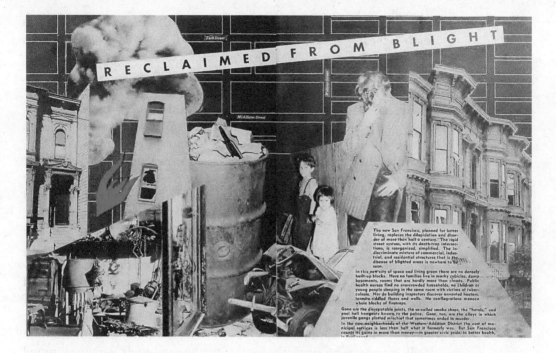

Inside the collage (small text block):

The new San Francisco, planned for better living, replaces the dilapidation and disorder of more than half a century. The rigid street system, with its death-trap intersections, is reorganized, simplified. The indiscriminate mixture of commercial, industrial, and residential structures that is the disease of blighted areas is nowhere to be seen.

In this new city of space and living green there are no densely built-up blocks. Here no families live in murky cubicles, damp basements, rooms that are hardly more than closets. Public health nurses find no overcrowded households, no children or young people sleeping in the same room with victims of tuberculosis. Nor do building inspectors discover unvented heaters, termite-riddled floors and walls. No conflagrations menace whole blocks of firetraps.

Gone are the disreputable joints, the so-called smoke shops, the "hotels," and pool hall hangouts known to the police. Gone, too, are the alleys in which juvenile gangs plotted mischief that sometimes ended in murder. In the new neighborhoods of the Western Addition District the cost of municipal services is less than half what it formerly was. But San Francisco counts its gains in more than money—in greater civic pride, in better health, ...

predominant. As landscape we saw an environment in which nature was predominant, but which had been welded together with expressions of human activity into a harmonious unit . . . and then there is nature, an environment untouched by human hand, either inaccessible only with some difficulty by footpath or primitive road."[6]

It bears noting that Gruen's good examples of "landscape" are still pastoral and Eurocentric, "the rolling hills of Pennsylvania and their farmhouses . . . rural New England areas accented by the slim fingers of church steeples . . . an Italian lake with colorful houses clinging to its steep shore."[7] He is less hospitable toward "transportationscape" of highways and "suburbscape," "the land of economic and racial segregation, with phony respectability and genuine boredom."

In Gruen's conceptualization, the most vital organs are in the city, with the urban core as the "heart" of all these functions:

It, too, works as a pump, supplying the cells and tissues located throughout the metropolitan area with life-giving energy. Most of all it supplies the brain of the city, represented by public and private leadership, by institutions of learning, by administration of all types . . . in the body urban this circulatory system is embodied in the veins and arteries of the communication apparatus, represented by mass transportation and individualized transportation for people and for goods; by tele-

Fig. 36. This photo collage from the pamphlet "New City: San Francisco Redeveloped" by the San Francisco City Planning Commission shows the danger of blight in the city: fire, trash, despair, and children in peril (1947). (San Francisco Public Library)

phone and telegraph lines; and by the postal system . . . if stagnation or congestion sets in, if the arteries or veins harden, then the heart cannot function properly and serious diseases result, with the danger of coronary thrombosis always present.[8]

Gruen's solution to repair the "tired heart of the city" was essentially a rebalancing and centralization (fig. 37). With more than a nod to the Garden City, he shows ten metropolises surrounding the urban core with direct circulation between them, a "cellular" structure that attempts to encompass the widening regionality that enhanced transportation infrastructure will bring.

Gruen's book shows that contrary to most scholarship asserting that medicine and city planning were unconcerned with issues of environmental public health, they were at least metaphorically interested in these issues, but that interest was more focused on the "health" of the physical city and increasingly decoupled with the actual health of humans, especially on the population level. The interdisciplinary, coordinated action that characterized the transformation of the landscape in the Industrial Revolution and Progressive Era had given way to the McCarthy era's increased atmosphere of conservatism and suspicion of "socialist" widespread government programs. Public health as a profession began to lose its authority as individualized medicine was increasingly the focus of funding and study. Architecture and urban planning also continued their trajectory of seeking ways to "scientize" their practice and gain legitimacy, and the language of biology and ecology appeared to offer that.

In 1960, the American Public Health Association's (APHA) Committee on the Hygiene of Housing published *Planning the Neighborhood*. The guide is decidedly a template for typical suburban neighborhoods of this time, although it purports to be a universal guide to planning, claiming that these "environmental standards for rural housing can be easily combined with those for urban and suburban housing."[9] The guidelines echo many of the tenets of the Garden City and its subsequent translations: neighborhood units based on school catchment areas, provisions for green space, and the separation of vehicle and pedestrian roads. The primary concerns here are not environmental hazards such as pollution and water quality, as these are assumed to be inner-city issues, but rather sanitation services and "moral hazards" such as taverns and nightclubs, shielding the planned community from some of the perceived causes of urban crisis. The booklet was fixated on ideal residential densities and lot size and floor/area equations, demonstrating that the ideal way of living can be achieved through quantification.[10]

The healthy suburb and unhealthy city binary would be made clear in coming decades, especially with the "urban crisis" that was a source of fixation for policy makers, city shapers, and the popular media alike. In 1977, the Centers for Disease Control (CDC) released *The Effect of the Man-Made Environment*

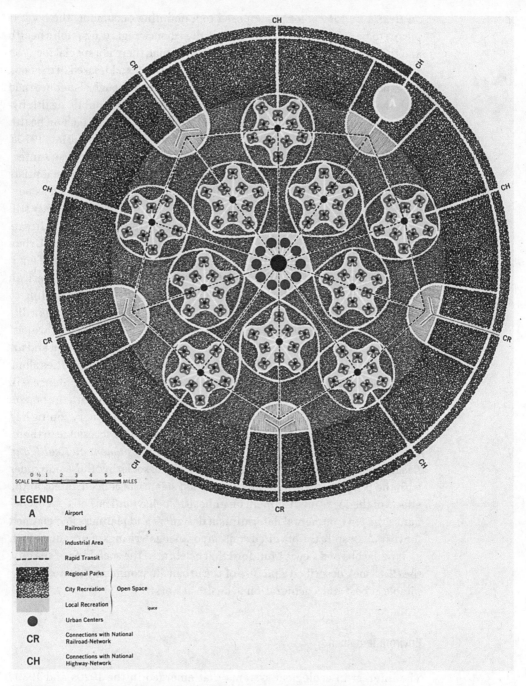

LEGEND

A   Airport

Railroad

Industrial Area

Rapid Transit

Regional Parks

City Recreation   Open Space

Local Recreation   ipace

●   Urban Centers

CR   Connections with National
Railroad-Network

CH   Connections with National
Highway-Network

Fig. 37. Planners and architects attempted to address the urban crisis using more advanced medical metaphors. In *The Heart of Our Cities: The Urban Crisis; Diagnosis and Cure* (1964), Victor Gruen makes this literal, warning of the city center's "tired heart" and comparing transportation circulation to the body's oxygen and blood circulation. (Victor Gruen Papers, American Heritage Center, University of Wyoming)

on Health and Behavior. As opposed to a planning document, the book is meant to be an overview of the state of the science regarding public health and the built environment. Like the APHA manual, there is a special focus on residential environments. Unlike the APHA, the issues addressed in the book are explicitly urban, with the results often negative. Although also concerned with the science of evaluating the built environment and public health hypotheses models on the physical and social environments' impact on health outcomes, the essays collectively show the vision of the city in the late 1970s. Research on chronic disease at this time was still relatively new, and infectious disease was controlled by microbiology. Subsequently, the scientists here are more concerned with the "disease" of social problems such as poverty and racial tensions but also with the environmental dangers the city still posed, such as traffic congestion, fossil fuel use, and the still unknown threats of nuclear power. In a chapter entitled "Community Health and the Urban Environment," Donald Kennedy stated outright that due to a number of environmental causes and the heterogeneity of the urban population, "American cities are unhealthy places in which to live, work, play or visit," leading to racial discrimination, civil disorder, crime.[11] The diversity of the city is a distinct negative. Kennedy goes on to note that the "serious problems [are] associated with black minority groups." In comparison to architectural and urbanist writings of the time, even this faintest recognition of inequities along racial divisions is significant. However, the passiveness of the sentence still leads the reader to believe that illness and violence originate with the person or population rather than their environment, when exclusionary zoning had all but made the preferred environment of the suburbs inaccessible to them. The takeaway from *The Effect of the Man-Made Environment on Health and Behavior* is that because a scientific model for associating those outcomes with the physical environment was lacking, scientists concentrated on the effects of the social environment on unhealthy behavior. The book openly debunks the environmental determinism designers and planners had claimed for years.[12] Despite the oft-cited contemporaneous writings of urbanists such as Jane Jacobs and Lewis Mumford that celebrated the social life of the city, the CDC book described a picture of the urban environment that was inhospitable at best and a denigration to health at worst.[13]

Environmentalism

The interest in ecological systems that emerged in the 1920s and 1930s expanded in the 1960s and 1970s to real environmental concerns. In previous eras, ecology provided a conceptual model for the urban landscape and health. These analogues continued as problems deepened. Mabel L. Walker, author of *Urban Blight and Slums,* was highly influenced by the Chicago School and saw the city as closed loop system that was "climaxing" as an ecosystem. In Walker's conceptualization, "blight" was a precursor stage to slums, and its spread would be inevitable without intervention.[14] In New York, the a twenty-block section of the Upper West Side known as the West Side Urban Renewal Area (WSURA) was able to stave off a mass bulldozing of the neighborhood by recasting it as an "urban habitat" and bringing up its diversity as a plus, as it is in an ecological community.[15] Jane Jacobs, the most famed urban critic of the time, while dismissing the "pseudoscience" of most urban analysis, exhorted people to look to life sciences and ecological sciences instead. Writer Rachel Carson published a series of coastal natural histories in the *New Yorker,* which eventually led to her work in the landmark 1962 book *Silent Spring* documenting the widespread and unintended effects of pesticide, notably DDT. Carson linked industry, poisons, environment, and illness in a framework that captured the zeitgeist of urban anxiety and environmentalism. Perhaps Carson was able to so viscerally describe the etiology of modern environmental disease because she herself suffered from and eventually succumbed to cancer.[16] Carson and Jacobs are rightly revered in the present day for having the foresight and courage to speak up against the relentless industrialization of the modern era, making their case through journalistic narrative and empathetic prose.

In a similar vein, Murray Bookchin, under the pseudonym Lewis Herber, published *Our Synthetic Environment* in 1962. He also linked rapid environmental change to the rise in chronic illness, hypothesizing that our bodies may be literally embodying our surroundings.

If it can be inferred from the complexity of man's metabolism that ill health can exist long before it becomes medically evident, it follows that the greatest care should be exercised in changing man's environment. Where changes are desirable, they should be preceded by meticulous and imaginative studies. And where changes are necessary, every precaution should be taken to minimize any ill effects they may have on the human body. It would be utter folly to introduce needless changes in man's diet, forms of work, habits, and physical surroundings without investigating their effects from the broadest perspective of public health. . . . Environmental changes should be studied not only in relation to the more dramatic effects they have on man; study should also be focused on the subtle changes produced in tissues and bodily functions.[17]

He notes the troubling rise in childhood cancers, which rose 28 percent between 1940 and 1955: "These statistics make it hazardous to say that the illness is essentially part of the aging process. Strong reasons exist for suspecting that environmental factors contribute significantly to increases in death from cancer among young people."[18]

The convergence of environmental ethics and rapidly developing technology presented a special case for the profession of landscape architecture. Ian McHarg's *Design with Nature* (1969) brought a deterministic angle to ecological analysis, isolating elements of the social and ecological context in separate layers to determine best suitability for interventions, focusing on, in the case of his most well-known work, a highway. His method, considered the precursor of modern geographical information systems (GIS) software, was actually predated by about four years by the work of architect Christopher Alexander and engineer Marvin Mannheim. Alexander and Mannheim also looked at a possible highway location, hand-drawing layers such as land costs, air pollution, drainage patterns, eyesores, and so forth.[19] Although McHarg, Alexander, and Mannheim expanded the view of how design and planning affected multiple systems, even landscape architecture was not immune to the oversights common to the other design professions as they sought to ground their field in a rational, positivist ideology. Namely, demographics were not a layer that figured into the spatial analysis. The environmental justice movement was still decades away from the environmentalism of the 1960s and 1970s. Even though Jacobs made her name advocating for the "strips of chaos" of the African American neighborhood of East Harlem, social equity issues were largely overlooked.

Chronic Disease as Urban Metaphor

The shift from the prevalence in infectious to chronic disease also marked a distinct shift in the conceptualization of how the built environment affected health. In the developed world, infectious disease as a cause of mortality began to wane under the proliferation of vaccines and biomedical research. Salk's polio vaccine perhaps represented the apex of microbial accomplishment, and the added support from the federal government in promoting and producing the vaccine was a victory for the field of public health.[20] At the same time, chronic diseases—illnesses that are noncommunicable, persistent, and, most crucially, without microbial cause[21]—began to rise as the primary causes of mortality in the United States. Although cancer has been recorded in accounts dating back to ancient Egyptian writings, Richard Nixon did not sign the National Cancer Act until 1971, the year after it had become the second leading cause of death in the country.[22] Other illnesses such as heart disease and diabetes have often been referred to as human-caused illnesses, or diseases of civilization, indicating that their murky origins can often be traced back to industry, environment, or byproducts thereof. Its emergence is also often tracked to economic production and increasing if inequitable prosperity. Most chronic disease is recognized as being multi-causal, a confluence of genetic, lifestyle, and environmental reasons. By this time, germ theory had been crystallized into "the epidemiological triangle," where incidence can be explained by the convergence of agent (microbial cause), host (the sick person), and vector (path of the disease). Moreover, although the symptoms of many chronic diseases overlap or are rooted in similar predispositions to illnesses, the strategies of treatment were mostly single-disease focused (and continue to be today).[23] Chronic disease lacks a clear model for eradication, even if it has dominated public health research for the past century. Post–World War II public health started to shift to study the multiple causes of chronic disease and redefining pathology. Epidemiology was at this time also becoming more established in American academia; in doing so, the language of "exposure" as predisposition to chronic disease was increasingly adopted, perhaps as a nod to the environmental movement at the time.[24] Epidemiologic historians Mervyn Susser and Zena Stein have also called the paradigm of chronic disease epidemiology a "black box" with unclear pathways between predisposing factors and outcomes. Not insignificantly, chronic diseases such as cancer and heart disease also affected middle-aged males more acutely, perhaps why it dominated the national conversation.[25] In *Illness as Metaphor* (1977), Susan Sontag confronts the late twentieth-century's preoccupation with cancer directly, saying:

Two diseases have been spectacularly, and similarly, encumbered by the trappings of metaphor: tuberculosis and cancer. The fantasies inspired by TB in the last century, by cancer now, are responses to a disease thought to be intractable and capricious—that is, a disease not understood—in an era in which medicine's central premise is that all diseases can be cured. Such a disease . . . Now it is cancer's turn to be the disease that doesn't knock before it enters, cancer that fills the role of an illness experienced as a ruthless, secret invasion—a role it will keep until, one day, its etiology becomes as clear and its treatment as effective as those of TB have become. Although the way in which disease mystifies is set against a backdrop of new expectations, the disease itself (once TB, cancer today) arouses thoroughly old fashioned kinds of dread.[26]

The unknowability of cancer and other chronic diseases is what made it so terrifying, but its unknowability also made it an apt way to communicate the direness of the urban condition and spur action.

The environmental movement and increasing prevalence of ecological thinking seemed appropriate to apply to the frustratingly indeterminant nature of chronic disease. In *Our Synthetic Environment,* Bookchin, using the pseudonym Herber, wrote, "Many physicians tend to approach the human organism with a fixed threshold of illness in mind. On one side of the threshold, the body is conceived as being in good health; on the other side, it is diseased and requires treatment. The line between health and disease is generally drawn as sharply as possible. The body ordinarily must reach a certain degree of disequilibrium and damage before it is regarded as ill. This approach would be excusable if it could be attributed merely to a fragmentary knowledge of the complex processes that take place in the human body."[27] Sontag's "dual kingdoms" would echo this critique of a particularly American view of wellness.

The difficulty of redefining health was clearly illustrated when the World Health Organization (WHO) was asked to undertake this task in 1948. Their response was that "health is a state of complete physical, mental and social wellbeing and not merely the absence of disease or infirmity."[28] Even so, the shift to specifically looking at social and economic factors of disease appeared to be more in Europe than in the United States. There were some outliers—John Gordon, a professor at Harvard medical school, said as early as the 1950s that epidemics could only be studied at the level of the population and spent his career seeking new models with multiple levels of causality.[29] Even so, an etiologic framework still predominated discussions of disease, although on the surface the new age of disease was unexplainable by any single or even multiple factors. Said Bookchin/Herber, "And here a typical disagreement arises. In the absence of conclusive evidence that a single factor contributes to all cases of an illness, many researchers are inclined to distrust the constellation as a whole. Complexity is regarded as "ambiguity," and the relationship between environment and degenerative illnesses is dismissed as "vague." This kind of thinking is characteristic of our modern Weltgeist. . . . The study of chronic and degenerative disorders still calls for imaginative departures from conventional approaches to disease."[30]

Chronic disease is a degenerative condition: slow, relentless, and often unbeatable, it is no wonder that many people saw parallels in the aging city. Many compared the issue of "blight" to cancer, eating cities from the inside out, although in most accounts it moved without discrimination and unceasingly—that is, without acknowledging the worst parts of the city were where the poorest and minorities, particularly African Americans and Latinos, lived. Mitchell Gordon, a reporter for the *Wall Street Journal,* published *Sick Cities: Psychology and Pathology of American Urban Life* in 1966, and on top of the familiar refrains about polluted air and water in the city, he also critiqued the lack of recreational opportunity and increasing commodification and construction in parks and zoos. In a departure from many books lamenting the health effects of the city, Gordon exhorted the government to squarely deal with inequality and race and dismissed aesthetic critiques of the suburbs as largely superficial, choosing instead to focus on their drain on the economy as well as how growing segregation threatened the health of all.[31] Said Gordon, "Regardless of what shape the urban mass of tomorrow takes, however, the dire danger of a continuing trend toward the accumulation of low-income, minority families in the core city and wealthier whites in the suburb must be recognized for what it threatens, politically, socially, and humanely, in terms of understanding and general wellbeing."[32]

Just as chronic diseases are multicausal, so were factors contributing to the urban crisis, namely years of policy favoring suburban growth and systemic racism. What was also apparent during this era is that while the fields of planning, design, and public health were operating in separate spheres, there was at least a shifting epistemology in public health to look at issues ecologically, whereas the former fields were still mostly a mired positivist and deterministic paradigm unsuited to the complex realities of human health during this era. Many only viewed the city itself as the locus of disease, without investigating sociopolitical causes.

Many urban scholars also used the language of disease and epidemiology to describe the spread of vacant buildings and their associated problems of squatters, fires, and so on. In a chapter in *Urban Policy Making and Metropolitan Development* (1976), Michael Dear stated:

The process of abandonment as it operates in space . . . suggests an initial broad scattering of abandoned structures, characterized internally by the occurrence of many small groups of abandoned houses. With the passage of time, this pattern is intensified; the broad scatter is maintained, although the small groups now contain a greater number of structures. A two-stage process is clearly suggested; the initial abandonments occur and later consolidation follows. . . . It suggests a 'leader-follower' sequence which resembles the propagation of plant species or the diffusion of information. It is essentially a contagious sequence . . . contagion has major implications for our understanding of the dynamics of abandonment, and for later policy considerations.[33]

With human epidemics assumed to be under control via vaccinations and other medical technologies, urban advocates now attempted to reappropriate the language of disease to propose treatments. The spread of blight is a fear that also predominates Saarinen's *The City,* claiming that cities have a natural organic order, but at a certain point when design or "expressive and correlative faculties are impotent to prevent disintegration of organic order, decline and death enters. This is true, no matter what happens in the microscopic tissues of cell-structure where cancer causes disintegration, or in the hearts of the large cities of today where compactness and confusion cause slums to spread."[34] As a vague metaphorical "illness" began to be applied to cities, the word was increasingly meant to stand in for blight, crime, and fear of minorities. As late as 1993, public health scholars Roderick and Deborah Wallace published a paper entitled "The Coming Crisis of Public Health in the Suburbs" for healthcare journal *Milbank Quarterly,* warning that through social networks and spatial epidemiology many of the urban diseases prevalent in the urban core—HIV/AIDS and mental health among them—could spread with the movement of poor and minority populations to the suburbs.[35]

The treatment of "blight" as a disease extended to its documentation. Much like cholera and yellow fever, "blight" was documented by public health agencies by going from door to door, or demarcating entire blocks or neighborhoods, although there still lacked real underlying theories about its spread. It bears noting that one way the standards were weighted against urban areas is that they originated with regulations for single-family homes, not multifamily.[36] The unspoken tension in all the literature surrounding slums and blight led to the question of whether they in themselves cause poor health, or were they a symptom of poverty and therefore larger systems? In her essay "The Costs of Bad Housing," housing reformer Edith Elmer Wood stated: "[Clifford] Shaw points out that while high delinquency rates and bad housing occur together, it does not necessarily follow that one is the cause of the other. Both may be the result of a tertium quid such as poverty. For practical purposes, he agrees that improved housing conditions in these areas would probably decrease delinquency and crime, provided whole neighborhoods were rebuilt at one time. In this proviso Shaw is, I think, justified, for it is bad associates rather than bad bricks and mortar that incite to delinquency."[37] The subsequent actions to combat them would be highly contradictory. While the language of urban renewal implies the physical environment was the problem, the actual actions that followed reinforced the idea that it was people. That argument dated back to the era of sanitation, but in the 1960s and 1970s the coupling of new disciplines such as sociology and ecology added new context. Those fields were interested in *why* the urban crisis happened and in examining those systems, but the fields were emerging and still largely based in conjecture or superficially co-opted by planners and designers. Either way, the disastrous moves in the urban environment that followed largely failed as they began to detach conditions of the environment from the health of people within them.

Urban Renewal: Quarantine and Elimination

The fear that the urban blight would spread to the suburbs lent both urgency and agency to urban renewal programs. As in disease epidemics of the past, when "immunizations" such as increased municipal services and attempts to enforce stricter building codes did not show immediate progress, the answer instead was to "eliminate" the source of disease by leveling neighborhoods altogether. The postmodern era reveals both the design and planning professions in flux when relating to public health matters. On one hand, while infectious disease had mostly been dealt with through germ theory research, the urban renewal programs recall the kind of neighborhood clearance seen in the era of the sanitary city, perhaps even at a larger scale. The key difference was that instead of eliminating a contagious epidemic such as cholera, governments were combating the less-defined epidemic of "blight," encompassing general disrepair and chaos, treating a social affliction as if its pathology was etiologic and could be eliminated at the source. Where policy, design, and planning went most astray was to treat the chronic diseases of blight, crime, and "social ills" in the same manner they treated infectious disease in an earlier era. Rather than fighting the causes of urban crisis, it instead treated the symptoms with twinned strategies of quarantine and elimination. Said Saarinen:

The slums he clears by piecemeal mending, and the old infects the new in short order. Urban conditions cannot be cured int his superficial manner. Deeper must the planner delve into his problems in order to discover the real cause of the difficulties, and then from these discoveries work out the proper methods of cure. The planner must know, as well as the doctor, that when the head aches the stomach might be out of order . . . and the planner must be aware of the fact as well as the doctor, that vitality cannot be transfused into a dead organ. The dead organ must be removed, and the transfusion effected in a healthy part of the body. . . . He must unearth the roots of the evil. He must amputate slums by a decisive surgery. And he must transfuse vitality only into those areas that are protected against contagion.[38]

Popular media would amplify these metaphors: ads in the *Saturday Evening Post* advertised a project by William Lescaze for Lower Harlem, referring to it as "Sure Surgery for Sick Slums," and a 1945 pamphlet for Pittsburgh's new city plans was entitled a "Civic Clinic for Better Living," depicting Benjamin Franklin as a proxy for the city, getting a checkup, and advocating for an infusion of new industry and homes for "nourishment."[39] Eventually, planners and designers would be even further empowered by the

Fig. 38. In a lecture titled "Slums and Blight . . . a disease of urban life," James W. Follin of the Urban Renewal Administration connected physical blight to infectious disease, using "Gussie," a child in peril as an emotional plea, who could only be saved by the "Gargantuan broom of code enforcement." Planning and public health have always been linked in order to exert control over the public realm (1955). (Urban Renewal Administration)

government with the Housing Act of 1949, which allowed for the housing-scale improvements of "urban redevelopment," and the Housing Act of 1954, which allowed for the more large-scale moves of "urban renewal."[40]

Just as in the sanitation era when advocates held up child mortality as a reason to act, the innocence of children subject to blight was also leveraged to communicate the metaphorical illness of blight. In a 1955 lecture to the University of Michigan School of Public Health and an accompanying publication, James W. Follin, commissioner of the Urban Renewal Administration, spoke on the topic "Slums and Blight . . . a disease of urban life" (fig. 38). He revolved his story around "Gussie," a cartoon depiction of a waif-like young white girl as proxy for the "deadly effect of slums on human lives." She is introduced standing on a pile of rubble, or "adrift on a sea of blight." The booklet shows a series of maps overlaying juvenile delinquency, lack of sanitation, tuberculosis, and population density, with the densest occurrences "always pointing to the center of cities."[41] Although much of the advocacy against decentralization of cities was inefficiencies of cost, Follin also used an economic argument, saying, "An eastern city, in one year, received $108 more in per capita revenue from good residential areas than it spent there, but its slums cost $88 more per person than they yielded. In one southern city, slum areas contributed only 5% percent of the city's property taxes, but required 53 percent of the city's health, police, fire and other service facilities."[42] Later in the publication, Gussie is shown wielding the "Gargantuan broom of code enforcement" of health and sanitation.

The mapping of blight was meant to convey its "contagious" spread as well. In his booklet, Follin showed urban ills as a black cloud. A 1951 *Architectural Forum article* entitled "Slum Surgery in St. Louis" showed "blighted" and "obsolete" districts beginning to spread over the rest of the city grid, with the former districts shaded completely as if to erase their existing characteristics. The same article praised the work of architects Leinweber, Yamasaki, & Hellmuth for their proposal of the now-infamous Pruitt Igoe housing complex, with a "river" of trees and plans to build "vertical neighborhoods for poor people . . . the new plan saves not only people, but money."[43] Another 1968 article regarding urban renewal by Shean O'Connell in *Official Architecture and Planning* showed planned new development in New Haven, Connecticut, in blood red, spatially clustered and then slowly spreading out, emphasizing the cellular nature of urban landscape "treatment." These depictions are not unlike the amorphous shading earlier surveyors used to convey the spread and uncertainty of cholera along the Eastern Seaboard or John Snow's advocacy for water pump replacement in urban areas.

The use of eminent domain also gave the government more power to clear land and people in the city. It should also be noted that many public health advocates were in favor of this flexing of government authority as some urban renewal allowed the building of large healthcare complexes.[44] Some municipalities even empowered their health officers to evict residents. In "A Workable Plan for Urban Renewal," published by the Boston City Planning Board in 1955, the text reads, "For the handling of extreme cases, the Health Commissioner is empowered . . . to 1) clean the premises at the expense of the owner or occupant, 2) force removal of the occupant, or 3) proceed in equity."[45] The government document also uses "surgery" as a term to describe the repair of houses. The problem of blight was so multifaceted, and people so fearful of its contagion, that many documents asserted that a "piecemeal" approach is useless. Continuing the medical metaphor, Follin said of urban renewal, "Each project can contain any or all of the three individual treatments for the blight disease—conservation, rehabilitation, and redevelopment, or in public health terms, prophylaxis, medical treatment and surgery."[46] The scale of the problem was such that surgery was wielded with a machete as opposed to a scalpel.

Graphic communication of the urban landscape was key to a 1947 urban renewal plan for the Fillmore (Western Addition) District of San Francisco (fig. 39). Proclaiming the neighborhood "Reclaimed by blight" a haphazard collage of fire, trash, and broken windows was overlaid on the urban grid, communicating the health and safety dangers of the neighborhood in its present state. Repeating the economic argument Follin also made in his lecture, the City Planning Commission stressed how crime will cost the city, noting that per capita police activity is $23.28, "compared with 26 cents in the Marina district, a 'good' area of similar size."[47] The chaos of the existing fabric is shown replaced with an illustration of tall buildings on a platform of green, not dissimilar to Le Corbusier's Radiant City. In other words, even for an "urban core" plan, it showed the marks of decentralization in its land-

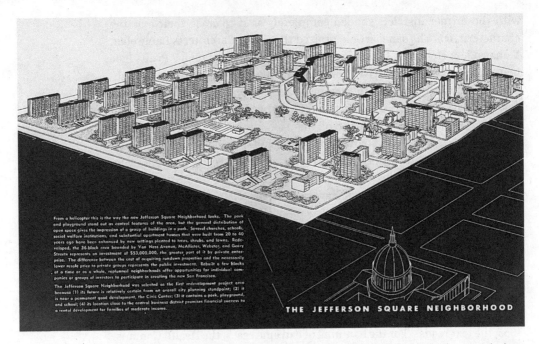

From a helicopter this is the way the new Jefferson Square Neighborhood looks. The park and playground stand out as central features of the area, but the general distribution of open space gives the impression of a group of buildings in a park. Several churches, schools, social welfare institutions, and substantial apartment houses that were built from 20 to 40 years ago have been enhanced by new settings planted to trees, shrubs, and lawns. Redeveloped, the 36-block area bounded by Van Ness Avenue, McAllister, Webster, and Geary Streets represents an investment of $53,000,000, the greater part of it by private enterprise. The difference between the cost of acquiring rundown properties and the necessarily lower resale price to private groups represents the public investment. Rebuilt a few blocks at a time or as a whole, replanned neighborhoods offer opportunities for individual companies or groups of investors to participate in creating the new San Francisco.

The Jefferson Square Neighborhood was selected as the first redevelopment project area because (1) its future is relatively certain from an overall city planning standpoint; (2) it is near a permanent good development, the Civic Center; (3) it contains a park, playground, and school; (4) its location close to the central business district promises financial success to a rental development for families of moderate income.

THE JEFFERSON SQUARE NEIGHBORHOOD

Fig. 39. In contrast to their earlier dire depictions of blight, the San Francisco City Planning Commission presented a clean, sterile alternative to the Jefferson Square neighborhood. The green spaces in between are similarly indistinguishable, but the combination of modern high rises and flat landscapes continues to convey the delivery of health via sun, fresh air, and "green" (1947). (San Francisco Public Library)

scape. Another renewal document from 1958 by the New York City Planning Commission showed buildings indiscriminately scattered across flat green lots with trees, but there is no other order besides a grid and no central nodes, and perhaps most importantly no people appear in either depiction. Even though the buildings are ostensibly built in the city, the plans showed no context; the Fillmore's Jackson Square plan is literally isolated from any existing fabric save for City Hall. Its historical context was also excised, although the Fillmore was a cultural center for the West Coast's small African American population.[48] Eighty percent of those removed by urban renewal were African American, with figures varying from city to city, although in Baltimore it was reported to be 100 percent.[49]

Even if urban renewal was meant to strategically eliminate blighted parts of the city, it is rare that its purported aims to rehouse the people living there were achieved; instead the core was replaced with luxury housing or commercial enterprises. This was largely intentional; it should be noted that trade groups were more involved with the more large-scale Housing Act of 1954.[50] *Building the American City,* a 1968 document by the National Commission on Urban Problems, partly reads as a postmortem on the age of urban renewal: "The Commission believes that the record clearly and unmistakably supports the view that the three primary purposes of the urban renewal title of the act of 1949 were: (a) to speed up the clearance of slums and badly blighted residential areas; (b) to facilitate the provision of decent, low-income housing by helping to finance the acquisition and preparation of appropriate sites, including insite preparation of public facilities that would contribute to 'a suitable living environment,' and (c) to give private enterprise 'maximum opportunity' to take part in redeveloping these areas"[51] (fig. 40). Later the commission stated: "This was justified on the ground that the process would replace a slum which was at once a health hazard, a moral cesspool, and an esthetic blight, with better buildings set in a more wholesome environment. As so often happens, idealism was called upon to justify self-interest. Most saw no inconsistency between the two, and by an amalgam of motives and schools of thought, the act was passed." The report deemed the failure to relocate or rehouse those evicted a weakness, although it says the "obliviousness" of urban renewal is not as destructive as the federal highway program. But the oversight to build new housing also enforces that most saw the people, not the environment, as the problem.

The corollary to urban elimination was the further damage wrought by

Fig. 40. The New York City Planning Commission also advocated for urban renewal, a total elimination of existing neighborhoods for purportedly healthier newer buildings, with green space filling any remnant space in between (1958). (Cover image of the Report on the West Side Urban Renewal Study used with permission of the New York City Planning Commission; all rights reserved)

the Federal Aid Highway Act of 1954. While the highways were not always explicitly health focused, they were the "circulatory systems" Saarinen described, and keeping them "unclogged" was the key to cities thriving again. Of course, the stories of freeway building are constant and similar. Wealthier neighborhoods were able to keep infrastructural intervention out, whereas poorer neighborhoods were sliced through and quarantined in a cloud of automobile pollution. The United States has yet to reconcile or heal the Latino neighborhoods of East Los Angeles, the Treme neighborhood of New Orleans, and the countless enclaves in New York cut through by Robert Moses's plans. These, too, were designed by the indisputable authority of "science," from the layered design investigations of McHarg, Alexander, and Mannheim, or by the calculations of the transportation engineers themselves. And although they are almost universally denigrated by designers today, there is an interesting overlap between the profession of landscape architecture and early freeways.[52] Extending past the research of McHarg and others, the possibility of the freeway was seductive even to famed designer Lawrence Halprin, who in 1966 wrote an entire book entitled *Freeways* and rhapsodized:

Freeways out in the countryside, with their graceful, sinuous, curvilinear patterns, are like great free-flowing paintings in which, through participation, the sensations of motion through space are experienced. In cities the great overhead concrete structures with their haunches tied to the ground and the vast flowing cantilevers rippling above the local streets stand like enormous sculptures marching the architectonic caverns. These vast and beautiful works of engineering speak to us in the language of a new scale, a new attitude in which high-speed motion and the qualities of change are not mere abstract conceptions but a vital part of our everyday experiences.[53]

He was conflicted, saying: "In the selection of routes, freeways have invariably been pushed through areas where the families were renters, not owners, areas usually occupied by groups who wielded little political power and were in no way vocal. The freeway in the city has been a great destroyer of neighborhood values. . . . Elevated freeways have done even worse damage to the areas through which they pass. They have blocked out light and air; they have brought blight into the city through their great shadows on the ground and through the noise of their traffic."[54]

The problems wrought by medical metaphors would persist well into the 1970s and early 1980s. Even when cities tried to intervene in vaccination-like ways, the myopic view of objective data and neutral models as problem-solver overlooked the messiness of urban life. The RAND Corporation, a think tank with roots in the defense industry, was hired by New York City to do an analysis of fire station need in the city. Largely looking at location, the researchers determined that efficient fire services could still be delivered if they were cut by almost 25 percent in some areas. Instead, fires between 1972 and 1976 increased 45 percent.[55] By the 1980s the craze for formal biomedical metaphors had dissipated. In *Good City Form* (1984) Kevin Lynch wrote:

Thinking of the city in vague disease terminology is problematic. . . . Cities are not organisms, any more than they are machines, and perhaps even less so. They do not grow or change of themselves or reproduce or repair themselves. They are not autonomous entities, nor do they run through life cycles, or become infected. . . . But it is more difficult, and more important, to see the fundamental ineptness of the metaphor and how it leads us unthinkingly to cut out slums to prevent their "infectious" spread, to search for an optimum size, to block continuous growth, to separate uses, to struggle to maintain greenbelts, to suppress competing centers, to prevent "shapeless sprawl", and so on.[56]

Ultimately the "decentralization" of the city was a way to give people with the means to leave a way out, and a way to keep minorities in. Slum clearance, urban renewal, and highway building cut large swaths through the city, not so much based on health need but on political voice and economic might. Even as "urban" diseases became more metaphorical, the treatments became more literal and were applied more bluntly. The working poor were often the first subjects of so-called scientific social planning; its "objectivity" was a way to gloss over these inequities.[57] Designers and planners, especially in the modernist era, were guilty of jumping on the rare promises of blank slates in which to execute their ideas. In the language of urban renewal, residents are faceless and raceless with the sins of the city inflicted upon them. Built on a rhetoric of improved health, urban renewal was supported by reassuring people living outside the city that their health would be preserved by stopping the contagion of blight. The glaring contradiction of this time period was that as those involved in the planning and design of and advocacy for the built environment became aware of ecology as actions to improve health in the city became more etiologic. The complexity and unknown factors of chronic disease allowed for this contradiction. The primary characteristic of chronic disease is that it is constant and unceasing, always present. It can be managed, but it is difficult to eliminate. Often preventive measures are the best guard against its worst effects, but we don't know its presence until the symptoms become acute. This was the real similarity between chronic disease and urban decay, but its treatment was too late and too narrowly focused, so the result was largely disastrous.

CHAPTER 6

Prescriptive Neighborhoods

The Maligned Suburb

As much as Progressive Era designers extolled the health and social benefits of the suburb, their architectural nature was always a hard sell to the larger design elite in general. Even as early as what would be considered the peak of suburbia in the 1950s and 1960s, while the popular culture of television and advertising celebrated the moral virtues of their lifestyles, prominent urbanite scholars including Jane Jacobs and Lewis Mumford decried sprawling growth as destructive to American communities and an incubator to social dysfunction. These critics defined the suburbs as a point-by-point rejection of what defined cities, chiefly in its density and diversity of buildings and the socioeconomic homogeneity of those who lived there. Although it was some years before the term "urban sprawl" would enter the popular lexicon, what these scholars seemed to fear most was the uncontrolled rapid growth. They were keen observers of the urban condition and human ecology, but their critiques of the suburbs were largely written from afar, which often led to conflicting conclusions about their implications on social conditions, or even agreement on what exactly was offensive about their environment. Employing an ecology metaphor, Jacobs likened cities to a mature, stable, diverse ecosystem with a "logical spatial organization" against the "dullness" of the suburbs. Jacobs and Lewis Mumford believed that their low density encouraged isolationism. Invoking Unwin's argument for the suburbs, Mumford said, "nothing gained by overcrowding, something lost by overspacing."[1] In *The Last Landscape* (1968), William Whyte recalls Unwin in a chapter called "The Case for Crowding," saying: "The stock justification is that lower densities mean healthier living, and planners of this persuasion make much of the correlation between the number of people per acre and the rate of crime and disease in slum neighborhoods. There is a correlation. But is there cause and effect?"[2] In a 1963 op-ed entitled "The Suburbs Are a Mess" for the *Saturday Evening Post,* Peter Blake, editor of *Architectural*

Forum, likens suburban development to the disorder of the cities of the Industrial Revolution:

The suburbs surrounding our major cities are in chaos. Housing developments are eating up land at a voracious rate, and the suburbs have lost the very qualities that people left the cities to find—privacy and free and open out-door space. Life in many suburbs, in fact has become only a little less intolerable than life on congested tenement streets . . . the front yard is completely unsuitable for outdoor living. The rear yard, on the other hand, is too small for growing children to play in, or for adults to entertain in, and frequently becomes nothing more than a place for hiding the garbage and hanging out the laundry.[3]

He even brings attention to the timeworn horror of "children playing in the streets," due to the lack of privacy and space in their own yards, although after that opening volley, he later decries the excess lot sizes of suburban homes and the distance between them.

Mumford's concerns with the suburbs were a natural outgrowth of his preoccupation with the historical rise and fall of cities. He saw parallels to the unrestricted growth and a subset of society that was ruled by "consumption and leisure" to the Hellenic cities before the fall of Rome.[4] More pointedly, rather than a blanket condemnation of suburban homogeneity, he noted that for all its problems, the city put people in constant contact with people of lower socioeconomic status and of different backgrounds, while the suburbs maintained the illusion of a world untouched by this. To confront the state of the city was also to find a common humanity. Blake also pointed to the centrality of shopping centers and the corresponding lack of visible "strong physical symbols of local government" as the reason for low civic participation.

Mumford was not strictly an urban evangelist; in fact he was a vocal advocate of the Garden Cities model and lived in Sunnyside Gardens, New York, for most of his life. Its emphasis on growth control via greenbelts was one of its most appealing aspects to him, although the Garden City's translation to American grounds failed to find its balance as a self-sustaining unit. Ebenezer Howard's promise of health via landscape, air, and sun was still the building block for the American suburb, alongside safety from urban crime and an escape from the congestion of the city. At some point the prototype of single-family houses and insulating swaths of yards had mutated to unceasing and unordered development. Whyte, Mumford, and Blake all trace the origin of the suburb to the Garden City ideal, but Whyte noted the standards that guided midcentury suburban development "are the legacy of a utopian concept which was never really intended for the city. It is the garden city ideal: difficult enough to achieve in suburbia, and wholly inapplicable to the city. In some respects, the original model was more realistic in its specifications than the current standards."[5]

Most of these writers were also opposed to the modernist, positivist style of grand urban planning of the time, but underlying these critiques is their view of the seemingly chaotic development of the suburbs not only as a rebuke of cities' density and diversity but also its control of the environment, its appearance, and the morals and health of its citizens.[6] To those who sought their own piece of property, it represented participation and success in the thriving American free market by building dream homes and showing off green lawns, and the desire for privacy, mobility, and choice.[7] Of course, the irony was that the explosive suburban growth of the mid- to late twentieth century was very much aided by government policy such as the Federal Housing Act of 1949, which expanded funding and made credit and mortgage issuance more freely available for suburban housing units. Whyte and Blake understood this contradiction; in his *Saturday Evening Post* op-ed, Blake duly places blame on the FHA for its guidelines on streets, landscaping, and density contributing to the "wasteland" appearance of the suburb, while Whyte noted that growth was not unplanned, even though it seemed to build with a "blind, lemminglike urge," but rather was the result of many decisions made by the federal government and developers.[8] Other policies made sure suburbs had the best schools and public services, effectively draining resources from the city and communities of color still living in them.[9] Additionally, the strict zoning codes first implemented in the city to prevent the spread of infectious disease, in particular the separation of industry, commercial, and residential land uses, were repeated and magnified in the suburbs, partly still in the name of health but also to protect market values.

Despite the apparent economic prosperity and healthy lifestyle offered by these neighborhoods, suburban ennui became a well-trod subject in literature and cinema by the 1970s. Writers such as Philip Roth, John Updike, and John Cheever restricted their view to the depression and restlessness of white, middle- to upper-class men, such as themselves. Some, such as in Richard Yates's *Revolutionary Road,* Rick Moody's *The Ice Storm,* or Anne Tyler's *The Amateur Marriage,* recast the dream images of suburbia from the 1950s and 1960s to explore how it limited the roles of women. Central to all these pieces of popular art is the imagery of expansive lawns, wooden fences, and shade trees, once signaling economic mobility and robust health, but now recast as cages. Mumford had been predictive when he forecast the malaise of a society required to do nothing but consume. If the suburbia of the late twentieth century had become strongly associated with mental illness in the white and affluent, just as cities had at the turn of the century, evidence soon emerged that the afflictions of suburbia could be physiological as well.

Moving into the 1980s and 1990s, it was not so much the original idea of the inner commuter suburb with which many of its critics took issue, but rather its cancerous cousin, sprawl. What differentiates "sprawl" from the suburbs? Whyte was thought to originate the term in a 1958 article for *Fortune* magazine, primarily decrying its further de-densification of buildings and land use, where "five acres is made to be doing the work of one." In the 1980s, where populations doubled in the outer suburbs, cars multiplied twice as fast as population, and land area used multiplied by four. Others have defined it as an urbanization pattern that is fully decoupled from a city center, a lack of open space, segregated land use, but, most of all, the predominance of automobile infrastructure, necessitating a car for even the most local of trips. Ironically, where designers and planners of the early suburbs were concerned with the automobile's threat to human health and safety, in many cases separating out driving thoroughfares completely from pedestrian paths, sprawl was built upon the apparent access and choice the automobile offered, but in doing so it increased the number of cars in a neighborhood, eliminating sidewalks and ceding green space for wider roads. It was not an intentional form of development, rather the peak realization of free-market and laissez-faire development, as well as the result of mass production, corporate expansion, and increasing availability of loans.[10]

Sprawl was the unintentional result of many factors, but primarily increasing access to technology (infrastructural, personal, societal) and consumer goods. So was the increasing obesity epidemic. The CDC reported that in the United States, the percentage of overweight adults hovered around 31 percent between 1960 and 1994, and the percentage of adults categorized as obese increased from 13 percent to 23 percent, meaning almost 55 percent of adults in the mid-1990s were overweight or obese.[11] Researchers started to draw connections between larger patterns of change in society, ranging from food availability and technological attachment, but a great deal of literature has pointed to sedentary lifestyles encouraged by the unabated suburban growth oriented around the automobile. While the previous eras shaped the environment around pandemic disease from identifiable sources, public health was now faced with predominantly human-created degenerative disease. While obesity is a complicated intersection of environmental, behavioral, and unavoidable hereditary causes, most public health experts agree it's one of the most highly preventable conditions. And while obesity in and of itself is not a cause of mortality, it can increase the risk of death, up to 2.5 times more than non-overweight/obese people, from other chronic diseases, namely cardiovascular disease, type 2 diabetes, stroke, various physiological disabilities, depression, and even many cancers. In 2005, it was estimated to incur over $190 billion, or almost 21 percent of all US healthcare expenditures.[12]

The epidemic also coincided with a major shift in American public health practice in the late 1980s and early 1990s that started to look at social determinants (or sometimes referred to as "upstream") causes of health. The World Health Organization defines these as "the conditions in which people are born, grow, live, work and age. These circumstances are shaped by the distribution of money, power and resources at global, national and local levels. The social determinants of health are mostly responsible for health inequities—the unfair and avoidable differences in health status seen within and between countries."[13] As discussed in detail in chapter 1, public health, as differentiated from the medical profession, has always been concerned with environmental conditions of health and disease. However, expanding programs to the poor were often politically stigmatized as "socialism," and support funding lagged. As described in chapter 4, in the midcentury the focus turned to medical treatment of the individual. The spate of "social diseases" in the urban crisis, and soon the rise of chronic disease, necessitated a turn back to its environmental roots. Once again, leaders in the field pointed to Europe, specifically the Healthy Cities initiative, as a model for integrating economic, social, and environmental conditions into the study of epidemics. In 1979, the Department of Health and Human Services published its first Healthy People framework, which set preventive care and disease priority areas for public health, namely reducing mortality across all age groups and reducing days of illness. Most importantly, the Healthy People initiatives were explicitly focused on the goal to "create social and physical environments that promote good health for all."[14] Shifting to what is often termed a "place-based" framework reinvigorated the examination of neighborhood, work, and school settings for their effects on wellness, as well as health inequities.

In a still-rare case of a designer publishing in the arena of public health, architect Roslyn Lindheim, alongside her colleague at the University of California Berkeley, sociologist Leonard Syme, published "Environments, People, and Health" in the *Annual Review of Public Health* in 1983. They noted that while many housing and city planning policies at the time purported to be based on conclusions about health, such policies were still based on nineteenth-century ideas about infectious disease and sanitation and did not take into account their possible effect on the chronic diseases of the modern era such as heart disease, mental illness, and cancer, among others. Lindheim is perhaps best known for her pioneering research on hospital design, but her nuanced observations on the wider environment are unfairly overlooked as they showed what was at the time (and, in some circles, still would be) a radical rethinking about disease causation and the role of the environment that would be valuable to both designers and the health community. Lindheim and Syme note: "Although in writing this paper we tried to define the environment by distinguishing between the man-made environment, the social environment, the natural environment, and the symbolic environment, we were forced to recognize that 'the environment' is none of these things independently. Rather, the environment is a result of the constant interaction between natural and man-made spatial forms, social processes, and relationships between individuals and groups."[15] Additionally, it is only a designer, working on the experiential level, rather than the high view of planning, who could make this distinction:

The basis for these [planning] policies is the belief that crowds and overcrowding increase the risk of both infectious and noninfectious disease as well as crime, mental illness, and other social pathologies. Most thinking on this topic has failed to distinguish between density within family units, numbers of households per housing unit, and density per acre. In any case, there is little evidence to show that increases in density or crowding are related to mental or physical ill health (except perhaps in the case of prisoners). Despite this lack of evidence, many current zoning and planning policies continue to be based on concepts of the "garden city," "open space," and "low density" first developed in response to problems of sanitation and later stimulated by efforts to reduce crowding. As shown below, these planning solutions fail to consider many other factors important to health and wellbeing.[16]

Instead of looking at the vectors of disease, Lindheim and Syme looked at how environments could build up "host-resistance" through social contacts and economic status. Looking at a number of case studies including Italian immigrants displaced from the West End of Boston, Japanese immigrants who had been Westernized and lost touch with culture, and residents of high-rise buildings and public housing, they found consistently that these groups, socially and economically isolated, bereft of control over their environments or disconnected from place, were more vulnerable to heart disease and other chronic conditions. They concluded that building connection to others and a physical and cultural place made one less susceptible to illness. Lindheim and Syme also pointed out that social isolation and lack of connections affected both city dweller and suburbanite alike, without distinguishing between the respective physical environments specifically.

Lindheim and Syme's theories about environment and health were analogous to the socioecological model, a framework first attributed to Urie Bronfenbrenner in the late 1970s and early 1980s. Stemming from the discipline's shift to examining social determinants of disease, this framework significantly widened the scope of public health intervention, looking at how seemingly distal initiatives, such as federal/state/local policies, were nested one within the other and had ripple effects through communities, social networks, and families, with the individual and their health outcomes at the center. While still holding that it was those factors closest to the individual (i.e., immediate family, friend, and home environments) that had the most impact on health, it considered the larger frameworks of history, culture, and policy that also shape one's daily life and actions.

Although the socioecological model had been used by public health experts for some time and for interventions as varied as early cancer detection to violence prevention, it had particular relevance to the obesity epidemic and specifically its relationship to the built environment. Using the model to study obesity has helped researchers understand more about its multifaceted causes, including socioeconomic status, stress, physical activity opportunity, food availability, and diet. Researcher James Sallis was one of the first to apply it specifically to obesity, positing that obesity was often a result of influences starting at the policy level, which in turn and respectively shape built environment, social and cultural environment, and ultimately the individual, particularly when it came to choices regarding physical activity and diet.[17] Increasingly, more public health experts began to study city planning, buildings, and landscapes at this time and even to act as advocates for more health-centric physical development.

That said, in the early 1990s the relationship between sprawl and obesity was more a strong hypothesis than proven cause and effect. But the undeniable intersection of the obesity crisis, unabated sprawl development, and public health experts' renewed focus on environment raised flags for many, centering on increasing use of personal automobiles and its direct and indirect effects. In the book *Urban Sprawl and Public Health,* two former CDC directors and physicians, Howard Frumkin and Richard Jackson, along with urban planning scholar Lawrence Frank, articulated how suburban and exurban development forced increasing car use leading to degraded environment and population health. They argue that low-density, far-reaching development that centers car use directly leads to air pollution (and its attendant respiratory and cardiovascular diseases), overtaxed water infrastructure, and pedestrian fatalities. Indirectly, they hypothesized that sprawl development not only prevents an active lifestyle but also enables a life dictated by driving and commutes leading to stress (from "road rage"), social isolation, and less social capital in communities.[18] On this last note, there has also turned out to be some merit to the argument put forth by the midcentury urban critics that sprawl would lead to low societal participation. Robert Putnam's wildly influential book, *Bowling Alone: The Collapse and Revival of American Community,* found that every ten minutes of driving time per day leads to a 10 percent decline in civic involvement (although it's key to note that this figure is presented alongside many, many other indicators and potential causes of declining participation). Public health experts were now explicitly putting out the call to designers and planners to come up with remedies to the hydra of disease, development, and social disintegration.

The New Urbanism Solution

Perhaps because it predominated so much of the development of the late twentieth century, "sprawl" was often undifferentiated from the "suburbs." Also, because the design elite was so dismissive of its seeming homogeneity and formlessness, a consideration of suburbia's specific morphology was largely absent from the literature, with the notable exception of Robert Venturi and Denise Scott Brown's *Learning from Las Vegas.* By the 1990s it would have been more myopic than usual to ignore the prevailing physical character of the American urban landscape. In 1991, husband and wife team Andres Duany and Elizabeth Plater-Zyberk, principals of the design and planning firm Duany Plater-Zyberk (DPZ), participated in the writing of the Ahwahnee Principles, a declaration led by the Local Government Commission of California that laid out a series of general principles revolving around resource efficiency. The Ahwahnee Principles in turn laid the foundation for the Charter and Congress for the New Urbanism (CNU) founded by Duany and Plater-Zyberk in 1993. The goals of the CNU were explicitly to reshape neighborhoods to a more "traditional" way of building to achieve environmental sustainability but also to return American neighborhoods to the professed "lost" ideals of engaged civics, social cohesion, and pedestrian travel through design, planning, and growth limits. The New Urbanists explicitly recommended returning to an older and centralized way of town building, evoking the neighborhood scale ethos of Clarence Perry when proposing neighborhoods centered around walking distance from schools and the values of Ebenezer Howard when proposing greenbelts, albeit in the context of the late twentieth century this was more to control development than for actual agricultural production.[19] In 2001, Duany and Plater-Zyberk, along with planner Jeff Speck, published *Suburban Nation: The Rise of Sprawl and the Decline of the American Dream,* a manifesto on how the design of the suburbs had contributed to ecological and societal destruction. Leaning on their professional experience with governments and communities, they state outright, "from mayors to average citizens, we have heard expressed a shared belief in a direct causal relationship between the character of the physical environment and the social health of families and the community at large."[20] Chief among their critiques was the contemporary American development dependence on the automobile, which in their view had permeated every aspect of design and planning from zoning to town layouts to individual dwellings, which now prominently featured multicar garages instead of front porches. Their observation that development had made us a nation of *motorists* not citizens was not inaccurate, and *Suburban Nation* pinpointed the upstream and downstream effects of unchecked, low-density development in a more direct way, and to a wider audience, than had yet to be seen in the research on sprawl published by academics, architects, and planners. It does not rely as much on numbers as it draws on emotion and observations, much as Jane Jacobs's *Death and Life of Great American Cities* was a reaction against the scientific rationalism of the modernists.

Earlier eras of design for health were defined by the elimination of waste, density, streets, and blight; the New Urbanist agenda sought to eliminate the automobile. The book makes accurate observations about how single-use zoning prevents active travel and demands auto use, effectively trapping "victims of sprawl"—children, teenagers, mothers, the elderly, commuters—in the car or in the home. They note how regulations prevent denser development, even the construction of backyard "granny flats." It is also a rebuke to the architectural profession for being overly focused on modernism and on the singular building, putting out a call to be "urbanists" and to be more cognizant and involved in local government and regional planning initiatives. Perhaps in the interest of giving their overall argument urgency, or to call attention to their "innovation" of reintroducing traditional building and planning, they also widely generalize that there are only "three different types of architecture: cutting edge modernist, authentic traditional, and a gigantic middle ground of compromise that includes lazy historicism, half-hearted modernism, and everything in between, most of which could be called kitsch."[21] Similarly, while Venturi and Scott Brown understood the more nuanced forces and even some of the cultural value of suburban development, advocates of New Urbanism presented a dichotomy where their design was the only alternative to more "crowded suburban arterials awash in strip malls, collector streets framed by blank privacy walls, and cul-de-sacs lined with garage doors."[22]

Suburban Nation was also a setup for introducing a physically based, highly specific urban and architectural code to build neotraditional neighborhoods. Although not directly referenced, the APHA's *Planning the Neighborhood* from some thirty years prior is an obvious predecessor to the New Urbanist literature, particularly in the APHA's preoccupation with density formulas and land use, as well as a concentration on housing types as the primary unit of the neighborhood and architectural form of the dwelling, with less attention on city planning or landscape architecture. In DPZ's words, to have such codes "frees up governments to govern," and there is no doubt the New Urbanists believed that their methodology would yield positive results, but it was also the first step in cementing their practice as foremost experts in building healthier neighborhoods. They and many other New Urbanist practices made their success on widely publishing practical guides and form-based codes for neighborhood building as well as holding design charettes for neighborhood visioning.[23]

The generalized observations and principles of *Suburban Nation* were truthful, commonsense, and even admirable in theory. But when enacted on the ground, they became almost immediately problematic. The New Urbanists' steadfast belief that "the old way of building" was best emphasized the historical blind spots of building for social change and uncritically doubled down on them, defining their superior traditionalism as European archetypes of architecture and town planning. Nor did they feel the need to update those forms, for the authors are critical of the Venice Charter for the Conservation and Restoration of Monuments and Sites (written in 1964), which advised that buildings, additions, and interventions should clearly be of their era instead of trying to blend into existing historic contexts. The early New Urbanists are particularly taken with regional interpretations of European architecture in the Deep South. Duany and Plater-Zyberk have stated that their inspirations came from a road trip to towns such as Savannah, Georgia, Charleston, South Carolina, and Natchez, Mississippi, but they don't reference the racial, social, or class systems inherent in the different forms of dwelling. They also quickly put aside the argument of possible socioeconomic fallout of new development, and acknowledged that it is difficult, but "fighting gentrification is tantamount to fighting *improvement;* revitalization will not occur without it" and would be counterproductive to existing residents.[24]

Pertaining to the subject at hand here, and most curious for a movement ostensibly centered around environmental sustainability, the New Urbanists are highly critical of the integration of landscape, and landscape architects in general. When discussing the importance of street trees for pedestrian comfort, *Suburban Nation* says:

This correlation makes clear what should be the first job of landscape architects: to correct the deficiencies they have inherited from the other professionals, who have failed to create comfortable street space. Unfortunately, this is precisely what most landscape architects leave undone. What they do instead is to prettify—to design something that is picturesque and photogenic, clusters of random varieties milling about an entrance gate. Straight lines and the repetition of trees, while beautiful in perspective, look boring on paper and thus are set aside in favor of a creative emulation of nature. . . . This is why the landscape budget is always the first thing in a project to be cut, and why landscape architects complain of not being taken seriously by their clients. Rather than performing an essential function—correcting for the spatial deficiencies of the urbanism, and complementing the linear relationship between building facades, sidewalks, and street—they have become exterior decorators."[25]

For the most part, they do not maintain the generalized reverence of urban nature as did Ebenezer Howard. In a later book, Jeff Speck would write: "Green spaces in cities are a lovely, salubrious, necessary thing. But they are also dull, at least in comparison to shopfronts and street vendors. Our kids may be suffering from nature deficit disorder, but they also know instinctively what we have been taught to ignore, which is that verdant landscapes do not entertain."[26] Duany would assert that rural nature has no place in the city, only squares and plazas.[27] This echoes Jane Jacobs's similar critiques of large parks for the sake of simply adding green space, except she used even sharper language, saying: "The first necessity in understanding how cities and their parks influence each other is to jettison confusion between real uses and mythical uses—for example. the science-fiction nonsense that parks are 'the lungs of the city.'"[28] Jacobs's assertion should be seen in context as a rebuke to the large-scale planning of the modern era, which cleared out entire neighborhoods in the name of large civic park gestures, but the New Urbanists appear to reinforce the binary that the country is inherently where nature resides, in opposition to the city. At the New Urbanist development Middleton Hills, Wisconsin, DPZ claimed they made every site decision from existing topography and watersheds, but the plan shows no such consideration; rather it is the same grid and semicircular layout of many other New Urbanist developments.

Most crucially, although recognizing that the physical properties of sprawl are responsible for health, environmental, and civic crises, New Urbanists simultaneously offered a prescription for said crises while claiming to be "only" architects and planners, therefore having plausible deniability for socioeconomic context, or effects of their work. They privileged a highly specific, culturally narrow definition of beauty as naturally bringing back genteelness to American neighborhoods and are as spatially deterministic as the most steadfast modernist, but they still presented their methods as a form of liberation for citizens from the car, or for governments from having to design. On one hand, Duany would claim that his work was separate from social ideology, instead arguing that it was modernist architects who associated traditional design with ideology and "moral overtones," asking if we reject classicism due to its attractiveness to the Third Reich. On the other, in *Towns and Town-Making Principles* (2006), Duany and Plater-Zyberk include an essay from Patrick Pinnell linking their work to Aristotelean ethics: "By deemphasizing the use of the automobile, they reduce the control of those outside interests which corrode autonomy and induce economic dependence; not only the automobile industry, but the oil and gas consorita; the highway lobby; the banks. . . . Theirs is work with a high degree of consistency in its technical means, in its chosen and invented forms, and in its consciously intended ends."[29]

These contradictions come into focus when surveying the landscape of built New Urbanist work. The existing fabric of urban sprawl proved to be resistant to change, and like the Garden City, or even Le Corbusier's unbuilt Radiant City, New Urbanist communities required massive land and financial commitment and an otherwise blank slate on which to build. Consequently, the best-known communities, such as Seaside (fig. 41) or Celebration, both in Florida, were often built far out from any existing metropolitan centers by private developers, despite *Suburban Nation's* advocacy for regional relationships. As a result, many of these communities function as towns made up largely as second homes, with the much-heralded public spaces controlled

Fig. 41. The landmark New Urbanist community Seaside, Florida, photographed from above by Alex MacLean, 2019. The architecture and planning firm Duany Plater-Zyberk laid out a manifesto and form-based code following "the old way of building," purporting to restore walkability, social cohesion, and civic engagement to American communities as a tonic to the unhealthy suburban sprawl that dominates the American landscape from the late twentieth century to today. (© Alex S. MacLean)

by covenants or private entities, with real estate ads for Seaside promising a leisure lifestyle, divorced from day-to-day work and ironically recalling early suburban advertisements centering its fresh air and distance from hectic urban stresses. There also lies an irony of using housing types and ornament derived from dwellings that used to house working-class, Black southerners and repurposing them in neighborhoods that were exclusive and majority white. Empirical research on the impact of New Urbanist developments found that most were under fifteen acres and housed roughly 1.4 million people, but up to half were built on greenfields, rendering the environmental argument largely moot.[30] Much like other utopian plans for cities, the initial message of "New Urbanism" has ultimately been diluted by developers who have used it as a catchall term for many new developments that only superficially follow the principles, so much so that the CNU installed a certification program for projects that truly adhere to their guidelines and ideals.[31]

For better or worse, DPZ would be most closely associated with their flagship project of Seaside but would still devote a great deal of effort to prove that New Urbanism was for all contexts and incomes. Over time Duany became the primary public face of the firm while Plater-Zyberk assumed an academic position at the University of Miami. The contradictions of their claims would become clearer through their attempts to house vulnerable populations. In the mid-1990s, New Urbanism was adopted as the standard architectural and planning style of public housing under the Clinton administration's HOPE VI development plans.[32] HOPE VI did attempt to take some lessons learned from the disastrous midcentury public housing developments, proposing a "scattered site" strategy that would strategically infill (often slightly higher-income) neighborhoods with smaller-scale single- or multifamily housing. But just as in the midcentury, the tactic of adopting a specific aesthetic for public housing, even if neotraditionalism instead of modernism, still served to visually stigmatize those within, while continuing to imply that those living in it will be uplifted and have their morals corrected through design. A joint CNU and Department of Housing and Urban Development (HUD) booklet, *Principles for Inner City Neighborhood Design: Hope VI and the New Urbanism,* begins, "The tools of New Urbanism can help housing agencies and developers build communities, rather than just buildings."[33] The CNU correctly pointed out that public housing of the past was too radically different from the existing context, and while the scale of this housing was often more amenable, the candy-colored housing still stands out as markedly different in places such as the Kalihi Housing in Honolulu (fig. 42), and in the post-Katrina Harmony Oaks Housing in New Orleans, even given the movement's European and southern roots. Architect Michael Pyatok, a leader in affordable housing design, decried both using New Urbanism and

Fig. 42. New Urbanist–style public housing in Kalihi Valley Homes, Honolulu, Hawaii. New Urbanist styles were used with a broad brush in public housing in the late twentieth and early twenty-first centuries despite differing urban contexts due to the Congress for the New Urbanism's close ties with the US Department of Housing and Urban Development, which latched onto the CNU's claim that community and health could be encouraged through design (2001). (Courtesy of Group 70)

the mixed-income strategy in general, saying: "Apparently, the designers sincerely believe that the unemployed and underemployed people need frozen, domestic stage sets from yesteryear that make them feel at home with their higher-income, employed new neighbors. Somehow, having a front porch is expected to catapult them into the middle class. . . . The Martha Stewarts of urban design are intruding on the lives of people like those that Studs Terkel documents—insulting their culture and ignoring their more significant economic needs."[34] Geographer and social theorist David Harvey makes a similar argument that "civics" can't come about via housing separate from economic realities, saying:

Put simply, does it not perpetuate the idea that the shaping of spatial order is or can be the foundation for a new moral and aesthetic order? Does it not presuppose that proper design and architectural qualities will be the saving grace not only of American cities but of social, economic, and political life in general? Few supporters of the movement would state so crude a thesis (although Kunstler comes close[35]). Yet this presumption pervades the writings of the New Urbanists as a kind of subliminal subtext. The movement does not recognize that the fundamental difficulty with modernism was its persistent habit of privileging spatial forms over social processes.[36]

Pyatok further accused the New Urbanists of "colluding with HUD and HOPE VI" not only in perpetuating a program that effectively displaced people from their neighborhoods to move them into others, and by noting that their restrictive and exacting codes in fact prevented them from making their own improvements and running home-based businesses.[37] As in the resort towns, New Urbanists considered only the living (dwelling) and not the work (economics). A century after physically sanitizing the city to rid it of infectious disease, Pyatok accused the New Urbanists of culturally and socially "sanitizing" the city, a connotation now meant to be wholly negative. Ironically, a few years before New Urbanists partnered with HUD, *Suburban Nation* made the same point about housing, "The problem is that the poor, who are presumed to be grateful to have any home at all, have been the object of fifty years of architectural and planning experimentation. With the best intentions, designers have responded to the affordable-housing challenge with the very latest in untested technology and style" and have even echoed Catherine Bauer's writing about stigmatizing the poor through grouping and design.[38] Duany, Plater-Zyberk, and Speck believed that returning to what they saw as a successful "traditional" form of building, which they assumed people wanted, overrode principles and ethics of housing the poor. Directly citing the modernist failures of Pruitt Igoe and Cabrini Green, Duany, Plater-Zyberk, and Speck state: "If one builds cities based on untested theories of flawed science, they are likely to fail. Good design may not generate good behavior, but bad design can generate bad behavior. . . . The real lesson is that the design of new places should be modeled on old places that work. Invention is welcome, but must be laid upon the solid foundation of precedent, as it is in medicine and jurisprudence."[39] However, this statement confuses precedent for research. Without casting a critical eye on history, the designers and government officials were only doomed to make the same mistakes again. And while it was a failure in administration rather than design, the well-documented effects of displacement wrought by the HOPE VI program as old high-density units were torn down to build new but less numerous midscale ones was one of the largest detriments to residents' health.[40] By the early twenty-first century, HUD abandoned the New Urbanist strategy in favor of what is termed the Choice Neighborhood Initiative, which aimed to better integrate public housing into existing neighborhood styles and more importantly aimed to replace each housing unit one-to-one, although that tenet has not proven to be entirely successful either.[41]

Duany's belief in code as cure also came into focus through his involvement in rebuilding after Hurricane Katrina. The situation would seem ripe for a New Urbanist rebuild. The housing stock demolished by the disaster was purportedly in the regional style in which DPZ specialized, and the scope of the devastation seemed to be a blank slate, but within an urban context rather than forcing an isolated development. DPZ's adeptness at partnering with local government also gave them a prominent role in the rebuilding process. Duany's eagerness to be involved was palpable, as he spent $150,000 of his own money to bring a team down and hold charettes, and in a community meeting as he referred to the rebuilding of New Orleans as "the planning Super Bowl."[42] Duany found himself less welcomed than he anticipated, though. Reed Kroloff, then dean of the architecture school at Tulane University in New Orleans, was quoted in the *New York Times* saying the New Urbanists "have now seduced Louisiana's hapless governor and been given the keys to the state."[43] Hired by Mississippi governor Haley Barbour, another firm associated with the Congress for New Urbanism, Urban Design Associates, produced a seventy-two- page book entitled *A Pattern Book for Gulf Coast Neighborhoods* available for free and distributed in Home Depot stores and other building supply stores. The *New York Times* wrote, "After living in tents and trailers, and negotiating the riddles of insurance and federal aid, many homeowners in the coming months will face questions of how exactly to reassemble houses of a certain historic vintage, like shotgun houses and Creole cottages. They are about to get some free design advice, whether they ask for it or not." Residents trying to rebuild as quickly as possible balked at the cost of window trims and balusters; David Buege, an architecture professor at Mississippi State University stated, "It troubles me that we have no credible proponents for urban forms that will have a longer useful life and that will be more deeply satisfying than New Urbanism."[44] As always, the attachment to style over strategy failed to take into account the vulnerability of the particular environment of the Gulf South, or future resiliency. In an interview, Duany conceded, "Apart from being costly, it is a challenge to create a walkable town that is essentially on stilts," and when pressed on the Gulf South's long legacy with the petrochemical industry, and the opportunity to push for more sustainable materials in rebuilding, he deferred: "The issues of materials policy and environmental justice are compatible with the New Urbanism movement, but they are not intrinsic to our movement. I am wary of stringing other agendas onto the New Urbanism."[45] None of these patterns became the required code for rebuilding, but the constant use of the words "appropriate" and "acceptable," in the pattern book and in most of DPZ's publications, signals a moral high ground through architectural style.

Duany made a larger miscalculation when wresting control of the vision plan of the New Orleans neighborhood of Gentilly. The solidly middle-class,

Fig. 43. Gentilly neighborhood in New Orleans, Louisiana, 2008. This middle-class diverse neighborhood, dominated by mid-century ranch houses built slab on grade, was flooded during Hurricane Katrina, necessitating a rebuilding plan. (Photograph by the author)

Fig. 44. Duany Plater-Zyberk proposed a typical New Urbanist town center plan for Gentilly, featuring romanticized European–American southern vernacular buildings and a formal town square, in a radical departure from its midcentury ranch and strip mall urban fabric (2006). (Ground-level perspective by Mike Thompson; Courtesy © DPZ CoDESIGN)

racially diverse neighborhood, built in the 1950s and 1960s, was primarily populated by single-story ranch-style and brick houses (fig. 43). On one hand, it was an opportunity for DPZ to transform a suburban neighborhood, albeit an older one well connected to an urban center and with less of the objectionable features of the kind of sprawl maligned by the New Urbanists. On the other, most of its housing units and commercial properties were structurally intact but in need of mold remediation and roof repairs after the flooding and being unoccupied for weeks and months when residents were not allowed to return. There are few of those existing buildings to be seen in DPZ's proposals. Duany suggested adding second stories to these homes and adding porches; what had previously been commercial strip malls are shown reoriented in a grid around a large green square lined with two rows of trees and reimagined as a nineteenth-century French Quarter–esque pastiche of fasciae, windows, and hipped roofs on two-story commercial buildings, and even a "civic building" that appears to be a church and bell tower, all rendered in DPZ's signature soft pastel watercolor[46] (fig. 44). None of these ideas would be implemented, for a variety reasons ranging from community pushback, the difficulty in effectively erasing a wide swath of the existing neighborhood, and the simple economic realities of the rebuilding process.

Given the relatively low amount of acreage granted to certified New Urbanist developments, it would almost seem that New Urbanism's most lasting impact was in the discourse *about* New Urbanism, in both advocacy from its boosters and critiques from skeptics and design elites.[47] Any article on New Urbanism ends up being a referendum on whether it "works" or not, perhaps because it proclaimed to do so much. While mostly dismissing the widespread opinion that their type of development is too form-centric, ignored more diverse or complex issues of place, and exacerbated economic inequalities, many New Urbanists also claim few of the projects built truly reflect their original intention.[48] For a style that had been so wholeheartedly embraced by private developers, it rings a bit hollow to claim that their main critics were free-market conservatives and libertarians, as urban planning scholar CNU member Cliff Ellis claimed in a piece that was essentially an item-by-item rebuttal of what he viewed as popular critiques. Of the much-debated historicism of the movement, Ellis parried with this statement: "'Nostalgia' has become a compromised term that obscures rather than illuminates.... New Urbanists do not support the return of the racial, economic, or gender inequalities of earlier times. Nor is there praise for the insularity of 19th-century small towns or neighbourhoods. New Urbanists fully expect the residents of their developments to live ungated, cosmopolitan lives, accessing cultural resources and social networks throughout the metropolis and the world. In short, the claim that New Urbanism is 'nostalgic' remains a debating maneuver rather than a serious argument."[49] While it is true that design and planning has always been a profession enamored with the new, and often eager to discard the old, New Urbanism's myopia never fully reckoned with the meaning of style, the environment, or the socioeconomic context of where they built and therefore only amplified its implications. That said, the message from the New Urbanists has expanded and softened in recent years. Where the first of their proposals and publications were arguably as utopian as Hygeia or any of the modernist schemes, Duany softened his approach to focus more on big-picture regional "Transect Planning," advising on ideal densities and open space/building mixes on an urban-rural gradient, later synthesized as "SmartCode." A recent CNU conference also saw Duany call to designers for an "incremental urbanism," a far cry from the type of top-down planning for which DPZ was best known, which previously dictated everything from zoning to window trim.[50]

Nevertheless, where the New Urbanists have remained most successful is convincing local governments and public health experts that they hold the solution for healthy development in the twenty-first century. The CNU conferences enlisted speakers with medical credentials, such as Richard Jackson, and researchers working on the urban sprawl and public health issue to speak at their conferences and confirm the claims made in *Suburban Nation:* the physical environment was going to have physical effects on population health. In 2010, they named their annual conference New Urbanism: Rx for Healthy Places and co-organized with the national Centers for Disease Control and Prevention, naming Dr. Howard Frumkin, then director of CDC's National Center for Environmental Health and the Agency for Toxic Substances and Disease Registry, the honorary chair of the eighteenth Annual Congress. Sessions focused on encouraging mobility, doing health assessments, and leveraging public health research to mount projects.[51] To their credit, they have made significant strides in changing street standards to more pedestrian-oriented activity, working closely with the Institute of Transportation Engineers (ITE).[52] The "Smart Growth Scorecard," which originated with the Congress for the New Urbanism, is still used by the Environmental Protection Agency (EPA) to evaluate projects.

The social, civic, and environmental effects of New Urbanism failed to materialize, but in the end the New Urbanism movement is still seen as an authority in creating "walkable" places. The question remains, is a New Urbanist approach *healthier* than other forms of development?

The Walking Cure

The obesity crisis continued to rise well into the 2010s. In 2016, the CDC reported that 39.8 percent (93.3 million) of all adults were obese, and 18.5 percent of children ages two to nineteen. The agency speculated that the annual medical cost of obesity was $147 billion.[53] Obesity had fully become the epidemic of preoccupation for a large swath of the United States. In an attempt to define how "wellness" is conveyed in the popular media, Carol-Ann Farkas found that a majority of articles in the magazines surveyed emphasized weight loss.[54] The growing health crisis and auto-oriented sprawl were the common causes that reunited the planning, design, and public health fields. They also agreed on a common cure: reintroducing active travel (walking and biking) into the fabric of neighborhoods. Walkability became a simple idea for researchers, designers, and policy makers to latch onto as a cure-all for both sustainability and health issues. Apart from the environmental destruction wrought by automobiles, public health experts would often rely on the maxim "walking has been engineered out of our environment"—in other words, ignored by decades of transportation engineers only looking at motorized transportation. In 1991, the Intermodal Surface Transportation Efficiency Act was passed, which gave metropolitan agencies more control over transportation funding and other pieces of legislation and explicitly included pedestrian environments as part of "multimodal" transportation infrastructure. Although most transportation funding is given to automobile- and highway-oriented projects, it opened opportunities to write policy and build for walking, biking, and public transit. In the early twenty-first century, cities such as Portland and Kansas City took the lead in writing walkability and pedestrian plans.[55]

Although the architecture and landscape architecture professions were increasingly taking up the issue of designing environmental sustainability, the charge to design for human health (and its significant overlaps with sustainability) had yet to be articulated. The push and evidence to reshape the built environment for wellness in the twenty-first century came from the public health side, followed by planning. In 2003, both the *American Journal of Public Health* and *American Journal of Health Promotion* published special issues on built environment, community design, and health. The *Journal of the American Planning Association* published a special issue on "Planning's Role in Building Healthy Cities" three years later. Steps were being taken to reconnect the fields, starting with building a body of empirical evidence. In an editorial for *AJPH* in 2013, Richard Jackson, Andrew Dannenberg, and Howard Frumkin, all trained physicians and public health scholars, noted that between 1993 and 2003, a PubMed search using the terms "health" and "built environment" yielded 39 results. Between 2003 and 2013, it yielded 675.[56] In late 2020, there were almost 4,000 results. Adding the term "physical activity" showed nearly 1,400 results, meaning over one-third of the studies are concerned with the issue.

Walking as prescription was of interest to the public health and medical communities for its seemingly innumerable mental and physical benefits. And while biking as active travel also increased health, it had a higher barrier to entry in cost and ability, as well as infrastructure provision. Generally, every able-bodied person can walk, but at some point, most were not doing enough walking to maintain even a baseline of wellness. In 2005, cardiologist David Sabgir founded the program Walk with a Doc, where doctors would meet patients in a trail or park and discuss health topics or even do health assessments such as blood pressure testing at the location. Sabgir was quoted as saying, "More than 90 percent of the diseases my patients and I tackle together in the office or the hospital are related to a sedentary lifestyle, yet it has been reported that only 3 percent of people are achieving the appropriate amount of exercise each week. . . . Frustrated by the inability to increase my patient's activity level, I told them I would be at the park on Saturday and would love for them to join me."[57] Sabgir's ideas have even extended to the rising popularity of doctors "prescribing" set amounts of time for their patients to walk, with varying degrees of success. Robert Zarr, a Washington, DC–area physician, launched DC Parks Rx, an online database that lets people search nearby parks by zip code and get safety and amenity information for each.[58] Park Rx, funded by the National Park Service and run by the Golden Gate National Parks Conservancy, also maintains a national database of similar park prescription programs.[59] The Robert Wood Johnson Foundation, the nation's largest public health nonprofit, founded the Active Living Research Initiative in 2001, with a special focus on research on children's settings and physical activity.

In 2014, building on over a decade of interest and research into study on walking and health, Surgeon General Vivek Murthy named "Healthy and Safe Community Environments" as one of the four core National Prevention Strategies. A year later, he launched a campaign called "Step It Up!" (fig. 45). In a rare move for a public health administrator, it was not only a call for individuals to engage in preventive health activities, but also for physical community improvements. Of the five strategic goals in the executive summary, "design communities that make it safe and easy to walk for people of all ages and abilities" and "fill surveillance, research, and evaluation gaps related to walking and walkability" directly opened the door again for cross-sector collaboration between not just academics in the fields but also local agencies and practitioners. The Executive Summary reported that only half of adults and 27 percent of high school students met the respective recommended physical activity levels of 150 minutes of moderate-intensity aerobic physical activity each week for adults and 60 minutes of physical activity a day for children and adolescents. "Challenging physical environments" was one stated barrier, alongside traffic danger, distance to destination, and perceptions of an unsafe neighborhood.[60]

What lessons could planners and designers take from this explosion of evidence and interest? The sheer amount of research on the topic alone would indicate that it is a more complicated issue than anticipated. Certainly, combating a multifaceted issue such as obesity, which lacks the single agent and vectors of infectious disease and is predicated on individual behavior as much as it is genetics, lacked the straightforwardness of sanitary campaigns. And like the specter of climate change, it is a slow-moving disaster in the making. It doesn't have the dramatic strike of other epidemics, nor the linear progression of some chronic diseases. And in studying but one of its probable causes, the built environment, researchers have more tools, but the frameworks aren't yet articulated. The availability and growing use of geospatial information system (GIS) software and digital data appear to make more definitive

Fig. 45. The US surgeon general's "Step It Up!" campaign encourages daily walking for health and in doing so advocates for and shows a "walkable" neighborhood, characterized by mid-rise housing, parks, and trees (2015). (Centers for Disease Control)

spatial correlations between health and place, but studies are often decoupled from a larger analysis of how policies, markets, and people form those places.

In the hundreds of papers looking at the topic, what does and does not make a "walkable" neighborhood? Most research understands that it is a combination of physical factors, both on the street itself and in the neighborhood context. Some take a macroscale approach, looking at zoning, land use, and changes by zip code. Others take a microscale approach, enumerating everything from number of benches to plantings to lights. Researchers at the University of Minnesota designed an index of over two hundred physical environment attributes, where others attempted to pin down the relationship to just one factor and walking behavior by controlling for all other attributes. What becomes clear is that fitting the alchemy of design into quantifiable, neutral, and discrete properties for research still leaves a great deal of ambiguity. In "Measuring the Unmeasurable: Urban Design Qualities Related to Walkability" (2009), a fascinating study for the *Journal of Urban Design* conducted by Reid Ewing and Susan Handy, the researchers attempted to transcend the quantitative by asking urban design experts to judge streets based on qualities derived from Kevin Lynch's landmark book *Image of the City:* enclosure, imageability, human scale, transparency, and complexity in order to "operationalize" them for design practice. For instance, the positive quality of "enclosure" consistently indicated proportions of street walls on either side of the street, sight lines, and visible sky. And out of all these studies, some consistent correlations emerged, such as the frequency of four-way intersections (indicating a gridded street network), mixed-use development, and amenities. This was perhaps summarized best in a paper by urban planning scholars Robert Cervero and Kara Kockleman, who coined the most consistent correlations to active travel as the "3 D's": design, diversity, and density.[61] Cervero would later amend those to add demographics, destinations, and distance, but again the simplicity of the message was attractive and often repeated across fields on how best to improve the built environment for walking.

This was somewhat of a validation for the New Urbanists, but how did their developments, which promised a human-scaled, walkable environment work on the ground? Many studies in this body of literature have examined New Urbanist (or regrettably categorized as "neotraditional") development. Self-contained, predicated on the promise of healthier lifestyles, and already of interest to public health researchers, much early scholarship on built environment sought to compare New Urbanist neighborhoods to "conventional" suburbs. Daniel A. Rodriguez, Asad J. Khattak, and Kelly R. Evenson (2006) compared two neighborhoods in North Carolina and found that those who lived in the New Urbanist neighborhood walked about fifty-five more minutes per week, but it was all incidental, that is, to get to specific destinations or amenities. They found no significant change in leisure time activity between the two.[62] Another study used the "New Urbanism Smart Scorecard" (adopted by EPA). Researchers looked at the scorecard's ideal measures for housing density, mixed-land use, number of intersections, and block lengths to test whether its claims resulted in more walking and found that the first three correlate with more walking behavior. Concerning the last factor of block lengths, where the scorecard rates blocks under 400 feet long as "excellent," researchers found that there was more walking on blocks that were 600 to 800 feet long. They also found that there was less walking associated with housing densities of 10–13 units per acre than in neighborhoods with more than 14 units per acre and with 7 to 9 units per acre.[63]

The Smart Scorecard is also just one example of a published evaluation tool rating the pedestrian friendliness of a neighborhood. The interest in such easy-to-use assessments bridged the vast amount of academic research on the topic to practice. Perhaps the best-known version of these tools is a company named Walk Score, founded in July 2007, which generates publicly available, online choropleth maps and ratings between 0 and 100 for major American cities. Interestingly, for the countless amounts of variables that had been studied in the literature on built environment and walking activity, Walk Score heavily weighted its algorithm based on one factor— "amenities" (primarily retail: grocery stores, coffee shops, restaurants, bars, movie theaters, schools, parks, libraries, book stores, fitness centers, drug stores, hardware stores, clothing/music) within a thirty-minute walk, with a decay function built in the farther away these locations were. They also measured the most commonly examined and easily attainable objective features in walkability research, chiefly population density, block length, and density of intersections. Although Walk Score is a privately held company, it claims to be based on academic research and validation in several studies.[64] Its ease of use, availability, and spatial clarity led to its use in many public health studies as a shorthand for the quality of the built environment, especially for a field yet unfamiliar with the syntax of planning and design.

Accordingly, around this same time there was more literature from the design world. Jeff Speck, coauthor of *Suburban Nation,* followed up with *Walkable City: How Downtown Can Save America, One Step at a Time* (2013) and *Walkable City Rules: 101 Steps to Making Better Places* (2018). Speck had since served terms as the director of design at the National Endowment for the Arts and the Mayors' Institute on City Design, and the books are a reiteration of the warnings outlaid in his books with DPZ and a straightforward set of objectives to aim for in reintroducing walkability in any town. Speck is a planner, and his books are not the didactic pattern books offered by his former partner Duany (in fact, there are no images in *Walkable City),* but rather a window into how the American urban landscape came to be and what political barriers exist in building for active rather than motorized travel. If Speck's book refrains from images, urban designer Julie Campoli's *Made for Walking: Density and Neighborhood Form* (2013) is pure visualization, looking at twelve neighborhoods in the United States and Canada and how they facilitate walking at the experiential scale. Campoli's book is meant to provide material for practitioners and community activists seeking to create or restore walkability to their own neighborhoods. Campoli strives for diversity in environments in her book, but nevertheless, there is a remarkable sameness in her book and those by Speck, alongside the many other walkability design guides published in recent years, that ties these together. Neighborhoods are dense, but not too dense (two to four stories), and there is a predominance of small-scale retail. Despite the lack of actual real estate devoted to New Urbanist development, clearly their work has influenced the aesthetic of walking. The downtowns idealized in these guides are those from the 1940s and 1950s, sociable without social media, an image of everyday life unaffected by millennial labor trends or workforce realities and geared toward an economic and consumerist middle class.

Herein lies the issue with much of the research on walkability. Despite vast amounts of literature devoted to the topic, the research has started to fold in on itself; the focus on isolated, objective measures on how it can be achieved leaves out many questions that transcend yet are affected by design. Almost all studies on walking and the built environment acknowledge that their studies are cross-sectional or only capture a moment in time. People move to different environments (or their environment becomes different), behavior patterns change for a myriad of reasons, and long-term health is a result of these changes over time. It would be incredibly difficult to capture these changes in the context of most scientific research in a way that directly relates health and the built environment, or given the relative newness of the field, we simply haven't seen that kind of longitudinal study yet. But the concentration on the same factors—number of intersections, building/population density, retail attractions, and destinations—or permutations thereof, obscure the nuances of the needs of different users, socioeconomic equity, and the realities of design and construction on an urban scale, especially when it comes to addressing large-scale health issues.

Speck says walking is a "simple, practical-minded solution to a host of complex problems we face as a society, problems that daily undermine our nation's economic competitiveness, public welfare, and environmental sustainability"[65]—a singular act with countless multiple benefits and engineered out due to nefarious or thoughtless transportation engineers or developers. But even walking does not follow universal rules. Studies have shown that walking for leisure (e.g., exercise) is influenced by different factors than walking for transportation (e.g., to run errands, to get to school or work). Despite an assertion from many urban designers that short block lengths, which translate into more intersections, increase walking, studies have shown that the elderly walk more in areas with long block lengths, specifically so that they can avoid intersections and can walk at their own pace without having to negotiate a timed crosswalk and traffic.[66] In another study on children walking to school, land-use mix (the diversity measure of the "3 D's") was associated with lower rates of walking; the researchers hypothesized this was because it added time to walking routes or because of child or parental fear of having to pass by busy commercial or isolated industrial properties.[67] Much of the walkability discussion focuses on how environments need to be "pleasant" and "leisurely," but those are qualities that would be valued most by someone with that leisure time to begin with. And for all the research and independently produced manuals on walking and design, there is still a mismatch between the conclusions drawn and the actual manuals that dictate street design. The *Highway Capacity Manual* biases limits for lower levels of pedestrians, not higher, and the AASHTO *Green Book* still sets design guidelines for speed, lighting, and street width for vehicles, not pedestrians.[68] Rare is the research framed in the effectiveness of current design policy.

Mobility researcher Mariela Alfonzo hypothesized a model for walking based on psychologist Abraham Maslow's hierarchy of human needs for motivation. Her triangular model suggests that the pleasurability of a walk is the last quality that needs to be satisfied for an individual to walk, coming after physical feasibility, accessibility, safety, and comfort. That is, trying to convert the phenomenology of walking into objective factors may be informative, but if those other basic needs aren't met first, it renders those efforts moot. What factors can be categorized into each of those levels also isn't straightforward. Walking is the result of so many contextual factors, continually interacting with each other, and this is precisely why it is so difficult to give directives for its design. Even so, the intense interest surrounding walking has made advocates out of the research community and, in turn, several disciplines that previously had little interest in architecture, landscape, and urban planning, and the vast amount of quantitative research has illuminated how many of these elements positively and negatively impact walking.

Many researchers are aware of the problematic legacy of trying to quantify design, especially in the interest of an agenda. Planning professor Emily Talen noted:

The inclination to be cautious about direct translations of social agendas is justified. The application of urban design to something like social justice has not always translated well. The complete, socially just Garden City became the sprawling, exclusive garden suburb, and garden suburbs eventually translated to sprawl, physical separation and car dependence. The failure of modernist urbanism's literal-minded articulation of equality in built form—sterile housing blocks and concrete towers—is another painful reminder of the failure of social ideas to translate well to built form. Yet contemporary imperatives based on principles of sustainability are forcing a reappraisal of the application of social goals in design terms.[69]

Harvard professor Ann Forsyth also noted that the word "walkability" is yet to be operationally defined. Are we measuring the conditions that support the act? Are we discussing the outcomes? Where it becomes most problematic is how over time walkability became the "proxy for better urban places," particularly as it relates to health, for reasons discussed in the next chapter.[70]

For all the ways walkability has been broken down to its base elements, it remains a dynamic act, indelibly connected to the landscape, that will always be difficult to capture through a neutral lens. Landscape architect Lawrence Halprin sketched observations and planned out his own works as walking music "scores," a notational sequence of emotions, movements, and changing views that interprets its phenomenology perhaps better than any other representation has.[71] And in comparison to the didactics of the New Urbanists, writer Rebecca Solnit poetically describes both the essentialism and urgency of ensuring walking remains a part of daily life, writing in her book *Wanderlust: A History of Walking:* "Perhaps walking is best imagined as an 'indicator species,' to use an ecologist's term. An indicator species signifies the health of an ecosystem, and its endangerment or diminishment can be an early warning sign of systemic trouble." Walking, and the restoration of walking, is to strike a delicate balance among people, place, and the wellness of both.

CHAPTER 7

Whose Wellness?

The Urban Renaissance and the Crisis of the Suburbs

In fifty years, the narrative of "healthy suburbs, sick cities" had flipped. In a large part, this had been supported by empirical health research, but it was reinforced by design and planning discourse. The literature of suburban repair came hand in hand with books celebrating the superiority of the city in matters of sustainability, health, and, implicitly, morals. While evidence grew that aspects of the physical environment in the suburbs could lead to degraded health, underlying assumptions about "choice" of location and the American ethics of personal responsibility recurred with as much frequency as they had during the sanitary campaigns of the Industrial Revolution or the urban crises of the midcentury. Through most of American history the "city" was posited as the antithesis of all that was healthy—that it lacked the green landscape and civic morals of "wilderness," that the rampant poverty and never ceasing industry of the city was a warning sign of excess, sure to descend into chaos at any point. To many town planners and designers at the turn of the century, the suburb was the compromise between civilization and nature.

Despite the many critiques leveled against the suburbs by the design and planning elite dating from the 1960s on, this was the dominant narrative through the late nineteenth and most of the twentieth centuries, and much of it was bolstered by claims of healthy lifestyles. As late as 1993, public health academics Wallace and Wallace, who previously had studied the infectious disease–like spread of blight and abandonment in the inner city, warned of a "coming crisis of health in the suburbs." Their concern was not about disease that originated in the suburbs, but rather that the "physical and social degradation" of inner-city neighborhoods and the "contagious and chronic disease, substance abuse, and violence" would make their way out of the cities to the suburbs as minorities, specifically Black urban residents, began to disperse outside the city but "hyper segregated" in enclaves that would be ignored by municipalities unequipped to deal with urban illness, doomed to "replicate" the health issues of the city without more holistic management of the urban to suburban gradient.[1]

Wallace and Wallace's predictions of an infectious suburban health crisis failed to take hold, and in fact the "city" as a locus of disease began to dissipate and even reverse as the new health concerns of obesity rose alongside sustainability and environmental ethics. Books such as David Owen's *Green Metropolis: Why Living Smaller, Living Closer, and Driving Less Are the Keys to Sustainability* (2009) argued that the density of the cities led to less energy use per capita, particularly in comparison to the auto dependency of the suburbs. Owen directly takes aim at America's long history of anti-urban environmentalists, from Jefferson to the Sierra Club, and like other suburban critics, he places the rampant use of the automobile as a chief cause of the environmental crisis. This argument for the environmental health of the city was further echoed in pieces such as Witold Rybczynski's "Green Case for Cities" in *The Atlantic* (2009), in which he stated: "A Thoreau-like existence in the great outdoors isn't green. Density is green." The physical presence of landscape was no longer a requirement to be "green." In fact, Owen states: "Environmentalists tend to focus on a handful of ways in which the city might be made to seem somewhat less oppressively man-made: by easing the intensity of development; by creating or enlarging open spaces around structures; by relieving traffic congestion and reducing the time that drivers spend aimlessly searching for parking spaces; by increasing the area devoted to parks, greenery and gardening; by incorporating vegetation into buildings themselves."[2] But he sees this as folly, when environmental performance and energy savings are the real key to sustainability. In a line of reasoning that would make Le Corbusier proud, both Owen and Rybczynski make pains to note high-rise living is more environmentally friendly, as an elevator uses less energy than the horizontal conveyance of a car. Beyond the city's environmental benefits, the superiority of their job market and "creative class" work was extolled by urban scholars such as Richard Florida. Despite Florida's deflections that he was simply a politically neutral analyst and commentator, Jamie Peck (2005) notes that many policy makers of the early twenty-first century would tout Florida's work as an urban revitalization strategy and were successful in implementing it.[3] Although literature and research are not *responsible* for the ever-attenuating inequities in health and economics, they both drive and reflect the interests of the moment of people working in the field and can consequently have long-term effects on how debates on a wider stage are framed and can influence investment. After over a hundred years of largely anti-urban sentiment, the United States instead embarked on an "urban renaissance" centering cities as the loci of innovation, wealth, and health.

Our image of the suburbs is largely the same one presented by Duany, Plater-Zyberk, and Speck's *Suburban Nation,* now over twenty years old. Its cultural hollowness comes not only from dispersed and homogenous landscape, but also from racial and economic homogeneity of the population. Many of our best-known urban scholars from Jane Jacobs to Richard Florida, and a rarefied group that might also be described as racially and economically homogeneous themselves, give self-congratulatory praise to the "diversity" of the city, but they often overlook the changing demographics of the suburbs. A Brookings Institution report analyzing 2010 census data identified trends of immigrants, minorities, and low-income families moving to the suburbs and young white wealthier residents moving back into city centers, much of it having to do with real estate prices.[4] Post–housing crash, suburban residents were essentially trapped in their neighborhoods.

Elizabeth Kneebone noted that the early twenty-first century was a significant "tipping point" in the geography of poverty, writing in a follow-up report, "In 2015, 16 million poor people lived in the suburbs, outnumbering the poor population in cities by more than 3 million, small metro areas by more than 6 million, and rural areas by more than 8 million."[5] The homes were purposely dispersed, built on a long-forgotten town planning model of maximizing individual exposure to air, green, and sun, and now relegated their residents to long commutes, lack of transit, and expensive car ownership. Ironically, many minorities and immigrants may have purposely sought a residence in the suburbs for its connotations of wealth, security, and health, only to find their situations worsened in other ways. *New York Times* columnist Paul Krugman, in an op-ed called "Stranded by Sprawl," and citing an Equality of Opportunity Project study led by Harvard and Berkeley economists, hypothesized that the loss of intergenerational upward mobility was partly due to sprawl—that is, less well-paying jobs where people lived.[6] Spatial location matters more so if you are poor. Over a century earlier, in the throes of the Industrial Revolution's health crisis, activist and clergyman Andrew Mearns noted in his pamphlet *The Bitter Cry of Outcast London* (1883) that the reason the poor congregated at the center of the city was that they could not move to cheaper housing or be further away from work. "The wretched people must live somewhere. They cannot afford to go out by train or tram into the suburbs. . . . Can they be expected—in addition to working twelve hours or more, for a shilling, or less—to walk three or four miles each way to take and fetch?"[7]

In 2017, Richard Florida, undeniably a driver of the recent literature on urban renaissance, issued a mea culpa of sorts in his book *The New Urban*

Crisis. Acknowledging his role in privileging the "creative class"—tech workers, artists, and the like—and leisure consumption in cities, he noted that the promised economic growth had only benefited the already rich.[8] The previous urban crises were ones of infectious disease, physical degradation, and social neglect, but in the twenty-first century, these issues had been pushed outside of the urban core to its outlying communities. And while the locale of these problems shifted, the group who suffered the brunt of them had not.

It is a uniquely American quality to operate under the assumption that people choose their neighborhoods, and that they are a direct reflection of their values and how they may act. While that is true for many, sociologist Herbert Gans said in his 1968 book *People and Plans:*

In modern society, where man's relationship to the land is indirect, diffuse, and often irrelevant, his life is shaped by the economy, the culture, and the power structure of his society. Whether he lives in a city or a suburb is much less important for understanding his behavior than his socioeconomic level and his life-cycle position, his job, income, education, and age. The people who can choose where to live will select the community that fits their way of life, and the crucial question to ask about communities is who chooses which, what makes people choose as they do, and what happens to people who have, for reasons of income and race, no choice at all.[9]

Urban scholar Becky Nicolaides also points out that both Louis Wirth and Lewis Mumford assigned blame to the urban and suburban environments, respectively, for the same problems of moral bankruptcy and isolation, Wirth relating these issues specifically to the city's physical and demographic diversity and Mumford to its supposed homogeneity.[10] Similarly, the debate around built environment and health acknowledge that the "city" and the "suburb" are different in some way, and the afflictions we have ascribed to them over time are also different and specific, but certainly not absolute, as these illnesses change over time. The more worrisome trend is that our most vulnerable populations—communities of color, immigrants, and the poor—have been repeatedly trapped in environments where they cannot become healthier. And as much as we have taken the empirical evidence on these places as proof that they make us healthy or sick, and even given that much of it may be true, the scope of the narrative must expand to look beyond physical attributes of the urban landscape.

The "suburbs" and the "city" have become shorthand for so much more, even when the patchwork American urban landscape defies a binary of "city" and "suburb" as much as it does "healthy" and "unhealthy." Much of this is due to the models set up between the 1930s and the 1960s, when emerging urban social sciences such as sociology, economics, and geography were under pressure to legitimize their field. A zonal model let them come up with a binary more suited to statistical testing instead of a recognizing a patchwork or gradient.[11] We may not know exactly what these connote, beyond a vague idea about density. But those connotations have effects that can radiate from one's self-image to policy. Kneebone notes that one of the complications that differentiates suburban poverty from urban is the "perceptions of affluence that complicate responses to growing poverty," as well as the lack of services to help the poor (food banks, shelters, etc.) that are commonplace in the city.[12] In the early twenty-first century, many urban scholars have sought to revise the conventional narrative of the suburbs to better reflect these changing demographics, presenting alternate views on its development, its technological economies, the heavy hand government policy played in its expansion, and the often overlooked history of Black and immigrant suburbanization.[13] In 2017, the American Housing Survey showed that 52 percent of people in the United States describe their neighborhood as suburban, far outnumbering those who would describe them as "urban," "rural," or unknown.[14] The problems located there by public health experts, designers, and planners are worthy of a closer look and in need of more nuanced and qualitative definitions to address them.

Health Becomes Commodity

Americans of a specific economic class are driven by the pursuit and consumption of wellness. Earlier chapters in this book have described how health was commodified through nature resorts and the packaging of early suburbs. Perhaps the impulse itself isn't unique to Americans, but if we put that pursuit in the context of an absent social healthcare system or a culture that equally celebrates individual responsibility and consumption, anything that provides a shortcut to health is valued. Not only were the connections between place and health redrawn in academic research, but findings have started to make their way into popular media. The walkability of neighborhoods and its ostensible relationship to weight loss and reduced risk of disease permeated many headlines in the first decades of the 2000s, with the assertion of medical experts to back it up. A similar strain of literature started to emerge alongside walkability evangelism that touted health and sustainability benefits of parks and outdoor spaces. Paralleling the New Urbanists' fondness for recalling how Ebenezer Howard and other European-influenced Progressive Era town builders "had it right," research on how parks act as preventive green doses for disease was often framed in the vast writings that Frederick Law Olmsted left behind regarding the health benefits of parks, marveling at his foresight. While parks and walkable streets likely never fell out of favor with the general public, the growing body of research focusing on the economic benefits of healthy urban landscapes also piqued the interest of developers and city builders.

Mainstream media continued to tout the superiority of cities, drawing connections between their ostensible health value, economic value, and the enlightened values of the people who lived within them. Articles by Richard Florida for *CityLab* such as "In the U.S., Walkability Is a Premium Good" touted that walkable neighborhoods were more affluent, dense, and educated and had more transit service. Florida cites a study done by another group of researchers for Smart Growth America that did not include a social equity factor but asserted that walkable places automatically have higher social equity since a hypothetical resident has better proximity to employment, density, and transit systems, which would "offset" steeper housing prices. Whether this balances out goes unquestioned by Florida.[15]

Certified healthy neighborhoods are becoming a commodity. Five years after the rating system's inception, a study found that neighborhoods in Seattle rated most walkable by Walk Score also had higher median monthly rental rates.[16] A year following that study, Walk Score was bought by real estate website Redfin. Today, high Walk Scores are often included in real estate listings as incentive. Some urban planners and engineers, most of them closely aligned with the Congress for the New Urbanism, have even mounted successful businesses as "walking consultants," educating communities about the benefits of walkable neighborhoods, helping community members run audits of their neighborhood, and helping them to figure out next steps.

Many of the early advocates of health and built environment saw this nascent demand as a validation of their research and urged leverage of this to bridge research to practice. A recent article for *Health Affairs* called for established health and wellness metrics that could be used by real estate developers who wanted to advertise health outcomes to demonstrate "value."[17] Citing Walk Score as an example, they urged readers to look at the success of the green building movement, in particular the Leadership in Energy and Environmental Design (LEED) standards, as a model. The LEED rating system, established in 1993 by the United States Green Building Council (USGBC), gave new buildings and building renovations points for including sustainable design and energy- and water-saving features, and depending on the number of points accrued, a building could achieve certified, silver, gold, or platinum status. The system was easy to adopt for many developers and municipalities. Cities such as San Francisco, Sacramento, and Houston made LEED a requirement for new construction or city projects or offered incentives such as height and density bonuses or tax breaks. In 2009, the USGBC launched a rating system for communities called LEED-ND (for Neighborhood Development). While the concentration of LEED-ND was on environmental sustainability and energy savings, there were features that provided the co-benefit of health, particularly the amenities that sought to reduce auto use and increasing walking and biking, such as being sited to housing and jobs proximity, providing transit, and reducing heat islands. Providing a baseline design for "walkable streets" was in fact a prerequisite to any level of certification, requiring that 90 percent of new buildings have entries to streets or public spaces (not parking lots), continuous sidewalks at least four to eight feet wide, and a specified building height to street centerline ratio of 1:1.5. More points could be achieved for walkable streets through additional regulations detailing facades, road speeds, and on-street parking. Landscape is not present in the requirements for walkable streets, but in a separate credit for "Tree-lined and shaded streetscapes." Environmental provisions such as protecting greenfields, habitat, and wetland conservation and ecological communities protection do seek to balance development and natural landscape concerns.[18]

In 2014, DELOS, a privately held company founded by financier Paul Scialla and with investment from the Clinton Global Initiative, would answer the call for a "LEED for health." The company's International WELL Building Institute (IWBI) launched the WELL Building Standard, a rating system similar to and designed to work with LEED building standards and offering its same levels of silver, gold, or platinum certification. DELOS touts its research credentials in improving the health of building dwellers, claiming, after "seven years of rigorous research and development working with leading physicians, scientists, and industry professionals, the WELL Building Standard is a performance-based certification system that marries best practices in design and construction with evidence-based medical and scientific research—harnessing the built environment as a vehicle to support human health and wellbeing."[19] At its launch, Scialla touted the much-repeated figure that we now spend "90 percent of our time indoors,"[20] but where in the past this figure had been used to exhort people to get outdoors more, DELOS leveraged it into keeping health at the building scale. DELOS's strategy recalls Le Corbusier's directives for pure air, sun, and optimal temperatures in his residential "cells," stressing health at the scale of the individual and with a view of the environment that is decidedly medical, focused on controlling infection and at the scale of the body. WELL's requisites are in the realms of Air, Water, Nourishment, Light, Movement, Thermal Comfort, Sound, Materials, Mind, Community, and Innovation. The Air, Water, and Thermal Comfort requirements lean heavily on the implementation of building infrastructure to achieve goals. Many other regulations have little to do with the design of the building at all but rather the administration of it. The category of Nourishment asks for food and beverages that are limited in sugars, refined grains, and trans fats and that "Promote Healthy Nutritional Messaging," among other things. Movement addresses the physical activity concerns by supporting commuters and providing physical activity equipment in the building. The Community category does encourage vaguely defined "civic engagement" and provision of public space, as well as new parent support, and even goes so far as asking certified buildings to provide immunizations to users. Its landscape provisions are limited to a regulation to provide "Access to Nature," categorized in the Mind category and limited to "requir[ing] the integration of nature into the project's interior and exterior through design elements that support direct access with nature using plants, water, light and views, and indirect access to nature using natural materials, patterns, colors or images."[21] An inventory of registered or certified WELL building projects in 2018 showed over a thousand buildings, the majority of them office projects. One Houston developer estimated that they could ask for a 20 percent rent premium over market rate for their WELL projects.[22] In 2018, IWBI branched out into a "Stay Well" consultancy for hoteliers and resorts looking to offer a "healthier travel experience" and a "Stay Well Shop" offering microbial linens, aromatherapy diffusers, and air purifiers, among other items.[23]

It would be unfair to criticize the WELL Building Standard for trying to do more than can reasonably be expected at the scale of the building, but in 2017, DELOS launched the "WELL Community Standard" pilot program, aiming to apply the same ten principles required of their buildings to the neighborhood scale. In a press release, IWBI chairman and CEO Rick Fedrizzi stated: "The WELL Community Standard is an important next step in what I like to call the 'second wave of sustainability,' whereby the environments we construct actively promote human health and wellness. . . . We are excited to unveil this program and believe that with its tremendous reach, the WELL Community Standard has a revolutionary capacity to truly enhance people's health and quality of life on the widest scale to date."[24] Unlike LEED-ND, which weights certain regulations like siting and neighborhood connectivity before getting into more granular details, the WELL Community Standard has prerequisites in each category but only assigns one point per other "optimization" feature, which means a quality such as public art or noise ordinances is allocated the same value as a holistic health impact assessment screening and sanitation. Landscape is curiously absent of regulation in the booklet, beyond being a supportive feature in air and water quality, pedestrian environments, and mitigating stress.

The WELL Community Standard is still in the pilot stage, so it is too early to evaluate the standard's impact on urban landscapes. The year before it unveiled its Community Standards, IWBI and developer Strategic Property Partners, LLC broke ground on constructing its own WELL building district from the ground up in Tampa, Florida, a $3 billion, fifty-six-acre mixed-use development anchored by a waterfront park, Amalie Arena (home to professional hockey team Tampa Bay Lightning), and the University of South Florida Morsani College of Medicine and Heart Institute. The public realm portion is planned to feature, among other amenities, wide sidewalks, a grocery and farmer's markets, free Wi-Fi, a community wellness center with "regular chef-led classes that will provide education on healthy cooking options," dimmable public realm lighting (to reduce light pollution), and water bottle refilling stations (fig. 46).[25] A release announcing the development played down the commercial features, instead saying: "The philosophy of WELL and its application to the Tampa project is straightforward: Better air and water, greener construction, and more healthful options for food and fitness—presented in the framework of a connected community—intend to help improve the physical and emotional health of the people living there. Research shows that people who live in walkable, connected neighborhoods have lower rates of obesity, diabetes, high blood pressure, and heart dis-

Fig. 46. The vision for the first WELL Certified Community District in Tampa, Florida (2019). (Courtesy of Reed Hilderbrand and Strategic Property Partners, LLC)

ease."[26] Reed Hilderbrand, the Cambridge, Massachusetts–based landscape architects tasked with the master planning and street design of the district, are well versed in designing vibrant public spaces, and for this project they were also tasked with essentially beta-testing what it means to translate the rigorous metrics for systems such as air and water from the controlled environment of the building to the spaces in between buildings. On a microlevel, this means specifying low-pollen trees and water fountains per linear foot and a focus on pedestrian comfort, with 650 oak trees planted and light paving used to mitigate Florida's intense heat.[27] The landscape architects found that achieving many of these wellness goals required alterations to Tampa's existing form-based code. The trees require at least 1,250 cubic feet of soil per tree at the size where they can both cast shade and stay healthy. Some streets even have two rows of trees; the result is a 45-foot-wide sidewalk that required changes to setback rules and floor area ratios. To manage storm run-off, Reed Hilderbrand at first specified open runnels, but a city law requiring any "interactive water feature" be thoroughly treated, extensively signed to warn against trash or waste being thrown in, and even showers to be provided nearby pushed them to redesign the system as planted rain gardens instead, in a sense a twenty-first-century reimagining of the clean streets that characterized the Industrial Revolution. While the concerns of water and health have remained the same, the methods through which they are treated here have become less medical and more ecological. Reed Hilderbrand also engaged in an intense study of other well-known and well-used public streets to understand their dimensions and design, from places as varied as Havana, Barcelona, Berlin, and their home base of Boston.[28]

Some might ask why Tampa is the locale for this experiment. It is being built with the full support of their progressive female mayor, who pointed out to the designers that the average age in Tampa is three to four years below the national average, and far below what we would think for a state known for its retirees. Also, as more and more young people are priced out of major cities into so-called secondary ones with more development-friendly environments, the potential to transform their urban landscapes into more walkable, more ecologically resilient places may be imminent. So is the risk for further displacement and exploitation of land. We still don't know what the result of all this engagement with the new metrics of urban landscape health will be. But the vision is clear from the developer and landscape architect's renderings, which show an abundance of pedestrians, overwhelmingly young professionals, and some children playing in minimal outdoor splash pad fountains. A mature urban forest mitigates the scale between them and soaring new towers. It is likely the ideal walkable, economically prosperous neighborhood that proponents of healthy design picture and a marked contrast to the larger context of Tampa's built environment. However, the realm designed by the landscape architect stops there, and it is ultimately the developer who will decide the mix of retail, jobs, and housing, as well as who gets to take advantage of the healthful amenities. The public realm of the development is powered by private investment and retail; its list of outdoor spaces includes "a rooftop lounge and terrace at the JW Marriott."[29] Who is granted access to this experiment in twenty-first-century wellness remains an unanswered but key question. In December 2020, Water Street's first apartments hit the market, with the lowest-priced one-bedrooms renting at $1,918 a month, more than two and a half times the price per square foot of an average rental in Tampa.[30]

As urban landscapes are reshaped for our contemporary needs for activity, food, and climate change mitigation, LEED-ND and the WELL Communities are still too new, too untested for an evaluation of their effectiveness. The first phase of the Tampa development is slated to be completed in 2022, a year after this book's publication. Even so, the ways in which they profess to improve health, and what they are not doing, are worthy of framing in the context of history. The impulse to improve urban landscapes in the name of health or abandon "unhealthy" landscapes for healthier ones almost always disadvantages the poor, minorities, and immigrants, even if through a series of unintended or even well-meaning decisions. The aesthetics or features of wellness uncoupled by larger social equity goals may uplift revenue, but not the health of populations. This is also symptomatic of a culture that views wellness as a set of consumer choices rather than a framework that guides the goals of policy and infrastructure. The twenty-first-century version of this pattern finds the intertwined goals of health and sustainability leading to a condition many called "green gentrification," a new name for something that has happened many times before. The High Line is perhaps the best-known example of this. This 1.5-mile-long linear park in New York City was built on an abandoned elevated rail line, injecting a carefully cultivated "wild" landscape, public gathering space, and pedestrian walking path through the formerly industrial meatpacking district. When it opened in 2009, the park was lauded by the press, initially popular with both locals and tourists, and hailed as a triumph of private-public partnerships. The runaway popularity of the park in turn led to skyrocketing rent prices alongside the park and forced out several long-term businesses. A resident of the nearby Chelsea-Elliot public housing tower told researchers that she was thankful for her food stamps, because she could no longer afford the food sold at the deli at which she worked. The effect was so fast some even referred to it as "hyper-gentrification." Even though many locals appreciated the new amenity and the security it had brought to the neighborhood, there remained an unease about how welcome

Fig. 47. The Atlanta BeltLine has successfully transformed an abandoned rail line into an active linear landscape, but not without tensions around its gentrification effects. (Photographs by Christopher Martin, 2009/2012; Courtesy Christopher Martin)

they would remain in the neighborhood. The Atlanta BeltLine is another linear park that had been praised by researchers for its health benefits in a planning impact assessment in 2012 (fig. 47). But in 2016, Ryan Gravel, the head planner of the project and board member of its partnership, stepped down, saying: "At this critical moment, however, we feel compelled to concentrate our efforts more directly on making sure that the Atlanta BeltLine lives up to its promise and potential, and specifically, that its investments and supporting policies become more intentional about who they will benefit. We know you agree that its advantages must accrue to everyone, especially those who are otherwise most vulnerable to the changes it brings. We fear, however, that without more urgent and deliberate attention to these communities, we'll end up building the Atlanta BeltLine without achieving its vision."[31]

LEED-ND or the WELL Community standards, while new, are also the most straightforward way available to communities or developers to certify their projects as sustainable or healthy, but their provisions for community benefits are diminished by the overwhelming concentration on building physical features, to say nothing of becoming an increasingly circular system that benefits certain manufacturer associations, material producers, and certified consultants. A study in the *Journal of the American Planning Association* surveyed and interviewed over 130 LEED professionals and found that only 40 percent of LEED-ND projects built by 2016 had affordable housing included. The survey revealed that most thought the incentives weren't strong enough to include them, and that the risks in including them in projects, as well as the cost of certification itself, outweighed potential savings down the line for benefits.[32] Many advocates of healthier and more sustainable communities trust that the demonstrable dividends in community improvements will attract enough investment that developers will absorb the cost of housing the poor or will be altruistic enough to contribute to a community good. The lesson demonstrated in the midcentury is that for all its touted "benefits," it is folly to entrust public health to private interests. It is also not a surprise that many of the large-scale landscape improvement projects pointed to as examples of green gentrification—New York's High Line, Houston's Buffalo Bayou, Chicago's 606 trail—lean heavily on private funding. Developers demand return on investment on a timeline much more rapid than even sustainability features can often demonstrate; health gains are still too nebulously defined and happen over a much longer time period than investors are willing to wait.

Gentrification in of itself has had proven health effects, such as the stress that comes from displacement or further depleted financial resources, diminished social capital, or limited access to amenities residents had previously enjoyed. As people are forced farther and farther away from their neighborhoods or urban centers, it can also lead to longer commute times, more driving, and less leisure time to exercise or rest. These health effects were significant enough for the CDC to recognize "Gentrification" as a health issue under its Healthy Community Design Initiative, an unfortunately short-lived program that ceased to be funded under the Trump administration, along with a dramatic decrease in the budget for the Environmental Protection Agency's Office of Environmental Justice. The excitement over receiving a healthy injection of landscape clouds its positive effects and clouds discussion over the negative long-term social and economic benefits, no matter how often the issue has played itself out time and time again.

Compounding the health equity issue, many studies have shown that neighborhoods that are predominantly white have more park access than Latino, African American, and Asian Pacific Islander neighborhoods and receive more funding for maintenance and improvements.[33] How can disadvantaged communities, already more vulnerable to built environment–based chronic disease, receive the benefits of landscape? Researchers Winifred Curran and Trina Hamilton, in a study of Newtown Creek in Greenpoint, Brooklyn, advocate for an approach they call "just green enough."[34] In their case, they pointed to how the Superfund site could be cleaned up to benefit the health of residents, while still retaining industrial uses in the area that, while not meeting a textbook definition of sustainability, needed to be retained to provide jobs. The Newtown Creek Nature Walk, the result of a community demand for open space from the Department of Environmental Protection in exchange for their building of a sewage plant in the neighborhood, provides a continuous walking path and access to the (still polluted) water. It is bereft of the kind of self-consciously "wild nature" aspects of the High Line, so much so that the *New York Times* dubbed it an "ironic nature walk" in a review of the space. In another exploration of how to be "just green enough," another group of researchers termed the urban revitalization issue the "green space paradox," wherein green space projects appear successful from a financial standpoint and even the perspective of nearby residents, while still excluding those who are most in need of its health benefits.[35] They cite the privileging of ecological health over social justice issues.

Perhaps the issue is that we have made "green" synonymous with health without probing deeper. The supposed co-benefits are often touted without interrogating where the values of environmental sustainability and human health may come into conflict. A more nuanced discussion of this has to start with a recognizance of how city planning, public health, and design have contributed to a discourse that often elevated physical improvements at the expense of community engagement and empowerment in the name of wellness. Although design does play a key part in communicating for whom a park is intended, ensuring neighborhood improvements do not result in displacement is just as much a product of the processes of building the park, including a strong community input process and follow-up, securing land trusts and economic opportunities for existing residences, cognizance of upstream and downstream effects of the built environment, and the scale or amount of land secured for the project itself. Successful ways of doing so are detailed in the next chapter.

Landscape architecture as a profession has changed in the past few decades, a far cry from Andres Duany's assertion that landscape architects' function is to "prettify" or merely frame the street for shade. Particularly in the face of climate change, most degree programs have recently been concentrating more on environmental performance and community-based design, returning to its roots in social justice inherent in Frederick Law Olmsted's work and writing, albeit largely without the critique that is probably due for hundred-year-old philosophies. Beyond his views on class and moral behavior, after all, it should be noted that he had built support for Central Park by touting not only its health benefits but also how it would elevate property values and contribute increased tax revenue to the city, foreseeing green gentrification as a benefit long before it had a name.[36]

Reckoning with Reconnection

Reconnecting the design and planning of cities to public health is an exciting prospect to architects, landscape architects, and health professionals alike. For public health, it represents a new realm of possibilities, collaboration, and tactics for preventive health. For designers and planners, it satisfies the ever-present utopian impulse to improve the lives of people who inhabit their work and demonstrate the validity of science for a profession that has long struggled to define and explain its disciplinary rigor to outsiders. For landscape architecture, a field that is often victim to value engineering or dismissed as a decorative art, it represents an opportunity to reclaim an agency lost since Olmsted's Progressive Era works. The intertwined issues of sprawling development, climate change, and obesity-related chronic disease is an urgent charge to think of solutions that transcend the fields. Evidence is mounting that even the kind of infrastructure we think is an objectively good—parks, walkable streets, trails—can have negative effects if other factors, specifically socioeconomic and more robust behavior models, aren't considered. The success of the sanitary movement and Progressive Era parks are often hailed as the largest successes of achieving health through the shaping of urban landscape. Less discussed are considerable displacement of the poor and the implied or even explicit moralism embedded in these sweeping changes. Without a more critical view of history and a more expansive view of invisible and physical contexts, these efforts will become circular at best and repeat the same mistakes at worst. Most of all, although each profession would claim to be neutral actors, acting on objective reasoning, the redesign of communities and, in turn, people's everyday lives is inherently political, a fact that would become painfully clear as the fields began to intersect and make their case to the general public.

In the early part of the twenty-first century, the momentum built behind shaping the environment for health, aided by cities and urban advisories. The economic and metropolitan policy think tank Brookings Institution published several papers on "the economic promise" of walkability, most authored by Christopher Leinberger. Leinberger and co-researcher Mariela Alfonzo note many of the mismatches in their research on walkable places— that real estate costs are higher (but transportation costs lower), and places with low walkability are also less affluent and have lower educational attainment. While they also note that there is "no significant difference in terms of transit access to jobs between poor and good walkable places," they also found that "walkable places benefit from being near other walkable places," which would seemingly indicate less walkable and more affordable neighborhoods being pushed further and further out. The report also specifically calls for lenders to consider "walkability" in their underwriting standards and for developers to include when determining economic prospects for sites.[37] In 2015, the Urban Land Institute (ULI), the real estate–focused research and education organization, published a *Building Healthy Places Toolkit,"* which codified much of the research that has been discussed here, clearly illustrated with examples of development from suburban shopping centers to urban downtowns, and covered a variety of strategies from making walkable places to ensuring healthy food access and air and water quality. "Social wellbeing," on the other hand, is relegated to three pages in the guide, on par with "Adopt pet-friendly policies."[38] It is far more complicated to take these steps than can be covered in even a wide-ranging toolkit. As the ULI toolkit states in its introduction, "These actors can play a role in crafting places that contribute to a healthier community fabric, places that promote better health for all and that will ultimately result in higher, more sustained market returns." Advocates of healthy places saw this real estate interest as a boon to planners and public health researchers that gave credence to their research, heavily leaned on by these economic analyses as "evidence-based" proof of their effectiveness as health strategies.

While investment shifted to the cities, the suburbs continued to be both the battlefield and hypothetical laboratory where some designers sought to address the past several decades of unchecked development. The early twenty-first century saw a great deal of literature on the issue of "suburban repair," albeit in more comprehensive and incremental ways than originally proposed by the New Urbanists. Books such as Paul Lukez's *Suburban Transformations* and Galina Tachieva's *Sprawl Repair Manual,* the latter of which was eventually adopted as part of the New Urbanist arsenal in its SmartCode (fig. 48), take a more nuanced look at types of suburban development beyond reducing them to big box stores and McMansions. June Williamson and Ellen Dunham-Jones's *Retrofitting Suburbia* discusses key policy changes that need to be made alongside formal ones. These were emphatically not blank slate approaches to design; they accepted the existing fabric and a degree of uncertainty and flexibility in execution.

Unfortunately, the recession of 2007 to 2012 left most Americans skittish to engage in any kind of development, let alone experimental strategies. But it also halted the conventional, market-driven ways of urban expansion, leaving swaths of half-constructed, abandoned subdivisions and economically devastated Americans. The crisis also spurred another opportunity for architects to engage in thought experiments on the future of urbanization and suburbanization in the spirit of Le Corbusier's Radiant City, Frank Lloyd Wright's Broadacre City, and, most notably, the ideas of Ebenezer Howard. In 2011, the Museum of Modern Art in New York City opened the

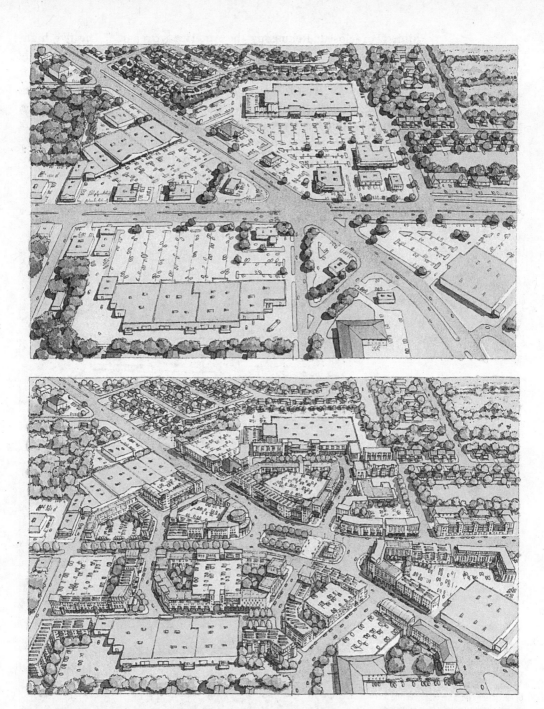

Fig. 48. Galina Tachieva's *Sprawl Repair Manual* shows with much specificity how a typical suburban shopping center can add density and redesign streets to encourage walking (2010). (Courtesy © DPZ CoDESIGN)

exhibit "Foreclosed: Rehousing the American Dream."[39] The five high-profile, architect-led design teams selected for the exhibit took a decidedly higher-density approach to living. Architecture firm MOS's proposal for The Oranges, New Jersey, shows ribbons of four-story buildings winding between single-family housing, claiming to share nodes of stairs, plumbing, and service. Studio Gang's proposal for Cicero, Illinois, recognizes the influx of immigrants, shows how to recombine existing bungalow structures into intergenerational housing, and offers a phytoremediation plan for an abandoned factory. WORKac's "Nature-City" places a spiral tower at the center of their proposal with mid-rise housing surrounding it, in the interest of leaving more land to reintroduce to the ecosystem an expanded urban forest or water

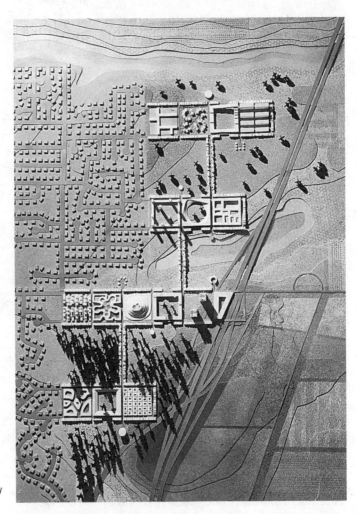

Fig. 49. WORKac's "Nature-City," from the Museum of Modern Art exhibit "Foreclosed," speculates on what can be done to save the "unhealthy" landscapes of suburbia, wracked by foreclosure during the recession. The firm proposes letting parts of it go to wilderness while densifying housing (2012). (Photograph by James Ewing; Courtesy of WORKac)

systems (fig. 49). The entry somewhat softens the approach to nature seen in Le Corbusier's towers in the park strategy by bringing residents closer to the ground and bringing green onto the roofs of the spiral tower. The nature depicted in their proposal is not the manicured lawns long associated with suburban landscapes, but rather a wilder green meant to symbolize wetlands and sublime urban forest—a compromise between the purified pastures associated with the City Beautiful movement and the idealization of wilderness described by Thoreau and Muir. They directly call back to Howard's proposal, claiming their design, "Nature-City, reinvents British urbanist Ebenezer Howard's 1899 concept of the Town-Country, a classic feature of the Garden City that combines the conveniences of urban life with the health benefits and access to agriculture of country living. Nature-City integrates density, diversity, a mixture of uses, and a variety of housing types ranging in affordability, and incorporates ecological infrastructure, sky gardens, urban farms, and public open space, including large swaths of restored native habitats."[40] Another high-profile design competition, the 2010 "Build a Better Burb," sponsored by the Long Island Index, emphasized the inclusion of a small-scale agricultural component in their design, harking back to Howard's original intents for the Garden City. There are many parallels between the solutions for suburban "abandonment" and the urban "blight" of forty years prior. In most cases, sleek, modernist design is meant to serve as a contrast and promise against crumbling residential fabric and a reinforcement of the refrain of greater efficiency by bundling infrastructure services. Automobile streets are replaced by superblocks and pedestrian paths. Where they differ most is in their treatment of nature. The pastoral green that characterized the image of the suburbs for so long gives way to a wilder, more "ecological" nature, allowing for riverbeds, taller grasses, and, in the case of WORKac's plan, "wildlife passages" that cut through apartment buildings.[41] The idea of an agricultural, productive nature tended to by residents seems to have finally been abandoned.

The most common factor among all the proposals is amplified residential density. Density is the most graspable concept, and the foundation of almost every argument about the built environment and health over time. It appears to be an objective quality of planning and design that is also easily measurable. But we have also let it define the difference between "city" and "suburb," perhaps to the neglect of cultural meanings and changing demographics. The perspective of density and its relationship to illness has changed as we shifted to urban infectious disease to chronic ones. While high density ignited the spread of cholera, yellow fever, and other diseases, low density appears to be where the obesity epidemic and its attendant illnesses have settled into the American fabric, and is much more difficult to eradicate. Density is of course only changed through zoning laws, which means negotiating layers of local and regional plans, public comment processes, and then eventual adoption. And only after then can the process of building start, which means it can be a decade plus before the fabric also starts to change. Underlying all of this is an issue that is rarely confronted by urbanists and public health advocates alike—"density" may appear to be a clear quality of the built environment for those working in the field, but it is still a nebulous, and even negative, concept for most Americans. Perhaps it still carries connotations of disease and crowding, inseparable from years of negative perceptions of the "city," even as wealth, demographics, and illness has shifted. The difference between units per area of land and people per unit is indistinguishable to most.

Meanwhile, interest in health and the built environment research has increased and even institutionalized through several efforts, although not without controversy. In 2014, the American Institute of Architects (AIA), through a partnership with the Clinton Global Initiative, convened a ten-year Design and Health initiative, with a board of experts across fields and a consortium supporting transdisciplinary research between schools of public health and architecture in several universities. They also formed a partnership with the then newly established Center for Advanced Urbanism at MIT to produce a report on the relationship between health and the built environment. However, the results of the report laid bare more complicated issues of reconnecting the fields. Many of the report's conclusions, as well as interviews given by center director and coauthor Alan Berger following its release, centered around his revelation that causality cannot be proved in the built environment, with special aim at the "prejudices" against the suburbs present in health and built environment research and study on food deserts. According to Berger in an interview with MIT News, "the idea of the food desert is largely fiction. There's access to decent food pretty much across the metropolitan areas. In our cities the proximity to fast food doesn't directly lead to poor urban health; there's proximity to fast food everywhere. The question is how you get people to choose the right foods."[42] It is perhaps not surprising that the report also brings up the self-selection caveat, and determines bluntly that "more obese people simply chose to live in the suburbs." The report seems to purposefully take aim at advocates' sacred cows, ending with the statement: "That regimen [the weekly 150 minutes of aerobic activity recommended by the CDC] will not be met through increased stair climbing instead of elevators and slightly more walking between parking lots and office buildings. These examples point to the need for reliable, meaningful research on ways to have design more effectively impact urban health."[43]

The report's assertions and surrounding publicity (a *CityLab* article by Emily Badger on its findings was titled "We Don't Know Nearly as Much about the Link between Public Health and Urban Planning as We Think We Do") did not sit well with researchers who had already spent well over a decade doing research on the topic and advocating for its importance. Howard Frumkin, Richard Jackson, and Andrew Dannenberg, perhaps the foremost researchers and spokespeople for the built environment on the public health side, published a fifteen-page rebuttal to the MIT report, citing shoddy and cherry-picked research assertions, lack of public health expertise in writing the report, and misrepresenting empirical conclusions as "prejudices." Where Berger cited the complexity of the built environment as preventing conclusive action, the physicians ended with the statement:

As the report emphasizes, this is an area of considerable complexity. Many factors determine the health of individuals and populations, many factors determine the quality of buildings, neighborhoods, and cities, and many factors determine the choices people make. Research design, data analysis, and conclusions must acknowledge this complexity. No evidence is ever perfect, partly owing to the complexity of the world, but that complexity must not be allowed to foster nihilism or paralysis. Casting gratuitous doubt is not only irresponsible; it can be dangerous. We know a great deal, we can act on what we know, and as we do, we can and should continually test our assumptions and improve our knowledge.[44]

Berger, for his part, issued his own rebuttal to *their* rebuttal, primarily restating the inconclusiveness of health and built environment research, calling out Jackson, Dannenberg, and Frumkin's association with the Congress for the New Urbanism (and therefore biased), denouncing the personal nature of the critique, and asserting he was not making "conclusions" but rather was adding to the already robust discussion.[45] The original report was taken off MIT's website, although Berger's rebuttal remains.

The numerous calls to action on health and the built environment issued in the early twenty-first century to reconnect the fields of design and health often end with suggestions for transdisciplinary collaboration. A major conclusion of the MIT *Health and Urbanism* report was that "the design and public health fields also face the challenge of the lack of a shared vocabulary to completely engage with each other on health issues."[46] But even more key is for both fields to confront their differing epistemologies and what the burden of proof is when altering neighborhoods, as well as advocating for a longer community engagement process. Amid the many, many personal attacks in the critiques lies a central question to the debate on health and built environment. How much and what knowledge do we need to act? Frumkin, Jackson, and Dannenberg argue that we have more than enough, and it is time to act, albeit carefully. Berger, in the tradition of architects and planners who have long sought to lend scientific credibility to their work, says only causality can drive decisions. All authors, in the MIT report or in other articles, acknowledge the origins of partnerships between the fields of design, planning, and public health in the Industrial Revolution, through the theoretical contributions of Ebenezer Howard and the vast built work of Olmsted. These are held up as unequivocal successes. The less heroic experiments in housing, the urban crisis, and urban renewal go unmentioned. Neither side recognized the damage that has been done, that *is* being done, when looking at the built environment isolated from socioeconomics, politics, and the United States' unique and complicated history with personal responsibility and morality.

For all the evangelism surrounding the power of the built environment, many public health researchers and those in the medical community remain skeptical of how influential it can be in shaping behavior. Perhaps this is why Frumkin, Jackson, and Dannenberg caution against the danger of "gratuitous doubt" in what is still an emerging field. The restrictions around public health research demand controls that the complexity of daily life and messiness of the everyday environment do not offer. Unwittingly, several public health studies have ended with the conclusion that certain relationships cannot be determined unless they are studied in "new communities"—but even new communities don't exist independent of people's relationship to where they work or the circumstances that led them there. This is not researchers demanding "causality" per se, but rather an attempt to fit the messiness of the built environment into a scientific paradigm. At the same time, designers and planners must confront the limits of environmental determinism and their complicated history with economics, race, and failed social engineering.

While it may help make the case, we should also not wholly rely on "real estate" or the financial benefits of building for health to drive research and development. The promise of design that purports to both improve the human condition and reap profits for those who invest in it has proved time and time again to eventually prioritize the profits over equity, available only to those who can afford it. In the 1930s, the housers promised that developers could increase revenues if they invested in affordable housing, only to find they were mutually incompatible goals. There is some promising research emerging on the healthcare side that investing in preventive care, including community environments, can yield savings, and these efforts are discussed in the next chapter. Measuring such savings can only happen over the long term and at the timescale of chronic disease, which is still largely unknown. For all the research done in the field, there are still many questions to be asked about our relationship to our environment, or at least how we frame those questions.

Reframing Walkability

What happens, then, if we recast the arguments for walkability in the context of current socioeconomic divides and the history of health and urban landscape? Walking has been presented as both a "simple" act and a singular element to redesigning healthy neighborhoods, unifying advocates from the design, planning, medicine, and public health fields, as well as ground-up action from communities, with real effects on policies. The advocacy around walkable built environments is ongoing and will take decades to evaluate for its effectiveness as a health strategy, but obesity is only our latest American epidemic with roots in the urban landscape. In the previous eras, we were similarly afflicted by cholera, respiratory and "nervous" diseases, and social ills. Walkability is the latest way we have tried to address a disease by reshaping the environment, after smoothing our streets, covering up our creeks, planning parks, building playgrounds, and clearing blight. Or to put it another way, we sought to eliminate waste, density, decay, and cars from the urban landscape. It's worth revisiting the issue of walkability as a lens through which we view this shift. It's not the only issue, but it fits into the recurring patterns and is driven by discourse and supported by research. It's an undeniably positive act with health benefits. But altering the environment to achieve said goal with a single-mindedness can have many unintended effects, largely negative. Even if those altering the environment have good intentions, changing the places where people live is going to be met with resistance, and residents who have traditionally been further disadvantaged by urban development are right to be skeptical of good intentions from distal sources.

Obesity is a confluence of environment, genetics, and behavior. Its inexorable spread is a mystery, not because we don't know what causes it, but rather we don't know how those known factors interact with each other. There are over sixty genetic markers that can predispose people to the condition, but researchers have found that the difference in body mass index (BMI) between those with high or low genetic risk is quite small, but the social or physical environment strongly attenuates the possible outcome of obesity and its attendant diseases.[47] Essentially, obesity is our first epidemic where researchers are exploring how we literally embody our environment. As such, the obesity epidemic has started to mimic many earlier health crises in that it appears to have a spatial clustering and affects poor and minority populations more acutely. While hardly conclusive, studies have consistently shown that obesity clusters tend to occur in neighborhoods that have low residential density and lower property values, indicating socioeconomic status.[48] Rarely have we interrogated the explicit connection between socioeconomic status and urban form.

Our view of disease, especially those diseases that disproportionately afflict the poor, has also shifted since the widespread acceptance of germ theory. Although obesity affects entire populations, the focus on addressing it tends to be wholly focused on the individual and their "choices," such as their diet and their physical activity levels. A typical health questionnaire one would receive at a doctor's office will not ask where the nearest source of fresh food is, how many hours a week one works, or if one is able to walk to a park. There is an undeniable tinge of moralism to this tactic of addressing disease, seeing fatness as a failing of proper nutrition or sufficient exercise, but it is rooted in the American viewpoint of individual responsibility and bootstraps philosophy. While the hygiene campaigns of the Industrial Revolution transformed entire parts of the city, there was also a strong and vocal contingent who attached the deadly illnesses that plagued tenements to the cleanliness habits of its poor and immigrant occupants. Even as infectious diseases waned in the latter half of the twentieth century, researchers still referred to urban epidemics such as violence, drug addiction, and blight as "contagions," meaning social influence but using a word that implies that mere physical proximity to these afflictions could result in passage. Similar language has been used to characterize the spread of obesity, putting the onus on people, not the places.[49] The treatment of American epidemics has shown our steadfast attachment to "healthism," a term coined by political economist Robert Crawford in 1980, which places all health outcomes as the responsibility of the individual and its achievement as a sign of being a good citizen, or even a "badge of honor." Conversely, those suffering from bad health are perceived as a burden on society. Some have coined the idea as the "neoliberal idea of wellness." Obesity, while not necessarily a signifier of bad health in of itself, appears to many to be an outward signifier of choices from what we eat to where we live, no matter how much those "choices" are dictated by the environment.

Of course, the history of urban landscape and health is predicated on a degree of environmental determinism, but the medicalization of chronic disease and the structure of scientific research demand a degree of a causality that may be impossible to prove. Where people live and what those environments look like do not fit easily into those constructs, and so bring the biggest caveat to any study on neighborhoods and health outcomes. Almost every study must couch its discoveries in the "self-selection bias," that perhaps sedentary lifestyles are a result of people selecting suburban neighborhoods because they prefer driving, a usurping of the larger responsibility of designers, planners, and policy makers to provide enough of those places in the first place. However, this has also been used to discredit the influence of the environment itself and, purposely or not, reinforces the idea of healthism. Most notably, a paper published in the *Journal of Urban Economics* titled "Fat City: Questioning the Relationship between Urban Sprawl and Obesity," which followed people who had moved from sprawling to "less sprawling" neighborhoods and found no difference in weight after a year, concluded:

Our results strongly suggest that urban sprawl does not cause weight gain. Rather, people who are more likely to be obese (e.g., because they do not like to walk) are also more likely to move to sprawling neighborhoods (e.g., because they can more easily move around by car). Of course, the built environment may still place constraints on the type of exercise that people are able to take or the nature of the diet that they consume. The key point is that individuals who have a lower propensity to being obese will choose to avoid those kinds of neighborhoods. . . . It follows immediately from our results that recent calls to redesign cities in order to combat the rise in obesity are misguided. Our results do not provide a basis for thinking that such re-designs will have the desired effect, and therefore suggest that resources devoted to this cause will be wasted. The public health battle against obesity is better fought on other fronts."[50]

While the paper in no way represents the bulk of research, the sentiment reflects much of the thinking on causes of obesity outside the spheres of public health and design, or even those within it, as this same paper was cited prominently in the MIT report.

The concentration on the supposed direct relationship between form and health outcomes or neighborhood choice also obscures intervening factors. Suburban design and planning doesn't simply preclude people from walking, but the long commutes infringe on free time, and the cost of owning a car can add additional financial pressure. With more time spent commuting or working, the poor also have a limited physical activity "budget," particularly when it comes to leisure activity.[51] Often this is posed as an attitudinal barrier instead of an economic one. While likely not the intention of any researchers, the consistent relationship between socioeconomic status and poor health, even if neighborhoods have the "right" form, only enforces the biases of healthism. Studies have shown that many low-income neighborhoods, especially in urban areas, can appear to be otherwise walkable via the common measurements of density and street intersections, but crime, or fear of crime, is a much stronger deterrent to walking.[52] Lower-income neighborhoods are also less likely to have simple pedestrian infrastructure such as traffic calming, crosswalks, and lighting.[53] Maintenance and cleanliness of streets has also proven to be a strong influence. A study that looked specifically at the differences in favorable walking environments between whites and Hispanics/Latinos in Tucson indicated that in a Mexican American neighborhood, 30 percent of respondents also thought that elements of social cohesion and community identity contributed to a walkable environment, compared to 6 percent of white respondents. These are all factors that can be designed, to an extent, but as the researchers point out, the lack of attention paid to these factors in the walkability literature reveals how many of these indices have been developed and validated in white neighborhoods.[54] Nevertheless, it isn't hard to read the overtones of much of the walkability advocacy literature, especially in the way it is written to flatter those making the healthy, correct, and moral choice to walk or live in a walkable neighborhood, and it is an amorphous, unhealthy "other" that prefers to drive everywhere for everything. A more complicated truth is that most people want walkable access to their jobs or errands—it's just that their version of walkability goes beyond a medium-density, tree-lined street (fig. 50).

Healthism specifically colors the dissemination of research on obesity and the built environment, even if unintentionally. Food availability and the issue of food deserts are the other primary tenets of research in this arena. The concentration on the easily measurable factor of spatial distribution, and not quality or offerings of grocery stores, while illuminating, can distract from the importance of built environment if presented without nuance. A 2014 Walk Score map showing availability of stores showed the expected cities with high densities of grocery outlets: New York, San Francisco, and Philadelphia. However, the map counted bodegas, which normally sell highly processed and packaged food, as grocery stores, so areas such as low-income neighborhoods in the Bronx rated high despite more qualitative research indicating them as food deserts. A widely cited report, partially supported by the US Department of Agriculture (USDA), found that after controlling for income level, differences in access explain only 10 percent of disparities in caloric consumption across education groups. It also found that introducing new stores carrying fresh food did not change purchasing habits.[55] Although true that change in the built environment alone would not combat the issue, the researchers have not called for education programs or acknowledged that low-income populations often have less time to go to the grocery store with the frequency that having fresh food demands, or to prepare foods from scratch. Instead, the title of the study itself, "Is the Focus on Food Deserts Fruitless?," and its dissemination online under headlines such as "More Doubt Cast on Food Deserts" on the City Observatory website, imply that individuals are responsible for their health.

The effort to clarify the relationship between built environment and behavior, and to legitimize forms of planning and design through scientific inquiry, too often relegates socioeconomic status to a control variable and in turn clouds the equity of housing and landscape. This not only obscures its significant effects on health but also inequities in the environment itself. A *Bridging the Gap* research report found in an examination of 10,177 streets across 154 American communities that 89 percent of high-income neighborhoods had continuous sidewalks as opposed to 49 percent of low-income neighborhoods.[56] Walkability indices rarely include crime statistics or environmental factors such as air quality, and the quality of "safety" is normally confined to auto collision. Results are rarely contextualized with demographic information. Most American walkability research has been confined to non-Hispanic white populations, which not only biases cultural preferences but further obscures further possible inequities.[57] Directly addressing the issue of self-selection, recent research has shown that there is also a significant issue of neighborhood "mismatch," where supply is not meeting demand. A survey of Houston residents conducted by the Rice University Kinder Institute showed that 50 percent of residents want smaller homes in walkable areas, but only 10 percent of existing US housing qualifies as such.[58] In an Atlanta-based survey, Lawrence D. Frank et al. (2007) also found mismatch between neighborhood preference and actual residence, pointing out that "the availability and cost of housing, real and perceived quality of schools, job location, and other preferences require compromise."[59]

Walking has repeatedly been presented as a prescriptive dose to physical illness. We often miss the point that is also the only free form of transportation. Streets, sidewalks, and public spaces can encourage social interaction and build social capital, empowering economically disadvantaged areas.[60] It is an environmental justice issue and an empowering act. If we posed it as such, would it change the urgency of the issue? Perhaps not, but the supposed objectivity of health and political neutrality of architecture and landscape, and the efforts to make it so, are myths that must be dismantled. The insistence on finding the "causality" of the built environment before enacting changes in zoning or large-scale interventions is understandable, particularly given the United States' fraught history of using urban design and planning as a policy lever. But if we recognize the fallout and try harder to look ahead to both positive and negative effects, perhaps we can do better.

Take for example the popular refrain to return to the mid-rise downtowns celebrated by the New Urbanists and walkability advocates. To many, Main Street is simply an urban typology. In a 2017 column for the *New York Times* titled "The Myth of Main Street," Louis Hyman discusses the parallels between the Trump campaign's "Make America Great Again" slogan and the

Fig. 50. These renderings show a reimagining of a suburban parking lot in Marin County, California, to be more active, relying on the standard images of bikers, small-scale retail, and trees used to convey healthy neighborhoods. (Courtesy of Steve Price at Urban Advantage, www.urban-advantage.com)

popular refrain "Bring Main Street Back," a comparison most walkability advocates would likely never cosign. Hyman asserts both mottos are fraught and simply out of step with the current economic reality, saying:

But nostalgia for Main Street is misplaced—and costly. Small stores are inefficient. Local manufacturers, lacking access to economies of scale, usually are inefficient as well. To live in that kind of world is expensive. . . . It's worth noting that the idealized Main Street is not a myth in some parts of America today. It exists, but only as a luxury consumer experience. Main Streets of small, independent boutiques and nonfranchised restaurants can be found in affluent college towns, in gentrified neighborhoods in Brooklyn and San Francisco, in tony suburbs—in any place where people have ample disposable income. Main Street requires shoppers who don't really care about low prices. The dream of Main Street may be populist, but the reality is elitist. "Keep it local" campaigns are possible only when people are willing and able to pay to do so."[61]

Hyman is not in any way specifically excoriating the efforts of the walkability movement, or even thinking about its effects on disease. But the reality he describes is absolutely a downstream effect of selling an aesthetic of healthy neighborhoods.

CHAPTER 8

The New Ecology of Health

Expanding the Research Landscape

Singular pursuits to eliminate perceived hazards in the built environment—waste, miasma, germs, blight, and cars—had success in transforming the urban landscape and even made demonstrable positive effects on health outcomes but have also yielded many unintended, malignant ones. It is difficult to determine which and how health crises have significantly altered the landscape. In many instances, it appears to be a demonstrable epidemic, whether it be cholera and other "filth diseases," pulmonary disease, social ills, or obesity. These epidemics become amplified through popular media and empirical research. This research and the perception of the problem are reflected and, more often, refracted through the lens of design. Walkability, and the connection of design to physical activity, have predominated over much of the current body of literature, but there are other frontiers to consider where some fascinating discoveries have been made about the links between urban landscape and wellness.

It is necessary to move to a new ecology of health in the urban landscape that encompasses empirical research, complex models of chronic disease causation, and that recognizes historic and present-day inequities. Social epidemiologists Nancy Krieger, A. J. McMichael, and Mervyn and Ezra Susser have all proposed frameworks of "ecosocial," "human ecology," and "eco-epidemiology," respectively, to understand health outcomes. These are all theories that take the term "ecology" to mean reciprocal and interwoven relationships between social, environmental, and individual factors. In Krieger's words, this model "explicitly incorporates constructs pertaining to political economy, political ecology, ecosystems, spatiotemporal scales and levels, biological pathways of embodiment, and the social production of scientific knowledge."[1] Krieger has also explained her theory of a "spiderless web of causation" where there are rarely predominant factors in chronic disease but rather many threads, all connected through the center.[2] While these researchers are all primarily concerned with social determinants of health, such as policy, racism, and economy, the built environment still exists as an intervening factor of influence between these invisible but acutely felt causes. If models of health can consider these myriad factors, how can a framework of design and planning also consider these larger systems? Failure to do so in the past has allowed "health" to be weaponized as a tool of exclusion and discrimination, whether intentional or not.

Moreover, *can* health be woven back into our landscape? This chapter highlights some other urgent topics we have to confront in the twenty-first century: the promising research in the arena of landscape and mental health, the expanding discourse of smart cities and optimized wellness, and, finally, the urgent issue of climate change and health. Confronting these dangers and thinking about how to mitigate these impacts will require a reexamination of the intertwined systems of our urban settlements, our ecosystems, and our own bodies.

This Is Your Brain on Green

A rapidly growing body of empirical research on neuroscience and landscape has verified much of the intuitive hypotheses about nature and "nervousness" hypothesized in the early days of cities, with even more resonance in our contemporary context. In 1869, physician John Rauch, making an argument for more public parks in the city, said:

We have thus far been considering the influence of parks and trees on the physical development; we now propose to call attention to their influence on the mental condition. In fact, there is such an intimate connection between the two, that they cannot well be separated, as a sound and vigorous mind is generally dependent on upon a healthy condition of the bodily organs, and without either, the object of life is but imperfectly attained. . . . We live in an atmosphere of excitement, more so, perhaps, than any other community in the world, and it is therefore more necessary that all prudent safeguards should be thrown around us to prevent the impairment of the vigor of the mind and the inroads of disease. . . . This is an age of great mental activity and nowhere is the mind more stimulated than in Chicago. While it is true that the judicious use of an organ increases its power and confirms its health; but excessive exercise which requires an undue share of vital energy, leads to an unhealthy condition.[3]

Rauch's description was more based in anecdotes and his own experiences, but more than 125 years later, these instincts have been proven correct by clinical trials and empirical research. Much of the most definitive research on landscape and health has come out of studying healthcare environments. In 1984, Roger Ulrich conducted a study looking at post-operative recovery times in hospitals. He found that compared to patients facing a wall, patients with a window facing the landscape had shorter recovery times, asked for fewer painkillers, and had more positive comments about the nursing staff. Later studies by Ulrich found that the underlying factor between the different outcomes was that views of landscape reduced stress, which was inhibiting recovery in the patients facing the wall.[4] The work of landscape architect and environmental psychologist Clare Cooper Marcus would articulate design elements of landscapes for specific aliments from reduced motor function to dementia, as well as expand on the usefulness of "horticultural therapy," or gardening for patients. Marcus, with writing partners Carolyn Francis, Marni Barnes, and Naomi Sachs, has written a series of definitive books and articles on healing gardens and therapeutic landscapes to aid in the treatment of patients.[5]

From the robust work on landscape in healthcare settings, two distinct fields of study have grown, with direct implications for the larger urban environment. Environmental psychology examines how we interact with our world, and how our world shapes our health and behaviors. The origins of the field date back to the late 1960s or early 1970s, and whereas the field at first largely concentrated on interior environments, namely homes and workplaces, in recent decades research has been dominated by linking the presence of nature to mental health outcomes.[6] Even more recently, there has been a growing interest in seeing how perceptions of nature and climate change can inform environmental values and conservation behavior. The even newer field of neurourbanism is an emerging discipline that brings together neuroscientists, cognitive psychologists, city planners, urban designers, architects, and landscape architects to explore the impact of the design of our cities on stress and psychological well-being.[7]

This work is strongly influenced by E. O. Wilson's 1984 book *Biophilia,* which links humans' apparent innate preferences for natural settings to evolutionary biology. Wilson's book has attracted a resurgence of interest as more scientific study has validated the connection between landscape and mental and physical health. In an interview marking the thirtieth anniversary of the book, Wilson told the *Washington Post:*

Now we've come all the way around and are beginning, especially through studies in brain science, and psychology, including social psychology, and archaeology and biology, we're coming to realize that there's something a lot more complicated and deep and wondrous in the development of the human mind, than what we had imagined even. So there is a new trend and biophilia is part of that, because we know that all other animals—mobile animals, that are able to move around—are programmed to go to the right environment. They do it with no training whatsoever or anything. They just know exactly where to go and what to do when they get there. Why should human beings not have at least a strong residue of those environments in which we evolved? And those are natural environments, we originated in wildlands with certain characteristics.[8]

Studies in environmental psychology have confirmed and further articulated Ulrich's original discoveries on landscape and stress. As discussed earlier, landscape architects and environmental psychologists Frances E. Kuo and William C. Sullivan, based at the University of Illinois at Urbana-Champaign, wrote a series of papers on the effect of landscape on stress in public housing environments. Looking at the Cabrini Green housing projects in Chicago, they found that residents living in units facing landscape were less likely to be involved in violent incidents and tended to have more positive social interactions. They hypothesized that the constant mental fatigue and depletion of the residents resulted in acts of aggression, and the view of the landscapes seemed to have a recharging effect that prevented altercations.[9] Kuo and Sullivan also studied the effects of landscapes on children. A 2001 study by the researchers found that being immersed in green play areas could possibly suppress some symptoms associated with attention deficit disorder, such as focus, task completion, listening, and distraction.[10] In another study, Dongying Li and Sullivan studied ninety-four students at five central Illinois high schools. Students were randomly assigned to one of three types of classrooms—windowless, with a window looking out onto built space (such as another building facade or a parking lot), or with a window looking out onto green space. Each type of classroom had a similar size, layout, and furniture. The students participated in one-on-one experiments in which they did thirty minutes of activities that included a proofreading exercise, a speech, and a mental math exercise. Following the activities, the students were given an attention test, a ten-minute break in the classroom, and then another attention test following the break. These tests asked students to repeat a series of numbers in the same and reverse order in which they heard the numbers. Li and Sullivan found that students did better on the attention tests given after the break if they were in a classroom with a green view; they showed a 13 percent increase in performance following the break. There was no statistical difference in performance for the students in the windowless room or the room with a view onto a built space. Similarly, the students in the room with the green view showed a greater physiological recovery from stress after the break than the other students.[11]

The theory linking these studies is what is often referred to as attention-restoration therapy, which has its roots in the theories of nineteenth-century psychologist William James. He hypothesized that there are two different attention levels: voluntary and involuntary. Voluntary or directed attention is purposeful, the kind of attention we would bring to a work task. Involuntary is a passive act—we are aware of our surroundings, but it is a state of engagement that lets your mind rest.[12] The theory would be further articulated by environmental psychologists Rachel and Steven Kaplan, who would contextualize this theory in both our interactions with nature and our increasing constant exposure to information and media.[13] Nature is restorative as we can notice the sound of water, the movement of trees, and the colors of landscape, but we don't need to actively engage them. This theory is also the basis of the Japanese practice of Shinrin-Yoku, or "forest bathing," immersing oneself in a natural environment for therapeutic purposes. The practice is ancient, but the name was given in 1982 by Japan's forestry agency. Today, Japan has sixty officially designated trails specifically for the practice.[14]

Neurourbanism, a much newer field, stresses its interdisciplinary characteristics and specifically looks at the neural signatures of different settings as people navigate their way around the city. This research has identified that certain settings favor relaxation, and others are characterized by high mental alertness and increased stress.[15] Citing the unique combination of "social density and social isolation" often found in cities, along with the lack of control that people often feel in urban places, neurourbanism studies have pinpointed more specific stressors in cities, along with the mitigating effect of urban landscapes. A study conducted by Neale et al. in 2019 had elderly subjects in Edinburgh wear electroencephalography (EEG) helmets while walking through environments that were categorized as "urban busy," "urban quiet," or "urban green" (fig. 51). The Emotiv brand mobile devices categorized EEG waves into five classifications of mental states: "frustration," "excitement," "engagement," "meditation," and "long-term excitement," which

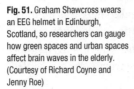

Fig. 51. Graham Shawcross wears an EEG helmet in Edinburgh, Scotland, so researchers can gauge how green spaces and urban spaces affect brain waves in the elderly. (Courtesy of Richard Coyne and Jenny Roe)

THE CHOROGRAPHY OF CHRONIC DISEASE

let the researchers label effects with more specificity. Slower alpha waves indicate more relaxed brain activity; higher beta waves indicate higher levels of alertness and more strain on attentional capacity. There were no significant differences between a quiet residential street and park in activating high beta waves, only a difference between these two and urban busy neighborhoods, indicating that street design and flows can have similar effects as parks. The researchers also found that for older adults, vigilance and engagement were still high in some parks, possibly due to degraded paths that were more difficult to walk and indicating a need for more nuanced study and design guidelines when it comes to the above-sixty-five age group.[16]

Studies on attention restoration theory have also found that even viewing nature on a screen, or in a virtual reality context, has had similar effects.[17] There are some critiques of the theory, namely the lack of specificity in kinds of natural environments and questioning the supposed evolutionary biology underpinnings of the theory.[18] Kaplan and Kaplan asserted our supposed attraction to environments with water and rich foliage is due to these being indicators of good habitats for survival. Wilson likewise posited the type of nature humans are attracted to most are savanna-like environments, due to our natural origins. More specific delineations in the kinds of landscapes that are most beneficial to our health have not really been explored. To most researchers in this area, "nature" remains a default generic pastoral (and European) ideal. In fact, many of our idealized urban landscapes, such as Central Park, are highly designed and engineered. Less "green" landscapes such as the deserts of the American Southwest, the wetlands of the Gulf South, and other landscape vernaculars are less explored in terms of their health benefits.

While this research is promising, it has, like much of the literature on health and built environment, been largely divorced from issues of race and socioeconomic status. In the context of most written American history to present-day scientific research and popular media, the kinds of nature that are most valued range from nineteenth-century pastoral to an image of American "wilderness," perhaps most embodied in our national parks system. Our view of the latter is perhaps most problematic. While most would hold national parks as central to our identity, they also represent the removal of Indigenous people from their own land (in effect, deeming their presence "unnatural"), and are a highly specific aesthetic that is exclusive to other landscapes that are just as "American," from southern wetlands to scrub forests.[19] There are very few studies done on the values of nature and wilderness from immigrant and minority perspectives. One by Cassandra Y. Johnson et al. (2004) showed that African Americans, Latinos, and recent immigrants were less likely than whites to indicate that they enjoyed viewing wilderness, or they planned to visit a wilderness area in the near future, or they agreed with the statement "I believe the trees, wildlife, free flowing water, rock formations, and meadows that wilderness protect have value themselves whether or not humans benefit from them." Interestingly, there was high agreement between both African Americans and whites in positively responding to the statement "Wilderness areas are important because they help to preserve plant and animal species that could have important scientific or human health values, such as new medicines."[20] Overall, the study most strongly indicates a lack of access to wilderness or large parks among minority and immigrant groups, a conclusion that has been supported by many other studies.[21] Carolyn Finney's *Black Faces, White Spaces: Reimagining the Relationship of African Americans to the Great Outdoors* looks at American environmental history through this perspective and at how the environment, and environmentalism, are framed as a white concern. To many African Americans, "wilderness" also signified something that has traditionally been unknown as well as a space of whiteness, and therefore it can provoke fear.[22] This addresses the often implied, rarely explicit assertion made from the Progressive Era that the "working class" (as African Americans are virtually invisible from these narratives) needed to be taught to properly appreciate nature for health and moral reasons. Even since then, we have rarely framed cultural perceptions or appreciations of nature through centuries of racism, nativism, and environmental injustice.

Beneficial landscapes can, and should, be present in a smaller and more distributed scale in urban areas and can have real effects. There is an expanding field of study on Adverse Childhood Experiences (ACEs). When children's bodies respond to difficult situations and environments by releasing stress-related chemicals, these responses in turn affect how the brain works and the body's capacity to ward off disease. The longer-term results can take many forms: problems with attention, decision-making, and behavior; depression; chronic illness; alcohol and substance abuse; reduced earnings; and shortened life expectancy.[23] The neighborhood environment is where the most difference can be made. The social environment is of course most applicable to this issue, but seeing how we can alter the urban landscape to address these issues is also key. Eugenia C. South et al. (2018) looked at the effects of greening on nearly 450 Philadelphia residents who lived near vacant lots (fig. 52). Over the course of eighteen months, some residents saw their nearby lots greened, meaning trash was removed, new grass and trees were planted, a fence was put in, and regular maintenance was done. Others saw only regular trash cleanup in their vacant lots. The final group's vacant lots remained untouched. For those residents near the greened lots, feelings of depression

Fig. 52. In a study of 450 Philadelphia residents, physician Eugenia C. South and her team performed a range of improvements on vacant lots and found that for those living near greened lots, feelings of depression decreased by 68 percent. (Courtesy of Pennsylvania Horticultural Society)

decreased by 68 percent. There was no improvement in the mental health of people living near lots where trash was cleaned up or nothing at all was done.[24]

There is undeniably a strong correlation between nature and mental health. For all the uncertainty around the built environment effects on behavior change, the intrinsic and measurable benefit of landscape on the brain appears to be one of the most conclusive subsets of contemporary research. To advance the work will take an expansion of concepts of nature and how its benefits are applied.

Health on the Ground: The Smart City and the Just City

A generalized, holistic ideal of "health" is still the goal of the contemporary city. We know that the multifaceted causes behind chronic disease are the results of systems that go far beyond the original. On a high level, many academics are still trying to conceptualize urban life as a predictive and automated system. This interest in finding conceptual models from biology or nature for the operation of the city is only the latest iteration of Howard's Garden City diagram, or writ larger in Saarinen's cellular concepts, or Park and Burgess's human ecologies. In the early twenty-first century there has been new interest from the fields of computer science and physics. Geoffrey West, a British physicist, has been a leader in advocating for a new science of cities. West rejects all previous models of cities as merely "theory." In an interview with the *New York Times Magazine,* West claimed he and colleague Luis Bettencourt had found the algorithm guiding urban growth, saying: "What we found are the constants that describe every city. . . . I can take these laws and make precise predictions about the number of violent crimes and the surface area of roads in a city in Japan with 200,000 people. I don't know anything about this city or even where it is or its history, but I can tell you all about it. And the reason I can do that is because every city is really the same." Although claiming to start with a blank slate and an ignorance of urban theory, West relied on the now familiar trope of comparing the body to the city, describing streets as blood vessels and alleys as capillaries. He refers to his growth model as "urban metabolism." West also decried traditional suburban development for its inefficiencies, saying of Phoenix: "When you look at some of these fast-growing cities, they look like tumors on the landscape. . . . They have these extreme levels of growth, but it's not sustainable growth."[25] Although West and his colleague Luis Bettencourt claim their scaling model solves for some diseases, that along with crime, illness increases by 15 percent as a city size doubles, urban metabolism otherwise appears largely unconcerned with the health of citizens.[26] The science of cities does attempt to address the complexity and plurality of connected urban systems but as of yet is narrowly concerned with scaling and flows of energy, goods, and information.

Twenty-first-century urban science looks to be a growing field. New York University's Center for Urban Science and Progress (CUSP) splashily launched a program in urban informatics in 2014. In 2018, the Massachusetts Institute of Technology announced its own program in urban science, jointly run by its well-established Departments of Urban Studies and Computer Science. But a look at both programs finds them largely bereft of history courses or urban theory, although MIT offers a single course in health and health equity. In an essay revisiting Jane Jacobs's "The Kind of Problem a City Is," Bettencourt points out that employing large-scale data to uncover urban patterns has always been used, mentioning Jacob Riis's use of statistics to build a social justice movement and the work of the RAND Corporation in allocating fire stations in New York, although he fails to mention the failings of the latter. It is also not the expertise of this new generation of urban scientists to think qualitatively, or even politically, about the city. Bettencourt realizes the limits of this application. And to some extent, schools are recognizing the false promise of "objectivity" when confronting complex urban issues.

As these schools work to make sure their programs are based in civics, the attempts to solve cities and provide consistent and neutral algorithms have proved attractive to the technology sector, which is starting to move into the urban realm. Many cities' forays into smart management include open data platforms for citizens to alert them to maintenance issues and crime and to access real-time information. But the issue of managing the public health of citizens, especially through algorithms, presents a particularly complex problem. For proponents of the smart or data-driven city, health is usually positioned as a natural outcome of spatial or economic optimization. In 2015, Google was a major backer of Sidewalk Labs, a start-up devoted to leveraging data and technology to solve complex urban issues. Health is central to the Sidewalk Labs mission; their related spinoff Cityblock is devoted to improving community health and is uniquely focused on Medicaid patients through community-based healthcare delivery and preventive health interventions. Cityblock is now a separate entity, but Sidewalk Labs kept "health" as a value for their first development, Sidewalk Toronto. A development on Toronto's Waterfront, Sidewalk Toronto was mired in controversy from its inception. Predicated on the notion that they could only achieve their goals if given a city to build "from the ground up"—as in any good utopian plan—Sidewalk Labs has been accused of circumventing the public input process and cutting backroom deals with the city government, and its use of technology and sensors, as well as the practices of their parent company, has many residents concerned about privacy issues.[27] In 2019, early renderings showed a public realm that appears inspired by and updates historical ideas. Sanitation trucks are shown in a separate tunnel running underneath the city, and gleaming modernist buildings have green on their roofs and bordering the streets. Pedestrians and bikers are foregrounded on the street. A health clinic with a transparent storefront is also shown. The style of the drawings is simple and in a bright watercolor palette, evoking the ideal small-scale, but bustling, urban environment (fig. 53).[28] Updated renderings released later that year showed a different vision of the optimized city, though. Architecture firm Heatherwick Studio designed a constructed mass timber forest of high-rises

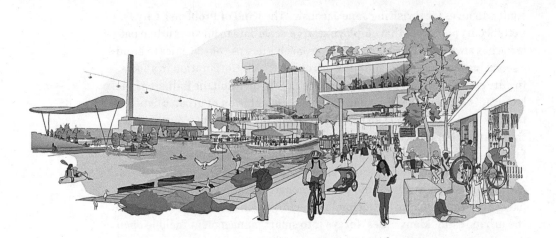

Fig. 53. Early illustrations of the planned Sidewalk Toronto development update historical ideas about health for the twenty-first century—separated waste systems, clean streets and water, and a thriving urban forest (2018). (Sidewalk Labs)

and glass walls above stone plazas. No green space is visible, nor does the apparent transparency of the architecture sway concerns about the surveillance aspect of constant data gathering.[29] Any obligatory nods to the more traditionally held aesthetics of health have been replaced by efficiency and the sway of new technologies. Ultimately, Sidewalk Labs pulled out of the project in mid-2020, citing economic uncertainty and that it would be too difficult to keep the project "financially viable without sacrificing core parts of the plan we had developed together with Waterfront Toronto to build a truly inclusive, sustainable community."[30]

Coworking company WeWork is similarly looking to enter the smart city arena with the promise of improving civic life. Much as DELOS sought to bring its WELL Building Standard to the urban realm, WeWork, which has rigorously studied the thermal comfort and mental well-being of its office spaces, announced, "What We has already done inside the building, take it outside, and reimagine a sort of connective tissue for 21st-century cities." Besides the reoccurring difficulty of translating the controlled environment of an office building to the public realm, the "connective tissue" WeWork is looking to strengthen still appears to be a narrowly targeted set of amenities. The company has already leveraged untold amounts of urban data in order to make real estate decisions, whether to judge the value of the space, nearby amenities, and its potential consumer base—largely young, wealthy professionals. In 2018, research scientist Carl Anderson described WeWork's efforts to evaluate places for expansion by using machine learning to give the properties a "thumbs up" or "thumbs down." Besides employing the problematic Walk Score metric, he stated, "So maybe we learn that having a Blue Bottle Coffee nearby is a good thing." Anderson added, "And a Western Union might be an indicator that it's not such a great block. Maybe it's proximity to rivers and parks. Or whatever. But we're trying to work that out."[31] The cultural and economic signifiers of a "good" neighborhood are made clear, and the language of urban improvement is used to (barely) hide a company's economic gain.

We have yet to see what these efforts will yield, especially as the COVID-19 pandemic has hollowed out business districts and temporarily made the idea of coworking a thing of the past. However, the idea that in the smart city, everything can be quantified from environments to bodies presents a danger to how we think about landscape. To conceptualize "green" as a dosage for our consumption neglects the nuances of designing for place and the wider picture of our own relationship to nature. In her essay "The Environment Is Not a System," artist and engineer Tega Brain points to the tech industry's interest in applying scientific management to environments:

As we scramble to understand and respond to a rapidly destabilizing environment characterized by human disturbance, climate change and extinction, we are simultaneously reveling in an unprecedented surplus of computing. It is therefore tempting (and lucrative) to make claims that neat technological fixes can address thorny existential problems, a modernist impulse that remains well and truly alive in projects like the smart city. . . . We must acknowledge these limits, but perhaps more significantly we must acknowledge how deeply entrenched we are within a computational worldview that assumes the systemacity of environments and under-acknowledges the indeterminacy of environmental encounters."[32]

Moreover, she points out that this technological approach often fails to see complex human interactions and, most of all, rarely acknowledges long histories of injustice.

On the other end of the scale, many communities are working to ensure health through ground-up work, cross-sector collaboration, and a combination of built environment transformation and policy. On a municipal level, forward-thinking departments of health and planning in cities such as San Francisco and Boston use health impact assessments (HIAs), essentially the health equivalent of a traditional environmental impact assessment, to understand how large new developments will impact resident health. In New York City, the city Departments of Design and Construction, Health and Mental Hygiene, Transportation, and City Planning and the Office of Management and Budget worked together to produce a guide to increasing "active design," or ways to encourage physical activity, in the public realm. And in 2007, Oklahoma City's Mayor Mick Cornett challenged the city to lose 1 million pounds and followed up with hundreds of millions of dollars in infrastructural investment, from building large parks to distributed community clinics to a rowing and kayaking building downtown. Mayor Cornett reached the million-pound goal in 2011.[33]

The emerging research on green space, trees, and health has also been crucial to hyperlocal initiatives. In 2015, members of the Massachusetts chapter of the American Planning Association's Sustainable Communities Division (APA-SCD) paired with Groundwork Lawrence, a community-based organization in Lawrence, Massachusetts, to implement and evaluate a tree-planting program in the town (figs. 54, 55). Members of the team polled residents on their top health concerns; the top answers were cancer and mental health, followed by asthma. After extensive public health research and tree canopy analysis, as well as more participatory meetings where community members were shown visual preference surveys of existing streets and edited images of those streets with trees, the APA-SCD helped Groundwork Lawrence with toolkits in both English and Spanish communicating the health advantages of trees, an infographic, and even a podcast to build support. Tree planting is often touted by advocates as a simple solution to improve health through the built environment. However, Groundwork Lawrence's admittedly ambitious plan to plant 2,400 trees in three years shows that even this "simple" act took extensive coalition building, necessary for the community's investment and long-term maintenance of the program. Beyond that, different tree species had to be carefully selected for benefits, to maintain a healthy ecology, and to ensure driving and pedestrian visibility.[34] The mostly volun-

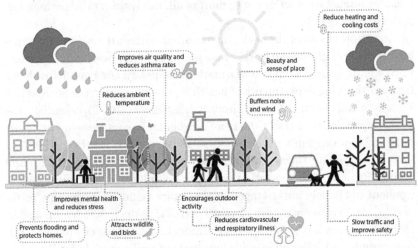

Fig. 54. The American Planning Association's Sustainable Communities Division and Groundwork Lawrence created this Green Streets Lawrence infographic in both English and Spanish to build support for its tree-planting program by connecting trees to resident health (2017). (Courtesy of Groundwork Lawrence and American Planning Association's Sustainable Communities Division)

THE CHOROGRAPHY OF CHRONIC DISEASE

Fig. 55. Before executing the Green Streets Plan, planners and designers polled residents on their specific health concerns to guide the research and design (2017). (Courtesy Groundwork Lawrence and American Planning Association's Sustainable Communities Division)

teer effort had to be realistic with identifying capacity and time frame. The APA-SCD team believe that partnering with an already existing community organization was key, especially in communicating the benefits of the program to residents. We still often take it for granted that the connections between landscape and health are known, but even for the researchers involved, the positive effects on mental health and crime reduction were a surprise, as were how the effects aligned with the residents' health concerns.[35]

The troubled history of public housing is also being rethought on local levels to promote health. In the demographically diverse neighborhood of High Point in Seattle, Washington, the Seattle Housing Authority undertook a series of housing and neighborhood upgrades that targeted residents' indoor air quality and asthma issues and increased opportunities for physical activity, using New Urbanism principles to guide them and a lengthy participatory process (fig. 56). An interdisciplinary public health team also helped form walking groups and provide information about routes. In addition to lower asthma rates, participants reported increasing walking time from 65 to 108 minutes per day, and in three months the number of participants who reported being moderately active for at least 150 minutes per week increased from 62 percent to 81 percent. Additionally, these residents reported fewer days of suffering from poor mental health.[36] In Denver, the Mariposa Housing Development, rebuilt from the ground up in the urban core of the city, used a social ecological model to guide its planning and integrated a grocery store, pharmacy, banks, and open space into the development. In a self-reported health survey for its

Fig. 56. In the High Point neighborhood of Seattle, Washington, planners and designers significantly increased physical activity and mental health and even decreased smoking rates through a community-based design process that emphasized active pathways, landscapes, and spaces for social cohesion (2017). (Seattle Housing Authority)

residents, smoking rates dropped by 6 percent, and 38 percent of residents reported improved health overall. They also found that reported incidences of crime per a thousand people decreased from 248 to 157.[37]

The Obama administration's Affordable Care Act (ACA) opened opportunities to expand health to the built environment. The policy incentivized healthcare companies to invest in preventive care outside the hospital in order to ward off more expensive emergency care. The ACA requires all hospitals to perform local community needs assessments each year and provides funds to address upstream causes of health; although it is not often they are put toward built environment improvements, this provides a possible pathway. The move away from fee-for-service models has spurred innovative partnerships among groups that heretofore had not been involved in health issues.

Boston's Conservation Law Foundation and the Massachusetts Housing Investment Corporation have been experimenting with the Healthy Neighborhood Equity Fund (HNEF) to funnel both public funds and private investment from philanthropic foundations and individual investors into developments rated for potentially high health impact. The mixed capital funds mean investment risk is somewhat mitigated, and HNEF has focused on proven healthy development strategies such as transit-oriented development in disadvantaged neighborhoods. In a project such as their Chelsea Flats apartment building, HNEF can work as owner/manager, taking in income from the rent but also ensuring over a quarter of the units remain affordable. HNEF also built the Brockton Neighborhood Health Center, which combined a health clinic with a grocery store that also teaches nutrition classes and

African and Caribbean cooking, the native cuisines of most of the residents. Brockton is a food desert, a third of the town's children are in poverty, and diabetes and heart disease there are above the national average. Rather than simply planting a grocery store in the neighborhood, the store's management worked in tandem with the health staff and thought of ways to address the specific health needs of the community; one solution they came up with was to offer a frequent shopper and awards program for healthy food purchases. The HNEF ensures the health of disadvantaged communities, especially in the face of rising housing costs in cities and gentrification.[38] Economics play a major part in their success, but they are not selling health or a health aesthetic; rather they are partnering with community organizations and leveraging the policy environment.

Some hospitals are starting to act as developers themselves. Healthcare leaders Kaiser Permanente announced a $200 million investment in housing in each of the eight states where it is located. Similarly, Nationwide Children's Hospital in Columbus, Ohio, also invested in its neighborhood's built environment, partnering with Community Development for All People, a local nonprofit. Nationwide distributed over $1 million for neighborhood residents to fix up and make repairs to their own houses. It has also bought and flipped homes, ensured affordable housing for its own employees, and improved roads and sidewalks.[39] Ironically, much of Nationwide's work is undoing the damage of the urban renewal and highway projects of the 1960s and 1970s, which isolated the neighborhood and let it deteriorate. Nationwide and its partners have formed an accountable care organization, a structure that allows it to get reimbursed for Medicare and Medicaid patients, but only per patient, not for each service. By ensuring a healthy environment outside of the hospital and reducing patient visits, the hospital can stay profitable. Both Kaiser's and Nationwide's initiatives are new, and their impacts are being measured, but in a few years results will show whether they yielded returns on health and investment.

The approaches described here are not fundamentally at odds but are two differing visions of how we approach health as the origins of disease have become less clear. More so, they are coming at the issue of health at radically different scales. The smart city uses hypergranular data to project abstract models of the city; the myriad community-level approaches here use "data" that is embedded in social and economic realities of neighborhoods for highly specific remedies. Where can they meet in the middle? We know that urban landscapes shaped around health, particularly in the age of more amorphous chronic disease, are most destructive when they fail to see the wider, ecological model of health, or when "health" is leveraged as an abstract concept to exclude or pass moral judgment. It would also be folly not to see what insights new technology and larger-scale data could yield. As ever, the issue of how health can shape our environment lies at a crossroads.

The Next Frontier: Climate Change and Health

The predominant narratives on health and built environment have often been singularly focused on a specific epidemic. Our present-day situation has the added urgency of climate change. Intensity and frequency of hurricanes, especially in the Atlantic Ocean, have increased since the 1980s, and the hurricane season is longer.[40] In the same time period, wildfires have increased by nearly fourfold and have consistently lasted longer and burned larger acreages.[41] A 2018 review of over 3,200 papers by a group of twenty-three NOAA scientists recognized ten climate hazards—warming, precipitation, floods, drought, heatwaves, fires, sea level, storms, changes in natural land cover, and ocean chemistry—that will impact virtually all aspects of our daily lives, among them health, food, water, infrastructure, economy, and security.[42] They also warned that current climate change predictions for temperature and sea level rise have likely been more conservative than what we will actually experience. Health, though, remains strangely decoupled from the conversation on climate change and built environment; strategies for resilience often toss off the word "health" as a co-benefit without thinking specifically about how health strategies and resilience strategies coincide or, worse, come into conflict. This is odd considering that it is now likely that every single person on this earth has tangibly felt the health effects of climate change, whether it is through increased heat, floods, or respiratory difficulties.

Since the early 1990s, the assertion that suburban development is particularly bad for health comes hand in hand with the argument that their planning and design are bad for the environment. This is undeniable. Urban development is a lead contributor to climate change. Residential, commercial, and industrial buildings contribute 43 percent of American carbon dioxide emissions, most of them coming from electricity use. Thirty-three percent of greenhouse gas emissions are due to transportation of all kinds, but chiefly from personal vehicles.[43] The distributed, disaggregated character of the suburban and exurban landscape strips greenfields, is detrimental to watershed systems, and disrupts habitat. The more we build and pave, the more the urban heat island effect will increase, along with the worldwide temperature rises we can expect from climate change. It is at times difficult to communicate to the general public how the deterioration of the environment will affect human health. Beyond the general air quality degradation from vehicles, rising temperatures will also increase levels of allergens and particulate matter in the air. For the more than 50 million Americans who suffer from allergic diseases, increased ozone can amplify these effects. It is estimated that airborne allergens cost the US healthcare system over $18 billion annually in 2017.[44] Increased heat will also attenuate the effects of illnesses such as heat stroke; those who will be most vulnerable are children, the elderly, and people with occupations that keep them outdoors for long periods of time.

How to best confront the challenge of climate change, at least in design or planning circles, is often framed as a battle between "urbanites" and "suburbanites," the choice to live in dense cities or sprawling neighborhoods, the choice to drive to work or take transit. This is magnified through the growing media influence of urbanists. Brent Toderian, a city planner and consultant based out of Vancouver, characterized suburbanites as consumerist and car-focused, tweeting, "If someone chooses to live in a smaller home in the inner city to avoid a commute, they generally don't pressure society to build them a bigger house with more stuff. So if you choose a bigger stuff-filled house in the suburbs, don't expect society to build you a fast commute. . . . Those choosing to live in the suburbs aren't entitled to free-flow car traffic capacity into the city at the expense of the taxes, health, safety & quality of life of city-dwellers."[45] Although these "choices" are ever more constrained by economic circumstance and years of policy, the argument that "smart growth" is good for both the environment and health persists in many public health studies on the built environment, perhaps because those in the field are not aware of the systemic change required to build to these requirements or to change the urban landscape we already have. This is not to say that we should abandon the principles of trying to reduce car usage, but it is time to take a harder look at who is most going to be affected by climate change and how we implement change through the built environment. Reducing auto use and increasing walkability has been held up as the panacea of public health and the environment for almost thirty years now, but we also have to consider a myriad of issues and prioritize. Obesity is in fact many ways a downstream effect of climate change. In a 2019 report, *The Lancet* Commission on Obesity used the word "syndemic" to describe the way climate change, obesity, and undernutrition are linked. The use of "syndemic" indicates "a synergy of epidemics, because they co-occur in time and place, interact with each other to produce complex sequelae, and share common underlying societal drivers." In their example, climate change will lead to more unpredictable weather, reducing agricultural yield and leading to more reliance on processed food.[46]

Climate change will also affect marginalized communities disproportionately. Communities of color have already historically been adjacent to roadways, downwind of industrial plants, or subject to polluted waters. Eric Klinenberg's landmark book *Heat Wave: A Social Autopsy of Disaster in*

Chicago showed that it was the elderly population that suffered the highest mortality rates in the city's 1995 heat wave; more recent research has shown that the poorest areas of cities are often the hottest and largely without air conditioning.[47] The increasing frequency of climate change events has also made it clear that marginalized populations are also in low-lying areas, with aging infrastructure that can't keep up with the rising intensity of effects. Hurricane Katrina, which hit New Orleans in 2005, and Hurricane Harvey, which hit Houston in 2017, disproportionately affected each city's sizable African American populations. After Hurricane Harvey, forty-three Superfund sites in Houston were also flooded, leaching unknown toxins into groundwater across the city. Analyses from Hurricane Katrina and other storm events have also shown that it is more difficult for the poor to evacuate, even temporarily. They are in service or low-wage jobs that do not give them the time to plan or leave, they do not have the extra money to stay in a hotel, or many times they don't have vehicles. Like the mental effects of gentrification, the economic stress of displacement, temporary or permanent, is acute and is added onto countless other daily stresses. There may be ambiguity as to whether people choose to live in environments that don't support physical activity, but no one chooses to live in a place that may be affected by flood or fire. While the predictive modeling of wildfires is less certain, the huge wildfires that struck Northern and Southern California in 2017 largely occurred at wildland and development interfaces, or what might be termed as exurban areas—neighborhoods that are lower in real estate value and therefore give a clue to socioeconomic status (fig. 57).

The most dramatic climate change effects go beyond suburban or urban communities. Many Indigenous communities, either pushed to the fringes of the urbanized landscape or located near the water since centuries before European settlement, will be the first to feel the effect of climate change. Isle de Jean Charles, Louisiana, home to the Biloxi-Chitimacha-Choctaw tribe, are the first case of climate refugees in the United States. The wetland and barrier island coastline of the state has significantly deteriorated and been overtaken by sea level rise in recent years, a crucial reason the damage from Hurricane Katrina was so devastating. The village on the southern tip of the state is largely populated by subsistence fishermen, but 90 percent of the island's landmass has disappeared, along with most of the population. The Department of Housing and Urban Development has $48 million to spend by 2022 to relocate the sixty or so people who remain there. Although this population number seems small, it's a bellwether for the future.[48] On the other side of the country, native Alaskans are experiencing a warming that is twice the rate of the rest of the country. The erosion of land, dying of the tundra, and coastal flooding will also have intractable effects on the economy and will

Fig. 57. Children in air masks escape the California Camp Fire. Climate change will be the largest threat to public health in our time and will disproportionately affect low-income communities of color (photograph by Gabrielle Lurie, 2018). (Gabrielle Lurie/San Francisco Chronicle/Polaris Images)

force them to move or to spend millions of dollars on infrastructure improvement, the effectiveness of which will be uncertain.[49]

In recent years the landscape architecture profession has changed its messaging to link landscape architecture to resilience. A blue-ribbon panel was assembled by the American Society of Landscape Architects in 2017. Their core principles advocate for incentive-based policies that build infrastructure that has multiple benefits, addresses environmental injustice and racial equity, and reflects community engagement, among other stipulations. The professional society has also advocated for green infrastructure and coastal resilience bills on the national level. The profession has, perhaps, been invigorated with a new urgency since the 2016 election, with the Trump administration seeking to dismantle federal environmental and health programs en masse. In a December 2016 editorial, Bradford McKee, then editor of *Landscape Architecture Magazine,* wrote:

There can scarcely be any overstating the threat the Trump presidency poses to the interests of the landscape architecture community, which center ardently on the welfare of human society and ecology and the planet. If design is the sum of all constraints, as Charles and Ray Eames said, this presidency will be the greatest constraint many of us will work under in our lifetimes, on the order of anathema to everything landscape architecture has ever stood for. We have to get right to work and be very canny about it, or the Trump administration, along with a Congress controlled by some of the most venal people ever to lodge themselves into American politics, will be a disaster well beyond the many ways we can name even now.[50]

The stance of the professional and academic community has stood in marked contrast to the recent inaction of the American Institute of Architects, whose national CEO offered President Trump architectural services for his "infrastructure plan," widely believed to end with a proposal for a border wall, and took weeks to write a statement opposing the EPA's deregulation of asbestos in buildings. The urban landscape, and landscape architects, will become central to thinking about solutions at the intersection of climate change and health.

The complexity and urgency of the issue will require large-scale thinking, collaborations, and an eco-social thinking that encompasses economics, environment, and demographics. The *Fourth National Climate Assessment* nods to this complexity, stating, "In addition, while climate-related risks such as heat waves, floods, and droughts have an important influence on these interdependent systems, these systems are also subject to a range of other factors, such as population growth, economic forces, technological change, and deteriorating infrastructure." For all the ways twentieth- and twenty-first-century science has advanced, it has largely been in silos. The decades-long myopia of design and planning is not isolated. The report goes on to say, "Although it is clear that climate-related and non-climate stressors impact multiple natural, built, and social systems simultaneously, thereby altering societal risks, the tools available for predicting these dynamics lag those that predict the dynamics of individual systems."[51] By all accounts, the lack of a "silver bullet" for health in the built environment, or the debate over causality versus correlation, is a straw man. It is time to do the difficult work of understanding how those of us who shape the urban landscape can encompass more diverse perspectives and models for collaborations and to advocate for the importance of our work while knowing the limits of our expertise.

What the urban landscape will look like in the face of climate change and worsening health crises is still unknown. What we do know is that we live in a landscape that has been largely shaped thus far by rapid scientific and technological advancement and hypercapitalism. Those advancements were successful in eradicating epidemics and temporarily controlling the environment. But each decade also saw a continuous fracturing of specialized fields, from planning to public health to medicine to sociology to ecology to architecture to landscape architecture, often borrowing from each other metaphorically, while neglecting to see recurring patterns of inequity and the damage wrought by positivist and technocratic ideology. Just as the devastation of cholera and other diseases of the Industrial Revolution indelibly shaped the cities and towns in which we live today, climate change, and how we do or do not confront it, will be the force that forms the landscape of the twenty-first century, even in the face of pandemic disease, present and future.

CONCLUSION

No Green Pill

One month after submitting the complete draft of this book, the first COVID-19 outbreaks were reported in New York City. As I write the final edits for this manuscript from Massachusetts, we're in our tenth month of lockdowns, the first glimmer of hope from a vaccine on the horizon. The evidence on the coronavirus is still very much emerging at this writing: its contagion, what kind of environments incubate it, why it barely affects some but kills others. The United States has not confronted an infectious pandemic since the 1918 Spanish Flu, and the response has so far been disastrous. Much of this blame can be placed on municipal and state authorities as well as the cruel negligence and outright denialism of the Trump administration. However, this is also a nation largely hostile to the idea of public health as a collective responsibility, and since the last pandemic, we have become complacent to the sacrifices, or even basic graces, that responsibility requires. The intersection of American individualism, disaster capitalism, and privatized healthcare that has now resulted in over 425,000 deaths is a incalculable tragedy, but hopefully one we will eventually learn from. We cannot overlook that the conditions for it have been laid for over a century, though. The pandemic simply ruptured structural faults that had thus far been held together by Band-Aids.

The past year has also been like watching the past 150 years of health narratives compressed into a few months, as COVID-19 somehow captures all the anxieties around disease spread discussed here. At first, the fear of germs led to us to sanitize groceries and quarantine mail. The contagiousness of the virus required immediate shifts in day-to-day behavior, with compliance or defiance becoming a marker of personal morals. Now that COVID's airborne transmission is known, the miasmic fears and responses of the late nineteenth century seem less out of date. As in the past, it will likely take at least a decade until we know the permanent marks COVID will leave on the urban landscape. Of course, it already has left marks in many ad hoc ways, from physical distancing stickers in grocery stores to plexiglass barriers to restaurants moving out onto the street, and the closure of offices and retail, a condition we still don't know will be permanent or not. In the world of architecture, the aesthetics of sterilization and quarantine have become a topic of interest once again. At the twenty-eighth Congress for New Urbanism conference, Andres Duany revealed plans for one of his latest projects, with homes emphasizing cross-ventilation but also featuring decontamination entry rooms with UV lights, washing machines, and sinks.[1] There was also immediate speculation on whether it was the city or the suburb that contributed to the most virulent spread. The first severe outbreaks in New York City and Boston saw elites immediately decamp for country homes or elsewhere. In April 2020, only a couple months after these outbreaks, the headline of an opinion article in the *Los Angeles Times* by Joel Kotkin declared, "Angelenos Love Suburban Sprawl: Coronavirus Proves Them Right."[2] Nine months later, Los Angeles's ICU capacity was at nearly zero, and restrictions on cremations meant to control air quality had to be lifted so that the city could address the backlog of bodies.[3] Rural regions, like my own home state of South Dakota, subsequently saw skyrocketing COVID rates, their already stretched and sparsely located healthcare resources struggling to keep up. Even so, the anti-urban undercurrent that drove much of the public's perception of healthy and unhealthy places through most of the twentieth century only needed the barest push to the forefront as the role of density entered the conversation once again. Like the vast generalizations of city and suburb, though, density and its relationship to COVID-19, and how we approach the concept, are virtually meaningless without more specifics. Emerging research seems to indicate that after controlling for population, density at the county level does not appear to be related to higher infection rates, and in fact more rural areas have higher mortality rates, likely due to the higher scarcity of health care. However, overcrowding, a living condition of many frontline workers, immigrants, and other communities of color who have been disproportionately killed by the coronavirus, is a factor largely invisible with available spatial data.

The inequitable environments and effects of COVID mortality also tell a familiar story. Two of the major co-morbidities of COVID-19 are obesity and pre-existing issues, primarily in Black and brown neighborhoods that already bore the environmental burden of decades of exclusion—air pollution, food deserts, heat islands, unsafe streets, and a paucity of green space. As we debate how homes will accommodate work and school from home or celebrate streets given over to dining, we must also remember that many are still without the basics of housing, fresh air, fresh water, and safe public spaces. A true landscape of wellness starts with these provisions available to all.

The specter of COVID-19 and future pandemics will likely define architecture and landscapes for decades forward, although perhaps as decades before, the possibility of the vaccine will halt the resurgence of interest in environmental factors. I hope not, if only because the patterns of "health-ful" landscapes of each era are so familiar by this point. A disease becomes a national preoccupation, emblematic of our particular point in time. A cause is identified, and planners and designers find ways to eliminate it through design. That design becomes a premium, excluding the same populations from the ostensible health benefits it offers, and instead they are blamed for their behavior or their "choice" to live in a neighborhood that is unhealthy. Even in the urban improvements ostensibly executed to cure those most vulnerable, there is a thin line between good intentions and paternalism. Just as design can no longer be extricated from its social and political contexts and effects, we as a country must come to accept that public health is also not a series of metrics, a dichotomy between "sick" and "well." In the excellent book *Against Health: How Health Became the New Morality,* Jonathan M. Metzl writes: "'Health' is a term replete with value judgments, hierarchies, and blind assumptions that speak as much about power and privilege as they do about well-being. Health is a desired state, but it is also a prescribed state and an ideological position. . . . Appealing to health allows for a set of moral assumptions that are allowed to fly stealthily under the radar."[4]

However, in many arenas, altering the built environment for health has also yielded successes and innovations, if not without collateral damage. The sanitary movement and eradication of cholera and yellow fever from American cities was a public health triumph. Frederick Law Olmsted's parks, envisioned as green tonics for the urban landscape, have largely been preserved and are both well loved and well used, and his ideas have become even more important as outdoor spaces that provide for mental respite and physical rejuvenation are at a premium in the pandemic. The work being done to retrofit suburban neighborhoods for walking and transit is key for more resilient futures. Finding lasting interventions for a post-pandemic, climate-changed landscape will require the political will to ingrain wellness in our public infrastructure rather than frame it as an individual pursuit.

The complicated history of our urban landscape and our health also mirrors the histories of the public health and design professions themselves. Both fields have become increasingly legitimized by large bodies of empirical evidence but are indelibly shaped by the messy and often non-empirical realities of human behavior. Some view the field of design as an alchemy, some view it as mathematic, but those in the day-to-day work know it is really based on best practices, lived experience, and ethics rather than exact science. Despite the efforts over the years to "scientize" the profession, human behavior and the relationship of our bodies to our environment are too complex to pin down causality. This should not deter us from the work of trying to make healthier environments—but the scope must widen to larger systems of populations, socioeconomics, and ecology. This is essentially the same shift that public health has made in recent years. A 2016 editorial in the *American Journal of Public Health* declared that it was time for "Public Health 3.0." Public Health 1.0 was defined in the Industrial Revolution, with the establishment and advancement of epidemiological science, the development of preventive and treatment strategies such as vaccines and antibiotics. Public Health 2.0 was a rearticulation of the field and its essential services in the wake of chronic disease. Public Health 3.0, write the authors, "emphasizes cross-sector collaboration and environmental, policy, and systems-level actions that directly affect the social determinants of health."[5] The health profession has scaled up and scaled out in terms of involvement and theoretical frameworks.

In the 1920s and 1930s, the dissemination and practice of germ theory necessitated a dramatic shift in the way medicine was practiced. Accordingly, design has always tried to find ways to lend scientific credulity to the profession, with mixed results. The profession of landscape architecture has expanded by leaps and bounds in recent decades, empowered by the interest in urban areas and how to combat the effects of climate change. It is, however, under the same pressure to quantify and empirically prove its worth and investment, often termed as "landscape performance." Quantifying the potential health benefits via the built environment has been a panacea in the Smart Cities movement justifying these interests. But it's been hard to prove, perhaps because it misses the larger web of environmental and societal interaction. The robustness of the ecosystem is not simply the sum total of carbon offsets each tree can yield, just as achieving public health goes beyond ensuring each person walks ten thousand steps a day (as important as this is). Attempts to view the landscape and our own health as a numerical exchange can yield significant blind spots. The early twentieth-century medical geographies, which tied place to health through narrative descriptions of the landscape, were not explicitly ecological but did hint at a larger truth about how humans embodied their environment. Public health historian Charles Rosenberg, discussing the method, wrote: "This style of explanation turned on a central irony: everything necessary to life was at the same time an occasion of vulnerability—wind, climate, water, food. Geography was in this sense destiny, providing indispensable components of existence."[6] Present-day medical geographers have called for the integration of societal frameworks into the study of place and health; unfortunately, the field remains largely an academic one, siloed from practice.[7] A recent study from a group of University of California researchers demonstrated we must reckon with how our social practice has long-lasting physiological effects. By overlaying mortgage companies' redlining maps with health data, they not only found that these neighborhoods were still largely occupied by people of color and immigrants, but that there remained a plethora of environmental hazards from air pollution to high lead content in soil—resulting in, among other disparities in health, an asthma rate three times higher in the Black population than the white.[8] It is sobering to think of the implications of this, and how little has changed in the 120 years since W. E. B. Du Bois wrote: "The most difficult social problem in the matter of Negro health is the peculiar attitude of the nation toward the well-being of the race. There have . . . been few other cases in the history of civilized peoples where human suffering has been viewed with such peculiar indifference. . . . There is a disposition among many to conclude that the rate is abnormal and unprecedented and that, since the race is doomed to early extinction, there is little left to do but moralize on inferior species."[9] The United States has a dark history of conscribing minorities and immigrants to landscapes of risk—legislatively, socially, and economically—only to blame them for their bad choices and failure to thrive.

The design field and often designers themselves think of themselves as neutral actors, uncoupled from politics. This is deeply problematic, as we have been compliant in a system that exacerbates social inequity. Countless studies continue to assert that those living near parks are healthier, better educated, and wealthier, without mentioning the socioeconomic status of neighborhoods or the green gentrification effect. Our American urban landscape and the growing segregation between rich and poor, healthy and unhealthy, are only symptomatic of larger histories of policies, power, and attitudes, but amplify and calcify them in built form. The question is not one of environmental determinism, but rather at what point is one conscribed to environmental inevitability. In almost two hundred years of American urban history, the nature of disease has changed. The seeds of modern-day chronic disease are cast at birth, spreading or diminishing based on where we live, go to school, and work. The widening chasms between these places have unfortunately only continued to grow.

Therein lies the dilemma. Health in development and design is often conceptualized as an amenity rather than an ethic; even Frederick Law Olmsted himself garnered support for his public parks by telling stakeholders that they would offer increased property values alongside their social benefits. This is at irrevocable odds with most other nations, which view it more as a measure of equity or basic right of citizens. We know undeniably that many landscape improvements lead to higher real estate values. The long-term health savings of healthy housing, walkable neighborhoods, and food availability is yet to be definitively calculated and will be illuminating, but thinking of urban landscape and wellness in terms of return on investment greatly simplifies or even obscures the complexity of the relationship. The efforts of forward-thinking healthcare conglomerates such as Kaiser Permanente to build housing and invest in parks shows that the idea has some basis in evidence, but in the long term it will likely take a larger national value shift in how we prioritize our health and the health of others.

And for all these advancements in specifying effects, what kinds of landscapes are considered "healthy" has remained relatively narrow, perhaps because its dominant narratives are so overwhelmingly Eurocentric. Witold Rybczynski chronicled how Steve Jobs reached out to landscape architect Laurie Olin to design the grounds of the new Apple headquarters in Cupertino. Jobs went seeking "the next Olmsted," and when Olin asked what he didn't want in the landscape, Jobs replied "nothing modern," despite the decidedly technologically sleek aesthetic of the campus. The unwritten narrative is that Jobs also likely knew he was gravely ill at the time, and Olin would later say that "health" for the workers was a primary value of the eventual design.[10] We have always sought a sense of healing in nature, but we can only envision its power in opposition to urbanity and through a narrow lens of aesthetics, even if that aesthetic is only achieved through massive feats of engineering. The pastoral predominates, with a romanticized view of our agricultural past, but to be held at a distance. Even one of our foremost American design futurists couldn't envision it otherwise. Although public landscape's necessity to our health is one of the few consistent narratives throughout medical, environmental, and landscape history, the scale and the myriad forms its design can take are less explored.[11] Nature has served as a metaphor for urban development and our bodies throughout history, and the theorists who have suggested that the health of our bodies is truly tied to the health of our ecosystem—Walter Cannon, Aldo Leopold, Roselyn Lindheim, to name a few—have traditionally been outliers. Of course, they are only outliers in the context of Western thought. Indigenous science, such as in Native American and Hawaiian cultures, has long espoused finding the balance between nature, spirituality, and ourselves, but this is at odds with the Western view of planning. Annette Koh and Konia Frietas, in a call to "decolonize" planning, noted: "A decolonial spatial imaginary would reject exclusion as the organizing principle. Decolonizing planning is essential for spatial justice—for public spaces open to all and housing accessible to the poorest."[12] In another commentary, Koh wrote that a decolonial framework "would make stewardship rather than ownership the most valuable relationship to land. It would foreground use rights and livelihoods, rather than enforce trespassing laws."[13] The Native Hawaiian concept of *pono* is often simply translated as "righteousness," but more colloquially it encompasses a sense of responsibility to the *ʻāina,* or land, which in turn indicates the well-being of those who live on it. Journalist and Native American activist Julian Brave Noisecat wrote: "Amid intersecting ecological, economic, political, and cultural catastrophes, Indigenous alternatives look increasingly appealing. Against the ecological crisis, the Indigenous suggest we understand land, water, and all living things not as resources, but as relatives."[14] In Indigenous science, the value of land and health transcends capital.

For all their differences in epistemology, the fields of both public health and design are also asked to be prognosticators. This has, historically, been a bad fit in a culture and government that tend to be reactionary to health crises. Americans have constantly sought a quick fix on health, preferably one that can be purchased. This goes against the prevailing view in medicine that most successful health interventions are preventive, that is, dependent on long-range planning. The Obama administration's Affordable Care Act embraced this strategy, opening health funding for more community partnerships, including those concerned with built environment improvements. In a wave of many Republican efforts to kill the ACA after Obama's term, Congress let the Preventive Health Fund expire, with one member dismissing it as "a slush fund for playgrounds." For all the interest that surrounded the role of the built environment in health outcomes in the early twenty-first century, the CDC has now ceased funding for the Healthy Community Design Initiative. In 2018, it also closed its Climate and Health program and attempted to dismiss its unit head before reassigning him to research on waterborne diseases. The Department of Interior and the Environmental Protection Agency have similarly been gutted; one program of note, the EPA's Environmental Justice program, which specifically looks at the vulnerability of minority and immigrant communities, has repeatedly been on the chopping block. There is still a need for advocacy on the importance of urban landscape and environment to health, but given the cyclical nature of interest, different strategies are needed. What's most troubling about our current era is that while support for holistic and social public health strategies waned in the early 1920s and 1930s due to the actual eradication of disease and vaccines, we have not eradicated the chronic physiological and mental illnesses that disproportionately affect the poor and communities of color—they have just been rendered more invisible.

Research on health and the built environment has expanded at an incredible rate over the past fifteen years. Most studies confirm what we seem to know intrinsically—exposure to and interaction with the landscape is good for our minds and our bodies. Now how do we make it actionable? How do we move forward on more complex questions, such as how to prioritize more vulnerable populations that have already been conscribed to the least healthy environments? What are the barriers to collaboration across not just the public health and design fields, but between researchers, policy makers, and communities? What are the limits to making changes to neighborhoods, in way that is not traumatizing or displaces the people who already live within it? Whose health values are we espousing and prioritizing? "Just green enough" may be an ethical approach, but is "just well enough"? Isn't everybody entitled to a home, a neighborhood, and a landscape that are healthy? These questions ultimately won't be answered by traditional empirical inquiry; rather, they require qualitative studies, reimagined narratives, and long-term monitoring in tandem with those studies. And once we ask these questions, we will have to walk the line between offering opportunity for health while mitigating risks. The true healthy landscape is one of negotiation, equity, and resilience, built from the ground up. Nor is landscape a metaphorical green pill, measured, packaged, and ready to be dosed at will. The effects of the landscape, both curative and harmful, are accrued over time and place until eventually it becomes embedded in our skin and bones.

NOTES

Introduction

1. Karen B. Desalvo et al., "Public Health 3.0: Time for an Upgrade," *American Journal of Public Health* 106, no. 4 (2016), https://doi.org/10.2105/AJPH.2016.303063.
2. Dan Buettner, *The Blue Zones: 9 Lessons for Living Longer from the People Who've Lived the Longest,* 2nd ed. (Washington, DC: National Geographic, 2012).
3. Preamble to the Constitution of the World Health Organization as adopted by the International Health Conference, New York, June 19–22, 1946, put into action April 1948.
4. Elizabeth Fee and Theodore M. Brown, "The Unfulfilled Promise of Public Health: Déjà Vu All Over Again," *Health Affairs* 21, no. 6 (2002), https://doi.org/10.1377/hlth aff.21.6.31.
5. In his book *The Urban Wilderness: A History of the American City,* Sam Bass Warner Jr. writes: "From this experience I have made the discovery that Americans have no urban history. They live in one of the world's most urbanized countries as if it were a wilderness in both time and space. Beyond some civic and ethnic myths and a few family and neighborhood memories, Americans are not conscious that they have a past and that by their actions they participate in making their future. As they tackle today's problems, either with good will or anger, they have no sense of where cities came from, how they grew, or even what direction the large forces of history are taking them. Whether one speaks to an official in Washington or to a neighborhood action group, the same blindness prevails. Without a sense of history, they hammer against today's crises without any means to choose their targets to fit the trends which they must confront, work with, or avoid." Samuel Bass Warner, *The Urban Wilderness: A History of the American City* (New York: Harper and Row, 1972), 4.
6. Dolores Hayden, *The Power of Place: Urban Landscapes as Public History* (Cambridge, MA: MIT Press, 1995).
7. Ibid.
8. Elizabeth Barlow Rogers, *Landscape Design: A Cultural and Architectural History* (New York, NY: Harry N. Abrams, 2001).
9. John Brinckerhoff Jackson, "The Word Itself," in *Landscape in Sight: Looking at America* (New Haven, CT: Yale University Press, 2000), 305.
10. Henri Lefebvre, *The Production of Space* (Oxford, UK Blackwell, 1991).
11. Susan Sontag, *Illness as Metaphor* (New York: Farrar, Straus and Giroux, 1978), 6.

12. Rachel Dodge, Annette Daly, Jan Huyton, and Lalage Sanders. "The Challenge of Defining Wellbeing." *International Journal of Wellbeing* 2, no. 3 (2012): 222–35.

13. Charles B. Corbin and Robert P. Pangrazi. "Toward a Uniform Definition of Wellness: A Commentary." *President's Council on Physical Fitness and Sports Research Digest,* series 3, no. 15 (2001): 1–10.

14. James William Miller, "A Historical Approach to Defining Wellness," *Spektrum Freizeit* 27 (2005): 84–106. It is also worth a significant note that Kellogg was an avowed eugenicist and a founder of the Race Betterment Foundation, which advocated for hygiene as a way to strengthen the race and was against interracial marriage due to the supposed lesser health of minorities. However, he also believed that a hygienic and healthy environment could overcome these lesser hereditary traits. For more on this topic see Brian Wilson's "Dr. Kellogg and Race Betterment," in *Dr. John Harvey Kellogg and the Religion of Biologic Living* (Bloomington: Indiana University Press, 2014), 133–70.

15. Carol-Ann Farkas, "'Tons of Useful Stuff': Defining Wellness in Popular Magazines," *Studies in Popular Culture 33,* no. 1 (2010): 113–32.

16. Lewis Mumford, *The Myth of the Machine* (New York: Harcourt, Brace & World, 1967), 16–17

1. Waste and Super-Infrastructure in the Urban Landscape

1. Jason Corburn, "Reconnecting with Our Roots: American Urban Planning and Public Health in the Twenty-First Century," *Urban Affairs Review* 42, no. 5 (2007), https://doi.org/10.1177/1078087406296390.

2. George E. Waring Jr., "The Cleaning of a Great City," *McClure's Magazine* ix., no. 5 (1897).

3. Ibid.; Steven Johnson, *The Ghost Map: The Story of London's Most Terrifying Epidemic—and How It Changed Science, Cities, and the Modern World* (New York: Riverhead Books, 2006), and Kari S. McLeod, "Our Sense of Snow: The Myth of John Snow in Medical Geography," *Social Science & Medicine* 50, no. 7–8 (2000): 923–935. McLeod in particular takes a critical examination of how Snow's work has been utilized in medical geography, public health, and planning as heroic narrative in spite of archival evidence revealing a more complex story.

4. Mervyn Susser and Zena Stein, *Eras in Epidemiology: The Evolution of Ideas* (Oxford: Oxford University Press, 2009).

5. Citizens' Association of New York, Council of Hygiene and Public Health, *Report of the Council of Hygiene and Public Health of the Citizens' Association of New York upon the Sanitary Condition of the City* (New York: D. Appleton, 1865).

6. R. Hewitt and B. Szczygiel, "Nineteenth-Century Medical Landscapes: John H. Rauch, Frederick Law Olmsted, and the Search for Salubrity," *Bulletin of the History of Medicine* 74, no. 4 (2000), 719.

7. Citizens' Association of New York, *Report of the Council,* 196.

8. Ibid., ciii.

9. Hippocrates, *Airs, Waters, Places,* Part 7. In more detail, he describes: "Such waters then as are marshy, stagnant, and belong to lakes, are necessarily hot in summer, thick, and have a strong smell, since they have no current; but being constantly supplied by rain-water, and the sun heating them, they necessarily want their proper color, are unwholesome and form bile; in winter, they become congealed, cold, and

muddy with the snow and ice, so that they are most apt to engender phlegm, and bring on hoarseness."

10. Citizens' Association of New York, *Report of the Council,* xv.
11. Tom Koch, *Disease Maps: Epidemics on the Ground* (Chicago: University of Chicago Press, 2011), 205.
12. Committee on the Expediency of Providing Better Tenements for the Poor, *Report of the Committee on the Expediency of Providing Better Tenements for the Poor* (Boston: American Periodicals Series 2, 1847).
13. Felix Driver, "Moral Geographies: Social Science and the Urban Environment in Mid-Nineteenth Century England," *Transactions of the Institute of British Geographers* 13, no. 3 (1988): 275–87.
14. Ibid.
15. Ibid.
16. Committee on the Expediency of Providing Better Tenements, *Report of the Committee,* 11.
17. Corburn, "Reconnecting with Our Roots."
18. Committee on the Expediency of Providing Better Tenements, *Report of the Committee.*
19. W. E. B. Du Bois, *The Philadelphia Negro: A Social Study* (Philadelphia: University of Pennsylvania, 1899), 297.
20. Committee on the Expediency of Providing Better Tenements, *Report of the Committee,* 11.
21. Edmund A. Parkes, *A Manual of Practical Hygiene: Prepared Especially for Use in the Medical Service of the Army* (London: J. Churchill & Sons, 1869); Citizens' Association of New York, *Report of the Council,* xvii.
22. Susser and Stein, *Eras in Epidemiology.*
23. Thaddeus E. Weckowicz and Helen P. Liebel-Weckowicz, eds., "The Scientific Revolution and the Beginnings of Modern Philosophy," *Advances in Psychology* 66, no. C (1990): 61–70, https://doi.org/10.1016/S0166-4115(08)61443-0.
24. Christopher Hamlin, "Predisposing Causes and Public Health in Early Nineteenth-Century Medical Thought," *Social History of Medicine* 5, no. 1 (1992), https://doi.org/10.1093/shm/5.1.43.
25. Susser and Stein, *Eras in Epidemiology.*
26. Alfredo Morabia, "Epidemiologic Interactions, Complexity, and the Lonesome Death of Max Von Pettenkofer," *American Journal of Epidemiology* 166, no. 11 (2007): 1233–38; and Alfredo Morabia, "Morabia Responds to 'The Context and Challenge of Von Pettenkofer's Contributions to Epidemiology,'" *American Journal of Epidemiology* 166, no. 11 (2007): 1242–43.
27. Hamlin, "Predisposing Causes and Public Health," 43–70.
28. Citizens' Association of New York, *Report of the Council.*
29. Ibid., 253.
30. Carl S. Smith, *City Water, City Life: Water and the Infrastructure of Ideas in Urbanizing Philadelphia, Boston, and Chicago* (Chicago: University of Chicago Press, 2013).
31. Hamlin, "Predisposing Causes and Public Health."
32. Susser and Stein, *Eras in Epidemiology.*
33. Driver, "Moral Geographies."
34. Hamlin, "Predisposing Causes and Public Health."

35. Benjamin Ward Richardson, *Hygeia: A City of Health* (London: Macmillan, 1876).

36. Martin V. Melosi, *The Sanitary City: Environmental Services in Urban America from Colonial Times to the Present* (Pittsburgh: University of Pittsburgh Press, 2008).

37. George E. Waring, *The Sanitary Drainage of Houses and Towns* (New York: Hurd and Houghton; Cambridge, Riverside Press, 1876), 10.

38. Waring, "Cleaning of a Great City."

39. Catherine Seavett Nordenson, "The Miasmist: George E Waring, Jr and the Evolution of Modern Public Health," *Landscape Research Record*, no. 5, 122. Nordenson also notes the irony of Waring dying of yellow fever, his body sealed in a casket and quarantined on Swinburne Island in contagionist practice.

40. Richard Sennett, *Flesh and Stone: The Body and the City in Western Civilization* (New York: W.W. Norton, 1994), 255–70.

41. Stanley K. Schultz and Clay McShane, "To Engineer the Metropolis: Sewers, Sanitation, and City Planning in Late-Nineteenth-Century America," *Journal of American History* 65, no. 2 (1978).

42. Corburn, "Reconnecting with Our Roots"; Melosi, *Sanitary City*.

43. Jon A. Peterson, "The Impact of Sanitary Reform upon American Urban Planning, 1840–1890," *Journal of Social History* 13, no. 1 (1979), 87.

44. Stuart Galishoff, "Drainage, Disease, Comfort, and Class: A History of Newark's Sewers," *Societas: A Review of Social History* 6, no. 2 (1976).

45. Peterson, "Impact of Sanitary Reform," 88.

46. Schultz and McShane, "To Engineer the Metropolis."

47. Ibid.

48. Waring, *Sanitary Drainage of Houses and Towns*, 15.

49. Schultz and McShane, "To Engineer the Metropolis."

50. Via Kathryn Staley, "Ameliorating Poverty," *Godey's Magazine* 133, no. 797 (1896). Gould went on to show a preoccupation with density: "Today the third commission finds that the crowding has grown beyond all precedent. In the East Side districts there is actually a greater density of population than exists in any other city in the world—in plain figures an average of 143.2 souls live there to the acre. The average for Paris is 125.2; for Berlin it is 113.6. In one ward in New York (the Tenth) the average reaches 626.26 per acre. In this sanitary district—and just why it may be classified as sanitary is not apparent—there are 986.4 persons to every one of thirty-two acres! There the conditions of health, comfort, and ordinary decency are reduced to the minimum. Fancy ninety-three per cent, of the whole ground area covered with brick and mortar; seven per cent, for fresh air, sunshine, and playground."

51. Sari Altschuler, *The Medical Imagination: Literature and Health in the Early United States* (Philadelphia: University of Pennsylvania Press, 2018).

2. Work and Play

1. An editorial in the *Chicago Tribune* dated March 12, 1862, and entitled "Abominable Water" described "Dead fish, newts, and various specimens of watery animalculae known to the books, are brought through the pipes in large numbers. Minnows large enough to bait a codfish hook, a few as much as four inches in length—some

alive and wriggling, others with backs broken, and others still dead and in the process of decomposition, are voided by the supply pipes" (4).

2. Ibid.; Anne Whiston Spirn, *The Granite Garden: Urban Nature and Human Design* (New York: Basic Books, 1984).

3. William Cronon, *Uncommon Ground: Rethinking the Human Place in Nature* (New York: W. W. Norton & Co., 1996); Leo Marx, "The Idea of Nature in America," *Daedalus* 137, no. 2 (2008), https://doi.org/10.1162/daed.2008.137.2.8.

4. Cronon, *Uncommon Ground,* 15.

5. Ralph Waldo Emerson. *Nature: Addresses, and Lectures* (Boston: Houghton, Mifflin, 1883).

6. J. B. Jackson, "Jefferson, Thoreau, and After," in *Landscape in Sight,* 176–77.

7. Ibid., 181. This is not to say Thoreau's views didn't also convey a sense of utopian sensibilities and control, says Jackson: "Our two utopias, the agrarian and the romantic, died because there were no longer Utopian men to inhabit them. What justified the grid and kept it valid for almost a century was the firm belief among Americans that it was possible to produce an ideal known as the Virtuous Citizen; what justified the elaborate landscaping of the romantics was the no less firmly held belief that it was possible to produce an ideal known as Man the Inhabitant of the Earth. Thoreau and Jefferson were poles apart in their definitions of human nature, but they agreed completely as to the possibility of defining it; and, having once defined it, of creating a suitable environment for it."

8. Roderick Nash, *Wilderness and the American Mind* (New Haven: Yale University Press, 2001); Joseph Knowles, *Alone in the Wilderness* (Boston: Small, Maynard, 1913).

9. Wilhelm Winternitz, "Hydrotherapeutics," in H. von Ziemssen, *Handbook of General Therapeutics in Seven Vols.,* vol. 5 (London: Smith, Elder, 1886), 273–606, 348. For more background on the medicinal utilization of the "water cure," see Jane M. Adams, "The Theory and Practice of the Water Cure," in *Healing with Water: English Spas and the Water Cure, 1840–1960* (Manchester: Manchester University Press, 2015), 23–58.

10. Gregg Mitman, "Hay Fever Holiday: Health, Leisure, and Place in Gilded-Age America," *Bulletin of the History of Medicine* 77, no. 3 (2003), https://doi.org/10.1353/bhm.2003.0127.

11. J. M. Adams, *Healing with Water.*

12. James M'Cabe, *Directions for Drinking the Cheltenham Waters* (Cheltenham: G. A. Williams, 1823), 17, qtd. in J. M. Adams, *Healing with Water,* 36.

13. "To Opium-Eaters, Arsenic-Takers, Etc." *Ballou's Dollar Monthly Magazine* 15, no. 1 (1862): 94.

14. J. M. Adams, *Healing with Water.*

15. Marshall Scott Legan. "Hydropathy in America: A Nineteenth Century Panacea." *Bulletin of the History of Medicine* 45, no. 3 (1971): 267–80.

16. Gregg Mitman and Ronald Numbers, "From Miasma to Asthma: The Changing Fortunes of Medical Geography in America," *History & Philosophy of the Life Sciences* 25, no. 3 (2003), 404.

17. "Round Hill Water Cure Establishment," *Boston Recorder* 32, no. 27 (1847): 106.

18. Joseph William Stickler, *The Adirondacks as a Health Resort: Showing the Benefit to Be Derived by a Sojourn in the Wilderness, in Cases of Pulmonary Phthisis, Acute*

and Chronic Bronchitis, Asthma, "Hay-Fever" and Various Nervous Affections (New York: G. P. Putnam's sons, 1886).

19. Conevery Bolton Valenčius, *The Health of the Country: How American Settlers Understood Themselves and Their Land* (New York: Basic Books, 2002).

20. Katherine M. Hunter, Bernard E. Hunter, and John Chumasero, "Some Notes on Berkeley Springs, West Virginia," *William and Mary Quarterly* 16, no. 3 (1936): 347–51.

21. "Round Hill Water Cure Institute," *Ballou's Pictorial Drawing—Room Companion* 9, no. 8 (1855): 120.

22. Mitman and Numbers, "From Miasma to Asthma: The Changing Fortunes of Medical Geography in America."

23. Carla C. Keirns, "Allergic Landscapes, Built Environments, and Human Health," in *Imperfect Health: The Medicalization of Architecture,* ed. Giovanna Borasi and Mirko Zardini (Montréal: Canadian Centre for Architecture; Zurich: Lars Müller, 2012).

24. Hewitt and Szczygiel, "Nineteenth-Century Medical Landscapes: John H. Rauch, Frederick Law Olmsted, and the Search for Salubrity."

25. F. R. Campbell, "The Relation of Meteorology to Disease," *Buffalo Medical and Surgical Journal* 26, no. 5 (December 1885).

26. City of Philadelphia, Public Playgrounds Commission, *Playgrounds for Philadelphia: Report of the Public Playgrounds Commission* (Philadelphia: Printed by the Commission, 1910).

27. Henry S. Curtis, *The Play Movement and Its Significance* (New York: Macmillan, 1917), 4.

28. G. Stanley Hall, "Recreation and Reversion," *Pedagogical Seminary* 22, no. 4 (1915): 510–20, https://doi.org/10.1080/08919402.1915.10533981.

29. Jacob A. Riis, "The Value of Playgrounds to the Community," *Public Health Journal* 4, no. 5 (1913).

30. Dominick Cavallo, *Muscles and Morals: Organized Playgrounds and Urban Reform, 1880–1920* (Philadelphia: University of Pennsylvania Press, 1981), 32.

31. Benjamin McArthur, "The Chicago Playground Movement: A Neglected Feature of Social Justice," *Social Service Review* 49, no. 3 (1975).

32. Jacob Riis, "Parks for the Poor," *Christian Union* (1870–1893) 44, no. 6 (1891).

33. Philadelphia, *Playgrounds for Philadelphia.*

34. Ibid.

35. Ibid.

36. Curtis, *Play Movement and Its Significance,* 23.

37. Riis, "Value of Playgrounds."

38. Curtis, *Play Movement and Its Significance,* 16.

39. Philadelphia, *Playgrounds for Philadelphia.*

40. Suzanne M. Spencer-Wood, "Turn of the Century Women's Organizations, Urban Design, and the Origin of the American Playground Movement," *Landscape Journal* 13, no. 2 (1994).

41. Curtis, *Play Movement and Its Significance,* 121.

42. Ibid., 119.

43. Philadelphia, *Playgrounds for Philadelphia.*

44. John Collins Warren, *Physical Education and the Preservation of Health* (Boston: William D. Ticknor, 1846), 5.

45. Joe L. Frost, *A History of Children's Play and Play Environments: Toward a Contemporary Child-Saving Movement* (New York: Routledge, 2012); see also Alexandra Lange, *The Design of Childhood* (London: Bloomsbury, 2018), chapter 4 on the progression from sand gardens to playgrounds.

46. Ibid.; Clarence Elmer Rainwater, *The Play Movement in the United States: A Study of Community Recreation* (Chicago: University of Chicago Press, 1922).

47. Benjamin McArthur, "The Chicago Playground Movement: A Neglected Feature of Social Justice," *Social Service Review* 49, no. 3 (1975).

48. Curtis, *Play Movement and Its Significance,* 101.

49. Ibid.

50. Ibid., 117.

51. Ibid.

52. Ocean Howell, "Play Pays: Urban Land Politics and Playgrounds in the United States, 1900–1930," *Journal of Urban History* 34, no. 6 (2008), https://doi.org/10.1177/0096144208319648.

53. Cavallo, *Muscles and Morals.*

54. Jane Addams, *The Spirit of Youth and the City Streets* (New York: Macmillan, 1909), 14.

55. Curtis, *Play Movement and Its Significance,* 101, 31–32.

56. Cavallo, *Muscles and Morals;* Howell, "Play Pays."

57. Chicago, Special Park Commission, *A Plea for Playgrounds: Issued by the Special Park Commission* (Chicago: W. J. Hartman, 1905), 13.

58. McArthur, "Chicago Playground Movement."

59. Howell, "Play Pays; Spencer-Wood, "Turn of the Century."

60. Spencer-Wood, "Turn of the Century."

61. Garrett Power, "Apartheid Baltimore Style: The Residential Segregation Ordinances of 1910–1913," *Maryland Law Review* 42, no. 2 (1983): 289–328.

62. Frost, *History of Children's Play,* 99.

3. Purified Air in the Progressive Era

1. Frederick Winslow Taylor, *The Principles of Scientific Management* (New York: Harper & Brothers, 1913), 11.

2. Walter Dwight Moody, *What of the City? America's Greatest Issue—City Planning, What It Is and How to Go about It to Achieve Success* (Chicago: McClurg, 1919), 21.

3. Ibid., viii.

4. Ibid., 72.

5. Henry Morgenthau, qtd. in Peter Geoffrey Hall, *Cities of Tomorrow: An Intellectual History of Urban Planning and Design in the Twentieth Century* (Oxford: Blackwell, 1996).

6. Thomas Bender, "The 'Rural' Cemetery Movement: Urban Travail and the Appeal of Nature," in *The Physical City: Public Space and the Infrastructure,,* ed. Neil Larry Shumsky, 2–17 (New York: Routledge, 1996); David Schuyler, *The New Urban Landscape: The Redefinition of City Form in Nineteenth-Century America* (Baltimore: Johns Hopkins University Press, 1986).

7. Schuyler, *New Urban Landscape.*

8. Wilson Flagg, *Mount Auburn: Its Scenes, Its Beauties, and Its Lessons* (Boston: J. Munroe, 1861), 86.

9. Schuyler, *New Urban Landscape,* 54–55.

10. William Cullen Bryant, *Letters of a Traveller; or, Notes of Things Seen in Europe and America* (London, 1850).

11. Bryant, *Letters of a Traveller.*

12. Hans Huth, *Nature and the American: Three Centuries of Changing Attitudes* (Berkeley: University of California Press, 1972).

13. Andrew Jackson Downing, *Rural Essays* (New York, 1853), 138.

14. Ibid.

15. Ibid., 147.

16. Andrew Jackson Downing, *Landscape Gardening,* ed. Frank Albert Waugh (New York: John Wiley & Sons, 1921).

17. Ibid., 148.

18. Catharine Ward Thompson, "Linking Landscape and Health: The Recurring Theme," *Landscape and Urban Planning* 99, no. 3 (2011), https://doi.org/10.1016 /j.landurbplan.2010.10.006. Also see Karen R. Jones, "'The Lungs of the City': Green Space, Public Health and Bodily Metaphor in the Landscape of Urban Park History," *Environment and History* 24, no. 1 (2018): 39–58, for a thorough deconstruction and of the phrase and thought in a European historical context.

19. James Jackson Jarves, qtd. in Huth, *Nature and the American.*

20. John H. Rauch, *Internments in Populous Cities and Their Influence Upon Health and Epidemics* (Chicago: Tribune Company, 1866), 28.

21. John H. Rauch, *Public Parks: Their Effects upon the Moral, Physical and Sanitary Condition of the Inhabitants of Large Cities, with Special Reference to the City of Chicago* (Chicago: S.C. Griggs, 1869), 44.

22. Ibid., 80–88.

23. Ibid.

24. Downing, *Landscape Gardening,* 151.

25. Ibid., 142.

26. Ibid., 346.

27. Thomas Fisher, "Frederick Law Olmsted and the Campaign for Public Health," *Places Journal,* November 2010, http://places.designobserver.com/feature /frederick-law-olmsted-and-the-campaign-for-public-health/15619/.

28. Peterson, "Impact of Sanitary Reform."

29. Citizens Association of New York, *Report of the Council,* 28.

30. Ibid., 213.

31. Peterson, "Impact of Sanitary Reform."

32. Geoffrey Blodgett, "Frederick Law Olmsted: Landscape Architecture as Conservative Reform," *Journal of American History* 62, no. 4 (1976), 873, https://doi.org/10 .2307/1903842.

33. Frederick Law Olmsted, *The Spoils of The Park: With a Few Leaves from the Deep-Laden Note-Books of "A Wholly Unpractical Man"* (Detroit, 1882); Lisa W. Foderaro, "The Parks That Made the Man Who Made Central Park," *New York Times,* October 30, 2019 Among other disagreements, the board of commissioners took issue with Olmsted's spending, and Olmsted was unhappy with the board interfering in the workforce he had carefully built and managed, among various other political machinations and controls Olmsted saw as antithetical to the democratic principles he sought to convey through design. The relationship between Olmsted and the board of commissioners deteriorated to the point where the board actually paid

for Olmsted to take a leave, during which he traveled to England to take a tour of the parks there.

34. Peterson, "Impact of Sanitary Reform," 197.
35. Blodgett, "Frederick Law Olmsted," 87.
36. Frederick Law Olmsted, *Civilizing American Cities: A Selection of Frederick Law Olmsted's Writings on City Landscapes* (Cambridge, MA: MIT Press, 1971).
37. Ibid.
38. Peterson, "Impact of Sanitary Reform."
39. Anne Whiston Spirn, "Constructing Nature: The Legacy of Frederick Law Olmsted," in *Uncommon Ground: Rethinking the Human Place in Nature,* ed. William Cronon (New York: W. W. Norton, 1996), 110.
40. Frederick Law Olmsted, "Public Parks and the Enlargement of Towns," *Journal of Social Science, Containing the Proceedings of the American Association (1869–1909)* 3 (1871): 32–33.
41. Hewitt and Szczygiel, "Nineteenth-Century Medical Landscapes," 73.
42. Allan S Galper, "Building Boston's Back Bay: Marriage of Money and Hygiene," *Historical Journal of Massachusetts* 23, no. 1 (1995); "Conditions That Menace Public Health," *Boston Globe,* June, 5, 1905, main ed.
43. "A Gigantic Cesspool," *Boston Globe* April 8, 1884, main ed.
44. Schuyler, *New Urban Landscape.*
45. Boston, City of, Department of Parks, *Notes on the Plan of Franklin Park and Related Matters* (Boston: Printed for the Department, 1886).
46. Olmsted, "Public Parks," 47–48.
47. Olmsted, *Spoils of the Park,* 36.
48. Schuyler, *New Urban Landscape,* 94.
49. Jones, "'Lungs of the City.'"
50. Frederick Law Olmsted, *A Consideration of the Justifying Value of a Public Park* (Boston: Tolman & White, 1881), 14.
51. Olmsted, "Public Parks," 44; also see Blodgett, "Frederick Law Olmsted," 75.
52. Frederick Law Olmsted, *Mount Royal* (New York, 1881), 26, qtd. in A. L. Murray, "Frederick Law Olmsted and the Design of Mount Royal Park, Montreal," *Journal of the Society of Architectural Historians* 26, no. 3 (1967): 163–71.
53. Boston, *Notes on the Plan.*
54. Olmsted, "Public Parks," 67–68.
55. "The Present Look of Our Great Central Park, *New York Daily Times,* July 9, 1856, 8.
56. Heather Gilligan, "An Entire Manhattan Village Owned by Black People Was Destroyed to Build Central Park: Three Churches, a School, and Dozens of Homes Were Demolished," https://timeline.com/black-village-destroyed-central-park-6356723113fa.
57. Julia Jacobs, "Their Land Became Part of Central Park. They're Coming Back in a Monument," *New York Times,* October 20, 2019, https://www.nytimes.com/2019/10/20/arts/lyons-seneca-village-monument.html.
58. Daniel Hudson Burnham et al., *Plan of Chicago* (New York: Princeton Architectural Press, 1993), 123.
59. Thomas J. Schlereth, "Burnham's *Plan* and Moody's *Manual* City Planning as Progressive Reform," *Journal of the American Planning Association* 47, no. 1 (1981), https://doi.org/10.1080/01944368108977091.
60. Ibid.

61. Moody, *What of the City?*, 71.
62. Walter Dwight Moody, *Wacker's Manual of the Plan of Chicago,* ed. Charles Henry Wacker and Commission for the Chicago Plan (Chicago: Printed by Calumet Publishing Company, 1916)., 7.
63. Burnham et al., *Plan of Chicago.*, 15.
64. Moody, *What of the City?*, 57.
65. P. G. Hall, *Cities of Tomorrow: An Intellectual History of Urban Planning and Design in the Twentieth Century.*
66. Moody, *Wacker's Manual,* 54.
67. Ibid., 105.
68. Burnham et al., *Plan of Chicago.*
69. Moody, *Wacker's Manual,* 103–4.
70. Margaret Garb, "Race, Housing, and Burnham's Plan: Why Is There No Housing in the 1909 Plan of Chicago?," *Journal of Planning History* 10, no. 2 (2011): 99, https://doi.org/10.1177/1538513210384453.
71. Ibid., 103.
72. P. G. Hall, *Cities of Tomorrow,* 41.
73. Ibid.
74. Ebenezer Howard and Frederic J. Osborn, *Garden Cities of To-morrow* (Cambridge, MA: MIT Press, 1965).
75. Raymond Unwin, *Nothing Gained by Overcrowding! How the Garden City Type of Development May Benefit Both Owner and Occupier* (London: Garden Cities and Town Planning Association, 1912), 5, 10.
76. Ibid.
77. Clarence Perry et al., *Neighborhood and Community Planning* (New York: Regional Plan of New York and Its Environs, 1929).
78. P. G. Hall, *Cities of Tomorrow.*
79. Robert Bruegmann, *Sprawl: A Compact History* (Chicago: University of Chicago Press, 2005).
80. Olmsted, "Public Parks," 23–25.
81. Ibid.
82. Olmsted and Vaux, *Preliminary Report upon the Proposed Suburban Village at Riverside, near Chicago* (New York: Sutton, Brown, 1868), 8–14.
83. Llewellyn Park real estate prospectus in Schuyler, *New Urban Landscape,* 157.
84. Downing, *Rural Essays.*
85. Olmsted, qtd. in Schuyler, *New Urban Landscape.*
86. Stebbins via Schuyler, *New Urban Landscape,* 178; and Frederick Law Olmsted and James Croes, New York City Board of the Department of Public Parks, "Document 72: Preliminary Report of the Landscape Architect and the Civil and Topographical Engineer, upon the Laying Out of the Twenty-Third and Twenty-Fourth Wards," December 20, 1876.
87. Russell Lopez, *Building American Public Health: Urban Planning, Architecture, and the Quest for Better Health in the United States* (New York, US: Palgrave Macmillan, 2012), doi:10.1057/9781137002440.
88. Schlereth, "Burnham's *Plan* and Moody's *Manual,*" 74.
89. "The Lungs of London," *The Albion, a Weekly Journal of News, Politics and Literature* 1, no. 38 (1839).
90. Ward Thompson, "Linking Landscape and Health."

91. Phyllis Allen Richmond, "American Attitudes toward the Germ Theory of Disease (1860–1880)," *Journal of the History of Medicine and Allied Sciences* 9, no. 4 (1954), https://doi.org/10.1093/jhmas/IX.4.428; Hewitt and Szczygiel, "Nineteenth-Century Medical Landscapes."

92. Hibbert Winslow Hill, *The New Public Health* (New York: Arno Press, 1977), 9.

93. Ibid., 33.

94. Fee and Brown, "Unfulfilled Promise of Public Health."

95. Samuel Hopkins Adams, "Guardians of the Public Health," *McClure's Magazine* 31, no. 3 (1908), 243.

4. Germ Theory and Environmental Compartmentalization

1. Charles E. Rosenberg, "Epilogue: Airs, Waters, Places; A Status Report," *Bulletin of the History of Medicine* 86, no. 4 (2012), https://doi.org/10.1353/bhm.2012.0082.

2. Robert E. Park, "The City: Suggestions for the Investigation of Human Behavior in the City Environment," *American Journal of Sociology* 20, no. 5 (1915), https://doi.org/10.1086/212433.600.

3. Clarence Stein, "Dinosaur Cities," *The Survey* 54, no. 3 (May 1, 1925): 134–38.

4. Henry Wright, "The Road to Good Houses," *The Survey* 54, no. 3 (May 1, 1925): 166–68, 189.

5. Ibid., 189.

6. Aldo Leopold, *For the Health of the Land: Previously Unpublished Essays and Other Writings,* ed. J. Baird Callicott and Eric T. Freyfogle (Washington, DC: Island Press, 2014), 219.

7. Walter B. Cannon, *The Wisdom of the Body* (New York: W. W. Norton, 1939).

8. Eliel Saarinen, *The City: Its Growth, Its Decay, Its Future* (Cambridge, MA: MIT Press, 1943), 9.

9. Robert E. Park, Ernest W. Burgess, and Roderick D. McKenzie, *The City* (Chicago: University of Chicago Press, 1967).

10. Richard Harris and Robert Lewis, "Constructing a Fault(Y) Zone: Misrepresentations of American Cities and Suburbs, 1900–1950," *Annals of the Association of American Geographers* 88, no. 4 (1998).

11. Jennifer S. Light, *Nature of Cities: Ecological Visions and the American Urban Professions, 1920–1960* (Baltimore: Johns Hopkins University Press, 2014).

12. Park, Burgess, and McKenzie, *The City,* 580.

13. Ibid., 582.

14. C.-E. A. Winslow, "Public Health at the Crossroads," *American Journal of Public Health* 16, no. 11 (1926), https://doi.org/10.2105/AJPH.16.11.1075-a.

15. Susser and Stein, *Eras in Epidemiology.*

16. H. Edmund Mathews, "Sanitation in Modern Architecture," *Journal of the Royal Society for the Promotion of Health* 55, no. 4 (1934): 150–56.

17. Margaret Campbell, "What Tuberculosis Did for Modernism: The Influence of a Curative Environment on Modernist Design and Architecture," *Medical History* 49, no. 4 (2005). Campbell's work and Beatriz Colomina's *X-Ray Architecture* (Zürich: Lars Müller, 2019) both discuss the influence of tuberculosis on modernism as a architectural style in depth.

18. Barbara Bates, *Bargaining for Life: A Social History of Tuberculosis, 1876–1938* (Philadelphia: University of Pennsylvania Press, 1992), 28–30.

19. Eric Mumford, "CIAM Urbanism after the Athens Charter," *Planning Perspectives* 7, no. 4 (1992): 391–417.

20. Le Corbusier, *La Charte d'Athènes* (repr., New York: Grossman, 1973), 57.

21. Le Corbusier, *The Radiant City; Elements of a Doctrine of Urbanism to Be Used as the Basis of Our Machine-Age Civilization* (New York: Orion Press, 1933); and Le Corbusier, *The City of Tomorrow and Its Planning* (Mineola, NY: Dover, 1929).

22. Le Corbusier, *Towards a New Architecture* (Mineola, NY: Dover, 1931), 58.

23. Ibid., 251.

24. Gerald Steyn. "Le Corbusier and the Human Body," *South African Journal of Art History* 27, no. 2 (2012): 259–72

25. Le Corbusier, *Towards a New Architecture,* 246.

26. Le Corbusier, *Radiant City;* and Le Corbusier, *City of Tomorrow and Its Planning.*

27. American Public Health Association, Committee on the Hygiene of Housing, *Basic Principles of Healthful Housing* (New York: American Public Health Association, 1941), 361.

28. José Luis Sert and International Congresses for Modern Architecture, *Can Our Cities Survive? An ABC of Urban Problems, Their Analysis, Their Solutions; Based on the Proposals Formulated by the C.I.A.M., International Congresses for Modern Architecture, Congrès Internationaux D'architecture Moderne* (Cambridge, MA: Harvard University Press; London: Oxford University Press, 1942), 20.

29. James C. Scott. *Seeing like a State: How Certain Schemes to Improve the Human Condition Have Failed* (New Haven: Yale University Press, 1998); and Le Corbusier, *Radiant City.*

30. Campbell, "What Tuberculosis Did for Modernism."

31. Sert and International Congresses, *Can Our Cities Survive?,* 23.

32. Philip Kennicott, "Le Corbusier at MOMA: A Love/Hate Relationship," *Washington Post,* July 12, 2013.

33. Scott, *Seeing like a State;* and Alexander von Hoffman, "High Ambitions: The Past and Future of American Low-Income Housing Policy," *Housing Policy Debate* 7, no. 3 (1996): 423–46.

34. "Public Housing and the USHA," *Architectural Forum* 70, no. 1 (January 1940), 10.

35. "Large Scale Housing Comes into Its Own via Private Enterprise as Metropolitan Life Lends a Hand and Fifty Million for U.S. Project No. 1," *Architectural Forum* 68, no. 5 (May 1938), 4.

36. Historic American Buildings Survey, Library of Congress, "Harbor Hills Housing Project, 7 Western Avenue, Lomita, Los Angeles County, CA," Lomita, California, 1933, photographs; https://www.loc.gov/item/ca2548/.

37. Historic American Buildings Survey, Library of Congress, "Lockefield Garden Apartments, 900 Indiana Avenue, Indianapolis, Marion County, IN," William Earl Russ and Merritt Harrison, creators, Indianapolis, Indiana, 1933, photographs; https://www.loc.gov/item/in0282/.

38. Landmarks Preservation Commission of New York, Williamsburg Housing, Addendum to LP-2135, February 10, 2004, http://s-media.nyc.gov/agencies/lpc/lp/2135A.pdf.

39. Historic American Buildings Survey, "Lockefield Garden Apartments."

40. Melosi, *Sanitary City.*

41. Catherine Bauer, "The Dreary Deadlock of Public Housing," *Architectural Forum* 87, no. 5 (May 1957): 141–42.

42. Ibid., 221.
43. Von Hoffman, "High Ambitions."
44. Eric Mumford. "The 'Tower in a Park' in America: Theory and Practice, 1920–1960," *Planning Perspectives* 10, no. 1 (1995): 17–41; and Mary C. Comerio, "Pruitt Igoe and Other Stories," *Journal of Architectural Education* 34, no. 4 (1981): 26–31.
45. F. Stuart Chapin, "An Experiment on the Social Effects of Good Housing," *American Sociological Review* 5, no. 6 (1940): 868–79; and von Hoffman, "High Ambitions."
46. United States, National Commission on Urban Problems, *Building the American City* (New York: Praeger, 1969), 119.
47. Henri Lefebvre, Neil Brenner, and Stuart Elden, *State, Space, World: Selected Essays* (Minneapolis: University of Minnesota Press, 2009), 169.
48. Ibid., 175.
49. Catherine Bauer, *Modern Housing* (Boston: Houghton Mifflin, 1934), 200. Ironically, we know more now about how landscape influences wellbeing, particularly in disadvantaged populations. More than 30 years after the condemnation of high-rise housing, researchers Frances Kuo and William Sullivan studied the relationship between crime and visible vegetation in Chicago's Cabrini Green projects (built between 1942 and 1962), and found that there were significantly more crimes reported on sides of the buildings that did not have views of green space than those that did, with even less crimes on sides with more robust vegetation (i.e., high canopy trees). They attributed the difference to vegetation's effect on mental fatigue, which over time could lead to more acts of aggression. Kuo and Sullivan's study highlighted two interesting points about the role of nature in disadvantaged neighborhoods. One, that the study discounted much of the crime prevention literature of that time period that asserted that more trees in high-crime neighborhoods encouraged crime as it could obscure undesirable activity. Two, for all that ultimately failed in the translation of modern design to the architecture of public housing, there was some credence to Le Corbusier's theory that just viewing nature was enough to have therapeutic benefits. These specific studies are discussed in more detail in chapter 8.
50. Charles Davis II, "When Public Housing Was White: William Lescaze and the Americanization of the International Style," in *Building Character: The Racial Politics of Modern Architectural Style* (Pittsburgh: University of Pittsburgh Press, 2019), 171–209.
51. Steven Lubar, "Trolley Lines, Land Speculation and Community-Building the Early History of Woodside Park, Silver Spring, MD," *Maryland Historical Magazine* 81, no. 4 (Winter 1986): 316–48.
52. Power, "Apartheid Baltimore Style."
53. Nayan Shah, *Contagious Divides: Epidemics and Race in San Francisco's Chinatown* (Berkeley: University of California Press, 2001).
54. Fee and Brown, "Unfulfilled Promise of Public Health."

5. Urban Decay and the Metaphorical Cancer of Blight

1. Morton Gabriel White and Lucia White, *The Intellectual versus the City: From Thomas Jefferson to Frank Lloyd Wright* (Cambridge, MA: Harvard University Press, 1962).
2. Frank Lloyd Wright, *The Living City* (New York: New American Library, 1970).

3. Lewis Mumford, "The Fourth Migration," *The Survey,* May 1, 1925, 132.
4. Ibid., 132.
5. William H. Whyte, *The Last Landscape* (Garden City, N.Y.: Doubleday, 1968), 337.
6. Victor Gruen, *The Heart of Our Cities: The Urban Crisis; Diagnosis and Cure* (New York: Simon and Schuster, 1964), 41–42.
7. Ibid.
8. Ibid., 49.
9. American Public Health Association, Committee on the Hygiene of Housing, *Planning the Neighborhood* (Chicago: Public Administration Service, 1960), vi.
10. Ibid.
11. Lawrence E. Hinkle and William C. Loring, eds., *The Effect of the Man-Made Environment on Health and Behavior: A Report of the Inter-University Board of Collaborators* (Atlanta: Center for Disease Control; Washington, DC: Public Health Service, U.S. Dept. of Health, Education, and Welfare, 1977), 9.
12. Ibid.
13. Becky Nicolaides, "How Hell Moved from the City to the Suburbs: Urban Scholars and Changing Perceptions of Authentic Community," in *The New Suburban History,* ed. Kevin M. Kruse and Thomas J. Sugrue (Chicago: University of Chicago Press, 2006).
14. Mabel L. Walker, with chapters by Henry Wright, *Urban Blight and Slums: Economic and Legal Factors in Their Origin, Reclamation, and Prevention,* Harvard City Planning Studies no. 12 (New York: Russell & Russell, 1971); Jonathan Norton Leonard, "Rachel Carson Dies of Cancer; 'Silent Spring' Author Was 56," *New York Times,* April 15, 1964, Books; Robert R. Gioielli, *Environmental Activism and the Urban Crisis: Baltimore, St. Louis, Chicago* (Philadelphia: Temple University Press, 2014), 15.
15. Jamin Creed Rowan, "The New York School of Urban Ecology: *The New Yorker,* Rachel Carson, and Jane Jacobs," *American Literature* 82, no. 3 (2010), https://doi.org/10.1215/00029831-2010-025.
16. Leonard, "Rachel Carson Dies of Cancer."
17. Murray Bookchin [Lewis Herber, pseud.], *Our Synthetic Environment* (New York: Knopf, 1962), 23.
18. Ibid., 7.
19. Margot Lystra, "Drawing Natures: US Highway Location, Representational Techniques and the Rise of Ecological Design," *Journal of Design History* 30, no. 2 (2016), https://doi.org/10.1093/jdh/epw013.
20. Susser and Stein, *Eras in Epidemiology.*
21. Garry Egger, "In Search of a Germ Theory Equivalent for Chronic Disease," *Preventing Chronic Disease* 9 (2012).
22. Barbara DeBuono, ed., *Milestones in Public Health: Accomplishments in Public Health over the Past 100 Years* (New York: Pfizer Global Pharmaceuticals, 2006), 83–84.
23. George Weisz, *Chronic Disease in the Twentieth Century: A History* (Baltimore: Johns Hopkins University Press, 2014), 236.
24. Susser and Stein, *Eras in Epidemiology.*
25. Ibid., 165.
26. Sontag, *Illness as Metaphor,* 5–6.
27. Bookchin, *Our Synthetic Environment,* 19.

28. Preamble to the Constitution of the World Health Organization as adopted by the International Health Conference, New York, June 19–22, 1946, put into action April 1948.

29. Susser and Stein, *Eras in Epidemiology.*

30. Bookchin, *Our Synthetic Environment,* 17–18.

31. Mitchell Gordon, *Sick Cities: Psychology and Pathology of American Urban Life* (New York: Macmillan, 1963); Gioielli, *Environmental Activism.*

32. Ibid., 418.

33. Michael Dear, qtd. in Rodrick Wallace and Deborah Wallace, "Origins of Public Health Collapse in New York City: The Dynamics of Planned Shrinkage, Contagious Urban Decay and Social Disintegration," *Bulletin of the New York Academy of Medicine* 66, no. 5 (1990).

34. Saarinen, *The City,* 15.

35. Rodrick Wallace and Deborah Wallace, "The Coming Crisis of Public Health in the Suburbs," *Milbank Quarterly* 71, no. 4 (1993), https://doi.org/10.2307/3350418.

36. Lopez, *Building American Public Health,* 127.

37. Edith Elmer Wood, "The Costs of Bad Housing," *Annals of the American Academy of Political and Social Science* 190, no. 1 (1937), 147, https://doi.org/10.1177/000271623719000117.

38. Saarinen, *The City,* 144.

39. Andrew Michael Shanken, *194X: Architecture, Planning, and Consumer Culture on the American Home Front* (Minneapolis: University of Minnesota Press, 2009), 70–74.

40. Alexander von Hoffman, "The Lost History of Urban Renewal," *Journal of Urbanism* 1, no. 3 (2008).

41. James W. Follin, "Slums and Blight . . . a disease of urban life," Sundwell Memorial Lecture, University of Michigan, May 3, 1955 (Washington, DC: Urban Renewal Administration, Housing and Home Finance Agency, 1956), 6.

42. Ibid., 7.

43. "Slum Surgery in St. Louis," *Architectural Forum,* April 1951, 128–29.

44. Russ P. Lopez, "Public Health, the APHA, and Urban Renewal," *American Journal of Public Health* 99, no. 9 (2009), https://doi.org/10.2105/AJPH.2008.150136.

45. Boston, City of, City Planning Board, "A Workable Plan for Urban Renewal" (Boston: City Planning Board, 1955) 15.

46. Follin, "Slums and Blight," 13.

47. San Francisco, City of, City Planning Commission, *New City: San Francisco Redeveloped* (San Francisco: City Planning Commission, 1947).

48. Walter Thompson, "How Urban Renewal Destroyed the Fillmore in Order to Save It," *Hoodline,* January 3, 2016, https://hoodline.com/2016/01/how-urban-renewal-destroyed-the-fillmore-in-order-to-save-it.

49. Lopez, "Public Health."

50. Von Hoffman, "Lost History of Urban Renewal."

51. United States, National Commission on Urban Problems, *Building the American City.*

52. Lystra, "Drawing Natures."

53. Lawrence Halprin. *Freeways* (New York: Van Nostrand Reinhold Inc, 1968), 17.

54. Ibid., 4.

55. Wallace and Wallace, "Origins of Public Health Collapse."

56. Kevin Lynch, *A Theory of Good City Form* (Cambridge, MA: MIT Press, 1981).
57. James C. Scott, *Seeing like a State.*

6. Prescriptive Neighborhoods

1. Lewis Mumford, *The City in History: Its Origins, Its Transformations, and Its Prospects* (New York: Harcourt, Brace & World, 1961), 553, 564, 572, 576.
2. Whyte, *Last Landscape,* 337.
3. Peter Blake, "The Suburbs Are a Mess," *Saturday Evening Post,* October 5, 1963, 14.
4. Mumford, *City in History;* Lawrence J. Vale, "Moralism and Urban Evolution: Excavating Mumford's the City in History," *Built Environment* 41, no. 3 (2015): 352–65, https://doi.org/10.2148/benv.41.3.352.
5. Whyte, *Last Landscape.*
6. Ibid. At least Whyte had the temerity to say, "When I am criticizing planners, the reader will understand that I do not mean all planners, but simply those with whose views I differ. Good planners are the ones with whose views I agree. This does not sound well put so baldly, but one might as well be frank."
7. Bruegmann, *Sprawl.*
8. Whyte, *Last Landscape,* 6.
9. David Freund, "Marketing the Free Market: State Intervention and the Politics of Prosperity in Metropolitan America," in *The New Suburban History* ed. Kevin M. Kruse and Thomas J. Sugrue (Chicago: University of Chicago Press, 2006), 11–32.
10. Oliver Gillham, *The Limitless City: A Primer on the Urban Sprawl Debate,* ed. Alex S. MacLean (Washington, DC: Island Press, 2002).
11. Centers for Disease Control and Prevention, "Overweight and Obesity," 2017, https://www.cdc.gov/obesity/index.html.
12. Adela Hruby and Frank Hu, "The Epidemiology of Obesity: A Big Picture," *PharmacoEconomics* 33, no. 7 (2015), https://doi.org/10.1007/s40273-014-0243-x.
13. World Health Organization, *Declaration of Alma-Ata, 1978* (World Health Organization, 2005).
14. DeBuono, *Milestones in Public Health.*
15. R. Lindheim and S. L. Syme, "Environments, People, and Health," *Annual Review of Public Health* 4 (1983), 337.
16. Ibid.
17. J. F. Sallis, N. Owen, and E. B. Fisher, "Ecological Models of Health Behavior," *Health Behavior and Health Education: Theory, Research, and Practice* 4 (2008).
18. Howard Frumkin, Lawrence D. Frank, and Richard J. Jackson, *Urban Sprawl and Public Health: Designing, Planning, and Building for Healthy Communities* (Washington, DC: Island Press, 2004).
19. Andres Duany, Elizabeth Plater-Zyberk, and Jeff Speck, *Suburban Nation: The Rise of Sprawl and the Decline of the American Dream* (New York: North Point Press, 2000), 144.
20. Ibid., xiii.
21. Ibid., 210.
22. Cliff Ellis, "The New Urbanism: Critiques and Rebuttals," *Journal of Urban Design* 7, no. 3 (2002), 265.
23. Michael Southworth, "New Urbanism and the American Metropolis," *Built Environment* 29, no. 3 (2003): 210–26.

24. Duany, Plater-Zyberk, and Speck, *Suburban Nation,* 172–73.
25. Ibid., 79–80.
26. Jeff Speck, *Walkable City: How Downtown Can Save America, One Step at a Time* (New York: Farrar, Straus and Giroux, 2012), 249.
27. Andres Duany and Emily Talen, "Transect Planning," *Journal of the American Planning Association* 68, no. 3 (2002).
28. Jane Jacobs, *The Death and Life of Great American Cities* (New York: Random House, 1961), 91.
29. Andres Duany and Elizabeth Plater-Zyberk, eds., *Towns and Town-Making Principles* (Cambridge, MA: Harvard University Graduate School of Design; New York: Rizzoli, 1991).
30. A. J. Khattak and D. Rodriguez, "Travel Behavior in Neo-Traditional Neighborhood Developments: A Case Study in USA," *Transportation Research Part A: Policy and Practice* 39, no. 6 (2005).
31. Southworth, "New Urbanism."
32. The CNU touted, "CNU's inner city task force, led by Ray Gindroz, established design criteria based on the Charter and organized training sessions and workshops for HUD employees of all disciplines. Through CNU's influence, the original HOPE VI Notice of Funds Availability specified New Urbanism by name, which guaranteed that many of the nation's top urban design firms would design thousands of units that were built in cities across the US." Congress for the New Urbanism, "HUD Hope VI," https://www.cnu.org/our-projects/hud-hope-vi.
33. Congress for the New Urbanism and U.S. Department of Housing and Urban Development, *Principles for Inner City Neighborhood Design: Hope Vi and the New Urbanism* (Washington, DC: Department of Housing and Urban Development, n.d.), 3.
34. Michael Pyatok, "Martha Stewart vs. Studs Terkel? New Urbanism and Inner Cities Neighborhoods That Work," *Places Journal.* 13, no. 1 (2000), 41.
35. James Howard Kunstler, author of *The Geography of Nowhere* (1994), was a prominent member of the Congress for the New Urbanism. While neither an architect nor planner, Kunstler was known for his firebrand editorials decrying automobile use and the "formless, soul-less, centerless, demoralizing mess" of the suburbs, although recently his written work has more closely focused on fossil fuel dependency and he has become more well known for espousing right-wing social views and conspiracy theories in public interviews and editorials.
36. David Harvey, "The New Urbanism and the Communitarian Trap: On Social Problems and the False Hope of Design," in *Sprawl and Suburbia: A Harvard Design Magazine Reader,* ed. William Saunders (Minneapolis: University of Minnesota Press, 2005).
37. Pyatok, "Martha Stewart vs. Studs Terkel?," 43.
38. Duany, Plater-Zyberk, and Speck, *Suburban Nation,* 53.
39. Ibid., 238–40.
40. James Hanlon, "Success by Design: HOPE VI, New Urbanism, and the Neoliberal Transformation of Public Housing in the United States," *Environment and Planning A* 42, no. 1 (2010): 80–98; and Danya Keene and E. Geronimus, "'Weathering' HOPE VI: The Importance of Evaluating the Population Health Impact of Public Housing Demolition and Displacement," *Journal of Urban Health* 88, no. 3 (2011): 417–35.

41. United States, Department of Housing and Urban Development, "Choice Neighborhoods," 2018, https://www.hud.gov/cn.

42. Douglas A. Blackmon and Thaddeus Herrick, "A New Urbanist Tries to Rebuild New Orleans Neighborhoods," *Chicago Tribune,* May 14, 2006.

43. Robin Pogrebin, "An Architect with Plans for a New Gulf Coast," *New York Times* May 24, 2006, Art & Design.

44. Ibid.

45. Bill Walsh, "Andres Duany on Rebuilding after Hurricane Katrina: Part I—The Gulf Coast," October 10, 2005, https://healthybuilding.net/blog/133-andres-duany-on-rebuilding-after-hurricane-katrina-part-i-the-gulf-coast.

46. New Orleans, City of, *Planning District 6 Rebuilding Plan,* Neighborhoods Rebuilding Plan, 2006.

47. Jeff Speck, "Why They Hate Us: A New Urbanist Dissects the Movement's Critics," *Architect,* June 2010, 68. Speck's editorial hypothesizes a "taxonomy" of New Urbanist critics as "the Libs [Libertarians], the Mods, and the Saints." Speck dismisses "the Libs" for their assertion that Americans to some extent want sprawl, but also for their ignorance of federal policies such as redlining and highway building that created the suburbs. Of "the Mods," i.e., most of the design elite, he notes what he feels is the undue emphasis on the formal style of New Urbanism and perceived hatred of "tradition" in building. Of the last group, he notes, "Finally there are the Saints, who are the hardest group to rebut because they are essentially right. The Saints, who wouldn't dirty their hands with conventional development practice, point to those New Urban communities that have failed to fully achieve the goals of the movement and call them "better-looking sprawl." Again, Speck is essentially right on all these counts, if also making vast generalizations, and admits that as a "reform" movement, New Urbanism is only as successful as the built environment that surrounds it, but still does not engage with the issues of equity, social history of its forms, nor its leaders' eagerness to capitalize on public housing and post-disaster landscapes.

48. Ellis, "New Urbanism."

49. Ibid., 268.

50. Andres Duany, "Thursday Morning Plenary," paper presented at the Living Community: The 21st Annual Event from the Congress of the New Urbanism, Salt Lake City, 2013.

51. Congress for the New Urbanism, "New Urbanism: Rx for Healthy Places," paper presented at the 18th Annual Congress for the New Urbanism, Atlanta, 2010.

52. Southworth, "New Urbanism."

53. Centers for Disease Control and Prevention, "Overweight and Obesity."

54. Farkas, "Tons of Useful Stuff."

55. Ria Hutabarat Lo, "Walkability: What Is It?," *Journal of Urbanism: International Research on Placemaking and Urban Sustainability* 2, no. 2 (2009).

56. R. J. Jackson, A. L. Dannenberg, and H. Frumkin, "Health and the Built Environment: 10 Years After," *American Journal of Public Health* 103, no. 9 (2013).

57. Mark Young, "Walk with a Doc," *Parks & Recreation* 48, no. 9 (2013), 20.

58. Frances Stead Stellers, "D.C. Doctor's Rx: A Stroll in the Park Instead of a Trip to the Pharmacy," *Washington Post,* May 15, 2015; and Park Rx America, https://parkrxamerica.org/.

59. Golden Gate National Parks Conservancy, "Park Prescriptions," ParkRx, 2019, https://www.parkrx.org/.

60. United States, Department of Health and Human Services, "Step It Up! The Surgeon General's Call to Action to Promote Walking and Walkable Communities" (Washington, DC: U.S. Department of Health and Human Services, Office of the Surgeon General, 2015), https://www.surgeongeneral.gov/library/calls/walking -and-walkable-communities/index.html.

61. Robert Cervero and Kara Kockelman, "Travel Demand and the 3Ds: Density, Diversity, and Design," *Transportation Research, Part D: Transport and Environment 2,* no. 3 (1997): 199–219.

62. Daniel A. Rodriguez, Asad J. Khattak, and Kelly R. Evenson, "Can New Urbanism Encourage Physical Activity? Comparing a New Urbanist Neighborhood with Conventional Suburbs," *Journal of the American Planning Association* 72, no. 1 (2006): 43–54.

63. Rob Boer et al., "Neighborhood Design and Walking Trips in Ten U.S. Metropolitan Areas," *American Journal of Preventive Medicine* 32, no. 4 (2007), https://doi.org /10.1016/j.amepre.2006.12.012.

64. Walk Score, "Walk Score Methodology," 2020, https://www.walkscore.com /methodology.shtml.

65. Speck, *Walkable City,* 11.

66. William A. Satariano et al., "Lower-Body Function, Neighborhoods, and Walking in an Older Population," *American Journal of Preventive Medicine* 38, no. 4 (2010).

67. Jason G. Su et al., "Factors Influencing Whether Children Walk to School," *Health & Place* (2013).

68. Lo, "Walkability."

69. Emily Talen, "The Geospatial Dimension in Urban Design," *Journal of Urban Design* 16, no. 1 (2011).

70. Ann Forsyth, "What Is a Walkable Place? The Walkability Debate in Urban Design," *Urban Design International* 20, no. 4 (2015), https://doi.org/10.1057/udi .2015.22.

71. Lawrence Halprin, *The RSVP Cycles; Creative Processes in the Human Environment* (New York: G. Braziller, 1970).

7. Whose Wellness?

1. Wallace and Wallace, "Coming Crisis of Public Health," include AIDS in their discussion, perhaps the most devastating and decidedly *the* urban health crisis of the 1980s. It is undiscussed here due to its infectious but largely non-environmental vectors. That said, since no government agency undertook the geographic mapping of the disease, it is wholly possible its spread had environmental factors that simply remained unknown.

2. David Owen, *Green Metropolis: What the City Can Teach the Country about True Sustainability* (New York: Riverhead Books, 2009).

3. Jamie Peck, "Struggling with the Creative Class," *International Journal of Urban and Regional Research* 29, no. 4 (2005), https://doi.org/10.1111/j.1468–2427.2005 .00620.x.

4. Elizabeth Kneebone and Emily Garr, *The Suburbanization of Poverty Trends in Metropolitan America, 2000 to 2008* (Washington, DC: Metropolitan Policy Program at Brookings, 2010).

5. Elizabeth Kneebone, "The Changing Geography of US Poverty," Testimony before the House Ways and Means Committee, Subcommittee on Human Resources, Feb-

ruary 15, 2017, https://www.brookings.edu/testimonies/the-changing-geography
-of-us-poverty/.

6. Paul Krugman, "Stranded by Sprawl," *New York Times,* July 28, 2013, A17; Nadarajan Chetty et al., "Where Is the Land of Opportunity? The Geography of Intergenerational Mobility in the United States," *Quarterly Journal of Economics* (2014) 129,
no. 4: 1553–1623, doi:10.1093/qje/qju022.

7. Andrew Mearns, *The Bitter Cry of Outcast London* (London: J. Clarke, 1883), 15.

8. Richard Florida, *The New Urban Crisis: How Our Cities Are Increasing Inequality,
Deepening Segregation, and Failing the Middle Class—and What We Can Do about
It* (New York: Basic Books, 2017).

9. Herbert J. Gans, *People and Plans; Essays on Urban Problems and Solutions* (New
York: Basic Books, 1968), 3.

10. Nicolaides, "How Hell Moved."

11. Harris and Lewis, "Constructing a Fault(Y) Zone."

12. Elizabeth Kneebone, "Confronting Suburban Poverty in America," ed. Alan Berube
(Washington, DC: Brookings Institution Press, 2013).

13. Kevin M. Kruse and Thomas J. Sugrue, eds., *The New Suburban History* (Chicago:
University of Chicago Press, 2006); Willow S. Lung-Amam, *Trespassers? Asian
Americans and the Battle for Suburbia* (Berkeley: University of California Press,
2017), doi:10.1057/9781137002440.

14. Shawn Bucholtz and Jed Kolko, "America Really Is a Nation of Suburbs," *CityLab,*
November 14, 2018, https://www.citylab.com/life/2018/11/data-most-american
-neighborhoods-suburban/575602/.

15. Richard Florida, "In the U.S., Walkability Is a Premium Good," *Bloomberg CityLab,*
June 16, 2016, https://www.bloomberg.com/news/articles/2016-06-16/the
-economic-benefits-of-walkable-neighborhoods-george-washington-university
-report; Tracy Hadden Loh, Christopher B. Leinberger, and Jordan Chafetz, *Foot
Traffic Ahead: Ranking Walkable Urbanism in America's Largest Metros* (Washington, DC: Center for Real Estate and Urban Analysis, George Washington University, 2019), https://smartgrowthamerica.org/resources/foot-traffic-ahead-2019.

16. David Moser, "Driven into Poverty: Walkable Urbanism and the Suburbanization of
Poverty," Citytank: Ideas for the City, March 8, 2013, http://citytank.org/2013/03
/08/driven-into-poverty-walkable-urbanism-and-the-suburbanization-of-poverty/.

17. Matthew J. Trowbridge et al., "Building Healthy Communities: Establishing Health
and Wellness Metrics for Use within the Real Estate Industry," *Health Affairs* 33, no.
11 (2014), https://doi.org/10.1377/hlthaff.2014.0654.

18. United States, Green Building Council, *LEED V4: Reference Guide for Neighborhood
Development* (Washington, DC: U.S. Green Building Council, 2018).

19. International WELL Building Institute, "The International WELL Building
Institute Launches the WELL Building Standard® Version 1.0," October 20, 2014
(press release), https://resources.wellcertified.com/articles/the-international-well
-building-institute-launches-the-well-building-standard-version-1-0/.

20. The 90 percent claim has been repeated in many outlets; it seems to have originated with E. Klepeis Neil et al., "The National Human Activity Pattern Survey
(NHAPS): A Resource for Assessing Exposure to Environmental Pollutants," *Journal of Exposure Analysis and Environmental Epidemiology* 11, no. 3 (2001), https://
doi.org/10.1038/sj.jea.7500165.

21. International WELL Building Institute, *WELL Building Standard v2* (New York,
NY: International WELL Building Institute, 2018).

22. Patricia Kirk, "Is WELL Certification Worth It for Developers?" *National Real Estate Investor,* July 10, 2017, https://www.nreionline.com/office/well-certification -worth-it-developers.
23. DELOS, "Stay Well," 2019, http://staywellrooms.com/.
24. Jamie Matos, "IWBI Launches the Well Community Standard™ to Promote Human Health and Wellness on a District Scale," WELL, September 5, 2017 (press release), https://www.wellcertified.com/en/articles/iwbi-launches-well-community -standard.
25. Strategic Property Partners, LLC and International WELL Building Institute, "Water Street Tampa First to Achieve WELL Design and Operations Designation for Global Wellness Standard for Communities," May 28, 2019 (press release). It is worth noting that Jeff Vinik, owner of the Tampa Bay Lightning, which has their arena in the development, is a partner in Strategic Property Partners.
26. Matos, "IWBI Launches the Well Community Standard™."
27. Ashley Gurbal Kritzer, "Here's What Water Street Tampa Will Look and Feel Like at Street Level," *Tampa Bay Business Journal,* June 28, 2018, https://www.bizjournals .com/tampabay/news/2018/06/28/heres-what-water-street-tampa-will-look-and -feel.html.
28. Elizabeth Randall, associate principal for Reed Hilderbrand, email correspondence and interview with author, November 7, 2019.
29. Strategic Property Partners, LLC and International WELL Building Institute, "Water Street Tampa."
30. Jay Cridlin, "Water Street Tampa's First Heron Apartments Hit Market, and They're Not Cheap," *Tampa Bay Times,* January 5, 2021.
31. Vanessa Quirk, "Citing Equity Issues, Founder of Atlanta Beltline Leaves Board," *Metropolis,* September 27, 2016, https://www.metropolismag.com/cities/landscape /citing-equity-issues-founder-of-atlanta-beltline-leaves-board/.
32. Nicola Szibbo, "Lessons for LEED® for Neighborhood Development, Social Equity, and Affordable Housing," *Journal of the American Planning Association* 82, no. 1 (2016), https://doi.org/10.1080/01944363.2015.1110709.
33. Jennifer R. Wolch, Jason Byrne, and Joshua P. Newell, "Urban Green Space, Public Health, and Environmental Justice: The Challenge of Making Cities 'Just Green Enough,'" *Landscape and Urban Planning* 125 (2014).
34. Winifred Curran and Trina Hamilton, "Just Green Enough: Contesting Environmental Gentrification in Greenpoint, Brooklyn," *Local Environment* 17, no. 9 (2012), https://doi.org/10.1080/13549839.2012.729569.
35. Wolch, Byrne, and Newell, "Urban Green Space."
36. Jeanne Haffner, "The Dangers of Eco-Gentrification: What's the Best Way to Make a City Greener?" *The Guardian,* May 6, 2015, http://www.theguardian.com/cities /2015/may/06/dangers-ecogentrification-best-way-make-city-greener.
37. Christopher Leinberger and Mariela Alfonzo, "Walk This Way: The Economic Promise of Walkable Places in Metropolitan Washington, D.C." (Washington, DC: Brookings Institution, 2012).
38. Urban Land Institute, *Building Healthy Places Toolkit* (Washington, DC: Urban Land Institute, 2015).
39. Barry Bergdoll and Reinhold Martin, *Foreclosed: Rehousing the American Dream* (New York,: Museum of Modern Art, 2012).
40. WORKac's "Nature-City" statement, in ibid.
41. Ibid.

42. Peter Dizikes, "3 Questions: Alan Berger on Cities and Health; New Report from Mit's Center for Advanced Urbanism Examines the Best Ways to Help Public Health in Metropolitan Areas," *MIT News,* November 21, 2013, http://news.mit.edu/2013/3q-alan-berger-on-cities-and-health-1121.

43. Alan Berger, *Report on the State of Health and Urbanism* (Cambridge, MA: Center for Advanced Urbanism, 2013), https://dusp.mit.edu/news/report-state-health-urbanism-0.

44. Howard Frumkin, Richard Jackson, and Andrew Dannenberg, "Critique of 'Report on the State of Health + Urbanism,'" *Architect,* April 11, 2014, https://www.architectmagazine.com/technology/critique-of-report-on-the-state-of-health-urbanism_o.

45. Alan Berger et al. "MIT's Center for Advanced Urbanism Counters Criticism of Its 2013 Report," May 5, 2014, https://www.architectmagazine.com/technology/mits-center-for-advanced-urbanism-counters-criticism-of-its-2013-report_o.

46. Berger, *Report on the State of Health.*

47. Hruby and Hu, "Epidemiology of Obesity."

48. V. Lathey, S. Guhathakurta, and R. M. Aggarwal, "The Impact of Subregional Variations in Urban Sprawl on the Prevalence of Obesity and Related Morbidity," *Journal of Planning Education and Research* 29, no. 2 (2009).

49. Kathleen Lebesco, "Neoliberalism, Public Health, and the Moral Perils of Fatness," *Critical Public Health* 21, no. 2 (2011), https://doi.org/10.1080/09581596.2010.529422.

50. J. Eid et al., "Fat City: Questioning the Relationship between Urban Sprawl and Obesity," *Journal of Urban Economics* 63, no. 2 (2008).

51. A. Forsyth et al., "Design and Destinations: Factors Influencing Walking and Total Physical Activity," *Urban Studies* 45, no. 9 (2008).

52. Emily Talen, "Pedestrian Access as a Measure of Urban Quality," *Planning Practice and Research* 17, no. 3 (2002).

53. Arlie Adkins, Carrie Makarewicz, et al., "Contextualizing Walkability: Do Relationships between Built Environments and Walking Vary by Socioeconomic Context?," *Journal of the American Planning Association* 83, no. 3 (2017), https://doi.org/10.1080/01944363.2017.1322527.

54. Arlie Adkins, Gabriela Barillas-Longoria, et al., "Differences in Social and Physical Dimensions of Perceived Walkability in Mexican American and Non-Hispanic White Walking Environments in Tucson, Arizona," *Journal of Transport & Health* 14 (2019): 1005–85.

55. Steven Cummins, Ellen Flint, and Stephen A. Matthews, "New Neighborhood Grocery Store Increased Awareness of Food Access but Did Not Alter Dietary Habits or Obesity," *Health Affairs (Project Hope)* 33, no. 2 (2014), https://doi.org/10.1377/hlthaff.2013.0512.

56. Kevin Gibbs et al., "Income Disparities in Street Features That Encourage Walking," *Bridging the Gap, Research Brief, March* (2012, http://www.bridgingthegapresearch.org/_asset/02fpi3/btg_street_walkability_FINAL_03-09-12.pdf.

57. Khattak and Rodriguez, "Travel Behavior"; Mia A. Papas et al., "The Built Environment and Obesity," *Epidemiologic Reviews* 29, no. 1 (2007).

58. Rice University, Kinder Institute for Urban Research, *The 32nd Kinder Institute Houston Area Survey: Tracking Responses to the Economic and Demographic Trans-*

formations (Houston, Texas, 2013), http://www.houston.org/newgen/Independent _Research/Klineberg-2013-Houston-Area-Survey.pdf.

59. Lawrence D. Frank et al., "Stepping towards Causation: Do Built Environments or Neighborhood and Travel Preferences Explain Physical Activity, Driving, and Obesity?," *Social Science and Medicine* 65, no. 9 (2007), 1900.

60. K. M. Leyden, "Social Capital and the Built Environment: The Importance of Walkable Neighborhoods," *American Journal of Public Health* 93, no. 9 (2003).

61. Louis Hyman, "The Myth of Main Street," *New York Times,* April 8, 2017, Opinion, SR1, https://www.nytimes.com/2017/04/08/opinion/sunday/the-myth-of-main -street.html.

8. The New Ecology of Health

1. Krieger, *Epidemiology and the People's Health,* Text 7–1.

2. Nancy Krieger, "Epidemiology and the Web of Causation: Has Anyone Seen the Spider?," *Social Science & Medicine* 39, no. 7 (1994).

3. Rauch, *Public Parks,* 80–81.

4. Roger S. Ulrich, "View through a Window May Influence Recovery from Surgery," *Science* 224 (1984).

5. Clare Cooper Marcus and Marni Barnes, *Healing Gardens: Therapeutic Benefits and Design Recommendations* (New York: Wiley, 1999).

6. D. Stokols, "Environmental Psychology," *Annual Review of Psychology.* 29, no. 1 (1978): 253–95, https://doi.org/10.1146/annurev.ps.29.020178.001345.

7. Mazda Adli et al., "Neurourbanism: Towards a New Discipline," *Lancet Psychiatry* 4 (2017), doi:10.1016/S2215-0366(16)30371-6.

8. Chris Mooney, "E. O. Wilson Explains Why Parks and Nature Are Really Good for Your Brain," *Washington Post,* September 30, 2015, https://www.washingtonpost .com/news/energy-environment/wp/2015/09/30/e-o-wilson-explains-why -experiencing-nature-is-good-for-the-human-mind/.

9. Frances E. Kuo and William C. Sullivan, "Environment and Crime in the Inner City: Does Vegetation Reduce Crime?," *Environment and Behavior* 33, no. 3 (2001); and Frances E. Kuo and William C. Sullivan, "Aggression and Violence in the Inner City: Effects of Environment via Mental Fatigue," *Environment and Behavior* 33, no. 4 (2001).

10. Andrea Faber Taylor, Frances E. Kuo, and William C. Sullivan, "Coping with ADD: The Surprising Connection to Green Play Settings," *Environment and Behavior* 33, no. 1 (2001).

11. Dongying Li and William C. Sullivan, "Impact of Views to School Landscapes on Recovery from Stress and Mental Fatigue," *Landscape and Urban Planning* 148 (2016), https://doi.org/10.1016/j.landurbplan.2015.12.015.

12. Stephen Kaplan, "The Restorative Benefits of Nature: Toward an Integrative Framework," *Journal of Environmental Psychology* 15, no. 3 (1995), https://doi.org /10.1016/0272-4944(95)90001-2.

13. Ibid.

14. Yoshifumi Miyazaki, *Shinrin-Yoku: The Japanese Art of Forest Bathing* (Portland, OR: Timber Press, 2018).

15. For more detail on these studies see Christopher Neale et al., "The Ageing Urban Brain: Analysing Outdoor Physical Activity Using the Emotiv Affectiv Suite in

Older People," *Journal of Urban Health,* 94, no. 6 (2017): 869–80; and Jenny J. Roe et al., "Engaging the Brain: The Impact of Natural versus Urban Scenes on Brain Activity Using Novel EEG Methods in an Experimental Setting," *Journal of Environmental Sciences* 1, no. 2 (2013): 93–10.

16. Neale et al., "Aging Urban Brain."
17. Andrew J. Kaufman and Virginia I. Lohr, "Does Plant Color Affect Emotional and Physiological Responses to Landscapes?," *Acta Horticulturae* 639 (2004): 229–33.
18. Yannick Joye and Siegfried Dewitte, "Nature's Broken Path to Restoration. A Critical Look at Attention Restoration Theory," *Journal of Environmental Psychology* 59 (2018), https://doi.org/10.1016/j.jenvp.2018.08.006.
19. Cronon, *Uncommon Ground.*
20. Cassandra Y. Johnson et al., "Wilderness Values in America: Does Immigrant Status or Ethnicity Matter?," *Society & Natural Resources* 17, no. 7 (2004), https://doi.org/10.1080/08941920490466585.
21. Jennifer Wolch, John P. Wilson, and Jed Fehrenbach, "Parks and Park Funding in Los Angeles: An Equity-Mapping Analysis," *Urban Geography* 26, no. 1 (2005).
22. Carolyn Finney, *Black Faces, White Spaces: Reimagining the Relationship of African Americans to the Great Outdoors* (Chapel Hill: University of North Carolina Press, 2014), 106.
23. Karen A. Kalmakis and Genevieve E. Chandler, "Adverse Childhood Experiences: Towards a Clear Conceptual Meaning." *Journal of Advanced Nursing* 70, no. 7 (2014): 1489–501, https://doi.org/10.1111/jan.12329.
24. Eugenia C. South et al., "Effect of Greening Vacant Land on Mental Health of Community-Dwelling Adults: A Cluster Randomized Trial," *JAMA Network Open* 1, no. 3 (2018), https://doi.org/10.1001/jamanetworkopen.2018.0298.
25. Jonah Lehrer, "A Physicist Solves the City," *New York Times Sunday Magazine,* December 17, 2010, https://www.nytimes.com/2010/12/19/magazine/19Urban_West-t.html.
26. Luis Bettencourt and Geoffrey West, "A Unified Theory of Urban Living," *Nature* 467, no. 7318 (2010).
27. Jim Balsillie, "Sidewalk Toronto Has Only One Beneficiary, and It Is Not Toronto," *Globe and Mail,* October 5, 2018, updated November 29, 2018, Opinion, https://www.theglobeandmail.com/opinion/article-sidewalk-toronto-is-not-a-smart-city/.
28. Sidewalk Labs, 2019, https://www.sidewalklabs.com/.
29. Leyland Cecco, "'Surveillance Capitalism': Critic Urges Toronto to Abandon Smart City Project," *The Guardian,* June 6, 2019, https://www.theguardian.com/cities/2019/jun/06/toronto-smart-city-google-project-privacy-concerns.
30. Daniel L. Doctoroff, "Why We're No Longer Pursuing the Quayside Project—and What's Next for Sidewalk Labs," Sidewalk Talk, May 7, 2020, https://medium.com/sidewalk-talk/why-were-no-longer-pursuing-the-quayside-project-and-what-s-next-for-sidewalk-labs-9a61de3fee3a.
31. Laura Bliss, "WeWork Wants to Build the 'Future of Cities': What Does That Mean?" *CityLab,* March 25, 2019, https://www.citylab.com/equity/2019/03/wework-smart-cities-machine-learning-coworking-urban-data/585343/. As of 2019, WeWork has been going through a slew of financial issues after a massive valuation cut shortly before a failed attempt to go public, and forced a resignation for its CEO, putting their larger vision for cities in doubt. However, this doesn't discount the

fact that the company still has massive amounts of urban data for its considerable real estate holdings.

32. Tega Brain, "The Environment Is Not a System," in "Research Values," special issue, *APRJA: A Peer Reviewed Journal About* 7, no. 1 (December 2017), https://researchvalues2018.wordpress.com/2017/12/20/tega-brain-the-environment-is-not-a-system/.

33. Ian Birrell, "How One of America's Most Overweight Cities Lost a Million Pounds," *The Atlantic,* October 14, 2015, https://www.theatlantic.com/health/archive/2015/10/how-one-of-americas-fattest-cities-lost-a-million-pounds/410371/.

34. American Planning Association and Groundwork Lawrence, *A Health Impact Assessment of the Lawrence Green Streets Program* (Lawrence, MA: American Planning Association and Groundwork Lawrence, March 2017).

35. Angela Cleveland, AICP, and Neil Angus, AICP, planners with Lawrence Green Streets Health Impact Assessment, interview with author conducted in Boston on October 10, 2019.

36. Joyce Buckner-Brown et al., "Using the Community Readiness Model to Examine the Built and Social Environment: A Case Study of the High Point Neighborhood, Seattle, Washington, 2000–2010," *Preventing Chronic Disease* 11, no. 11 (2014), https://doi.org/10.5888/pcd11.140235.

37. Urban Land Institute, "ULI Case Studies: Mariposa" (Urban Land Institute, 2017), https://casestudies.uli.org/mariposa/.

38. Kathleen Costanza, "Investing with Health in Mind," *Crosswalk Magazine,* December 11, 2015, https://medium.com/bhpn-crosswalk/investing-with-health-in-mind-f9a07416d7f1.

39. Laura Bliss, "When a Hospital Plays Housing Developer," *CityLab* September 21, 2018, https://www.citylab.com/equity/2018/09/when-a-hospital-plays-housing-developer/569800/.

40. National Climate Assessment, "Changes in Hurricanes," U.S. Global Change Research Program, 2014, https://nca2014.globalchange.gov/node/5665.

41. Union of Concerned Scientists, "Is Global Warming Fueling Increased Wildfire Risks?," August 22, 2018, https://www.ucsusa.org/global-warming/science-and-impacts/impacts/global-warming-and-wildfire.html.

42. C. Mora et al., "Broad Threat to Humanity from Cumulative Climate Hazards Intensified by Greenhouse Gas Emissions," *Nature Climate Change* 8, no. 12 (2018), https://doi.org/10.1038/s41558-018-0315-6.

43. Margalit Younger et al., "The Built Environment, Climate Change, and Health," *American Journal of Preventive Medicine.* 35, no. 5 (2008).

44. American College of Allergy, Asthma, and Immunology, "Allergy Facts," updated January 16, 2015, https://acaai.org/news/facts-statistics/allergies.

45. Brent Toderian (@BrentToderian), Twitter thread, December 8, 2017.

46. Boyd A. Swinburn, Vivica I. Kraak, Steven Allender, Vincent J. Atkins, Phillip I. Baker, Jessica R. Bogard, Hannah Brinsden, et al., "The Global Syndemic of Obesity, Undernutrition, and Climate Change: *The Lancet* Commission Report," *The Lancet* 393, no. 10173 (February 23, 2019), https://doi.org/10.1016/S0140-6736(18)32822-8.

47. Meg Anderson and Sean McMinn, "As Rising Heat Bakes U.S. Cities, the Poor Often Feel It the Most," *All Things Considered,* National Public Radio, September 3, 2019,

https://www.npr.org/2019/09/03/754044732/as-rising-heat-bakes-u-s-cities-the
-poor-often-feel-it-most.

48. Coral Davenport and Campbell Robertson, "Resettling the First American 'Climate
Refugees,'" *New York Times,* May 2, 2016, A1, https://www.nytimes.com/2016/05
/03/us/resettling-the-first-american-climate-refugees.html.

49. Erica Goode, "A Wrenching Choice for Alaska Towns in the Path of Climate
Change," *New York Times,* November 29, 2016, https://www.nytimes.com
/interactive/2016/11/29/science/alaska-global-warming.html.

50. Bradford McKee, "Get Ready," *Landscape Architecture Magazine,* November 15,
2016, https://landscapearchitecturemagazine.org/2016/11/15/get-ready/.

51. US Global Change Research Program, *Fourth National Climate Assessment,* 2 vols.
(Washington, DC: US Global Change Research Program, 2018), 640, 654.

Conclusion

1. Lloyd Alter, "What Will Our Homes Be Like after the Pandemic?," *Treehugger,*
June 29, 2020, https://www.treehugger.com/what-will-our-homes-be-like-after-the
-pandemic-5069963.

2. Joel Kotkin, "Angelenos Love Suburban Sprawl: Coronavirus Proves Them Right,"
Los Angeles Times, April 26, 2020.

3. Julia Carrie Wong, "Los Angeles Lifts Air-Quality Limits for Cremations as Covid
Doubles Death Rate," *The Guardian,* January 18, 2021.

4. Jonathan M. Metzl and Anna Kirkland, eds. *Against Health: How Health Became
the New Morality* (New York: New York University Press, 2010), 1–2.

5. Karen B. DeSalvo, Patrick W. O'Carroll, Denise Koo, John M. Auerbach, and
Judith A. Monroe, "Public Health 3.0: Time for an Upgrade," *American Journal of
Public Health* 106, no. 4 (2016): 621–22.

6. Rosenberg, "Epilogue," 662.

7. Robin A. Kearns, "Place and Health: Towards a Reformed Medical Geography,"
Professional Geographer 45, no. 2 (1993): 139–47.

8. Laura Klivans and Matthew Green, "Asthma Rates Higher in California's Historically Redlined Communities, New Study Finds," *KQED News: The California
Report,* May 23, 2019, https://www.kqed.org/news/11749299/asthma-rates-higher
-in-californias-historically-redlined-communities-new-study-finds; and Andrew
Urevig, "What Old Maps Say about Environmental Racism," in "Maps," special
issue of *Lateral,* no. 27 (June 3, 2018), http://www.lateralmag.com/articles/issue-27
/what-old-maps-say-about-environmental-racism.

9. Du Bois, *Philadelphia Negro,* 163.

10. Witold Rybczynski, "The Untold Story of Apple Park," *Architect Magazine,* November 9, 2018, https://www.architectmagazine.com/Design/the-untold-story-of
-apple-park_o.

11. Adds Karen Jones: "Significant here is the presence of a consistent historical narrative stretching from nineteenth-century park designers, health reformers and
period commentators to contemporary park practitioners, advocates and analysts
that fixes the park as a vital socio-environmental unit or biotic 'organ.' Latter-day
critics may have written off landscape planners with their illusions of creating *rus
in urbe* as idealistic romantics, captivated by the countryside, or anti-modernists
horrified by the urban world, but recent evidence from the medical and physical

sciences corroborates their germinating arguments as essentially sound." In Jones, "'Lungs of the City,'" 58.

12. Annette Koh and Konia Freitas, "Is Honolulu a Hawaiian Place? Decolonizing Cities and the Redefinition of Spatial Legitimacy," *Planning Theory and Practice* 19, no. 2 (2018): 280–83. Importantly, the authors write: "Second, we must demonstrate that decolonial practices and indigenous urbanism are not counter-factual fantasies that require a time machine. The Hawaiian proverb '*I ka wā ma mua, i ka wā ma hope*' can be translated as 'The future is in the past.' . . . To speculate about the past is to make the present strange and open up possibilities of decolonization that could subordinate property paradigms to Native Hawaiian understandings of land as responsibility rather than commodity" (282).

13. Annette Koh, "Decolonial Planning in North America," *Progressive City,* March 4, 2019, https://www.progressivecity.net/single-post/2019/03/04/DECOLONIAL -PLANNING-IN-NORTH-AMERICA.

14. Julian Brave Noisecat, "We Need Indigenous Wisdom to Survive the Apocalypse," *The Walrus,* November 2019, https://thewalrus.ca/we-need-indigenous-wisdom -to-survive-the-apocalypse/.

BIBLIOGRAPHY

Adams, Jane M. *Healing with Water: English Spas and the Water Cure, 1840–1960.* Manchester: Manchester University Press, 2015.

Adams, Samuel Hopkins. "Guardians of the Public Health." *McClure's Magazine* 31, no. 3 (1908): 241.

Addams, Jane. *The Spirit of Youth and the City Streets.* New York: Macmillan, 1909.

Adkins, Arlie, Gabriela Barillas-Longoria, Deyanira Nevárez Martínez, and Maia Ingram. "Differences in Social and Physical Dimensions of Perceived Walkability in Mexican American and Non-Hispanic White Walking Environments in Tucson, Arizona." *Journal of Transport & Health* 14 (2019): 1005–85.

Adkins, Arlie, Carrie Makarewicz, Michele Scanze, Maia Ingram, and Gretchen Luhr. "Contextualizing Walkability: Do Relationships between Built Environments and Walking Vary by Socioeconomic Context?" *Journal of the American Planning Association* 83, no. 3 (2017): 296–314. https://doi.org/10.1080/01944363.2017.1322527.

Adli, Mazda, Maximilian Berger, Eva-Lotta Brakemeier, Ludwig Engel, Joerg Fingerhut, Ana Gomez-Carrillo, Rainer Hehl, et al. "Neurourbanism: Towards a New Discipline." *Lancet Psychiatry* 4 (2017). doi:10.1016/S2215–0366(16)30371–6.

Alter, Lloyd. "What Will Our Homes Be Like after the Pandemic?" *Treehugger,* June 29, 2020, https://www.treehugger.com/what-will-our-homes-be-like-after-the-pandemic-5069963.

Altschuler, Sari. *The Medical Imagination: Literature and Health in the Early United States.* Philadelphia: University of Pennsylvania Press, 2018.

American College of Allergy, Asthma, and Immunology. "Allergy Facts." Updated January 16, 2015. https://acaai.org/news/facts-statistics/allergies.

American Planning Association and Groundwork Lawrence. *A Health Impact Assessment of the Lawrence Green Streets Program.* Lawrence, MA: American Planning Association and Groundwork Lawrence, March 2017.

American Public Health Association, Committee on the Hygiene of Housing. *Basic Principles of Healthful Housing.* New York: American Public Health Association, 1941.

——. *Planning the Neighborhood.* Chicago: Public Administration Service, 1960.

Anderson, Meg, and Sean McMinn. "As Rising Heat Bakes U.S. Cities, the Poor Often Feel It the Most." *All Things Considered.* National Public Radio, September 3, 2019. https://www.npr.org/2019/09/03/754044732/as-rising-heat-bakes-u-s-cities-the-poor-often-feel-it-most.

Balsillie, Jim. "Sidewalk Toronto Has Only One Beneficiary, and It Is Not Toronto."

Globe and Mail, October 5, 2018; updated November 29, 2018, Opinion. https://www
.theglobeandmail.com/opinion/article-sidewalk-toronto-is-not-a-smart-city/.

Bates, Barbara. *Bargaining for Life: A Social History of Tuberculosis, 1876–1938.* Philadelphia: University of Pennsylvania Press, 1992, 28–30.

Bauer, Catherine. "The Dreary Deadlock of Public Housing." *Architectural Forum* 87,
no. 5 (May 1957): 141–42.

———. *Modern Housing.* Boston: Houghton Mifflin, 1934.

Bender, Thomas. "The 'Rural' Cemetery Movement: Urban Travail and the Appeal of
Nature." In *The Physical City: Public Space and the Infrastructure,* edited by Neil
Larry Shumsky, 2–17. New York: Routledge, 1996.

Bergdoll, Barry, and Reinhold Martin. *Foreclosed: Rehousing the American Dream.* New
York: Museum of Modern Art, 2012.

Berger, Alan. *Report on the State of Health and Urbanism.* Cambridge, MA: Center for
Advanced Urbanism, MIT, 2013. https://dusp.mit.edu/news/report-state-health
-urbanism-0.

Berger, Alan, et al. "MIT's Center for Advanced Urbanism Counters Criticism of Its
2013 Report." May 5, 2014. https://www.architectmagazine.com/technology/mits
-center-for-advanced-urbanism-counters-criticism-of-its-2013-report_o.

Bettencourt, Luis, and Geoffrey West. "A Unified Theory of Urban Living." *Nature* 467,
no. 7318 (2010): 912–13.

Birrell, Ian. "How One of America's Most Overweight Cities Lost a Million Pounds." *The
Atlantic,* October 14, 2015. https://www.theatlantic.com/health/archive/2015/10
/how-one-of-americas-fattest-cities-lost-a-million-pounds/410371/.

Bliss, Laura. "WeWork Wants to Build the 'Future of Cities': What Does That Mean?"
CityLab, March 25, 2019: https://www.citylab.com/equity/2019/03/wework-smart
-cities-machine-learning-coworking-urban-data/585343/.

———. "When a Hospital Plays Housing Developer." *CityLab,* September 21, 2018.
https://www.citylab.com/equity/2018/09/when-a-hospital-plays-housing-developer
/569800/.

Blackmon, Douglas A., and Thaddeus Herrick. "A New Urbanist Tries to Rebuild New
Orleans Neighborhoods." *Chicago Tribune,* May 14, 2006.

Blake, Peter. "The Suburbs Are a Mess." *Saturday Evening Post,* October 5, 1963, 14–16.

Blodgett, Geoffrey. "Frederick Law Olmsted: Landscape Architecture as Conservative
Reform." *Journal of American History* 62, no. 4 (1976): 869–89. https://doi.org/10
.2307/1903842.

Boer, Rob, Yuhui Zheng, Adrian Overton, Gregory K. Ridgeway, and Deborah A. Cohen.
"Neighborhood Design and Walking Trips in Ten U.S. Metropolitan Areas." *American Journal of Preventive Medicine* 32, no. 4 (2007): 298–304. https://doi.org/10
.1016/j.amepre.2006.12.012.

Bookchin, Murray [Lewis Herber, pseud.]. *Our Synthetic Environment.* New York:
Knopf, 1962.

Boston, City of. City Planning Board. "A Workable Plan for Urban Renewal." Boston:
City Planning Board, 1955.

Boston, City of. Department of Parks. *Notes on the Plan of Franklin Park and Related
Matters.* Boston: Printed for the Department, 1886.

Brain, Tega. "The Environment Is Not a System." In "Research Values," special issue,
APRJA: A Peer Reviewed Journal About 7, no. 1 (2017). https://researchvalues2018
.wordpress.com/2017/12/20/tega-brain-the-environment-is-not-a-system/.

Bruegmann, Robert. *Sprawl: A Compact History*. Chicago: University of Chicago Press, 2005.

Bryant, William Cullen. *Letters of a Traveller; or, Notes of Things Seen in Europe and America*. London, 1850.

Bucholtz, Shawn, and Jed Kolko. "America Really Is a Nation of Suburbs." *CityLab*, November 14, 2018. https://www.citylab.com/life/2018/11/data-most-american -neighborhoods-suburban/575602/.

Buckner-Brown, Joyce, Denise Tung Sharify, Bonita Blake, Tom Phillips, and Kathleen Whitten. "Using the Community Readiness Model to Examine the Built and Social Environment: A Case Study of the High Point Neighborhood, Seattle, Washington, 2000–2010." *Preventing Chronic Disease* 11, no. 11 (2014): E194. doi: 10.5888 /pcd11.140235. https://www.cdc.gov/pcd/issues/2014/14_0235.htm.

Buettner, Dan. *The Blue Zones: 9 Lessons for Living Longer from the People Who've Lived the Longest*. 2nd ed. Washington, DC: National Geographic, 2012.

Burnham, Daniel Hudson, Edward H. Bennett, Charles Moore, and Chicago Commercial Club. *Plan of Chicago*. New York: Princeton Architectural Press, 1993.

Campbell, Margaret. "What Tuberculosis Did for Modernism: The Influence of a Curative Environment on Modernist Design and Architecture." *Medical History* 49, no. 4 (2005): 463–88.

Cannon, Walter B. *The Wisdom of the Body*. New York: W.W. Norton, 1939.

Cavallo, Dominick. *Muscles and Morals: Organized Playgrounds and Urban Reform, 1880–1920*. Philadelphia: University of Pennsylvania Press, 1981.

Cecco, Leyland. "'Surveillance Capitalism': Critic Urges Toronto to Abandon Smart City Project." *The Guardian*, June 6, 2019. https://www.theguardian.com/cities /2019/jun/06/toronto-smart-city-google-project-privacy-concerns.

Centers for Disease Control and Prevention. "Healthy People." National Center for Health Statistics, 2017. https://www.cdc.gov/nchs/healthy_people/index.htm.

———. "Overweight and Obesity." 2017, https://www.cdc.gov/obesity/index.html.

Cervero, Robert, and Kara Kockelman. "Travel Demand and the 3Ds: Density, Diversity, and Design." *Transportation Research, Part D: Transport and Environment 2*, no. 3 (1997): 199–219.

Chapin, F. Stuart. "An Experiment on the Social Effects of Good Housing." *American Sociological Review* 5, no. 6 (1940): 868–79.

Chetty, Nadarajan, Nathaniel Hendren, Patrick Kline, and Emmanuel Saez. "Where Is the Land of Opportunity? The Geography of Intergenerational Mobility in the United States." *Quarterly Journal of Economics* 129, no. 4 (2014): 1553–623. doi:10.1093/qje/qju022.

Chicago, City of. Special Park Commission. *A Plea for Playgrounds: Issued by the Special Park Commission*. Chicago: W. J. Hartman, 1905.

Citizens Association of New York, Council of Hygiene and Public Health. *Report of the Council of Hygiene and Public Health of the Citizens' Association of New York upon the Sanitary Condition of the City*. New York: D. Appleton, 1865.

Comerio, Mary C. "Pruitt Igoe and Other Stories." *Journal of Architectural Education* 34, no. 4 (1981): 26–31.

Committee on the Expediency of Providing Better Tenements for the Poor. *Report of the Committee on the Expediency of Providing Better Tenements for the Poor*. Boston: American Periodicals Series 2, 1847.

"Conditions That Menace Public Health." *Boston Globe*, June 5, 1905, Main ed., 1.

Congress for the New Urbanism. "HUD Hope VI." https://www.cnu.org/our-projects
/hud-hope-vi.

——. "New Urbanism: Rx for Healthy Places." Paper presented at the 18th Annual
Congress for the New Urbanism, Atlanta, 2010.

Congress for the New Urbanism and U.S. Department of Housing and Urban Development. *Principles for Inner City Neighborhood Design: Hope VI and the New Urbanism.* Washington, DC: Department of Housing and Urban Development, n.d.

Corbin, Charles B., and Robert P. Pangrazi. "Toward a Uniform Definition of Wellness:
A Commentary." *President's Council on Physical Fitness and Sports Research Digest,*
series 3, no. 15 (2001): 1–10.

Corburn, Jason. "Reconnecting with Our Roots: American Urban Planning and Public
Health in the Twenty-First Century." *Urban Affairs Review* 42, no. 5 (2007): 688–713.
https://doi.org/10.1177/1078087406296390.

Costanza, Kathleen. "Investing with Health in Mind." *Crosswalk Magazine,* December 11, 2015. https://medium.com/bhpn-crosswalk/investing-with-health-in-mind
-f9a07416d7f1.

Cridlin, Jay. "Water Street Tampa's First Heron Apartments Hit Market, and They're
Not Cheap." *Tampa Bay Times,* January 5, 2021.

Cronon, William. *Uncommon Ground: Rethinking the Human Place in Nature.* New
York: W. W. Norton, 1996.

Cummins, Steven, Ellen Flint, and Stephen A. Matthews. "New Neighborhood Grocery
Store Increased Awareness of Food Access but Did Not Alter Dietary Habits or Obesity." *Health Affairs* 33, no. 2 (2014): 283. https://doi.org/10.1377/hlthaff.2013.0512.

Curran, Winifred, and Trina Hamilton. "Just Green Enough: Contesting Environmental Gentrification in Greenpoint, Brooklyn." *Local Environment* 17, no. 9 (2012):
1027–42. https://doi.org/10.1080/13549839.2012.729569.

Curtis, Henry S. *The Play Movement and Its Significance.* New York: Macmillan, 1917.

Davenport, Coral, and Campbell Robertson. "Resettling the First American 'Climate
Refugees.'" *New York Times,* May 2, 2016, A1. https://www.nytimes.com/2016/05/03
/us/resettling-the-first-american-climate-refugees.html.

Davis, Charles, II. *Building Character: The Racial Politics of Modern Architectural
Style.* Pittsburgh: University of Pittsburgh Press, 2019.

DeBuono, Barbara, ed. *Milestones in Public Health: Accomplishments in Public Health
over the Past 100 Years.* New York: Pfizer Global Pharmaceuticals, 2006.

DELOS. "Stay Well." 2019. http://staywellrooms.com/.

Desalvo, Karen B., Patrick W. O'Carroll, Denise Koo, John M. Auerbach, and Judith
A. Monroe. "Public Health 3.0: Time for an Upgrade." *American Journal of Public
Health* 106, no. 4 (2016): 621. https://doi.org/10.2105/AJPH.2016.303063.

Dizikes, Peter. "3 Questions: Alan Berger on Cities and Health; New Report from MIT's
Center for Advanced Urbanism Examines the Best Ways to Help Public Health in
Metropolitan Areas." *MIT News,* November 21, 2013. http://news.mit.edu/2013/3q
-alan-berger-on-cities-and-health-1121.

Doctoroff, Daniel L. "Why We're No Longer Pursuing the Quayside Project—and
What's Next for Sidewalk Labs." Sidewalk Talk, May 7, 2020. https://medium.com
/sidewalk-talk/why-were-no-longer-pursuing-the-quayside-project-and-what-s
-next-for-sidewalk-labs-9a61de3fee3a.

Dodge, Rachel, Annette Daly, Jan Huyton, and Lalage Sanders. "The Challenge of
Defining Wellbeing." *International Journal of Wellbeing* 2, no. 3 (2012): 222–35.

Downing, Andrew Jackson. *Landscape Gardening.* Edited by Frank Albert Waugh. New York: John Wiley Sons, 1921.

——. *Rural Essays.* New York, 1853.

Driver, Felix. "Moral Geographies: Social Science and the Urban Environment in Mid-Nineteenth Century England." *Transactions of the Institute of British Geographers* 13, no. 3 (1988): 275–87.

Duany, Andres. "Thursday Morning Plenary." Paper presented at the Living Community: The 21st Annual Event from the Congress of the New Urbanism, Salt Lake City, 2013.

Duany, Andres, and Elizabeth Plater-Zyberk, eds. *Towns and Town-Making Principles.* Cambridge, MA: Harvard University Graduate School of Design; New York: Rizzoli, 1991.

Duany, Andres, Elizabeth Plater-Zyberk, and Jeff Speck. *Suburban Nation: The Rise of Sprawl and the Decline of the American Dream.* New York: North Point Press, 2000.

Duany, Andres, and Emily Talen. "Transect Planning." *Journal of the American Planning Association* 68, no. 3 (2002): 245–66.

Du Bois, W. E. B. *The Philadelphia Negro: A Social Study.* Philadelphia: University of Pennsylvania, 1899.

Egger, Garry. "In Search of a Germ Theory Equivalent for Chronic Disease." *Preventing Chronic Disease* 9 (2012): E95.

Eid, J., M. A. Turner, H. G. Overman, and D. Puga. "Fat City: Questioning the Relationship between Urban Sprawl and Obesity." *Journal of Urban Economics* 63, no. 2 (2008): 385–404.

Ellis, Cliff. "The New Urbanism: Critiques and Rebuttals." *Journal of Urban Design* 7, no. 3 (2002): 261–91.

Emerson, Ralph Waldo. *Nature: Addresses, and Lectures.* Boston: Houghton, Mifflin, 1883.

Farkas, Carol-Ann. "'Tons of Useful Stuff': Defining Wellness in Popular Magazines." *Studies in Popular Culture* 33, no. 1 (2010): 113–32.

Fee, Elizabeth, and Theodore M. Brown. "The Unfulfilled Promise of Public Health: Déjà Vu All Over Again." *Health Affairs* 21, no. 6 (2002): 31. https://doi.org/10.1377/hlthaff.21.6.31.

Finney, Carolyn. *Black Faces, White Spaces: Reimagining the Relationship of African Americans to the Great Outdoors.* Chapel Hill: University of North Carolina Press, 2014. doi:10.5149/northcarolina/9781469614489.001.0001.

Fisher, Thomas. "Frederick Law Olmsted and the Campaign for Public Health." *Places Journal,* November 2010. http://places.designobserver.com/feature/frederick-law-olmsted-and-the-campaign-for-public-health/15619/.

Flagg, Wilson. *Mount Auburn: Its Scenes, Its Beauties, and Its Lessons.* Cambridge, MA: J. Munroe, 1861.

Florida, Richard. "In the U.S., Walkability Is a Premium Good." *Bloomberg CityLab,* June 16, 2016. https://www.bloomberg.com/news/articles/2016-06-16/the-economic-benefits-of-walkable-neighborhoods-george-washington-university-report.

——. *The New Urban Crisis: How Our Cities Are Increasing Inequality, Deepening Segregation, and Failing the Middle Class—and What We Can Do about It.* New York: Basic Books, 2017.

Follin, James W. "Slums and Blight . . . a disease of urban life." Sundwell Memorial

Lecture, University of Michigan, May 3, 1955. Washington, DC: Urban Renewal Administration, Housing and Home Finance Agency, 1956.

Forsyth, A., M. Hearst, J. M. Oakes, and K. H. Schmitz. "Design and Destinations: Factors Influencing Walking and Total Physical Activity." *Urban Studies* 45, no. 9 (2008): 1973–96.

Forsyth, Ann. "What Is a Walkable Place? The Walkability Debate in Urban Design." *Urban Design International* 20, no. 4 (2015): 274–92. https://doi.org/10.1057/udi .2015.22.

Frank, L. D., B. E. Saelens, K. E. Powell, and J. E. Chapman. "Stepping towards Causation: Do Built Environments or Neighborhood and Travel Preferences Explain Physical Activity, Driving, and Obesity?" *Social Science and Medicine* 65, no. 9 (2007): 1898–914.

Freund, David. "Marketing the Free Market: State Intervention and the Politics of Prosperity in Metropolitan America." In Kruse and Sugrue, *New Suburban History,* 11–32.

Frost, Joe L. *A History of Children's Play and Play Environments: Toward a Contemporary Child-Saving Movement.* New York: Routledge, 2012.

Frumkin, Howard, Lawrence D. Frank, and Richard J. Jackson. *Urban Sprawl and Public Health: Designing, Planning, and Building for Healthy Communities.* Washington, DC: Island Press, 2004.

Frumkin, Howard, Richard Jackson, and Andrew Dannenberg. "Critique of 'Report on the State of Health + Urbanism.'" *Architect,* April 11, 2014. https://www .architectmagazine.com/technology/critique-of-report-on-the-state-of-health -urbanism_o.

Galishoff, Stuart. "Drainage, Disease, Comfort, and Class: A History of Newark's Sewers." *Societas: A Review of Social History* 6, no. 2 (1976): 121–38.

Galper, Allan S. "Building Boston's Back Bay: Marriage of Money and Hygiene." *Historical Journal of Massachusetts* 23, no. 1 (1995): 61.

Gans, Herbert J. *People and Plans; Essays on Urban Problems and Solutions.* New York: Basic Books, 1968.

Garb, Margaret. "Race, Housing, and Burnham's Plan: Why Is There No Housing in the 1909 Plan of Chicago?" *Journal of Planning History* 10, no. 2 (2011): 99–113. https:// doi.org/10.1177/1538513210384453.

Gibbs, Kevin, S. J. Slater, L. Nicholson, D. Barker, and F. J. Chaloupka. "Income Disparities in Street Features That Encourage Walking." *Bridging the Gap,* Research Brief, March 2012. http://www.bridgingthegapresearch.org/_asset/02fpi3/btg_street _walkability_FINAL_03-09-12.pdf.

"A Gigantic Cesspool." *Boston Globe,* April 8, 1884, Main ed., 1.

Gillham, Oliver. *The Limitless City: A Primer on the Urban Sprawl Debate.* Edited by Alex S. MacLean. Washington, DC: Island Press, 2002.

Gilligan, Heather. "An Entire Manhattan Village Owned by Black People Was Destroyed to Build Central Park: Three Churches, a School, and Dozens of Homes Were Demolished." Timeline, February 22, 2017. https://timeline.com/black-village -destroyed-central-park-6356723113fa.

Gioielli, Robert R. *Environmental Activism and the Urban Crisis: Baltimore, St. Louis, Chicago.* Philadelphia: Temple University Press, 2014.

Golden Gate National Parks Conservancy. "Park Prescriptions." ParkRx, 2019. https:// www.parkrx.org/.

Goode, Erica. "A Wrenching Choice for Alaska Towns in the Path of Climate Change." *New York Times,* November 29, 2016. https://www.nytimes.com/interactive/2016 /11/29/science/alaska-global-warming.html.

Gordon, Mitchell. *Sick Cities: Psychology and Pathology of American Urban Life.* New York: Macmillan, 1963.

Gruen, Victor. *The Heart of Our Cities: The Urban Crisis; Diagnosis and Cure.* New York: Simon and Schuster, 1964.

Haffner, Jeanne. "The Dangers of Eco-Gentrification: What's the Best Way to Make a City Greener?" *The Guardian,* May 6, 2015. http://www.theguardian.com/cities /2015/may/06/dangers-ecogentrification-best-way-make-city-greener.

Hall, G. Stanley. "Recreation and Reversion." *Pedagogical Seminary* 22, no. 4 (1915): 510–20. https://doi.org/10.1080/08919402.1915.10533981.

Hall, Peter Geoffrey. *Cities of Tomorrow: An Intellectual History of Urban Planning and Design in the Twentieth Century.* Oxford: Blackwell, 1996.

Halprin, Lawrence. *Freeways.* New York: Van Nostrand Reinhold, 1968.

———. *The RSVP Cycles: Creative Processes in the Human Environment.* New York: G. Braziller, 1970.

Hamlin, Christopher. "Predisposing Causes and Public Health in Early Nineteenth-Century Medical Thought." *Journal of the Society for the Social History of Medicine* 5, no. 1 (1992): 43. https://doi.org/10.1093/shm/5.1.43.

Hanlon, James. "Success by Design: HOPE VI, New Urbanism, and the Neoliberal Transformation of Public Housing in the United States." *Environment and Planning* A 42, no. 1 (2010): 80–98.

Harris, Richard, and Robert Lewis. "Constructing a Fault(Y) Zone: Misrepresentations of American Cities and Suburbs, 1900–1950." *Annals of the Association of American Geographers* 88, no. 4 (1998): 622–39.

Harvey, David. "The New Urbanism and the Communitarian Trap: On Social Problems and the False Hope of Design." In *Sprawl and Suburbia: A Harvard Design Magazine Reader,* edited by William Saunders. Minneapolis: University of Minnesota Press, 2005.

Hayden, Dolores. *The Power of Place: Urban Landscapes as Public History.* Cambridge, MA: MIT Press, 1995.

Hewitt, R., and B. Szczygiel. "Nineteenth-Century Medical Landscapes: John H. Rauch, Frederick Law Olmsted, and the Search for Salubrity." *Bulletin of the History of Medicine* 74, no. 4 (2000): 708–34.

Hill, Hibbert Winslow. *The New Public Health.* New York: Arno Press, 1977.

Hinkle, Lawrence E., and William C. Loring, eds. *The Effect of the Man-Made Environment on Health and Behavior: A Report of the Inter-University Board of Collaborators.* Atlanta: Center for Disease Control; Washington, DC: Public Health Service, U.S. Dept. of Health, Education, and Welfare, 1977.

Historic American Buildings Survey, Library of Congress. "Harbor Hills Housing Project, 7 Western Avenue, Lomita, Los Angeles County, CA." Lomita, CA, 1933. Photographs. https://www.loc.gov/item/ca2548/.

———. "Lockefield Garden Apartments, 900 Indiana Avenue, Indianapolis, Marion County, IN." William Earl Russ and Merritt Harrison, creators. Indianapolis, IN, 1933. Photographs. https://www.loc.gov/item/in0282/.

Howard, Ebenezer, and Frederic J. Osborn. *Garden Cities of To-Morrow.* Cambridge, MA: MIT Press, 1965.

Howell, Ocean. "Play Pays: Urban Land Politics and Playgrounds in the United States, 1900–1930." *Journal of Urban History* 34, no. 6 (2008): 961–94. https://doi.org/10.1177/0096144208319648.

Hruby, Adela, and Frank Hu. "The Epidemiology of Obesity: A Big Picture." *Pharmaco-Economics* 33, no. 7 (2015): 673–89. https://doi.org/10.1007/s40273-014-0243-x.

Hunter, Katherine M., Bernard E. Hunter, and John Chumasero. "Some Notes on Berkeley Springs, West Virginia." *William and Mary Quarterly* 16, no. 3 (1936): 347–51.

Huth, Hans. *Nature and the American: Three Centuries of Changing Attitudes.* Berkeley: University of California Press, 1972.

Hyman, Louis. "The Myth of Main Street." *New York Times,* April 8, 2017, Opinion, SR1. https://www.nytimes.com/2017/04/08/opinion/sunday/the-myth-of-main-street.html.

International WELL Building Institute. "The International WELL Building Institute Launches the WELL Building Standard® Version 1.0." Press release, October 20, 2014. https://resources.wellcertified.com/articles/the-international-well-building-institute-launches-the-well-building-standard-version-1-0/.

———. *WELL Building Standard v2.* New York: International WELL Building Institute, 2018.

Jackson, John Brinckerhoff. *Landscape in Sight: Looking at America.* New Haven: Yale University Press, 2000.

Jackson, R. J., A. L. Dannenberg, and H. Frumkin. "Health and the Built Environment: 10 Years After." *American Journal of Public Health* 103, no. 9 (2013): 1542–44.

Jacobs, Jane. *The Death and Life of Great American Cities.* New York: Random House, 1961.

Jacobs, Julia. "Their Land Became Part of Central Park: They're Coming Back in a Monument." *New York Times,* October 20, 2019. https://www.nytimes.com/2019/10/20/arts/lyons-seneca-village-monument.html.

Johnson, Cassandra Y., J. M. Bowker, John C. Bergstrom, and H. Ken Cordell. "Wilderness Values in America: Does Immigrant Status or Ethnicity Matter?" *Society & Natural Resources* 17, no. 7 (2004): 611–28. https://doi.org/10.1080/08941920490466585.

Johnson, Steven. *The Ghost Map: The Story of London's Most Terrifying Epidemic—and How It Changed Science, Cities, and the Modern World.* New York: Riverhead Books, 2006.

Jones, Karen R. "'The Lungs of the City': Green Space, Public Health and Bodily Metaphor in the Landscape of Urban Park History." *Environment and History* 24, no. 1 (2018): 39–58.

Joye, Yannick, and Siegfried Dewitte. "Nature's Broken Path to Restoration: A Critical Look at Attention Restoration Theory." *Journal of Environmental Psychology* 59 (2018): 1–8. https://doi.org/10.1016/j.jenvp.2018.08.006.

Kalmakis, Karen A., and Genevieve E. Chandler. "Adverse Childhood Experiences: Towards a Clear Conceptual Meaning." *Journal of Advanced Nursing* 70, no. 7 (2014): 1489–501. https://doi.org/10.1111/jan.12329.

Kaplan, Stephen. "The Restorative Benefits of Nature: Toward an Integrative Framework." *Journal of Environmental Psychology* 15, no. 3 (1995): 169–82. https://doi.org/10.1016/0272-4944(95)90001-2.

Kaufman, Andrew J., and Virginia I. Lohr. "Does Plant Color Affect Emotional and Physiological Responses to Landscapes?" *Acta Horticulturae* 639 (2004): 229–33.

Kearns, Robin A. "Place and Health: Towards a Reformed Medical Geography." *Professional Geographer* 45, no. 2 (1993): 139–47.

Keene, Danya, and E. Geronimus. "'Weathering' HOPE VI: The Importance of Evaluating the Population Health Impact of Public Housing Demolition and Displacement." *Journal of Urban Health* 88, no. 3 (2011): 417–35.

Keirns, Carla C. "Allergic Landscapes, Built Environments, and Human Health." In *Imperfect Health: The Medicalization of Architecture,* edited by Giovanna Borasi and Mirko Zardini, 97–116. Montréal: Canadian Centre for Architecture; Zurich: Lars Müller, 2012.

Kennicott, Philip. "Le Corbusier at MOMA: A Love/Hate Relationship." *Washington Post,* July 12, 2013.

Khattak, A. J., and D. Rodriguez. "Travel Behavior in Neo-Traditional Neighborhood Developments: A Case Study in USA." *Transportation Research Part A: Policy and Practice* 39, no. 6 (2005): 481–500.

Kirk, Patricia. "Is WELL Certification Worth It for Developers?" *National Real Estate Investor,* July 7, 2017. https://www.nreionline.com/office/well-certification-worth-it -developers.

Klivans, Laura, and Matthew Green. "Asthma Rates Higher in California's Historically Redlined Communities, New Study Finds." KQED News: The California Report, May 23, 2019. https://www.kqed.org/news/11749299/asthma-rates-higher-in -californias-historically-redlined-communities-new-study-finds.

Kneebone, Elizabeth. "The Changing Geography of US Poverty." Testimony before the House Ways and Means Committee, Subcommittee on Human Resources, February 15, 2017. https://www.brookings.edu/testimonies/the-changing-geography-of -us-poverty/.

———. "Confronting Suburban Poverty in America." Edited by Alan Berube. Washington, DC: Brookings Institution Press, 2013.

Kneebone, Elizabeth, and Emily Garr. *The Suburbanization of Poverty Trends in Metropolitan America, 2000 to 2008.* Washington, DC: Metropolitan Policy Program at Brookings, 2010.

Knowles, Joseph. *Alone in the Wilderness.* Boston: Small, Maynard, 1913.

Koch, Tom. *Disease Maps: Epidemics on the Ground.* Chicago: University of Chicago Press, 2011.

Koh, Annette. "Decolonial Planning in North America." *Progressive City,* March 4, 2019. https://www.progressivecity.net/single-post/2019/03/04/DECOLONIAL -PLANNING-IN-NORTH-AMERICA.

Koh, Annette, and Konia Freitas. "Is Honolulu a Hawaiian Place? Decolonizing Cities and the Redefinition of Spatial Legitimacy." *Planning Theory and Practice* 19, no. 2 (2018): 280–83.

Kotkin, Joel. "Angelenos Love Suburban Sprawl: Coronavirus Proves Them Right." *Los Angeles Times,* April 26, 2020.

Krieger, Nancy. *Epidemiology and the People's Health: Theory and Context.* New York: Oxford University Press, 2011.

———. "Epidemiology and the Web of Causation: Has Anyone Seen the Spider?" *Social Science & Medicine* 39, no. 7 (1994): 887–903.

Kritzer, Ashley Gurbal. "Here's What Water Street Tampa Will Look and Feel Like at Street Level." *Tampa Bay Business Journal,* June 28, 2018. https://www.bizjournals .com/tampabay/news/2018/06/28/heres-what-water-street-tampa-will-look-and -feel.html.

Krugman, Paul. "Stranded by Sprawl." *New York Times,* July 28, 2013, A17.

Kruse, Kevin M., and Thomas J. Sugrue. *The New Suburban History.* Chicago: University of Chicago Press, 2006.

Kuo, Frances E., and William C. Sullivan. "Aggression and Violence in the Inner City: Effects of Environment via Mental Fatigue." *Environment and Behavior* 33, no. 4 (2001): 543–71.

———. "Environment and Crime in the Inner City: Does Vegetation Reduce Crime?" *Environment and Behavior* 33, no. 3 (2001): 343–67.

Landmarks Preservation Commission of New York. Williamsburg Housing. Addendum to LP-2135, February 10, 2004. http://s-media.nyc.gov/agencies/lpc/lp/2135A.pdf.

Lange, Alexandra. *The Design of Childhood.* London: Bloomsbury, 2018.

"Large Scale Housing Comes into Its Own via Private Enterprise as Metropolitan Life Lends a Hand and Fifty Million for U.S. Project No. 1." *Architectural Forum* 68, no. 5 (May 1938), 4.

Lathey, V., S. Guhathakurta, and R. M. Aggarwal. "The Impact of Subregional Variations in Urban Sprawl on the Prevalence of Obesity and Related Morbidity." *Journal of Planning Education and Research* 29, no. 2 (2009): 127.

Lebesco, Kathleen. "Neoliberalism, Public Health, and the Moral Perils of Fatness." *Critical Public Health* 21, no. 2 (2011): 153–64. https://doi.org/10.1080/09581596.2010.529422.

Le Corbusier. *The City of Tomorrow and Its Planning.* Mineola, NY: Dover, 1929.

———. *La Charte d'Athènes.* 1942; repr., New York: Grossman, 1973.

———. *The Radiant City; Elements of a Doctrine of Urbanism to Be Used as the Basis of Our Machine-Age Civilization.* New York: Orion Press, 1933.

———. *Towards a New Architecture.* Mineola, NY: Dover, 1931.

Lefebvre, Henri. *The Production of Space.* Oxford: Blackwell, 1991.

Lefebvre, Henri, Neil Brenner, and Stuart Elden. *State, Space, World: Selected Essays.* Minneapolis: University of Minnesota Press, 2009.

Legan, Marshall Scott. "Hydropathy in America: A Nineteenth Century Panacea." *Bulletin of the History of Medicine* 45, no. 3 (1971): 267–80.

Lehrer, Jonah. "A Physicist Solves the City." *New York Times Sunday Magazine,* December 17, 2010. https://www.nytimes.com/2010/12/19/magazine/19Urban_West-t.html.

Leinberger, Christopher, and Mariela Alfonzo. "Walk This Way: The Economic Promise of Walkable Places in Metropolitan Washington, D.C." Washington, DC: Brookings Institution, 2012.

Leonard, Jonathan Norton. "Rachel Carson Dies of Cancer; 'Silent Spring' Author Was 56." *New York Times,* April 15, 1964, Books.

Leopold, Aldo. *For the Health of the Land: Previously Unpublished Essays and Other Writings.* Edited by J. Baird Callicott and Eric T. Freyfogle. Washington, DC: Island Press, 2014.

Leyden, K. M. "Social Capital and the Built Environment: The Importance of Walkable Neighborhoods." *American Journal of Public Health* 93, no. 9 (2003): 1546.

Li, Dongying, and William C. Sullivan. "Impact of Views to School Landscapes on Recovery from Stress and Mental Fatigue." *Landscape and Urban Planning* 148 (2016): 149–58. https://doi.org/10.1016/j.landurbplan.2015.12.015.

Light, Jennifer S. *Nature of Cities: Ecological Visions and the American Urban Professions, 1920–1960.* Baltimore: Johns Hopkins University Press.

Lindheim, R., and S. L. Syme. "Environments, People, and Health." *Annual Review of Public Health* 4 (1983): 335–59.

Lo, Ria Hutabarat. "Walkability: What Is It?" *Journal of Urbanism: International Research on Placemaking and Urban Sustainability* 2, no. 2 (2009): 145–66.

Loh, Tracy Hadden, Christopher B. Leinberger, and Jordan Chafetz. *Foot Traffic Ahead: Ranking Walkable Urbanism in America's Largest Metros, 2019.* Washington, DC: Center for Real Estate and Urban Analysis, George Washington University, 2019. https://smartgrowthamerica.org/resources/foot-traffic-ahead-2019.

Lopez, Russell. *Building American Public Health: Urban Planning, Architecture, and the Quest for Better Health in the United States.* New York: Palgrave Macmillan, 2012. doi:10.1057/9781137002440.

Lopez, Russ P. "Public Health, the APHA, and Urban Renewal." *American Journal of Public Health* 99, no. 9 (2009): 1603. https://doi.org/10.2105/AJPH.2008.150136.

Lubar, Steven "Trolley Lines, Land Speculation and Community-Building: The Early History of Woodside Park, Silver Spring, Maryland." *Maryland Historical Magazine* 81, no. 4 (Winter 1986): 316–48.

Lung-Amam, Willow S. *Trespassers? Asian Americans and the Battle for Suburbia.* Berkeley: University of California Press, 2017. doi:10.1525/california/97805202 93892.001.0001.

"The Lungs of London." *The Albion, A Weekly Journal of News, Politics, and Literature* 1, no. 38 (1839): 299.

Lynch, Kevin. *A Theory of Good City Form.* Cambridge, MA: MIT Press, 1981.

Lystra, Margot. "Drawing Natures: US Highway Location, Representational Techniques and the Rise of Ecological Design." *Journal of Design History* 30, no. 2 (2016). https://doi.org/10.1093/jdh/epw013.

Marcus, Clare Cooper, and Marni Barnes. *Healing Gardens: Therapeutic Benefits and Design Recommendations.* New York: Wiley, 1999.

Marshall, Aarian. "Cities Are Watching You—Urban Sciences Graduates Watch Back." *Wired,* June 25, 2018. https://www.wired.com/story/mit-urban-sciences -program/.

Marx, Leo. "The Idea of Nature in America." *Daedalus* 137, no. 2 (2008): 8–21. https:// doi.org/10.1162/daed.2008.137.2.8.

Mathews, H. Edmund. "Sanitation in Modern Architecture." *Journal of the Royal Society for the Promotion of Health* 55, no. 4 (1934): 150–56.

Matos, Jamie. "IWBI Launches the Well Community Standard™ to Promote Human Health and Wellness on a District Scale." WELL, press release, September 5, 2017. https://www.wellcertified.com/en/articles/iwbi-launches-well-community -standard.

McArthur, Benjamin. "The Chicago Playground Movement: A Neglected Feature of Social Justice." *Social Service Review* 49, no. 3 (1975): 376–95.

McKee, Bradford. "Get Ready." *Landscape Architecture Magazine,* November 15, 2016. https://landscapearchitecturemagazine.org/2016/11/15/get-ready/.

McLeod, Kari S. "Our Sense of Snow: The Myth of John Snow in Medical Geography." *Social Science & Medicine* 50, no. 7–8 (2000): 923–35. https://doi.org/10.1016/S0277 -9536(99)00345-7.

Mearns, Andrew. *The Bitter Cry of Outcast London.* London: J. Clarke, 1883.

Melosi, Martin V. *The Sanitary City: Environmental Services in Urban America from Colonial Times to the Present.* Pittsburgh: University of Pittsburgh Press, 2008.

Metzl, Jonathan M., and Anna Kirkland, eds. *Against Health: How Health Became the New Morality*. New York: New York University Press, 2010.

Miller, James William. "A Historical Approach to Defining Wellness." *Spektrum Freizeit* 27 (2005): 84–106.

Mitman, Gregg. "Hay Fever Holiday: Health, Leisure, and Place in Gilded-Age America." *Bulletin of the History of Medicine* 77, no. 3 (2003): 600–635. https://doi.org/10.1353/bhm.2003.0127.

———. "In Search of Health: Landscape and Disease in American Environmental History." *Environmental History* 10, no. 2 (2005): 184–210. http://www.jstor.org/stable/3986112.

Mitman, Gregg, and Ronald Numbers. "From Miasma to Asthma: The Changing Fortunes of Medical Geography in America." *History & Philosophy of the Life Sciences* 25, no. 3 (2003): 391–412.

Miyazaki, Yoshifumi. *Shinrin-Yoku: The Japanese Art of Forest Bathing*. Portland, OR: Timber Press, 2018.

Moody, Walter Dwight. *Wacker's Manual of the Plan of Chicago*. Edited by Charles Henry Wacker and Commission for the Chicago Plan. Chicago: Calumet, 1916.

———. *What of the City? America's Greatest Issue—City Planning, What It Is and How to Go about It to Achieve Success*. Chicago: McClurg, 1919.

Mooney, Chris. "E. O. Wilson Explains Why Parks and Nature Are Really Good for Your Brain." *Washington Post,* September 30, 2015. https://www.washingtonpost.com/news/energy-environment/wp/2015/09/30/e-o-wilson-explains-why-experiencing-nature-is-good-for-the-human-mind/.

Mora, C., D. Spirandelli, E. C. Franklin, J. Lynham, M. B. Kantar, W. Miles, C. Z. Smith, et al. "Broad Threat to Humanity from Cumulative Climate Hazards Intensified by Greenhouse Gas Emissions." *Nature Climate Change* 8, no. 12 (2018): 1062–71. https://doi.org/10.1038/s41558-018-0315-6.

Morabia, Alfredo. "Epidemiologic Interactions, Complexity, and the Lonesome Death of Max Von Pettenkofer." *American Journal of Epidemiology* 166, no. 11 (2007): 1233–38.

———. "Morabia Responds to 'The Context and Challenge of Von Pettenkofer's Contributions to Epidemiology.'" *American Journal of Epidemiology* 166, no. 11 (2007): 1242–43.

Moser, David. "Driven into Poverty: Walkable Urbanism and the Suburbanization of Poverty." Citytank: Ideas for the City, March 8, 2013. http://citytank.org/2013/03/08/driven-into-poverty-walkable-urbanism-and-the-suburbanization-of-poverty/.

Mumford, Eric. "CIAM Urbanism after the Athens Charter." *Planning Perspectives* 7, no. 4 (1992): 391–417.

———. "The 'Tower in a Park' in America: Theory and Practice, 1920–1960." *Planning Perspectives* 10, no. 1 (1995): 17–41.

Mumford, Lewis. *The City in History: Its Origins, Its Transformations, and Its Prospects*. New York: Harcourt, Brace & World, 1961.

———. "The Fourth Migration." *The Survey,* May 1, 1925, 130–33.

———. *The Myth of the Machine*. New York: Harcourt, Brace & World, 1967.

Murray, A. L. "Frederick Law Olmsted and the Design of Mount Royal Park, Montreal." *Journal of the Society of Architectural Historians* 26, no. 3 (1967): 163–71.

Nash, Roderick. *Wilderness and the American Mind*. New Haven: Yale University Press, 2001.

National Climate Assessment. "Changes in Hurricanes." U.S. Global Change Research Program, 2014. https://nca2014.globalchange.gov/node/5665.

Neale, Christopher, P. A. Aspinall, Jennifer Roe, et al. "The Ageing Urban Brain: Analysing Outdoor Physical Activity Using the Emotiv Affectiv Suite in Older People." *Journal of Urban Health* 94, no. 6 (2017): 869–80.

Neil, E. Klepeis, William C. Nelson, Wayne R. Ott, John P. Robinson, Andy M. Tsang, Paul Switzer, Joseph V. Behar, Stephen C. Hern, and William H. Engelmann. "The National Human Activity Pattern Survey (NHAPS): A Resource for Assessing Exposure to Environmental Pollutants." *Journal of Exposure Analysis and Environmental Epidemiology* 11, no. 3 (2001): 231–52. https://doi.org/10.1038/sj .jea.7500165.

New Orleans, City of. *Planning District 6 Rebuilding Plan.* Neighborhoods Rebuilding Plan, 2006. https://nolaplans.com/plans/Lambert%20Intermediate/District _6_Plan_FINAL%20PLAN%20REPORT%20Planning%20District%206%20Profile %2010-04-06.pdf.

Nicolaides, Becky. "How Hell Moved from the City to the Suburbs: Urban Scholars and Changing Perceptions of Authentic Community." In Kruse and Sugrue, *New Suburban History,* 80–98.

Noisecat, Julian Brave. "We Need Indigenous Wisdom to Survive the Apocalypse." *The Walrus,* November 2019. https://thewalrus.ca/we-need-indigenous-wisdom-to -survive-the-apocalypse/.

Nordenson, Catherine Seavett. "The Miasmist: George E Waring, Jr. and the Evolution of Modern Public Health." *Landscape Research Record,* no. 5, 117–26.

Olmsted, Frederick Law. *Civilizing American Cities: A Selection of Frederick Law Olmsted's Writings on City Landscapes.* Cambridge, MA: MIT Press, 1971.

——. "Public Parks and the Enlargement of Towns." *Journal of Social Science, Containing the Proceedings of the American Association* 3 (1871): 1.

——. *The Spoils of the Park: With a Few Leaves from the Deep-Laden Note-Books of "A Wholly Unpractical Man."* Detroit, 1882.

Olmsted and Vaux. *Preliminary Report upon the Proposed Suburban Village at Riverside, near Chicago.* New York: Sutton, Brown, Printers, 1868.

Owen, David. *Green Metropolis: What the City Can Teach the Country about True Sustainability.* New York: Riverhead Books, 2009.

Papas, Mia A., Anthony J. Alberg, Reid Ewing, Kathy J. Helzlsouer, Tiffany L. Gary, and Ann C. Klassen. "The Built Environment and Obesity." *Epidemiologic Reviews* 29, no. 1 (2007): 129–43.

Park, Robert E. "The City: Suggestions for the Investigation of Human Behavior in the City Environment." *American Journal of Sociology* 20, no. 5 (1915): 577–612. https:// doi.org/10.1086/212433.

Park, Robert E., Ernest W. Burgess, Roderick D. McKenzie. *The City.* Chicago: University of Chicago Press, 1967.

Parkes, Edmund A. *A Manual of Practical Hygiene: Prepared Especially for Use in the Medical Service of the Army.* 3rd ed. London: J. Churchill & Sons, 1869. https:// catalog.hathitrust.org/Record/011713661. http://hdl.handle.net/2027/uc1.b527 4189.

Park Rx America. https://parkrxamerica.org/.

Paumgarten, Nick. "The Message of Measles," *New Yorker,* August 26, 2019, 38–47.

Peck, Jamie. "Struggling with the Creative Class." *International Journal of Urban and*

Regional Research 29, no. 4 (2005): 740–70. https://doi.org/10.1111/j.1468-2427
.2005.00620.x.

Perry, Clarence, et al. *Neighborhood and Community Planning.* New York: Regional
Plan of New York and Its Environs, 1929.

Peterson, Jon A. "The Impact of Sanitary Reform upon American Urban Planning,
1840–1890." *Journal of Social History* 13, no. 1 (1979): 83–103.

Philadelphia, City of. Public Playgrounds Commission. *Playgrounds for Philadelphia:
Report of the Public Playgrounds Commission.* Philadelphia: Printed by the Commission, 1910. http://hdl.handle.net/2027/hvd.32044096987110.

Pogrebin, Robin. "An Architect with Plans for a New Gulf Coast." *New York Times,*
May 24, 2006, Art & Design.

Power, Garrett. "Apartheid Baltimore Style: The Residential Segregation Ordinances of
1910–1913." *Maryland Law Review* 42, no. 2 (1983): 289–328.

"The Present Look of Our Great Central Park." *New York Daily Times,* July 9, 1856, 8.

"Public Housing and the USHA." *Architectural Forum* 70, no. 1 (January 1940), 10.

Pyatok, Michael. "Martha Stewart vs. Studs Terkel? New Urbanism and Inner Cities
Neighborhoods That Work." *Places Journal* 13, no. 1 (2000): 40–43.

Quirk, Vanessa. "Citing Equity Issues, Founder of Atlanta Beltline Leaves Board."
Metropolis, September 27, 2016. https://www.metropolismag.com/cities/landscape
/citing-equity-issues-founder-of-atlanta-beltline-leaves-board/.

Rainwater, Clarence Elmer. *The Play Movement in the United States: A Study of Community Recreation.* Chicago: University of Chicago Press, 1922.

Rauch, John H. *Internments in Populous Cities and Their Influence upon Health and
Epidemics.* Chicago: Tribune, 1866.

———. *Public Parks: Their Effects upon the Moral, Physical and Sanitary Condition
of the Inhabitants of Large Cities; with Special Reference to the City of Chicago.*
Chicago: S.C. Griggs, 1869.

Rice University, Kinder Institute for Urban Research. *The 32nd Kinder Institute Houston Area Survey: Tracking Responses to the Economic and Demographic Transformations.* Kinder Institute for Urban Research, 2013. https://scholarship.rice.edu
/bitstream/handle/1911/105182/2013-report.pdf?sequence=1&isAllowed=y.

Richardson, Benjamin Ward. *Hygeia: A City of Health.* London: Macmillan, 1876.

Richmond, Phyllis Allen. "American Attitudes toward the Germ Theory of Disease
(1860–1880)." *Journal of the History of Medicine and Allied Sciences* 9, no. 4 (1954):
428–54. https://doi.org/10.1093/jhmas/IX.4.428.

Riis, Jacob. "Parks for the Poor." *Christian Union* 44, no. 6 (1891): 272.

———. "The Value of Playgrounds to the Community." *Public Health Journal* 4, no. 5
(1913): 267–71.

Rodriguez, Daniel A., Asad J. Khattak, and Kelly R. Evenson. "Can New Urbanism
Encourage Physical Activity? Comparing a New Urbanist Neighborhood with Conventional Suburbs." *Journal of the American Planning Association* 72, no. 1 (2006):
43–54.

Roe, Jenny J., Peter A. Aspinall, Panagiotis Mavros, and Richard Coyne. "Engaging the
Brain: The Impact of Natural versus Urban Scenes on Brain Activity using Novel
EEG Methods in an Experimental Setting," *Journal of Environmental Sciences* 1,
no. 2 (2013): 93–10. http://dx.doi.org/10.12988/es.2013.3109.

Rogers, Elizabeth Barlow. *Landscape Design: A Cultural and Architectural History.* New
York: Harry N. Abrams, 2001.

Rosenberg, Charles E. "Epilogue: Airs, Waters, Places; A Status Report." *Bulletin of the History of Medicine* 86, no. 4 (2012): 661–70. https://doi.org/10.1353/bhm.2012.0082.

"Round Hill Water Cure Establishment." *Boston Recorder* 32, no. 27 (1847): 106.

"Round Hill Water Cure Institute." *Ballou's Pictorial Drawing—Room Companion* 9, no. 8 (1855): 120.

Rowan, Jamin Creed. "The New York School of Urban Ecology: The *New Yorker,* Rachel Carson, and Jane Jacobs." *American Literature* 82, no. 3 (2010): 583. https://doi.org /10.1215/00029831-2010-025.

Rybczynski, Witold. "The Untold Story of Apple Park." *Architect Magazine,* November 9, 2018. https://www.architectmagazine.com/Design/the-untold-story-of-apple -park_o.

Saarinen, Eliel. *The City: Its Growth, Its Decay, Its Future.* Cambridge, MA: MIT Press, 1943.

Sallis, J. F., N. Owen, and E. B. Fisher. "Ecological Models of Health Behavior." *Health Behavior and Health Education: Theory, Research, and Practice* 4 (2008): 465–86.

San Francisco, City of. City Planning Commission. *New City: San Francisco Redeveloped.* San Francisco: City Planning Commission, 1947.

Satariano, William A., Susan L. Ivey, Elaine Kurtovich, Melissa Kealey, Alan E. Hubbard, Constance M. Bayles, Lucinda L. Bryant, Rebecca H. Hunter, and Thomas R. Prohaska. "Lower-Body Function, Neighborhoods, and Walking in an Older Population." *American Journal of Preventive Medicine* 38, no. 4 (2010): 419–28.

Saunders, William S. *Sprawl and Suburbia: A Harvard Design Magazine Reader.* Minneapolis: University of Minnesota Press, 2005.

Schlereth, Thomas J. "Burnham's *Plan* and Moody's *Manual* City Planning as Progressive Reform." *Journal of the American Planning Association* 47, no. 1 (1981): 70–82. https://doi.org/10.1080/01944368108977091.

Schultz, Stanley K., and Clay McShane. "To Engineer the Metropolis: Sewers, Sanitation, and City Planning in Late-Nineteenth-Century America." *Journal of American History* 65, no. 2 (1978): 389–411.

Schuyler, David. *The New Urban Landscape: The Redefinition of City Form in Nineteenth-Century America.* Baltimore: Johns Hopkins University Press, 1986.

Scott, James C. *Seeing like a State: How Certain Schemes to Improve the Human Condition Have Failed.* New Haven: Yale University Press, 1998.

Sennett, Richard. *Flesh and Stone: The Body and the City in Western Civilization.* New York: W. W. Norton, 1994.

Sert, José Luis, and International Congresses for Modern Architecture. *Can Our Cities Survive? An ABC of Urban Problems, Their Analysis, Their Solutions; Based on the Proposals Formulated by the C.I.A.M., International Congresses for Modern Architecture, Congrès Internationaux D'architecture Moderne.* Cambridge, MA: Harvard University Press; London: Oxford University Press, 1942.

Shah, Nayan. *Contagious Divides: Epidemics and Race in San Francisco's Chinatown.* Berkeley: University of California Press, 2001.

Shanken, Andrew Michael. *194X: Architecture, Planning, and Consumer Culture on the American Home Front.* Minneapolis: University of Minnesota Press, 2009.

Sidewalk Labs. 2019. https://www.sidewalklabs.com/.

Small, Andrew. "CityLab Daily: This Election Year, Density Is Destiny." *CityLab,* October 5, 2018. https://www.citylab.com/newsletter-editions/2018/10/citylab-daily -suburbs-will-swing-elections/572257/.

Smith, Carl S. *City Water, City Life: Water and the Infrastructure of Ideas in Urbanizing Philadelphia, Boston, and Chicago.* Chicago: University of Chicago Press, 2013.

Sontag, Susan. *Illness as Metaphor.* New York: Farrar, Straus and Giroux, 1978.

South, Eugenia C., Bernadette C. Hohl, Michelle C. Kondo, John M. Macdonald, and Charles C. Branas. "Effect of Greening Vacant Land on Mental Health of Community-Dwelling Adults: A Cluster Randomized Trial." *JAMA Network Open* 1, no. 3 (2018), https://doi.org/10.1001/jamanetworkopen.2018.0298.

Southworth, Michael. "New Urbanism and the American Metropolis." *Built Environment* 29, no. 3 (2003): 210–26.

Speck, Jeff. *Walkable City: How Downtown Can Save America, One Step at a Time.* New York: Farrar, Straus and Giroux, 2012.

———. "Why They Hate Us: A New Urbanist Dissects the Movement's Critics." *Architect,* June 2010, 68.

Spencer-Wood, Suzanne M. "Turn of the Century Women's Organizations, Urban Design, and the Origin of the American Playground Movement." *Landscape Journal.* 13, no. 2 (1994): 125.

Spirn, Anne Whiston. "Constructing Nature: The Legacy of Frederick Law Olmsted." In *Uncommon Ground: Rethinking the Human Place in Nature,* edited by William Cronon, 91–113. New York: W. W. Norton, 1996.

———. *The Granite Garden: Urban Nature and Human Design.* New York: Basic Books, 1984.

Staley, Kathryn. "Ameliorating Poverty." *Godey's Magazine* 133, no. 797 (1896): 510.

Stein, Clarence. "Dinosaur Cities." *The Survey* 54, no. 3 (May 1, 1925), 134–38.

Stellers, Frances Stead. "D.C. Doctor's Rx: A Stroll in the Park instead of a Trip to the Pharmacy." *Washington Post,* May 15, 2015.

Steyn, Gerald. "Le Corbusier and the Human Body." *South African Journal of Art History* 27, no. 2 (2012): 259–72.

Stickler, Joseph William. *The Adirondacks as a Health Resort: Showing the Benefit to Be Derived by a Sojourn in the Wilderness, in Cases of Pulmonary Phthisis, Acute and Chronic Bronchitis, Asthma, "Hay-Fever" and Various Nervous Affections.* New York: G.P. Putnam's Sons, 1886.

Stokols, D. "Environmental Psychology." *Annual Review of Psychology* 29, no. 1 (1978): 253–95. https://doi.org/10.1146/annurev.ps.29.020178.001345.

Strategic Property Partners, LLC and International WELL Building Institute. "Water Street Tampa First to Achieve WELL Design and Operations Designation for Global Wellness Standard for Communities." Press release, May 28, 2019.

Su, Jason G., Michael Jerrett, Rob McConnell, Kiros Berhane, Genevieve Dunton, Ketan Shankardass, Kim Reynolds, Roger Chang, and Jennifer Wolch. "Factors Influencing Whether Children Walk to School." *Health & Place* 22 (2013): 153–61. https://www.sciencedirect.com/science/article/abs/pii/S1353829213000609?via %3Dihub.

Susser, Mervyn, and Zena Stein. *Eras in Epidemiology: The Evolution of Ideas.* Oxford: Oxford University Press, 2009.

Swinburn, Boyd A., Vivica I. Kraak, Steven Allender, Vincent J. Atkins, Phillip I. Baker, Jessica R. Bogard, Hannah Brinsden, et al. "The Global Syndemic of Obesity, Undernutrition, and Climate Change: *The Lancet* Commission Report." *The Lancet* 393, no. 10173 (February 23, 2019). https://doi.org/10.1016/S0140–6736 (18)32822–8.

Szibbo, Nicola. "Lessons for LEED® for Neighborhood Development, Social Equity, and Affordable Housing." *Journal of the American Planning Association* 82, no. 1 (2016): 37–49. https://doi.org/10.1080/01944363.2015.1110709.

Tachieva, Galina. *Sprawl Repair Manual.* Washington, DC: Island Press, 2010.

Talen, Emily. "The Geospatial Dimension in Urban Design." *Journal of Urban Design* 16, no. 1 (2011): 127–49.

———. "Pedestrian Access as a Measure of Urban Quality." *Planning Practice and Research* 17, no. 3 (2002): 257–78.

Taylor, Andrea Faber, Frances E. Kuo, and William C. Sullivan. "Coping with ADD: The Surprising Connection to Green Play Settings." *Environment and Behavior* 33, no. 1 (2001): 54–77.

Taylor, Frederick Winslow. *The Principles of Scientific Management.* New York: Harper & Brothers, 1913.

Thompson, Walter. "How Urban Renewal Destroyed the Fillmore in Order to Save It." *Hoodline,* January 3, 2016, https://hoodline.com/2016/01/how-urban-renewal -destroyed-the-fillmore-in-order-to-save-it.

"To Opium-Eaters, Arsenic-Takers, Etc." *Ballou's Dollar Monthly Magazine* 15, no. 1 (1862): 94.

Trowbridge, Matthew J., Sarah Gauche Pickell, Christopher R. Pyke, and Douglas P. Jutte. "Building Healthy Communities: Establishing Health and Wellness Metrics for Use within the Real Estate Industry." *Health Affairs* 33, no. 11 (2014): 1923. https://doi.org/10.1377/hlthaff.2014.0654.

Ulrich, Roger S. "View through a Window May Influence Recovery from Surgery." *Science* 224 (1984): 420.

Union of Concerned Scientists. "Is Global Warming Fueling Increased Wildfire Risks?" August 22, 2018. https://www.ucsusa.org/global-warming/science-and-impacts /impacts/global-warming-and-wildfire.html.

United States. Department of Health and Human Services. "Step It Up! The Surgeon General's Call to Action to Promote Walking and Walkable Communities." Washington, DC: U.S. Department of Health and Human Services, Office of the Surgeon General, 2015. https://www.surgeongeneral.gov/library/calls/walking-and -walkable-communities/index.html.

———. Department of Housing and Urban Development. "Choice Neighborhoods." 2018. https://www.hud.gov/cn.

———. Green Building Council. *LEED V4: Reference Guide for Neighborhood Development.* Washington, DC: United States Green Building Council, 2018.

———. National Commission on Urban Problems. *Building the American City: Report.* New York: Praeger, 1969.

Unwin, Raymond. *Nothing Gained by Overcrowding! How the Garden City Type of Development May Benefit Both Owner and Occupier.* London: Garden Cities and Town Planning Association, 1912.

Urban Land Institute. *Building Healthy Places Toolkit.* Washington, DC: Urban Land Institute, 2015.

———. "ULI Case Studies: Mariposa." Urban Land Institute, 2017. https://casestudies .uli.org/mariposa/.

Urevig, Andrew. "What Old Maps Say about Environmental Racism." In "Maps," special issue of *Lateral,* no. 27 (June 3, 2018). http://www.lateralmag.com/articles/issue-27 /what-old-maps-say-about-environmental-racism.

US Global Change Research Program. *Fourth National Climate Assessment.* 2 vols. Washington, DC: US Global Change Research Program, 2018.

Vale, Lawrence J. "Moralism and Urban Evolution: Excavating Mumford's *The City in History.*" *Built Environment* 41, no. 3 (2015): 352–65. https://doi.org/10.2148/benv .41.3.352.

Valenčius, Conevery Bolton. *The Health of the Country: How American Settlers Understood Themselves and Their Land.* New York: Basic Books, 2002.

von Hoffman, Alexander. "High Ambitions: The Past and Future of American Low-Income Housing Policy." *Housing Policy Debate* 7, no. 3 (1996): 423–46.

———. "The Lost History of Urban Renewal." *Journal of Urbanism* 1, no. 3 (2008): 281–301.

Walker, Mabel L., with chapters by Henry Wright. *Urban Blight and Slums; Economic and Legal Factors in Their Origin, Reclamation, and Prevention.* Harvard City Planning Studies, no. 12. New York: Russell & Russell, 1971.

Walk Score. "Walk Score Methodology." 2020. https://www.walkscore.com /methodology.shtml.

Wallace, Rodrick, and Deborah Wallace. "The Coming Crisis of Public Health in the Suburbs." *Milbank Quarterly* 71, no. 4 (1993): 543–64. https://doi.org/10.2307 /3350418.

———. "Origins of Public Health Collapse in New York City: The Dynamics of Planned Shrinkage, Contagious Urban Decay and Social Disintegration." *Bulletin of the New York Academy of Medicine* 66, no. 5 (1990): 391.

Walsh, Bill. "Andres Duany on Rebuilding after Hurricane Katrina: Part I—The Gulf Coast." Healthy Building Network, October 10, 2005. https://healthybuilding.net /blog/133-andres-duany-on-rebuilding-after-hurricane-katrina-part-i-the-gulf -coast.

Ward Thompson, Catharine. "Linking Landscape and Health: The Recurring Theme." *Landscape and Urban Planning* 99, no. 3/4 (2011): 187–95. https://doi.org/10.1016/j .landurbplan.2010.10.006.

Waring, George, E. "The Cleaning of a Great City." *McClure's Magazine* 9, no. 5. (1897): 4.

———. *The Sanitary Drainage of Houses and Towns.* New York: Hurd and Houghton; Cambridge, Riverside Press, 1876.

Warner, Sam Bass. *The Urban Wilderness: A History of the American City.* New York: Harper & Row, 1972.

Warren, John Collins. *Physical Education and the Preservation of Health.* Boston: William D. Ticknor, 1846.

Weckowicz, Thaddeus E., and Helen P. Liebel-Weckowicz, eds. "The Scientific Revolution and the Beginnings of Modern Philosophy." *Advances in Psychology* 66, no. C (1990): 61–70. https://doi.org/10.1016/S0166-4115(08)61443-0.

Weisz, George. *Chronic Disease in the Twentieth Century: A History.* Baltimore: Johns Hopkins University Press, 2014.

White, Morton Gabriel, and Lucia White. *The Intellectual versus the City: From Thomas Jefferson to Frank Lloyd Wright.* Cambridge, MA: Harvard University Press, 1962.

Whyte, William H. *The Last Landscape.* Garden City, NY: Doubleday, 1968.

Wilson, Brian C. "Dr. Kellogg and Race Betterment." In *Dr. John Harvey Kellogg and the Religion of Biologic Living.* Bloomington: Indiana University Press, 2014, 133–70.

Winslow, C.-E. A. "Public Health at the Crossroads." *American Journal of Public Health* 16, no. 11 (1926): 1075–85. https://doi.org/10.2105/AJPH.16.11.1075-a.

Winternitz, Wilhelm. "Hydrotherapeutics." In *Handbook of General Therapeutics,* by H. von Ziemessen. Vol. 5: 273–606. London: Smith, Elder, 1886.

Wolch, Jennifer R., Jason Byrne, and Joshua P. Newell. "Urban Green Space, Public Health, and Environmental Justice: The Challenge of Making Cities 'Just Green Enough.'" *Landscape and Urban Planning* 125 (2014): 234–44.

Wolch, Jennifer, John P. Wilson, and Jed Fehrenbach. "Parks and Park Funding in Los Angeles: An Equity-Mapping Analysis." *Urban Geography* 26, no. 1 (2005): 4–35.

Wong, Julia Carrie. "Los Angeles Lifts Air-Quality Limits for Cremations as Covid Doubles Death Rate." *The Guardian,* January 18, 2021.

Wood, Edith Elmer. "The Costs of Bad Housing." *Annals of the American Academy of Political and Social Science* 190, no. 1 (1937): 145–50. https://doi.org/10.1177 /000271623719000117.

World Health Organization. Declaration of Alma-Ata, International Conference on Primary Health Care, Alma-Ata, USSR, September 6–12, 1978. https://www.who.int /publications/almaata_declaration_en.pdf.

———. "Improving Vaccination Demand and Addressing Hesitancy." WHO, World Health Organization, updated June 17, 2020. https://www.who.int/immunization /programmes_systems/vaccine_hesitancy/en/.

Wright, Frank Lloyd. *The Living City.* New York: New American Library, 1970.

Wright, Henry. "The Road to Good Houses." *The Survey* 54, no. 3 (May 1, 1925): 166– 68, 189.

Young, Mark. "Walk with a Doc." *Parks & Recreation* 48, no. 9 (2013): 20.

Younger, Margalit, Heather R. Morrow-Almeida, Stephen M. Vindigni, and Andrew L. Dannenberg. "The Built Environment, Climate Change, and Health." *American Journal of Preventive Medicine* 35, no. 5 (2008): 517–26.

INDEX

Italicized page numbers refer to illustrations.

automobiles: and air pollution, 86; degraded environment and health, 134; and environmentalism, 156; and Fourth Migration, 110; in Garden Cities, 77, 78; highway planning, 116, 126; and suburban sprawl, 109, 131, 134–35, 229n35; as target of New Urbanist movement, 136; and unchecked, low-density development, 135–36
Autumnal Catarrh (Wyman), 38–39

Ballou's Dollar Monthly Magazine, 35
Baltimore, Maryland: germ theory of disease and segregation, 104; race and urban renewal, 124; sanitary sewer system, 55
Barbour, Haley, 143
Barham, C., 43
Barnes, Marni, 186
Basic Principles of Healthful Housing (APHA), 85
Bass, Sam, 213n5
Bauer, Catherine, 101–2, 103
Berger, Alan, 174, 175–76
"Berkeley Springs, West Virginia" (Moray and Hoen), *40*
Bettencourt, Luis, 192, 193
Better Tenements for the Poor (1846), 18–19, 20, 27–28
Bigelow, Jacob, 58
Biophilia (Wilson), 186–87
Bitter Cry of Outcast London, The (Mearns), 157
Blackwood's Edinburgh, 61
Blake, Peter, 128–29, 130
Blue Zones Project, 1
Bookchin, Murray (Lewis Herber), 115–16, 118
Boston, Massachusetts: Back Bay Fens, 65–66, 68, 72; disparity between poor and wealthy neighborhoods, 18; elites during Covid-19, 206; Emerald Necklace, 68; first cemetery outside city limits, 58; as hybrid of industrial and agricultural activity, 11; sand garden, 49; sewer system, 27; use of HIAs, 195; "A Workable Plan for Urban Renewal," 123
Boston Globe, 65, 66
Boston Medical and Surgical Journal, 34
Boston Recorder, 36
Bowling Alone: The Collapse and Revival of American Community (Putnam), 134–35
"Boys Enjoying the Amusements of a Public Playground" (Hine), *50*
Bradburn, Norman, 6
Brain, Tega, 195
Brave Noisecat, Julian, 211
Broadacre City, 109
Bronfenbrenner, Urie, 133–34

Brooklyn, New York: Greenwood Cemetery, 58; Newton Creek Superfund site (Greenpoint), 167–68; Ten Eyck Houses (Williamsburg Houses), 98, *98, 99,* 104
Bryant, William Cullen: as advocate for public parks, 58–59, 60; growing rates of economic inequality, 59; parks of England, 82
Buege, David, 143
"Build a Better Burb" (Long Island Index), 173
buildings, as self-contained cities, 90
Building the American City (National Commission on Urban Problems), 124–25
built environment: and Affordable Care Act, 198; and health, 3, 147–50, *149,* 152–53, 174–76, 209; myriad community-level approaches used to improve health through, 195–99, *196, 197, 198;* quantifying potential health benefits from, 208; relationship with behavior, 180–81; research on effect of, 169–70, 174–76, 178–85, *182,* 190–91, *191;* unintended consequences of altering, 177; use of language of disease for, 84, 86, 112, 119–20, 126, 178. *See also* urban landscapes
Burgess, Ernest, zonal model, 87–88, *88*
Burnham, Daniel: aesthetic concerns of, 71, 72, 73; background, 63–64; benefits of parks, 74; Chicago plans by, 72, *74,* 74–75; commercial and elite from cities moving to suburbs, 78; as epitome of Progressive Era city planners, 63; Hausmann's Paris as template for, 72, *73, 74,* 82; legacy, 82; plans for suburbs, 75; San Francisco plans by, 72; urban density and need for parks, 71; White City in 1893 Columbian Exposition, 71

Cabrini Green, Chicago, Illinois, 142, 225n49
Campbell, F. R., 43
Campoli, Julie, 151–52
Cannon, Walter B., 87
Can Our Cities Survive? (CIAM), 91–92, 94–95
capitalism: parks' benefits to, 68; public space as product of, 5; and urban renewal, 124–25
Carson, Rachel, 115
Case, John, illustration from *Compendium Anatomicum, 2*
catarrh (hay fever), 34, 35–36, 38–39, *40,* 43
Celebration, Florida, 139
cemeteries: in cities, 57, 61; first, outside city limits, 58; as places of leisure, 58, 61
Center for Advanced Urbanism (MIT), 174
Center for Urban Science and Progress (CUSP, New York University), 192
Centers for Disease Control (CDC), 112, 114, 131, 146, 167, 211

Central Park, New York City: construction of, *69,* 71; displacement of African Americans and of poor to build, 68, *69,* 71; health benefits of, 71; "natural" topography and features, *70;* and Olmsted, 64, 220n33; Vaux as agricultural and drainage engineer for, 63; "walled off" from city by trees, *70*

Cervero, Robert, 150

Chadwick, Edwin, 24–25

Channing, Walter, 25

Chapin, F. Stuart, 102

Charter and Congress for the New Urbanism (CNU), 135, 140, 145, 146, 229n32

Chicago, Illinois: Burnham's plans for, 72, *73, 74,* 74–75, 82; Cabrini Green, 187, 225n49; Drainage Canal as money saver and example of health preparedness, 57; Hull House sand garden, 49; as hybrid of industrial and agricultural activity, 11; 1995 heat wave in, 201–2; playgrounds, 45–46; "A Plea for Playgrounds," 51, 53; School of Sociology at University of Chicago, 87–88; sewer system, 27; *Wacker's Manual for the Plan of Chicago,* 71–72; White City in 1893 Columbian Exposition, 71

Chicago Playground Association, 45–46

Chicago Settlement House movement, 44–45

Chicago Tribune, 216n1

Choice Neighborhood Initiative, 142

cholera: burial of victims, 58; and English sanitation, 13–14; epidemics in nineteenth-century America, 13, 23; mapping and spread of, *22,* 22

chronic diseases: causes of, 117, 118, 184; in cities, 90–91; and disconnection from and loss of control over environment, 133; and environment, 115–16; epidemiology of, as "black box," 117; and gender, 117; obesity epidemic, 131, 134; policies and, 134; preoccupation with cancer, 117; primary causes of mortality, 116; primary characteristic, 127; and urban blight, 118–23, *122*

cities: ability to escape, for healthy nature, 37; adverse effect on morality of, 79, 158; algorithm guiding growth of, 192, 193; American historical view of, as being antithesis of health, 155; animals in nineteenth-century cities, 11, *13,* 16; arguments for and against decentralization of, 122; building of sewer systems, 28; Burgess zonal model, 88, *88;* cemeteries in, 57, 61; chronic diseases in, 90–91; and climate change, 200; as closed ecosystem, 114–15; conditions in, leading to disease, 21; and COVID-19, 206;

data-driven ("smart"), 192–95, *194,* 201; decentralization of, 110–12, 123–24, *124,* 127; as decoupled from human health, 112; diseases of, spreading to suburbs, 155–56, 231n1; diseases of late 1970s, as social, 114; diseases of upper classes in, 34, 35–36; and ecological view of health, 1, 16, 64; economic class and departure from, during epidemics, 14; effect of health of each urbanite on all, 29; environmental health of, 156; evaluating walkability, 150–51; food deserts in, 174, 180, 199; germs in, 48; health and science models and metaphors used, 84, 86–89, *88, 89,* 92, 110–12, *113,* 126–27, 192; health in, as worse than in country, 78–79; housing density as defining difference between, and suburbs, 173; Howard's model, 88; as hybrid of industrial and agricultural activity, 11–12, *12,* 16; and immigrants' rural backgrounds, 33; increasing poverty of poor in American, could lead US to becoming like European, 18; as intellectually stimulating and therefore requiring green spaces, 62; legitimizing through scientific models, 85; measures separating, from natural environment, 31; mortality studies, 13, 14; myriad community-level approaches used in, to improve health through built environment, 195–99, *196, 197, 198;* nature as binary of, 54; nature's efforts to reclaim landscape of, 33, 216n1; nodes and networked circulation of streets, 26–27; nostalgia for agrarian US and anti-urban perceptions, 109; as origins of disease, 39, 86; period of most rapid growth of, 11; poverty in, as different from suburban poverty, 159; power of nature viewed as in opposition to, 210; privatized services, 28; Progressive Era ideal, 75; race and building of sewer systems, 55; Saarinen and organic models of, 87, *89;* sanitary infrastructure construction, 26–27, 28, 31; spread of diseases to suburbs, 120, 155–56, 231n1; street systems and human heart, 27; suburbs as binary of, 88, 112, 114, 128, 158–59; suburbs' relationship to, 78, 79. *See also entries beginning with* urban

citizenship and play, 47

City, The: Its Growth, Its Decay, Its Future (Saarinen), 87, 119–20

City Beautiful movement, 75, 85, 173

Cityblock, 193

CityLab, 160

City of Tomorrow and Its Planning (Le Corbusier), 92–93

climate change and health, 200–204

and privatized municipal services, 28; and Progressive Era ideal city, 75; and reconnecting with nature, 54; replacement of housing for poor with housing for wealthy, 124–25; and residence, 157–58; and urban blight, 118–19; and walkability, 169–70, 179–80, 181; and way of life, 158; and WELL Certified Communities, 165. *See also* poverty

economy, 2–3, 5, 7. *See also* industry and industrialization

Effect of the Man-Made Environment on Health and Behavior, The (CDC), 112, 114

efficiency, 56, 57

Emerson, Ralph Waldo, 33

England: cholera and London water system, 13–14; Garden City in Letchworth, 77; London, 14, 59, 61; parks of, 60–61, 82

environmental determinism, 99, 114, 174–76, 178, 208

environmental justice movement, 116, 181, 211

Environmental Protection Agency (EPA), 146, 150, 211

environmental psychology, 186–91, *188*

environment and environmentalism: automobiles and degradation of, 134; and cholera and yellow fever epidemics, 23; chronic disease and disconnection from and loss of control over, 133; and chronic illness, 115–16; defining, 133; and density of cities, 156; and diseases, 1, 21, 132, 146; dismissed as cause of disease by germ theory proponents, 43; and "green gentrification," 165–67, *166;* health and degradation of, 200–201; and industry, 115–16; LEED and sustainability, 160–61; poor as victims of, 20; scientific management of, 192–95, *194;* use of bodily and wellness metaphors in, 87

"Environment Is Not a System, The" (Brain), 195

"Environments, People, and Health" (Lindheim and Syme), 132–33

epidemics: burial practices, 57–58; economic class and departure from cities during, 14; landscapes as vector of, 4; in nineteenth-century America, 13, 23; professionalization of urban planning and public health to combat, 3; as result of individual choices, 3; syndemic, 201; urban landscape movements as reactions to specific urban, 5. *See also specific epidemics by name*

"epidemiological triangle," 117

"Epilogue: Airs, Waters, Places; A Status Report" (Rosenberg), 84–85

etiological individual, 82–83, 84–85

Europe: establishment of CIAM, 91; germ theory acceptance in, 23; grand boulevards in cities in, 26–27; Hausmann's Paris plans as template, 72, *73, 74;* health resorts in, as model for America, 41–42; Healthy Cities and integration of economic, social, and environmental conditions into study of epidemics, 152; increasing poverty of poor in American cities could lead to becoming like cities in, 18; landscapes of, as examples of good, 110–11; and New Urbanist movement, 137; parks in the great cities of, 59–60; and public housing in US, 85; sewer systems as example for American cities, 28; social and economic factors of disease, 118; social housing in, 104; translating trends from, while forming American ethos toward urban green space, 60; and view of healthy landscapes, 210. *See also* England

Ewing, Reid, 150

"Experiment on the Social Effects of Good Housing, An" (Chapin), 102

"Fat City: Questioning the Relationship between Urban Sprawl and Obesity" (Eid), 179

Federal Aid Highway Act (1954), 126

Federal Housing Act (1949), 130

Fedrizzi, Rick, 162

Fellheimer, Alfred, 98

Fillmore (Western Addition) District renewal, San Francisco, California, 123–24, *124*

Finney, Carolyn, 190

Flagg, Wilson, 58

Flesh and Stone (Sennett), 27

Florida, Richard, 156, 157–58, 160

Follin, James W., "Slums and Blight," *122,* 122, 123

Forbes, 131

"Foreclosed: Rehousing the American Dream" (Museum of Modern Art, New York City), 170, *172,* 172–74

Forsyth, Ann, 154

"Fourth Migration, The" (Mumford), 109–10

Fourth National Climate Assessment, 204

Fracastoro, Girolamo, 21

Francis, Carolyn, 186

Frank, Lawrence D., 134, 181

Freeways (Halprin), 126

Frumkin, Howard, 134, 146, 147, 175

Gans, Herbert, 158

Garden Cities: American, by Stein and Wright, 77–78; automobiles in, 77, 78; housing density as basis of, 133; Howard's plans, 76–77,

Garden Cities (*continued*)
78; and Mumford, 129; preservation of rural landscape, 34; public housing links to, *96, 96-98, 97, 98;* tenets of, in APHA guidelines for suburbs, 112; "Town-Country" as best of "Town" and "Country," 76–77; Unwin's in Letchworth, England, 77

Garden Cities of To-morrow (Howard), 76, 92

gardening, 186

gender: and chronic diseases, 117; morality attributed to women, 48; and playgrounds and playground movement, 48, 50, 53; and public health and planning versus housing reformers, 75; women and plumbing functions, 23; women in suburbs, 130

Gentilly neighborhood, New Orleans, Louisiana, 143–44, *144*

gentrification: and displacement, 167; "green," 165–67, *166,* 168

Geography of Nowhere, The (Kunstler), 141

germ theory of disease: acceptance in Europe of, 23; air and sunlight in, 91; as clarifying argument of miasmists, 24; dirt and germs of urban streets, 48; and dismissal of environmental causes of disease, 43; as justification for housing covenants and neighborhood controls, 104–5; modern split of public health from urban design, 82–83, 84; and shift of study of public health from external to internal causes, 90

Godey's Lady's Book, 23, 29

Good City Form (Lynch), 127

Good Health: A Journal of Hygiene, illustration from, *12*

Good Housekeeping, 44

Google, Sidewalk Labs, 193–94; Sidewalk Toronto, *194*

Gordon, John, 118

Gordon, Mitchell, 118–19

Gould, E. K. L., 29, 216n50

Graunt, John, 14

Gravel, Ryan, 166

"green." *See* environment and environmentalism; nature

"Green Case for Cities" (Rybczynski), 156

"green gentrification," 165–67, 168, 209

Green Metropolis: Why Living Smaller, Living Closer, and Driving Less Are the Keys to Sustainability (Owen), 156

Green Streets, Lawrence, Massachusetts, *196,* 196–97, *197*

Greenwood Cemetery, Brooklyn, New York, 58

Gropius, Walter, 91

Groundwork Lawrence, Green Streets Lawrence, *196,* 196–97, *197*

Gruen, Victor, *The Heart of Our Cities: The Urban Crisis; Diagnosis and Cure,* 110–12, *113*

"Guardians of Public Health" (Adams), 83

Gulick, Luther, 43–44, 45

Hall, G. Stanley, 44, 45, 47

Hall, Peter, 75

Halprin, Lawrence, 126, 154

Halsted, H., 41

Hamilton, Trina, 167–68

Handy, Susan, 150

Harbor Hills Housing Project, Lomita, Los Angeles County, California, 96, *96,* 97

Harlem, New York, urban renewal, 121

Harmony Oaks Housing, New Orleans, Louisiana, 140

Harper's Weekly, 69

Harris, Elisha, 65

Harrison, Merritt, Lockefield Gardens, Indianapolis, Indiana, 96–97, *97*

Harvey, David, 141–42

Haskell, Llewellyn, 79

Hausmann, Georges-Eugène, 72, 82

Hayden, Dolores, 4

hay fever (catarrh), 34, 35–36, 38–39, 40, 43

Hay Fever and Paroxysmal Sneezing (Mackenzie), 34, 35–36

health: Affordable Care Act, 198, 211; American historical view of cities as being antithesis of health, 155; American search for quick fix for, 211; in cities as worse than in country, 78–79; of cities decoupled from human, 112; and climate change, 200–204; disease as binary of, 118; ecological view, 1, 16, 64, 65, 66, 67, 84; effect of, of each urbanite on all, 29; as ethic in built environment, 209; as fundamental human right, 1–2; gentrification as issue of, 167; guidelines to encourage, in built environment, 3, 150; individual responsibility for, 7, 19, 20, 178, 180; and influence of built environment, 174–76; medical geographies' connections between, and place, 37–38; and morality, 20, 207; myriad community-level approaches used in cities to improve, through built environment, 195–99, *196, 197, 198;* natural outcome of spatial or economic optimization, 193; nature as synonymous with, 168; parks as benefiting, 60–61, 63, 64, 71, 72–74; pathological view of, 84; and playgrounds, 46–47, 48–49; poverty associated with ill, 54; pre-existing respiratory issues and COVID-19, 206; quantifying potential, benefits from built environment, 208; redefinition of, 118, 227n28; safeguarding, of citizens as nation's greatest asset, 57; shaping built environment for, 147–50, 149, 152–53; social determinants ("upstream"), 132–35; of suburban residents, 129, 130; tension between humanistic thinking technocratic and scientific solutions for, 31; traditional view, 1; urban blight as cause of poor health, 120; as weight loss in popular media, 146; World Health Organization definition, 1; zip code as indicator, 1. *See also* commodification of health; Garden Cities; walking and walkability

Health Affairs, 160

Health and Urbanism (MIT), 175

Health and Wealth of the City of Wheeling, The (Reeves), 39

health impact assessments (HIAs), 195

"healthism," 178–79, 180

health resorts: Adirondacks, 36, 39–40; and economic class, 42; European, as model for American, 41–42; as medical treatment and vacation, 41; railroads and growth of, 37; sanitoriums as advancement on, for germ theory era, 91; urbanization of, 41; "water cure," 35, 36, 36–37, 37, 41; western US, 41–42; West Virginia, 39, 40; White Mountains of New Hampshire, 38, 38–39

"Healthy and Safe Community Environments," 148

Healthy Community Design Initiative (CDC), 167, 211

Healthy People initiatives (HHS), 132

Heart of Our Cities, The: The Urban Crisis; Diagnosis and Cure (Gruen), 110–12, 113

Heat Wave: A Social Autopsy of Disaster in Chicago (Klinenberg), 201–2

Herber, Lewis (Murray Bookchin), 115–16, 118

"High Ambitions: The Past and Future of American Low-Income Housing Policy" (Hoffman), 104

High Line, New York City, 165–66, 168

Hill, Hibbert Winslow, 82–83

Hippocrates, 16, 21, 34, 214n9

Hoen, A., "Berkeley Springs, West Virginia," 40

Hoffman, Alexander von, 104

HOPE VI, 140, 142, 229n32

"horticultural therapy," 186

hot and mineral springs, 36–37, 37, 41

housing: APHA guide to healthful, 93; Burn-

ham's Chicago plans absence of, 75; choice and race, 20; costs and walkability ratings, 160; covenants and segregation, 104; and economic class, 157–58; healthcare industry investments in, 199; influence of sanitoriums on, 91; Le Corbusier's individualization of, 92–93; and miasmic gases, 25; mismatch between desired, and existing, 181; mixed-income strategy in, 141–42; for poor as experiments, 142; for poor replaced with, for wealthy, 124–25; "scientific," 93, 94; for workers, 27–28. *See also* public housing

Housing Act (1954), 124

housing density: and air ventilation, 23; Americans' connotations of, 174; as basis of Garden Cities, 133; as defining difference between cities and suburbs, 128, 173; and disease, 17–18, 64–65, 93, 133, 173; and environmentalism, 156; and Garden Cities, 76, 77; and higher mortality rate, 43; and need for parks, 71; Olmsted and, 64–65; playgrounds to reduce, 46; and suburban regulations, 136; tenements, 29, 216n50; and walkability, 152

Howard, Ebenezer: background, 76; and Le Corbusier, 92; and New Urbanists, 135; Town-Country concept, 78, 173. *See also* Garden Cities

human body: as metaphor for city, 87, 92, 110–12, 113, 192; understanding through nature, 2

humoral models of diseases, 21

hydropathy, 35, 36, 36–37, 37, 41

"Hydrotherapeutics" (Winternitz), 34

Hygeia: A City of Health (Richardson), 25, 76

hygiene: appearance of, 28; of poor and disease, 29; utopian city of Hygeia, 25

Hyman, Louis, 181–83

illness. *See* diseases; epidemics

Illness as Metaphor (Sontag), 6, 117, 118

Image of the City (Lynch), 150

immigrants: assimilation of, in suburbs, 78; as bringers of disease, 18–19, 19; as contributors to playground movement, 53; and COVID-19, 8, 206; and improvement of urban landscapes for health, 165; and nature, 189–90; rural backgrounds, 33; and walkability, 180

Indigenous communities: balance with nature of, 210, 239n12; and climate change, 202–3; and decolonial framework for planning, 210–11, 239n12; removal of, to establish national parks, 189; and wilderness, 33

individual responsibility: and commodification of health, 159, 165; epidemics as
result of, 3; for health, 7, 19, 20, 178, 180;
and mythic American landscape, 7; and
obesity, 174
industry and industrialization: Burnham's
plans for, 75; cities as hybrid of, and
agricultural activity, 11–12, *12,* 16; as destructive to body and soul, 44; and diseases,
115–16; of economy of health, 41; housing
for workers, 27–28; longing for nature as
reaction against, 32; parks and playgrounds
movements as backlash to, 54; rapid growth
of, 11, 12; as self-governing enterprise with
little oversight, 12
Intellectual versus the City, The (White and
White), 109
Intermodal Surface Transportation Efficiency
Act (1991), 147
International Congresses for Modern Archi-
tecture (CIAM), 91, 93, 94–95
International Journal of Wellbeing, 6
International WELL Building Institute
(IWBI), 161–65; first Certified Community
District, Tampa, Florida, *163*
*Intramural Interments in Populous Cities and
Their Influence upon Health and Epidemics*
(Rauch), 61

Jackson, John Brinckerhoff, 4, 33, 217n7
Jackson, Richard, 134, 146, 147, 175
Jacobs, Jane, 103, 115, 128, 136, 137–38
James, William, 188
Jarves, James Jackson, 61
Jefferson, Thomas, 33–34, 109, 217n7
Jefferson Square urban renewal plan, San
Francisco, California, *124,* 124
Jensen, Jens, 46
Jobs, Steve, 210
Johnson, David, *White Mountains from
Conway, NH, 38*
Johnson, George, 45, 47
Johnson, Reginald D., Harbor Hills Housing
Project, Lomita, Los Angeles County, Cali-
fornia, 96, *96,* 97
Journal of the American Planning Association,
147, 166–67
Journal of Urban Design, 150
Journal of Urban Economics, 179
"Justifying Value of a Public Park, The"
(Olmsted), 67

Kaiser Permanente, 199
Kalihi Housing, Honolulu, Hawaii, 140, *141*

Kaplan, Rachel, 188, 189
Kaplan, Steven, 188, 189
Kellogg, John Harvey, 7, 214n14
Kennedy, Donald, 114
Khattak, Asad J., 150
"Kind of Assisted Emigrant We Can Not Afford
to Admit, The" (*Puck*), 19, *19*
Klinenberg, Eric, 201–2
Kneebone, Elizabeth, 157, 159
Knowles, Joseph, 34
Koch, Robert, 21
Kockleman, Kara, 150
Kotkin, Joel, 206
Krieger, Nancy, 184–85
Krugman, Paul, 157
Kunstler, James Howard, 141, 229n35
Kuo, Frances E. (Ming), 187, 225n49

Ladies Home Journal, 23
Lady's Annual Register, 23
Lancet, The, 201
Landscape Architecture Magazine, 203
landscapes: basic tenet of theory of, 5; and
crime, 225n49; Eurocentric view of, 210;
inclusion of grass, trees, etc. in playgrounds,
50, 51, *52;* individual responsibility and
mythic American, 7; and LEED-ND, 161; and
New Urbanist movement, 137–38; pastoral
and European examples of good, 110–11; and
recovery times in healthcare environments,
186; as reflecting changing health concepts,
4; relationship to neurology, 62; research
on effect of "green," on health, 185–91, *191;*
as responsibility, 239n12; trees as index of
living conditions, 95; trees as walling off
parks from city, 67, *70;* and WELL Community Standard, 162–65, *163*
Last Landscape, The (Whyte), 110, 128
Lawrence, Massachusetts, *196,* 196–97, *197*
Learning from Las Vegas (Venturi and Scott
Brown), 135
Le Corbusier: influence of, in US, 95; influence
of tuberculosis sanitoriums, 91; and nature,
94, 95; and optimization of individual,
92–93, 103; Plan Voison, 99, *100;* political
views of, 94; purpose of street to, 93; Radiant
City (Ville Radieuse), 34, 93, *94;* therapeutic
benefits of viewing nature, 225n49; use of
body metaphor by, 92; Vitruvian Man for the
Modern Age, 92
Lee, Joseph, 47
LEED (Leadership in Energy and Environmental Design) and LEED-ND, 160–61, 162,
166–67

Lefebvre, Henri, 5, 103
Leinberger, Christopher, 169–70
leisure: cemeteries as places of, 58, 61; to increase efficiency of workers, 57; and parks and playgrounds movements, 54; technology and time for, 32; walking for, 152, 153
L'Enfant, Pierre Charles, 27
Leopold, Aldo, 87
Lescaze, William, Williamsburg Houses (Ten Eyck Houses), Brooklyn, New York, 98, *98, 99,* 121
Letchworth, England, 77
Letters of a Traveller (Bryant), 59
Li, Dongying, 187
Lindheim, Roslyn, 132–33
Living City, The (Wright), 109
Llewellyn Park, New Jersey, 79
Local Government Commission of California, 135
Lockefield Gardens, Indianapolis, Indiana, 96–97, *97*
Los Angeles Times, 206
Lukez, Paul, 170
"Lungs of London, The" (*Blackwood's Edinburgh*), 61
Lynch, Kevin, 127, 150

Mackenzie, Morell, 34, 35–36
Made for Walking: Density and Neighborhood Form (Campoli), 151–52
Mannheim, Marvin, 116, 126
Marcus, Clare Cooper, 186
Marin County, California, *182*
Mark West Hot Springs, California, *37*
Massachusetts, 46, 198–99
Massachusetts Housing Investment Corporation, 198–99
Massachusetts Institute of Technology (MIT), 174, 175, 192–93
M'Cabe, James, 35
McClure's Magazine, 12–13, 26, 83
McHarg, Ian, 116, 126
McKee, Bradford, 203
McMichael, A. J., 184, 185
Mearns, Andrew, 157
medical geographies/topographies: connections between place and health, 37–38; current calls for integration of societal framework into, 208–9; described, 37, 38; dissemination of findings, 38–39; and germ theory, 43; and human embodiment of environment, 208; methodology, 43; as official field, 15; as part travel brochures, 41–42; research, 37
"medical imagination," 31

miasma theory of disease: and contagion theory, 21–22; germ theory of disease as clarifying, 24; and housing, 25; and winds, 16–17, 61–62
Middleton Hills, Wisconsin, 138
Milbank Quarterly, 120
mineral springs, 36–37, *37,* 41
Mineral Waters of the United States and Their Therapeutic Uses, The (Crook), 41
Modern Housing (Bauer), 101
Modulor, Le (Le Corbusier), 92
Moody, Walter Dwight: Hausmann's Paris plans as template for Chicago, 72, *73, 74;* parks as encouraging good behavior and health, 72–73, 74; parks as encouraging good morality, 63; promotion of power of urban planning, 71–72; scientific management in urban planning, 56–57; selling Burnham's plan for Chicago, 75
"Moral Influence of Graves" (Flagg), 58
morality and moralism: in APHA guidelines for suburbs, 112; attributed to women, 48; city's adverse effect on, 79; city streets as danger to, of youth, 43–44; and cleanliness, 23; as connected to wellness, 35; and disease, 6; and health, 20, 207; and housing density, 18; and nature, 32, 33, 217n7; parks as encouraging good, 63, 72–74; and playgrounds, 47–48; poverty associated with, 54; and primitive psyche, 47; Progressive Era ideas about, 81, 82; public parks and playgrounds and, 53, 59–60; of urban dwellers and good mental health of upper classes, 62; and urban planners, 57; and walkability, 180. *See also* individual responsibility
Moray, John, "Berkeley Springs, West Virginia," *40*
Morgenthau, Henry, 57
mortality, *17;* of children, 19; chronic diseases as primary cause of, 116; contagious diseases as cause of, 23; COVID-19, 205; density and disease and higher urban, 43; and economic class, 14; extensive sewer systems in Europe and low rates of, 28; and housing density, 18; and obesity epidemic, 131; and race, 55; studies of urban, 13, 14
Mount Auburn, Cambridge, Massachusetts, 58
Muir, John, 33
Mumford, Lewis: Burnham's plan for Chicago, 75; Garden Cities model, 129; migration stages, 109–10; moral bankruptcy of suburbs, 158; negative aspects of suburbs, 128, 129; opinion of urban planners, 228n6; unplanned neighborhoods, 86

Murthy, Vivek, 148
Museum of Modern Art, New York City, "Foreclosed: Rehousing the American Dream," 170, *172,* 172–74

National Cancer Act (1971), 116
National Commission on Urban Problems, 102, 124–25
national parks, 189
Nationwide Children's Hospital, 199
Native Americans. *See* Indigenous communities
Natural and Political Observations made upon the Bills of Mortality (Graunt), 14
nature: ability to escape cities for, 33, 37; and agrarian production, 34; biological connections between health and, 65; city as binary of, 54; consistent study of health effect of, 210, 238n11; as curing disease, 33, 34, 39, 42; defining, 189; different conceptions of, 173; economic class and reconnecting with, 54; efforts of, to reclaim urban landscape, 33, 216n1; and Green Streets, *196,* 196–97, *197;* and Indigenous communities, 210, 239n12; and Le Corbusier, 94, 95; longing for, as reaction against industrialization, 32; measures separating cities from, 31; and morality, 32, 33, 217n7; parks and playgrounds movements type of, 54; power of, viewed as in opposition to urbanity, 210; research on effect of, 185–91, *191;* as restorative by its existence, 188; role of, in disadvantaged neighborhoods, 225n49; romanticization of, *38;* as synonymous with health, 168; understanding human body through, *2;* wilderness, 33, 109, 189–90
"Nature-City" (WORKac), *172,* 172–73
Neale, Christopher, 188–89
neurourbanism, *188,* 188–89
Newark, New Jersey, sewer system, 27
New Orleans, Louisiana: burials in, 58; effect of hurricanes on, 143–45, *144,* 202; Harmony Oaks Housing, 140
New Public Health (Hill), 82–83
Newton Creek Superfund site, Greenpoint, Brooklyn, 167–68
New Urban Crisis, The (Florida), 157–58
New Urbanist movement: automobiles as target of, 136; communities, 138, 139, *139,* 140–41, *141;* critics of, 230n47; and European architecture, 137; foundation of, 3; goals, 135, 136; and green spaces, 137–38; impact of, 145–46; mixed-income strategy in housing as subtext of, 141–42; neighborhood

codes, 137; and *Planning the Neighborhood,* 136; and public housing, 140–42; rebuilding of New Orleans after Hurricane Katrina, 143–45, *144;* and Seattle public housing approach, 197, *198;* SmartCode, 145, 170, *171;* socioeconomic effects of works of, 137, 138, 142, 145; and sprawl, 139–40; as used by developers, 140; and walkability of communities, 150–51, 152; and walkability scores, 160
New York City: Active Design Guidelines, 3; early playgrounds, *45,* 46, *46,* 49; elites during Covid-19, 206; ground conditions (1865), 15–16; guide to increasing "active design," 195; High Line, 165–66, 168; as hybrid of industrial and agricultural activity, 11, *13,* 16; mortality survey (1863), 14; plans for Staten Island, 65; Queensbridge Housing (Queens), 98–99, *100–101;* sanitary surveys (nineteenth-century), 3, 11, *15;* sanitation during nineteenth century in, 12–13, *13,* 14–16; sewer system, 27; Stuyvesant Town, 96; Sunnyside Gardens, 129; West Side Urban Renewal Area (WSURA), 115, *125;* "White Wings" street sweepers and trash collectors, 26. *See also* Brooklyn, New York; Central Park, New York City
New York Daily Times, 68, 71
New York Evening Post, 58–59
New York Illustrated News, 41
"New York Park, The" (Downing), 60
New York (state) "small parks" law, 46
New York Times, 68, 143, 157, 168, 181–83
New York Times Magazine, 192
Nicolaides, Becky, 158
Nothing Gained by Overcrowding!: How the Garden City Type of Development May Benefit Both Owner and Occupier (Unwin), 77

obesity epidemic: campaign against, 147–50, *149;* causes, 131, 134, 177, 179; and climate change, 201; and COVID-19, 206; and economic class, 178, 179–80; extent, 146; and food deserts, 174, 180; and individual responsibility, 174, 178; mortality, 131; walking as cure, 146
Oklahoma City, 195–96
Olin, Laurie, 210
Olmsted, Frederick Law: background, 63, 64; Boston Back Bay Fens plans, 66; Central Park project, 64, 220n33; and Chicago playgrounds, 46; density as root cause of diseases, 64–65; ecological view of cities, 64, 65, 66, 67, 84; as epitome of Progressive

sprawl: and automobiles, 131, 229n35; and
COVID-19, 206; decentralization of cities,
127; and intergenerational upward mobility,
157; and New Urbanists, 139–40; and obesity,
179; and public health, 134; "repair" of, 170,
171, 172, 172–74; and socioeconomic effects
of New Urbanists' works, 138; suburban, 109,
131, 134–36, 229n35; as threat to social ordering and sensible resource management,
87, 110, 128, 134–35

Sprawl Repair Manual (Tachieva), 170, *171*
Squatters in Central Park (Wyand), *69*
Stebbins, Henry, 80
Stein, Clarence, 86; Garden Cities, 77–78;
Harbor Hills Housing Project, Lomita, Los
Angeles County, California, 96, *96,* 97
Stein, Zena, 117
"Step It Up!" campaign, 148, *149*
Stickler, Joseph W., 36, 39–40
Strategic Property Partners, LLC, 163, 233n25
Stuyvesant Town, New York City, 96
*Suburban Nation: The Rise of Sprawl and the
Decline of the American Dream* (Duany,
Plater-Zyberk, and Speck), 135–38, 139, 142
Suburban Transformations (Lukez), 170
suburbs: abandonment of productive nature
in, 173; Americans defining neighborhood
as, 159; APHA template for, 112, 114;
architectural code for, 136–37; assimilation
of immigrants in, 78; Burnham's plans for,
75; city as binary of, 88, 112, 114, 128, 158–59;
and climate change, 200; diseases of cities
spreading to, 120, 155–56, 231n1; economic
class and migration to, 78, 86; health of residents, 129, 130; housing density as defining
difference between cities and, 173; housing
density regulations, 136; as ideal rural-urban
hybrid, 80; infrastructure dangers in, 86;
as mark of success of residents, 130; media
image of, 201; moral bankruptcy of, 158; negative aspects of, 128–30, 157; as not solution
to urban problems, 86; and obesity epidemic,
131; and Olmsted, 76; peak of, 128; poverty
in, as different from urban poverty, 159;
racial diversity in, 157; relationship to cities,
78, 79; "repair" of unchecked development,
170, *171, 172,* 172–74; and sprawl, 109, 131,
134–36, 229n35; urban renewal as "immuni-
zation" against spread of urban blight to, 121;
winding roads of, 79; women in, 130
"Suburbs Are a Mess, The" (Blake), 128–29
Sullivan, Louis, 109
Sullivan, William C., 187, 225n49
Sumner Fields Homes, Minneapolis, Minnesota, 102

sunlight, 42, 90–91
Sunnyside Gardens, New York City, 129
Survey, The (ed. Mumford), 86
Susser, Ezra, 184, 185
Susser, Mervyn, 117, 184, 185
Sydenham, Thomas, 21
Syme, Leonard, 132–33

Tachieva, Galina, *Sprawl Repair Manual,*
170, *171*
Talen, Emily, 153
Tampa, Florida, *163,* 163–65, 233n25
Taylor, Frederick Winslow, 56
Taylor, Graham, 45
technology: and ability to build bigger and with
increased control of internal environment,
90; and accessibility to nature, 33; and
Fourth Migration, 110; and leisure time, 32;
and obesity epidemic, 131; scientific man-
agement of environment, 192–95, *194*
Tenement House Commission, 46
tenements: air in, 17–18, 29, 216n50; physical
and moral environment of, 20; and sewer
systems, 28
Ten Eyck Houses (Williamsburg Houses),
Brooklyn, New York, 98, *98, 99,* 104
Thoreau, Henry David, 33, 217n7
"Three Magnets" (Garden City), 76
Toderian, Brent, 201
Toronto, Canada, 193–94, *194*
Towards a New Architecture (Le Corbusier),
92–93, 94
"Town-Country," 76–77
Towns and Town-Making Principles (Duany
and Plater-Zyberk), 138–39
"townsite consciousness," 64, 66
"Transect Planning," 145
transportation: and climate change, 200;
funding, 147; and Olmsted, 66; railroads and
growth of resort towns, 37. *See also* automo-
biles; walking and walkability
Travis, John, 7
Trump, Donald, 203, 204, 205
tuberculosis, 55, 117
typhus, and Chicago Drainage Canal, 57

Ulrich, Roger, 186, 187
United States Green Building Council
(USGBC), 160–61
Unwin, Raymond, 77
urban blight, *110, 111;* as cause of poor health
or symptom of poverty and larger systems,
120; causes of, 119; and chronic diseases, 127;
and city as closed ecosystem, 115; language
of disease and epidemiology to describe,

119–20, 178; racism and economic class, 118–19; urban renewal fighting disease of, 118–23, *122*

Urban Blight and Slums (Walker), 115

urban density. *See* housing density

Urban Design Associates, 143

urban green space. *See* cemeteries; parks and parks movement

urban history: accounts of, 3–4; Americans' lack of awareness of, 213n5; consistent study of effect of parks and nature, 210, 238n11; landscapes as public, 4; language of disease and epidemiology, 119–20, 178; Public Health 1.0–3.0, 208; reevaluation of redesign of communities, 169; suburban and urban binary, 88, 128, 158–59

Urban Land Institute (ULI), 170

urban landscapes: and call for public health more etiologically oriented, 82–83; as consumer choice, 7; early understanding of relationship of, to health of residents, 16; as machines, 65–66; models for future empirical research, 184–85; as public history, 4; as reactions to specific urban epidemics, 5; as tenet of well-being, 7

urban planners and planning: Athens Charter of 1933, 91; benefits of, 72; and climate change, 203–4; compliance of, in system exacerbating social inequity, 209; concern about strain on infrastructure of unplanned building, 86; and consideration of community, 168; decolonial framework for, 210–11, 239n12; elimination of breeding grounds of socialism, 57; failures, 57; good intentions and unintended consequences, 207; health and science models and metaphors used, 84, 86–89, *88, 89,* 92, 110–12, *113,* 126–27, 192; highway planning, 116, 126; job of planners, 57; and landscape architects, 168; modern split with public health, 82–83, 84; Mumford's opinion of, 228n6; as part of sanitary movement, 26; planning as social ordering and sensible resource management, 87, 110, 128; professionalization of, to combat epidemics, 3, 26; in Progressive Era, 81; promotion of, by Moody, 71–72; and public housing, 95; as "scientific," 56–57, 85; and suspicion of government programs as socialist, 105, 112; use of medical and ecological language, 84, 86, 112, 126, 178. *See also specific individuals by name*

Urban Policy Making and Metropolitan Development (Dear), 119

Urban Redevelopment Act (1949), 102

urban renaissance and environmentalism, 156

urban renewal: and decentralization, 123–24, *124;* eminent domain, 123; fighting disease of urban blight, 118–23, *122;* and race, 124; and residents, 127

Urban Sprawl and Public Health (Frumkin, Richard Jackson, and Frank), 134

urban youth: city streets as dangerous to, 43–44, 48; mortality of children, 19; playgrounds as salvation of, 44–45, 49, 51, 53; as workers, 44, 55

US Department of Agriculture (USDA), 180

US Department of Health and Human Services (HHS), 132

US Department of Housing and Urban Development (HUD), 140, 142, 202

US Department of Interior, 211

US Sanitary Commission, 63

"Value of Playgrounds to Community, The" (Riis), 44

Vaux, Calvert, 63, 67; Riverside, Illinois, 79, *80*

Venice Charter for the Conservation and Restoration of Monuments and Sites, 137

Venturi, Robert, 135

Vergara, Camilo Jose, *Fifth Ave at 110th St East Harlem, 110*

Vinik, Jeff, 233n25

Vitruvian Man for the Modern Age, 92

Wacker, Charles, 71

Wacker's Manual for the Plan of Chicago (Moody), 71–72

Wald, Lillian, 45

Walden (Thoreau), 33

Walkable City: How Downtown Can Save America, One Step at a Time (Speck), 151

Walkable City Rules: 101 Steps to Making Better Places (Speck), 151

Walker, Mabel L., 115

walking and walkability: and commodification of health, 160; as cure for obesity epidemic, 146; defining, 153, 154; and economic class, 169–70, 179–80, 181; elements making neighborhood, 179–80; as engineered out of environment, 146–47; as environmental justice issue, 181; and ethnicity, 179–80; evaluating cities', 150–51; in LEED neighborhoods, 161; for leisure versus for transportation, 152, 153; and Main Street, 181–83, *182;* Newtown Creek Nature Walk, 168; and New Urbanist movement, 150–51, 152; as part of "multimodal" transportation infrastructure, 147; Portland and Kansas City as leaders, 147; promotion of, 147–48, 159; research on, 152–53, 169–70; trees for, 137–38